Jon E. Lewis is a historian and writer, whose books on history and military history are sold worldwide. He is also the editor of many *The Mammoth Book of* anthologies, including the bestselling *On the Edge*.

Recent Mammoth titles

The Mammoth Book of Chess
The Mammoth Book of Alternate Histories
The Mammoth Book of New IQ Puzzles
The Mammoth Book of Fun Brain-Training
The Mammoth Book of Dracula
The Mammoth Book of Best British Crime 8
The Mammoth Book of Tattoo Art
The Mammoth Book of Bob Dylan
The Mammoth Book of Mixed Martial Arts
The Mammoth Book of Codeword Puzzles
The Mammoth Book of New Sherlock Holmes Adventures
The Mammoth Book of Historical Crime Fiction
The Mammoth Book of Best New SF 24
The Mammoth Book of Really Silly Jokes
The Mammoth Book of Best New Horror 22
The Mammoth Book of Undercover Cops
The Mammoth Book of Weird News
The Mammoth Book of Lost Symbols
The Mammoth Book of Conspiracies
The Mammoth Book of Muhammad Ali

The Mammoth Book of

ANTARCTIC JOURNEYS

Edited by Jon E. Lewis

ROBINSON

RUNNING PRESS
PHILADELPHIA · LONDON

Constable & Robinson Ltd
55–56 Russell Square
London WC1B 4HP
www.constablerobinson.com

First published in the UK by Robinson,
an imprint of Constable & Robinson Ltd, 2012

A copy of the British Library Cataloguing in Publication

Data is available from the British Library

UK ISBN 978-1-84901-722-0 (paperback)
UK ISBN 978-1-78033-134-8 (ebook)

1 3 5 7 9 10 8 6 4 2

First published in the United States in 2012 by Running Press
Book Publishers, a member of the Perseus Books Group

Books published by Running Press are available at special discounts for bulk
purchases in the United States by corporations, institutions, and other organizations.
For more information, please contact the Special Markets Department at the
Perseus Books Group, 2300 Chestnut Street, Suite 200, Philadelphia, PA 19103,
or call (800) 810-4145, ext. 5000, or e-mail special.markets@perseusbooks.com

9   8   7   6   5   4   3   2   1
Digit on the right indicates the number of this printing

US Library of Congress Control number: 2010941556
US ISBN 978-0-7624-4275-1

Running Press Book Publishers
2300 Chestnut Street
Philadelphia, PA 19103-4371

Visit us on the web!
www.runningpress.com
Printed and bound in the UK

"I am just going outside and may be some time."
Captain Laurence "Titus" Oates, *c.* 16 March 1912

Contents

Introduction: the South Pole

The South Pole, the southern end of the earth's axis, lies within Antarctica, the world's most hostile continent. This Geographical South Pole, distinct from the Magnetic South Pole (currently wandering Antarctica's Adélie Coast), is at an elevation of 9,300 feet, with 8,850 of those feet comprised of ice. James Cook, the English naval officer and explorer, was the first to cross the Antarctic Circle, a blasting berg-strewn experience which caused him to remark in his *A Voyage Towards the South Pole* (1777) that "no man will ever venture further than I have done". Cook was wrong: *A Voyage Towards the South Pole* caught the European imagination and created a self-denying prophecy. Man upon man clamoured to sail South to see the sights described by Cook – and to best his Southing record. There was money in it, too, for Cook had discovered seal- and whale-rich grounds around South Georgia. In 1820 Fabian Bellinghausen of Russia and Edward Bransfield of England, both sighted the Antarctic continent itself. James Ross's Royal Navy expedition of 1839 made the first Antarctic landfall, after which the British took a markedly proprietorial view of the white continent, just as they did of the Arctic. Thus the Norwegian Amundsen's successful attempt on the South Pole in 1911, beating Scott of the Royal Navy, was a national tragedy, all the more so because Scott and his companions died in the doing. (There was also the British lament that Amundsen's bid was not quite "proper", for he had used dogs, rather than manhauling his sledges as the British did). Scott's journal of his last expedition – assuredly one of the true masterpieces of travel-writing – recorded an epic struggle against bad luck and Nature and preserved, to this day, the public opinion of the Antarctic as the fantasy ice palace of Heroes.

Which, of course, is not wide of the mark. Mawson,

Shackleton, and Byrd – to pick three post-Scott explorers at random – all endured extraordinary struggles against the white death with a resoluteness of body and soul that can only inspire. But there is more to seek in Antarctica than the physical and mental limits of humankind. Scott's own expedition was (almost) as much about scientific research as it was polar conquest; to the very end Scott and his companions pulled along their weighty geological specimens. Today, the uninhabited continent is inhabited by some twenty scientific bases, prime among them the Amundsen-Scott base at 90° South, established to understand Antarctica's geology, ecosystem and weather. There is irony, even tragedy, in the scientific exploration of Antarctica: As David Helvarg finds in "Melting Point", global warming is causing sections of the Antarctic ice-shelves to break off and glaciers to retreat: Where the Edwardian Antarctic explorers landed on a foreshore of ice, the modern visitor can step onto rocky beach. The immortal Antarctica of the heroes, in other words, is disappearing – literally – before our eyes.

Southing

Captain James Cook RN

In 1768 Captain James Cook, instructed by the Admiralty to find the Southern Continent speculated by geographers, made his first voyage towards the South Pole. Journeying due south from Tahiti to latitude 60 degrees, he disproved the existence of a temperate continent in the southern Pacific; for additional proof of the non-existence of such a continent he sailed south from the Cape of Good Hope in 1772, crossing the Antarctic circle without sighting land. The extracts below are from Cook's 1772 voyage.

Floating Rocks

Dangerous as it is to sail among these floating rocks (if I may be allowed to call them so) in a thick fog; this, however, is preferable to being entangled with immense fields of ice under the same circumstances. The great danger to be apprehended in this latter case, is the getting fast in the ice; a situation which would be exceedingly alarming. I had two men on board that had been in the Greenland trade; the one of them in a ship that lay nine weeks, and the other in one that lay six weeks, fast in this kind of ice; which they called packed ice. What *they* call field ice is thicker; and the whole field, be it ever so large, consists of one piece. Whereas this which *I* call field ice, from its immense extent, consists of many pieces of various sizes both in thickness and surface, from 30 or 40 feet square, to 3 or 4; packed close together; and in places heaped one upon another. This, I am of opinion, would be found too hard for a ship's side, that is not properly armed against it. How long it may have lain, or will lie here, is a point not easily determined. Such ice is found in the Greenland seas all the summer long; and I think it cannot be colder there in the summer, than it is here. Be this as it may, we certainly had no thaw; on the contrary, the mercury in Fahrenheit's thermometer kept generally below the freezing point, although it was the middle of summer.

"I can be bold enough to say that no man will venture farther than I have done"

For I firmly believe that there is a track of land near the Pole which is the source of most of the ice that is spread over this vast Southern Ocean. I also think it probable that it extends farthest to the North opposite the Southern Atlantic and Indian Oceans; because ice was always found by us farther to the North in these oceans than any where else, which I judge could not be, if there were not land to the South; I mean a land of considerable extent. For if we suppose that no such land exists, and that ice may be formed without it, it will follow of course that the cold ought to be every where nearly equal round the Pole, as far as 70° or 60° of latitude, or so far as to be beyond the influence of any of the known continents; consequently we ought to see ice every where under the same parallel, or near it: and yet the contrary has been found. Very few ships have met with ice going round Cape Horn; and we saw but little below the sixtieth degree of latitude, in the Southern Pacific Ocean. Whereas in this ocean, between the meridian of 40° West and 50° or 60° East, we found ice as far North as 51°. Bouvet met with some in 48°; and others have seen it in a much lower latitude. It is true, however, that the greatest part of this southern continent (supposing there is one), must lie within the polar circle, where the sea is so pestered with ice that the land is thereby inaccessible. The risque one runs in exploring a coast, in these unknown and icy seas, is so very great, that I can be bold enough to say that no man will ever venture farther than I have done; and that the lands which may lie to the South will never be explored. Thick fogs, snow storms, intense cold, and every other thing that can render navigation dangerous, must be encountered; and these difficulties are greatly heightened, by the inexpressibly horrid aspect of the country; a country doomed by Nature never once to feel the warmth of the sun's rays, but to lie buried in everlasting snow and ice. The ports which may be on the coast, are, in a manner, wholly filled up with frozen snow of vast thickness; but if any should be so far open as to invite a ship into it, she would run a risque of being fixed there for ever, or of coming out in an ice island. The islands and floats on the coast, the great falls from the ice cliffs in the port, or a heavy snow storm attended with a sharp frost, would be equally fatal.

LAND!

Edward Bransfield RN

An English naval officer, Bransfield (c. 1795–1852) is generally credited with having discovered the Antarctic continent on 30 January 1820, although the Russian explorer Fabian Bellinghausen may have pipped him by two days.

At noon we threw a bottle overboard, containing a paper bearing the following inscription: "This bottle was hove overboard from the *Williams,* an English brig, on a voyage of discovery, to the southward, on 12 January 1820, in latitude 57° 48' and longitude 69° 55' W. Should any vessel pick this up at sea, it is requested the master will note the latitude and longitude, putting it overboard again; or should it be found on any coast or harbour, the person so finding it will, I hope, inclose this paper to the Board of Longitude, in London, stating when, where, and how he came by it; signed Edward Bransfield, master of HMS *Andromache* . . ."

Several shoals of seals and a few penguins being seen, we tried for soundings about eight o'clock, but obtained no bottom with 120 fathoms. During the night we kept the lead going two hours, but unsuccessfully, still passing through and by large shoals of seals and penguins. So great a sign of land being in the neighbourhood made it necessary to keep a very vigilant look-out, when about eight o'clock in the morning, land was discovered making in a moderate height, and partly covered with snow. At nine we hove too, and sounded with 55 fathoms brown sand and ooze, the extremes of the land bearing from east to SSE; filled and bore up E.b.S. for a supposed entrance to a spacious bay, or at least where we thought we might bring up and water. In standing in, an unconnected chain of rocks, detached from the main, presented themselves, forming in very remarkable shapes. When within a mile or a mile and a half of the land, we hove to and hoisted the whale-boat out, put leads and lines, and armed her, when Mr Smith took her to go in search of an anchorage where we might lie in security . . .

The breakers in smooth water are scarcely perceptible, except at intervals when the sea breaks. A short distance to the eastward of the cape is a small island pierced through, resembling the arch of a bridge. After determining the latitude of Cape Shireff, we ran to the eastward until abreast of an island, which, from its barren, uncomfortable appearance, was named the Island of Desolation. Its latitude is 62° 27' S and longitude 60° 35' and 10 miles due east of the last cape. Previous to the going down of the sun, we determined the variation, by an excellent azimuth, to be 23° 52' east, and an amplitude soon after 22° 30' east. During the time we were prosecuting our pursuits, we were surrounded by shoals of seals and penguins. From Desolation Island we ran in a NE direction for a cluster we perceived, which, when abreast of, were supposed to be the same seen by Mr Smith in the month of February 1819. The whole of these islands, along the part of the coast which we had already seen, were composed of black rock, and above the reach of the water patches of snow made but a dismal aspect. The main entirely capped which gave us but very faint hopes of ever being able to speak well of its fertility . . .

At 1.30, an island was observed nearly clear of snow, bearing WSW; at four, the bluff bow [sic] NE. At five, observing the land to the SW of the island appear like a bay, we made sail, steering WSW with a moderate breeze. The necessary precautions were taken by keeping the lead going and a hand forward to look out for foul ground, and ice being taken, we rounded the island, and at 7.30 brought up with the chain cable in sixteen fathoms, coarse sand, with black gravel, the eastern point of the island bearing NE.b.E.; a small island near the bottom of the bay W.b.N. and the southern point of the bay SW. While rounding the island we observed its shore covered with penguins, whose awkward movement had the most strange appearance, and at the same time the most intolerable stench assailed our noses that I ever smelt, arising from these gentry. As soon as everything was secure, we hoisted the boats out, manned and armed the whale-boat, and after breakfast Mr Bransfield proceeded in her to effect a landing, where he might plant the Jack, and take possession of it by the name of New South Britain, in the name and behalf of HM George IV, his heirs and successors. At eight o'clock, observed the boat land on a shingle beach, which bore from the brig NNW; observed soon after, with the aid of our glasses, the Jack planted; we hoisted on board the brig, our ensign and pendant, and fired a gun; he likewise buried a bottle, containing several coins of the realm, given by different people for that purpose.

Dog Days

Robert F. Scott

A torpedo officer in the Royal Navy with no experience of polar travel, Robert Falcon Scott was chosen to lead the British National Antarctic Expedition (1901–4). Scott's chief qualification for the job – aside from being an officer and a gentleman, these being the age's bywords for honour, courage and duty – was that he was an acquaintance of Sir Clements Markham, the president of the Royal Geographical Society and the expedition's sponsor. In truth, Markham was more fortunate than he understood; Scott was capable of inspiring extraordinary love and loyalty. He was also courageous almost beyond measure. Scott certainly had faults but these were the faults of his class; his dilettantish approach to expedition organization was entirely of a stripe with the Edwardian upper class's belief that sport and exploration were the preserves of the amateur.

From his expedition base at McMurdo Sound Scott, Edward Wilson and Ernest Shackleton made the first extensive land exploration of the white continent, reaching 82 degrees 17' south, 500 miles from the Pole. On this occasion, Scott used a team of dogs, nineteen in number: Nigger, Jim, Spud, Snatcher, FitzClarence, Stripes, Birdie, Nell, Blanco, Grannie, Lewis, Gus, Joe, Wolfe, Vic, Bismarck, Kid, Boss and Brownie. Below is Scott's diary of his southing record.

November 27. Today it is beautifully bright, clear, and warm, the temperature up to +20°; but, alas! this morning we found that the dogs seemed to have derived no benefit from their rest. They were all snugly curled up beneath the snow when we went out, but in spite of their long rest we had to drag them out of their nests; some were so cramped that it was several minutes before they could stand. However, we shook some life into them and started with the full load, but very soon we had to change back into our old routine, and, if anything, the march was more trying than ever. It becomes a necessity now to reach the land soon in hopes of making a depot, so our course has been laid to the westward of S.W., and this brings the bold bluff cape on our port bow. I imagine it to be about fifty miles off, but hope it is not so much; nine hours' work today has only given us a bare four miles.

It was my turn to drive today; Shackleton led and Wilson pulled at the side. The whole proceedings would have been laughable enough but for the grim sickness that holds so tight a grip on our poor team: Shackleton in front, with harness slung over his shoulder, was bent forward with his whole weight on the trace; in spite of his breathless work, now and again he would raise and half-turn his head in an effort to cheer on the team. "Hi, dogs," "Now then," "Hi lo-lo-lo . . ." or any other string of syllables which were supposed to produce an encouraging effect, but which were soon brought to a conclusion by sheer want of breath. Behind him, and obviously deaf to these allurements, shambled the long string of depressed animals, those in rear doing their best to tread in the deep footprints of the leaders, but all by their low-carried heads and trailing tails showing an utter weariness of life. Behind these, again, came myself with the whip, giving forth one long string of threats and occasionally bringing the lash down with a crack on the snow or across the back of some laggard. By this time all the lazy dogs know their names, as well they ought; I should not like to count the number of times I have said, "Ah, you, 'Wolf,'" or "Get on there, 'Jim,'" or "'Bismarck', you brute"; but it is enough to have made me quite hoarse tonight, for each remark has to be produced in a violent manner or else it produces no effect, and things have now got so bad that if the driver ceases his flow of objurgation for a moment there is a slackening of the traces. Some names lend themselves to this style of language better than others; "Boss" can be hissed out with very telling effect, whereas it is hard to make "Brownie" very emphatic. On the opposite side of the leading sledge was Wilson, pulling away in grim silence. We dare not talk on such occasions as the dogs detect the change of tone at once; they seize upon the least excuse to stop pulling. There are six or eight animals who give little trouble, and these have been placed in the front, so that the others may be more immediately under the lash; but the loafers are growing rather than diminishing in numbers. This, then, is the manner in which we have proceeded for nine hours today – entreaties in front and threats behind – and so we went on yesterday, and so we shall go on tomorrow. It is sickening work, but it is the only way; we cannot stop, we cannot go back, we must go on, and there is no alternative but to harden our hearts and drive. Luckily, the turn for doing the actual driving only comes once in three days, but even thus it is almost as bad to witness the driving as to have to do it.

Tonight we discussed the possibility of getting some benefit by marching at night; it was very warm today in the sun, and the air temperature was up to +25°.

November 29. Shortly after four o'clock today we observed the most striking atmospheric phenomenon we have yet seen in these regions. We were enveloped in a light, thin stratus cloud of small ice-crystals; it could not have extended to any height, as the sun was only lightly veiled. From these drifting crystals above, the sun's rays were reflected in such an extraordinary manner that the whole arch of the heavens was traced with circles and lines of brilliant prismatic or white light. The coloured circles of a bright double halo were touched or interesected by one which ran about us parallel to the horizon; above this, again, a gorgeous prismatic ring encircled the zenith; away from the sun was a white fog-bow, with two bright mock suns where it intersected the horizon circle. The whole effect was almost bewildering, and its beauty is far beyond the descriptive powers of my sledging pencil. We have often seen double halos, fog-bows, mock suns, and even indications of other circles, but we have never been privileged to witness a display that approaches in splendour that of today. We stopped, whilst Wilson took notes of the artistic composition, and I altitudes and bearings of the various light effects. If it is robbed of some of the beauties of a milder climate, our region has certainly pictures of its own to display.

November 29 (continued). Both in the first and second advance today we noticed that the points of starting and finishing were in view of one another, but that in travelling between them either end was temporarily lost to sight for a short time. This undoubtedly indicates undulation in the surface, but I should think of slight amount, probably not more than seven or eight feet, the length of the waves being doubtful, as we cannot be certain of the angle at which we are crossing them; they cannot exceed two miles from crest to crest, and are probably about one.

We had rather a scare tonight on its suddenly coming over very thick just as Wilson and I were coupling up the second load to bring it on; all our food and personal equipment had been left with Shackleton in the advanced position, and, of course, we could see nothing of it through the haze. We followed the old tracks for some way, until the light got so bad that we repeatedly lost sight of them, when we were obliged to halt and grope round for them. So far we were only in danger of annoying delays, but a little later a brisk breeze sprang up, and to our consternation rapidly drifted up the old tracks; there was nothing for it but to strike out a fresh course of our own in the direction in which we supposed the camp to lie, which we did, and, getting on as fast as possible, had the satisfaction of sighting the camp in about half an hour. 'All's well that ends well,' and luckily the fog was not very thick; but the incident has set us thinking that if very thick weather were to come on, the party away from the camp might be very unpleasantly situated, so in future we shall plant one or two flags as we advance with the first load, and pick them up as we come on with the second.

December 2. We noticed again today the cracking of the snow-crust; sometimes the whole team with the sledges get on an area when it cracks around us as sharply and as loudly as a pistol shot, and this is followed by a long-drawn sigh as the area sinks. When this first happened the dogs were terrified, and sprang forward with tails between their legs and heads screwed round as though the threatened danger was behind; and, indeed, it gave me rather a shock the first time – it was so unexpected, and the sharp report was followed by a distinct subsidence. Though probably one dropped only an inch or two, there was an instantaneous feeling of insecurity which is not pleasant. Digging down tonight Shackleton found a comparatively hard crust two or three inches under the soft snow surface; beneath this was an air space of about an inch, then came about a foot of loose snow in large crystals, and then a second crust. There is a good deal that is puzzling about these crusts.

December 3. . . . Our pemmican bag for this week by an oversight has been slung alongside a tin of paraffin, and is consequently strongly impregnated with the oil; one can both smell and taste the latter strongly; it is some proof of the state of our appetites that we really don't much mind!

We are now sufficiently close to the land to make out some of its details. On our right is a magnificent range of mountains, which we are gradually opening out, and which must therefore run more or less in an east-and-west direction. My rough calculations show them to be at least fifty miles from us, and, if so, their angle of altitude gives a height of over 10,000 feet. The eastern end of this range descends to a high snow-covered plateau, through which arise a number of isolated minor peaks, which I think must be volcanic; beyond these, again, is a long, rounded, sloping snow-cape, merging into the Barrier. These rounded snow-capes are a great feature of the coast; they can be seen dimly in many places, both north and south of us. They are peculiar as presenting from all points of view a perfectly straight line inclined at a slight angle to the horizon. North of this range the land still seems to run on, but it has that detached appearance, due to great distance, which we noted before, and we can make little of it. The south side of the range seems to descend comparatively abruptly, and in many cases it is bordered by splendid high cliffs, very dark in colour, though we cannot make out the exact shade. Each cliff has a band of white along its top where the ice-cap ends abruptly; at this distance it has a rather whimsical resemblance to the sugaring of a Christmas cake. The cliffs and foothills of the high range form the northern limit of what appears to be an enormous strait; we do not look up this strait, and therefore cannot say what is beyond, but the snow-cape on this side is evidently a great many miles from the high range, and there appears to be nothing between. This near snow-cape seems to be more or less isolated. It is an immense and almost dome-shaped, snow-covered mass; only quite lately could we see any rock at all, but now a few patches are to be made out towards the summit, and one or two at intervals along the foot. It is for one of these that we have now decided to make, so that we may establish our depot there, but at present rate of going we shall be a long time before we reach it.

South of this isolated snow-cape, which is by far the nearest point of land to us, we can see a further high mountainous country; but this also is so distant that we can say little of it. One thing seems evident – that the high bluff cape we were making for is not a cape at all, but a curiously bold spur of the lofty mountain ranges, which is high above the level of the coastline, and must be many miles inland. It is difficult to say whether this land is more heavily glaciated than that which we have seen to the north; on the whole, I think the steeper surfaces seem equally bare. There is a consolation for the heavier surface and harder labour we are experiencing in the fact that each day the scene gets more interesting and more beautiful.

Today, in lighting the Primus, I very stupidly burnt a hole in the tent; I did not heat the top sufficiently before I began to pump, and a long yellow flame shot up and set light to the canvas. I do not think I should have noticed what had happened at first, but luckily the others were just approaching and rushed forward to prevent further damage. As it was, there was a large hole which poor Shackleton had to make shift to repair during our last lap; it is not much fun working with a needle in the open at the midnight hours, even though the season happens to be summer.

December 4. After a sunshiny day and with the cooler night hours there comes now a regular fall of snow-crystals. On a calm night there is nothing to indicate the falling crystals save a faint haze around the horizon; overhead it is quite clear. Suddenly, and apparently from nowhere, a small shimmering body floats gently down in front of one and rests as lightly as thistle-down on the white surface below. If one stoops to examine it as we have done many times, one finds that it is a six-pointed feathery star, quite flat and smooth on either side. We find them sometimes as large as a shilling, and at a short distance they might be small hexagonal pieces of glass; it is only on looking closely that one discovers the intricate and delicate beauty of their design.

The effect of these *en masse* is equally wonderful; they rest in all positions, and therefore receive the sun's rays at all angles, and in breaking them up reflect in turn each colour of the spectrum. As one plods along towards the midnight sun, one's eyes naturally fall on the plain ahead, and one realizes that the smile of a gem-strewn carpet could never be more aptly employed than in describing the radiant path of the sun on the snowy surface. It sparkles with a myriad points of brilliant light, comprehensive of every colour the rainbow can show, and is so realistic and near that it often seems one has but to stoop to pick up some glistening jewel.

We find a difficulty now in gaining even four miles a day; the struggle gets harder and harder. We should not make any progress if we did not pull hard ourselves; several of the dogs do practically nothing, and none work without an effort. Slowly but surely, however, we are 'rising' the land. Our sastrugi today, from the recent confused state, have developed into a W.N.W. direction; it looks as though there was a local wind out of the strait.

December 5. At breakfast we decided that our oil is going too fast; there has been some wastage from the capsizing of the sledge, and at first we were far too careless of the amount we used. When we came to look up dates, there was no doubt that in this respect we have outrun the constable. We started with the idea that a gallon was to last twelve days; ours have averaged little over ten. As a result we calculate that those which remain must be made to last fourteen. This is a distinct blow, as we shall have to sacrifice our hot luncheon meal and to economize greatly at both the others. We started the new routine tonight, and for lunch ate some frozen seal-meat and our allowance of sugar and biscuit. The new conditions do not smile on us at present, but I suppose we shall get used to them.

The events of the day's march are now becoming so dreary and dispiriting that one longs to forget them when we camp; it is an effort even to record them in a diary. Tonight has been worse than usual. Our utmost efforts could not produce more than three miles for the whole march, and it would be impossible to describe how tiring the effort was to gain even this small advance. We have an idea we are rising in level slightly, but it is impossible to say so with certainty.

Shackleton broke the glass of his watch yesterday afternoon; the watch still goes, but one cannot further rely on it, and I am therefore left with the only accurate time-keeper. It is a nuisance to lose a possible check on future observations, but luckily my watch seems to be a very trustworthy instrument; its rate on board the ship was excellent, and I have no reason to suppose that it has altered much since we left. My watch was presented to me by Messrs. Smith & Son, of the Strand, and I believe it to be an exceptionally good one, but the important observations which we take ought not to depend on a single watch, and future expeditions should be supplied with a larger number than we carry.

December 6. . . . A dire calamity today. When I went outside before breakfast I noticed that "Spud" was absent from his place. I looked round and discovered him lying on the sledge with his head on the open mouth of the seal-meat bag; one glance at his balloon-like appearance was sufficient to show what had happened. As one contemplated the impossibility of repairing the mischief and of making him restore his ill-gotten provender, it was impossible not to laugh; but the matter is really serious enough: he has made away with quite a week's allowance of our precious seal-meat. How he could have swallowed it all is the wonder, yet, though somewhat sedate and somnolent, he appeared to suffer no particular discomfort from the enormously increased size of his waist. We found of course that he had gnawed through his trace, but the seal-meat bag will be very carefully closed in future.

Whilst we were making preparations for a start last night we were overtaken by a blizzard and had to camp again in a hurry. The barometer has been falling for two days, and Wilson has had twinges of rheumatism; the former we took for a sign that we were rising in altitude, but we ought to have been warned by a further drop of two-tenths of an inch whilst we were in camp. The blizzard was ushered in with light flaky snow and an increasing wind, and a quarter of an hour later there was a heavy drift with strong wind. We have been completing our calculations of what is to be left at the depot and what carried on to the south.

December 8. . . . Our poor team are going steadily downhill; six or seven scarcely pull at all, perhaps five or six do some steady work, and the remainder make spasmodic efforts. The lightening of the load is more than counter-balanced by the weakening of the animals, and I can see no time in which we can hope to get the sledges along without pulling ourselves. Of late we have altered our marching arrangements; we now take the first half-load on for four miles, then return for the other half, eating our cold luncheon on the way back. Today it took us three and a half hours to get the advance load on, and I who remained with it had to wait another five and a half before the others came back – nine hours' work to gain four miles.

Before supper we all had a wash and brush-up. We each carry a tooth-brush and a pocket-comb, and there is one cake of soap and one pocket looking-glass amongst the party; we use our tooth-brushes fairly frequently, with snow, but the soap and comb are not often in request, and the looking-glass is principally used to dress our mangled lips. Snow and soap are rather a cold compound, but there is freshness in the glowing reaction, and we should probably use them oftener if the marches were not so tiring. Tonight the tent smells of soap and hazeline cream.

December 10. Yesterday we only covered two miles, and to get on the second load at all we had to resort to the ignominious device of carrying food ahead of the dogs.

"Snatcher" died yesterday; others are getting feeble – it is terrible to see them. The coast cannot be more than ten or twelve miles, but shall we ever reach it? and in what state shall we be to go on? The dogs have had no hesitation in eating their comrade; the majority clamoured for his flesh this evening, and neglected their fish in favour of it. There is the chance that this change of diet may save the better animals.

This evening we were surprised by the visit of a skua gull; even our poor dogs became excited. We are nearly 180 miles from any possible feeding-ground it may have, and it is impossible to say how it found us, but it is curious that it should have come so soon after poor "Snatcher" has been cut up.

December 11. Last night I had a terrible headache from the hot work in the sun and the closeness of the tent. I couldn't sleep for a long time, though we had the tent open and our bags wide; sleep eventually banished the headache, and I awoke quite fit. The weather has improved, for although still hot a southerly breeze has cooled the air. In covering three and a half miles we have altered several bearings of the land, so that it cannot now be far off. As we travel inward the snow-covered ridges of our cape are blocking out the higher range to the north.

About 1 a.m. a bank of stratus cloud came rapidly up from the south; it looked white and fleecy towards the sun and a peculiar chocolate-brown as it passed to the northward and disappeared. It must have been travelling very fast and about two or three thousand feet above us; in an hour we had a completely clear sky.

Hunger is beginning to nip us all, and we have many conversations as to the dainties we could devour if they were within reach.

December 14. We have arrived at a place where I think we can depot our dog-food, and none too soon; I doubt if we could go on another day as we have been going. We have just completed the worst march we have had, and only managed to advance two miles by the most strenuous exertions. The snow grows softer as we approach the land; the sledge-runners sink from three to four inches, and one's feet well over the ankles at each step. After going a little over a mile things got so bad that we dropped one sledge and pushed on to bring some leading marks in line. Then Shackleton and I brought up the second half-load with the dogs somehow; after which, leaving the dogs, we all three started back for the sledge that had been dropped. Its weight was only 250 lbs., yet such was the state of the surface that we could not drag it at the rate of a mile an hour.

The air temperature has gone up to +27°, and it feels hot and stuffy; the snow surface is +22°. It would be difficult to convey an idea of what marching is like under present conditions. The heel of the advanced foot is never planted beyond the toe of the other, and of this small gain with each pace, two or three inches are lost by back-slipping as the weight is brought forward. When we come to any particularly soft patch we do little more than mark time.

The bearings of our present position are good but distant. To the west we have a conspicuous rocky patch in line with one of three distant peaks, and to the north another small patch in line with a curious scar on the northern range. The back marks in each case are perhaps twenty or thirty miles from us, and, though they will be easy enough to see in clear weather, one cannot hope to recognize them when it is misty. It is for this reason that I propose tomorrow to take our own food, on which our safety depends, closer in to the land, so that there may be no chance of our missing it.

December 15 (3.15 a.m.). As soon as we had lightened our load last night we started steering straight for the rocky patch to the westward. The sky was overcast and the light bad, and after proceeding about a quarter of a mile we found that we were crossing well-marked undulations. Still pushing on, we topped a steep ridge to be fronted by an enormous chasm filled with a chaotic confusion of ice-blocks. It was obvious that we could go no further with the sledges, so we halted and pitched camp, and after eating our meagre lunch set forth to explore. The light was very bad, but we roped ourselves together, and, taking our only ice-axe and the meat-chopper, descended cautiously over a steep slope into the rougher ice below. Taking advantage of the snow between the ice-blocks we wended our way amongst them for some distance, now and again stepping on some treacherous spot and finding ourselves suddenly prone with our legs down a crevasse and very little breath left.

At first we could get some idea of where these bad places lay, but later the light grew so bad that we came on them quite without warning, and our difficulties were much greater, whilst the huge ice-blocks about us swelled to mountainous size in the grey gloom, and it was obvious that we could make no useful observations in such weather. We stumbled our way back with difficulty, and, cutting steps up the slope, at length caught a welcome view of the camp.

The dogs were more excited than they have been for many a day; poor things, they must have been quite nonplussed when we suddenly vanished from sight. We can make little out of the chasm so far, except that it quite cuts us off from a nearer approach to the land with our sledges, so that we shall have to depot our own food with the rest of the dog food and trust to fortune to give us clear weather when we return.

December 16. There was bright, clear sunshine when we awoke yesterday afternoon, and we not only had a good view of the chasm, but Shackleton was able to photograph it. It looks like a great rift in the Barrier which has been partly filled up with irregular ice-blocks; from our level to the lowest point in the valley may be about a hundred feet, and the peaks of some of the larger blocks rise almost to our level. The rift is perhaps three-quarters of a mile broad opposite to us, but it seems to narrow towards the south, and there is rather a suggestion that it ends within a few miles. The general lie of the rift is N.N.W. and S.S.E.; on the other side the surface appears to be level again, and probably it continues so for five or six miles to the land; however, it is certainly not worth our while to delay to ascertain this fact. In the sunlight the lights and shadows of the ice-blocks are in strong contrast, and where the sun has shone on blue walls, caverns have been melted and icicles hang over glassy, frozen pools. We found some of the icicles still dripping.

Intent on wasting no more of our precious time, we got back to our depot as quickly as possible, and set about rearranging the loads, taking stock, and fixing up the depot. Whilst we were thus employed a very chill wind came up from the south, and we did not escape without some frost-bitten fingers; however, after luncheon we got away and started head to wind and driving snow at 11 p.m. At midnight I got an altitude which gives the latitude as 80.30, and at 1.30 we camped, as we have decided now to start our marches earlier every day until we get back into day routine.

As I write I scarcely know how to describe the blessed relief it is to be free from our relay work. For one-and-thirty awful days have we been at it, and whilst I doubt if our human endurance could have stood it much more, I am quite sure the dogs could not. It seems now like a nightmare, which grew more and more terrible towards its end.

I do not like to think of the difference between the state of our party now and as it was before we commenced this dreadful task; it is almost equally painful to think of the gain, for during all this time we have advanced little more than half a degree of latitude, though I calculate we have covered 330 miles (380 statute miles).

But it is little use thinking of the past; the great thing is to make the best of the future. We carry with us provisions for four weeks and an odd day or two, a little dog-food, our camp equipment, and, for clothing, exactly what we stand in.

At the depot, which I have now called Depot "B", we have left three weeks' provision and a quantity of dog-food. This should tide us over the homeward march, so that the present stock can all be expended before we return to Depot "B"; and all will be well if we can get back within four weeks, and if we have a clear day to find the spot.

Poor "Vic" was sacrificed tonight for the common good.

December 17. We roused out yesterday afternoon at 3 p.m. in very bright sunshine. To our astonishment, a couple of hundred yards behind us lay the end of the chasm which stood between us and the coast; it gradually narrows to a crevasse, which in places is bridged over with snow, but in others displays a yawning gulf. We must have crossed it within a few feet of such a gulf; our sledge track could be seen quite clearly leading across the bridge. Not suspecting anything of this sort we were quite regardless of danger during our last march, and unconsciously passed within an ace of destruction. It certainly has been a very close shave, as we could scarcely have escaped at the best without broken limbs had we fallen into the hole, and one doesn't like to contemplate broken limbs out here.

This new light on the chasm seems to show that it is caused by a stream of ice pressing out through the strait to the north against the main mass of the Barrier; this would naturally have such a rending effect on either side of the entrance. We have got the dogs on seven miles tonight; they need a lot of driving, especially as the surface has become irregular, with wavy undulations. It is almost impossible to make out how these waves run. As the chill of the evening comes on now, a mist arises along the whole coast-line and obscures the land; for this reason we are the more anxious to get back into day-marches, and we shall make a much earlier start tomorrow.

December 18. Started at 5 p.m. and finished at midnight. The short hours are to get to earlier marches, but I begin to doubt whether we shall ever be able to work the dogs for much more than eight hours again; the poor creatures are generally in a healthier state with the fresh food, but all are very weak and thin. With such a load as we now have there would have been no holding them when we left the ship; as someone said today, "If only we could come across some good, fat seals. We could camp for a week and start fair again." It is curious to think that there is possibly not a living thing within two hundred miles of us. Bad as the dog-driving is, however, the fact that each mile is an

advance, and has not to be covered three times, is an inexpressible relief.

We are gradually passing from the hungry to the ravenous; we
cannot drag our thoughts from food, and we talk of little else.
The worst times are the later hours of the march and the nights;
on the march one sometimes gets almost a sickly feeling from
want of food, and the others declare they have an actual gnawing
sensation. At night one wakes with the most distressing feeling of
emptiness, and then to reflect that there are probably four or five
hours more before breakfast is positively dreadful. We have all
proved the efficacy of hauling our belts quite tight before we go
to sleep, and I have a theory that I am saved some of the worst
pangs by my pipe. The others are non-smokers, and, although
they do not own it, I often catch a wistful glance directed at my
comforting friend; but, alas! two pipes a day do not go far, even
on such a journey as ours.

December 19. We are now about ten miles from the land, but
even at this distance the foothills cut off our view of the higher
mountains behind, save to the north and south. Abreast of us the
sky-line is not more than three or four thousand feet high, though
we know there are loftier peaks behind. The lower country which
we see strongly resembles the coastal land far to the north; it is a
fine scene of a lofty snow-cap, whose smooth rounded outline is
broken by the sharper bared peaks, or by the steep disturbing fall
of some valley. Here and there local glaciers descend to Barrier
level; the coastline itself winds greatly, forming numerous headlands and bays; we are skirting these and keeping our direct
course, a little to the east of south. The coast is fringed with
white snow-slopes, glaciers, and broken ice-cascades; but in
many places black rocky headlands and precipitous uncovered
cliffs serve more clearly to mark its windings. Perhaps one of the
most impressive facts is that we see all this above a perfectly level
horizon line. Everywhere apparently there is as sharp and definite a line between the land and the level surface of the Barrier as
exists on an ordinary coastline between land and water. When it
becomes at all thick or gloomy the rocks stand out and the white,
snowy surfaces recede, giving rise to curious optical illusions.
The high, curiously shaped rocky patches seem to be suspended
in mid-air; there was one a few days ago, long and flat in shape,

which appeared to be so wholly unsupported that it was named "Mahomet's Coffin", but when the weather cleared we could see that the snow about it was really closer than the rock itself.

Wilson is the most indefatigable person. When it is fine and clear, at the end of our fatiguing days he will spend two or three hours seated in the door of the tent sketching each detail of the splendid mountainous coast-scene to the west. His sketches are most astonishingly accurate; I have tested his proportions by actual angular measurement and found them correct. If the fine weather continues we shall at least have a unique record of this coastline. But these long hours in the glare are very bad for the eyes; we have all suffered a good deal from snow-blindness of late, though we generally march with goggles, but Wilson gets the worst bouts, and I fear it is mainly due to his sketching.

"Wolf" was the victim tonight. I cannot say "poor 'Wolf,'" for he has been a thorn in the flesh, and has scarcely pulled a pound the whole journey. We have fifteen dogs left, and have decided to devote our energies to the preservation of the nine best; we have done nearly eight miles today, but at such an expenditure of energy that I am left in doubt as to whether we should not have done better without any dogs at all.

December 20. . . . Poor "Grannie" has been ailing for some time. She dropped today. We put her on the sledge, hoping she might recover, and there she breathed her last; she will last the others three days. It is little wonder that we grow more and more sick of our dog-driving.

The sky has been overcast with low stratus cloud, but it is wonderfully clear below; we have had this sort of weather for some time. One looks aloft and to the east and finds the outlook dull and apparently foggy, when it is surprising to turn to the west and get a comparatively clear view of all the low-lying rocks and snow-slopes which are now ten or a dozen miles from us.

My tobacco supply is at such "low water" that today I have been trying tea-leaves: they can be described as nothing less than horrid.

December 21. We are now crossing a deep bay, but the sky is still overcast and our view obscured; the surface was particularly heavy today, and our poor dogs had an especially bad time. After a few miles we determined to stop and go on at night again, as the heat was very great; the thermometer showed 27°, but inside the instrument-box, which is covered with white canvas, it showed 52°. There must be an astonishing amount of radiation, even with the sun obscured. Starting again at 8 p.m., we found that matters were not improved at all. Very few of the dogs pulled, whilst 'Stripes' and 'Brownie' were vomiting. Things began to look very hopeless, so we thought it would be wise to see what we could do alone without assistance from our team. We found that on ski we could just move our own sledges, but only just; on foot, after going for ten minutes, we found we were doing something under a mile an hour, but only with much exertion. After this experiment we camped again, and have been discussing matters. We calculate we were pulling about 170 lbs. per man; either the surface is extraordinarily bad or we are growing weak. It is no use blinding ourselves to facts: we cannot put any further reliance on the dogs. Any day they might all give out and leave us entirely dependent on ourselves. In such a case, if things were to remain just as they are, we should have about as much as we could do to get home; on the other hand, will things remain just as they are? It seems reasonable to hope for improvement, we have seen so many changes in the surface; at any rate, we have discussed this matter out, and I am glad to say that all agree in taking the risk of pushing on.

Misfortunes never come singly; since starting we have always had a regular examination of gums and legs on Sunday morning, and at first it seemed to show us to be in a very satisfactory condition of health, but tonight Wilson told me that Shackleton has decidedly angry-looking gums, and that for some time they have been slowly but surely getting worse. He says there is nothing yet to be alarmed at, but he now thought it serious enough to tell me in view of our future plans. We have decided not to tell Shackleton for the present; it is a matter which must be thought out. Certainly this is a black night, but things must look blacker yet before we decide to turn.

December 22. . . . This morning we had bright sunshine and a clear view of the land; the coastline has receded some way back in a deep bay, beyond which the land rises to the magnificent mountain ranges which evidently form the backbone of the whole continent. There are no longer high snow-covered foothills to intercept our view of the loftier background; it is as though at this portion of the coast they had been wiped out as a feature of the country, though farther to the south where the coastline again advances they seem to recur.

But just here we get an excellent view of the clean-cut mountain range. Abreast of us is the most splendid specimen of a pyramidal mountain; it raises a sharp apex to a height of nine thousand feet or more, and its precisely carved facets seem to rest on a base of more irregular country, fully four thousand feet below. With its extraordinary uniformity and great altitude it is a wonderfully good landmark. Close to the south of this is an equally lofty table mountain, the top of which is perfectly flat though dipping slightly towards the north; this tabular structure is carried on, less perfectly, in other lofty mountain regions to the south; we have not seen it so well marked on any part of the coast since the land we discovered south of Cape Washington, which seems to indicate some geological alliance with that part. We can now see also the high land that lies beyond the foothills we have lately been skirting; it is more irregular in outline, with high snow-ridges between the sharper peaks. To the south one particular conical mountain stands much closer to the coast than the main ranges. It looks to be of great height, but may not be so distant as we imagine; it will form our principal landmark for the next week. It is noticeable that along all this stretch of coast we can see no deep valley that could contain a glacier from the interior ice-cap (if there is one).

The beauty of the scene before us is much enhanced when the sun circles low to the south: we get then the most delicate blue shadows and purest tones of pink and violet on the hill-slopes. There is rarely any intensity of shade – the charm lies in the subtlety and delicacy of the colouring and in the clear softness of the distant outline.

We have decided to cease using our bacon and to increase the seal allowance, as the former seems the most likely cause of the scurvy symptoms. To Shackleton it was represented as a preventive measure, but I am not sure that he does not smell a rat. The exchange is not quite equal in weight; we again lose a little. We cannot certainly afford to lose more, as we are already reduced to starvation rations. Our allowance on leaving the ship ran to about 1.9 lb. per man per day, but various causes have reduced this. At first we went too heavy on our biscuit; then we determined to lay by two extra weeks out of eleven; then 'Spud' had his share of the seal-meat bag; altogether I calculate we are existing on about a pound and a half of food a day; it is not enough, and hunger is gripping us very tightly. I never knew what it was like before, and I shall not be particularly keen on trying it again.

Our meals come regularly enough, but they are the poorest stop-gaps, both from want of food and want of fuel. At breakfast now we first make tea – that is to say, we put the tea in long before the water boils, and lift and pour out with the first bubbling. The moment this is over we heap the pemmican and biscuit into the pot and make what we call a "fry"; it takes much less time than a hoosh. The cook works by the watch, and in twenty minutes from the time it is lighted the Primus lamp is out; in two or three more the breakfast is finished. Then we serve out luncheon, which consists of a small piece of seal-meat, half a biscuit, and eight to ten lumps of sugar. Each of us keeps a small bag which, when it contains the precious luncheon, is stowed away in the warmth of a breast-pocket, where it thaws out during the first march. Absurd as it may sound, it is terribly difficult not to filch from this bag during the hours of the march. We have become absolutely childish in this. We know so perfectly the contents of the bags that one will find oneself arguing that today's piece of seal is half an inch longer than yesterday's; ergo, if one nibbles half an inch off, one will still have the same lunch as yesterday.

Supper is of course the best meal; we then have a hoosh which runs from between three-quarters to a whole pannikin apiece, but even at this we cannot afford to make it thick. Whilst it is being heated in the central cooker, cocoa is made in the outer. The lamp is turned out directly the hoosh boils, usually from twenty-eight to thirty minutes after it has been lighted; by this time the chill is barely off the contents of the outer cooker, and of course the cocoa is not properly dissolved, but such as it is, it is the only drink we can afford. We have long ceased criticizing the quality of our food; all we clamour for now is something to fill up, but, needless to say, we never get it. Half an hour after supper one seems as hard set as ever.

My companions get very bad "food dreams"; in fact, these have become the regular breakfast conversation. It appears to be a sort of nightmare; they are either sitting at a well-spread table with their arms tied, or they grasp at a dish and it slips out of their hand, or they are in the act of lifting a dainty morsel to their mouth when they fall over a precipice. Whatever the details may be, something interferes at the last moment and they wake. So far, I have not had these dreams myself, but I suppose they will come.

When we started from the ship we had a sort of idea that we could go as we pleased with regard to food, hauling in automatically if things were going too fast; but we soon found that this would not do at all – there must be some rigid system of shares. After this we used to take it in turns to divide things into three equal portions; it is not an easy thing to do by eye, and of course the man who made the division felt called upon to make certain that he had the smallest share. It was when we found that this led to all sorts of absurd remonstrances and arguments that Shackleton invented the noble game of "shut-eye", which has solved all our difficulties in this respect. The shares are divided as equally as possible by anyone; then one of the other two turns his head away, the divider points at a 'whack' and says, 'Whose is this?' He of the averted head names the owner, and so on. It is a very simple but very efficacious game, as it leaves the matter entirely to chance. We play it at every meal now as a matter of course, and from practice we do it very speedily; but one cannot help thinking how queer it would appear for a casual onlooker to see three civilized beings employed at it.

December 23. We have been getting on rather faster than we thought, though we had a suspicion that the sledge-meter was clogging in the very soft snow. Our latitude is now about 81½° S. Today I had to shift the balance-weight on the theodolite compass needle; the dip must be decreasing rapidly. Theodolite observations are now difficult, as the tripod legs cannot be solidly planted. I find it a good plan to leave it up for the night, as in the morning there is always a little cake of ice under each leg. The surface is so soft that one can push the shaft of the ice-axe down with a finger.

The dogs of course feel it much, but the leaders have the worst time, for they have to make the foot-prints; the others step carefully into them, and are saved the trouble of making their own. Several times lately, and especially today, the dogs have raised their heads together and sniffed at the breeze; with a northerly wind one might suppose that their keen scent might detect something, but it is difficult to imagine what they can find in air coming from the south. Shackleton, who always declares that he believes there is either open water or an oasis ahead, says that the dogs merely confirm his opinion.

We felt the chill wind in our faces much, owing to their very blistered state. We have especial trouble with our nostrils and lips, which are always bare of skin; all our fingers, too, are in a very chapped, cracked condition. We have to be very economical with our eyes also, after frequent attacks of snow-blindness; all three of us today had one eye completely shaded, and could see only by peering with the other through a goggle. But all our ailments together are as nothing beside our hunger, which gets steadily worse day by day.

December 24. Wilson examined us again this morning. I asked him quietly the result, and he said, "A little more." It is trying, but we both agree that it is not time yet to say "Turn." But we have one fact to comfort us tonight – we have passed on to a much harder surface, and though it still holds a layer of an inch or two of feathery snow, beneath that it is comparatively firm, and we are encamped on quite a hard spot; the sastrugi are all from the S.S.E. parallel to the land. If the dogs have not improved, they have not grown much worse during the past day or two; their relative strength alters a good deal, as the following tale will show: "Stripes" and "Gus" pull next one another; a week ago one had great difficulty in preventing "Stripes" from leaping across and seizing "Gus's" food. He was very cunning about it; he waited till one's back was turned, and then was over and back in a moment. Time has its revenges: now "Gus" is the stronger, and tonight he leapt across and seized "Stripes's" choicest morsel. At other times they are not bad friends these two; loser and winner seem to regard this sort of thing as part of the game. After all, it is but "the good old rule, the simple plan," but of course we right matters when we detect such thefts.

Tonight is Christmas Eve. We have been thinking and talking

about the folk at home, and also much about our plans for tomorrow.

December 25, Christmas Day. . . . For a week we have looked forward to this day with childish delight, and, long before that, we decided that it would be a crime to go to bed hungry on Christmas night; so the week went in planning a gorgeous feed. Each meal and each item of each meal we discussed and redis-cussed. The breakfast was to be a glorious spread; the Primus was to be kept going ten or even fifteen minutes longer than usual. Lunch for once was to be warm and comforting; and supper! – well, supper was to be what supper has been.

In fact, we meant this to be a wonderful day, and everything has conspired to make it so.

When we awoke to wish each other "A merry Christmas" the sun was shining warmly through our green canvas roof. We were outside in a twinkling, to find the sky gloriously clear and bright, with not a single cloud in its vast arch. Away to the westward stretched the long line of gleaming coastline; the sunlight danced and sparkled in the snow beneath our feet, and not a breath of wind disturbed the serenity of the scene. It was a glorious morn-ing, but we did not stay to contemplate it, for we had even more interesting facts to occupy us, and were soon inside the tent sniff-ing at the savoury steam of the cooking-pot. Then breakfast was ready, and before each of us lay a whole pannikin-full of biscuit and seal-liver, fried in bacon and pemmican fat. It was gone in no time, but this and a large spoonful of jam to follow left a sense of comfort which we had not experienced for weeks, and we started to pack up in a frame of mind that was wholly joyful.

After this we started on the march, and felt at once the improvement of surface that came to us last night; so great was it that we found we three alone could draw the sledges, and for once the driver was silent and the whip but rarely applied. The dogs merely walked along with slack traces, and we did not attempt to get more out of them. No doubt an outsider would have thought our procession funereal enough, but to us the relief was inexpressible; and so we trudged on from 11.30 to 4 p.m., when we thoroughly enjoyed our lunch, which consisted of hot cocoa and plasmon with a whole biscuit and another spoonful of jam. We were off again at 5.30, and marched on till 8.30, when

we camped in warmth and comfort and with the additional satisfaction of having covered nearly eleven miles, the longest march
we have made for a long time.

Then we laid ourselves out for supper, reckless of consequences, having first had a Christmas wash and brush-up.
Redolent of soap, we sat around the cooking-pot, whilst into its
boiling contents was poured a double "whack" of everything. In
the hoosh that followed one could stand one's spoon with ease,
and still the Primus hissed on, as once again our cocoa was
brought to the boiling-point. Meanwhile I had observed
Shackleton ferreting about in his bundle, out of which he presently produced a spare sock, and stowed away in the toe of that
sock was a small round object about the size of a cricket ball,
which when brought to light, proved to be a noble "plum-
pudding". Another dive into his lucky-bag and out came a
crumpled piece of artificial holly. Heated in the cocoa, our plum-
pudding was soon steaming hot, and stood on the cooker-lid
crowned with its decoration. For once we divided food without
"shut-eye".

I am writing over my second pipe. The sun is still slowly
circling our small tent in a cloudless sky, the air is warm and
quiet, all is pleasant without, and within we have a sense of
comfort we have not known for many a day; we shall sleep well
tonight – no dreams, no tightening of the belt.

We have been chattering away gaily, and not once has the
conversation turned to food. We have been wondering what
Christmas is like in England – possibly very damp, gloomy, and
unpleasant, we think; we have been wondering, too, how our
friends picture us. They will guess that we are away on our sledge
journey, and will perhaps think of us on plains of snow; but few, I
think, will imagine the truth, that for us this has been the reddest
of all red-letter days.

December 26. . . . Poor Wilson has had an attack of snow-
blindness, in comparison with which our former attacks may be
considered as nothing; we were forced to camp early on account
of it, and during the whole afternoon he has been writhing in
horrible agony. It is distressing enough to see, knowing that one
can do nothing to help. Cocaine has only a very temporary effect,

and in the end seems to make matters worse. I have never seen an eye so terribly bloodshot and inflamed as that which is causing the trouble, and the inflammation has spread to the eyelid. He describes the worst part as an almost intolerable stabbing and burning of the eyeball; it is the nearest approach to illness we have had, and one can only hope that it is not going to remain serious.

Shackleton did butcher tonight, and "Brownie" was victim. Poor little dog! his life has been very careworn of late, and it is probably a happy release.

December 27. Late last night Wilson got some sleep, and this morning he was better; all day he has been pulling alongside the sledges with his eyes completely covered. It is tiresome enough to see our snowy world through the slit of a goggle, but to march blindfolded with an empty stomach for long hours touches a pitch of monotony which I shall be glad to avoid. We covered a good ten miles today by sledge-meter, though I think that instrument is clogging and showing short measure. The dogs have done little, but they have all walked, except "Stripes", who broke down and had to be carried on the sledge; he was quite limp when I picked him up, and his thick coat poorly hides the fact that he is nothing but skin and bone. Yesterday I noticed that we were approaching what appeared to be a deeper bay than usual, and this afternoon this opening developed in the most interesting manner.

On the near side is a bold, rocky, snow-covered cape, and all day we have been drawing abreast of this; as we rapidly altered its bearing this afternoon it seemed to roll back like some vast sliding gate, and gradually there stood revealed one of the most glorious mountain scenes we have yet witnessed. Walking opposite to Wilson I was trying to keep him posted with regard to the changes, and I think my reports of this part must have sounded curious. It was with some excitement I noticed that new mountain ridges were appearing as high as anything we had seen to the north, but, to my surprise, as we advanced the ridges grew still higher, as no doubt did my tones. Then, instead of a downward turn in the distant outline came a steep upward line; Pelion was heaped on Ossa, and it can be imagined that we pressed the pace to see what would happen next, till the end came in a gloriously sharp double peak crowned with a few flecks of cirrus cloud.

We can no longer call this opening a bay; it runs for many miles in to the foot of the great range, and is more in the nature of an inlet. But all our thoughts in camp tonight turn to this splendid twin-peaked mountain, which, even in such a lofty country, seems as a giant among pigmies. We all agree that from Sabine to the south the grandest eminences cannot compare in dignity with this monster. We have decided that at last we have found something which is fitting to bear the name of him whom we must always the most delight to honour, and "Mount Markham" it shall be called in memory of the father of the expedition.

December 28. Sights today put us well over the 82nd parallel (82.11 S.). We have almost shot our bolt. If the weather holds fine tomorrow, we intend to drop our sledges at the midday halt and push on as far as possible on ski. We stopped early this after-noon in order to take photographs and make sketches. Wilson, in spite of his recent experiences, refuses to give in; whatever is left unsketched, and however his eyes may suffer, this last part must be done.

It is a glorious evening, and fortune could not have provided us with a more perfect view of our surroundings. We are looking up a broad, deep inlet or strait which stretches away to the south-west for thirty or forty miles before it reaches its boundary of cliff and snow-slope. Beyond, rising fold on fold, are the great névé fields that clothe the distant range; against the pale blue sky the outline of the mountain ridge rises and falls over numerous peaks till, with a sharp turn upward, it culminates in the lofty summit of Mount Markham. To the north it descends again, to be lost behind the bluff extremity of the near cape. It seems more than likely that the vast inlet before us takes a sharp turn to the right beyond the cape and in front of the mountains, and we hope to determine this fact tomorrow.

The eastern foothills of the high range form the southern limit of the strait; they are fringed with high cliffs and steep snow-slopes, and even at this distance we can see that some of the rocks are of the deep-red colour, whilst others are black. Between the high range and the Barrier there must lie immense undulat-ing snow-plateaux covering the lesser foothills, which seem rather to increase in height to the left until they fall sharply to the Barrier level almost due south of us.

To the eastward of this, again, we get our view to the farthest south, and we have been studying it again and again to gather fresh information with the changing bearings of the sun. Mount Longstaff we calculate as 10,000 feet. It is formed by the meeting of two long and comparatively regular slopes; that to the east stretches out into the Barrier and ends in a long snow-cape which bears about S. 14 E.; that to the west is lost behind the nearer foothills, but now fresh features have developed about these slopes. Over the western ridge can be seen two new peaks which must lie considerably to the south of the mountain, and, more interesting still, beyond the eastern cape we catch a glimpse of an extended coastline; the land is thrown up by mirage and appears in small white patches against a pale sky.

We know well this appearance of a snow-covered country; it is the normal view in these regions of a very distant lofty land, and it indicates with certainty that a mountainous country continues beyond Mount Longstaff for nearly fifty miles. The direction of the extreme land thrown up in this manner is S. 17 E., and hence we can now say with certainty that the coastline after passing Mount Longstaff continues in this direction for at least a degree of latitude. Of course one cannot add that the level Barrier surface likewise continues, as one's view of it is limited to a very narrow horizon; but anyone who had travelled over it as we have done, and who now, like us, could gaze on these distant lands beyond its level margin, could have little doubt that it does so.

It is fortunate to have had such glorious weather to give us a clear view of this magnificent scene, for very soon now we must be turning, and though we may advance a few miles we cannot hope to add largely to our store of information.

It has been a busy evening, what with taking angles, sketching, and attending to our camp duties, but hours so full of interest have passed rapidly; and now the sun is well to the south, and from all the coast is rising the thin night mist exactly as it does after a hot day in England, so we are preparing to settle down in our sleeping-bags, in the hope that tomorrow may prove equally fine.

A great relief comes to us in this distant spot at finding that our slight change of diet is already giving a beneficial result; late tonight we had another examination of our scurvy symptoms, and there is now no doubt that they are lessening.

December 29. Instead of our proposed advance we have spent the day in our tent, whilst a strong southerly blizzard has raged without. It is very trying to the patience, and tonight, though the wind has dropped, the old well-known sheet of stratus cloud is closing over us, and there is every prospect of another spell of overcast weather which will obscure the land. This afternoon for the third time we have seen the heavens traced with bands and circles of prismatic light, and, if anything, the phenomenon has been more complicated than before; it was a very beautiful sight.

Only occasionally today have we caught glimpses of the land, and it is not inspiriting to lie hour after hour in a sleeping-bag, chill and hungry, and with the knowledge that one is so far from the region of plenty.

December 30. We got up at six this morning, to find a thick fog and nothing in sight; to leave the camp was out of the question, so we packed up our traps and started to march to the S.S.W. This brought us directly towards the mouth of the strait, and after an hour we found ourselves travelling over a disturbed surface with numerous cracks which seemed to radiate from the cape we were rounding. After stumbling on for some time, the disturbance became so great that we were obliged to camp. If the fates are kind and give us another view of the land, we are far enough advanced now to see the inner recesses of our strait.

After our modest lunch Wilson and I started off on ski to the S.S.W. We lost sight of the camp almost immediately, and were left with only our tracks to guide us back to it, but we pushed on for perhaps a mile or more in hopes that the weather would clear; then, as there was no sign of this, and we could see little more than a hundred yards, we realized there might be considerable risk and could be no advantage in proceeding, and so turned and retraced our footsteps to the camp.

This camp we have now decided must be our last, for we have less than a fortnight's provision to take us back to Depot "B", and with the dogs in their present state it would be impossible to make forced marches; we have, therefore, reached our southerly limit. Observations give it as between 82.16 S. and 82.17 S.; if this compares poorly with our hopes and expectations on leaving the ship, it is a more favourable result than we anticipated when those hopes were first blighted by the failure of the dog team.

Whilst one cannot help a deep sense of disappointment in reflecting on the "might have been" had our team remained in good health, one cannot but remember that even as it is we have made a greater advance towards a pole of the earth than has ever yet been achieved by a sledge party.

We feel a little inclined to grumble at the thick weather that surrounds us; it has a depressing effect, and in our state of hunger we feel the cold though the temperature is +15°; but we must not forget that we had great luck in the fine weather which gave us such a clear view of the land two days ago.

December 31. As we rose this morning the sun was still obscured by low stratus cloud, which rapidly rolled away, however; first the headlands and then the mountains stood out, and we could see that we had achieved our object of yesterday in opening out the inlet; but in this direction the cloud continued to hang persistently, so that it was to little purpose that we had obtained such a position. We could see now that the inlet certainly turned to the north of west; on either side the irregular outlines of the mountains were clear against a blue sky, and, descending gradually towards the level, left a broad gap between, but low in this gap hung the tantalizing bank of fog, screening all that lay beyond. By turning towards the strait we had partly obscured our clear view of Mount Longstaff and quite cut off the miraged images of the more distant land, but we had approached the high cliffs which formed the southern limit of the strait, and in the morning sun could clearly see the irregular distribution of red and black rock in the steep cliff faces.

In hope that the fog-bank to the west would clear, we proceeded with our packing in a leisurely manner, and when all was ready, turned our faces homewards. It was significant of the terrible condition of our team that the turn produced no excitement. It appears to make no difference to them now in which direction they bend their weary footsteps; it almost seems that most of them guess how poor a chance they have of ever seeing the ship again. And so we started our homeward march, slowly at first, and then more briskly as we realized that all chance of a clearance over the strait was gone.

In the flood of sunlight which now illumined the snow about us, we were able to see something of the vast ice upheavals caused by the outflow of ice from the strait; pushing around the cape, it is raised in undulations which seem to run parallel to the land. We directed our course towards the cape with the hopes of getting to the land, but were obliged to keep outwards to avoid the worst disturbances; this brought us obliquely across the undulation, and as we travelled onward they rose in height and became ridged and broken on the summit. Now, too, we came upon numerous crevasses which appeared to extend radially from the cape, and these, with the cracks and ridges, formed a network of obstruction across our path through which we were forced to take a very winding course.

We extended our march until we had passed the worst of this disturbance, and by that time we were well to the north of the cape and abreast of one of the curious rocky groins that occur at intervals along the coast. This showed samples of both the red and the black rock, which seem to constitute the geological structure of the whole coast, and we decided to pitch our camp and make an excursion to the land on our ski. By the time that we had swallowed our luncheon the clouds had rolled away, leaving us in the same brilliant sunshine that we have enjoyed so frequently of late, and in which even at a distance of five or six miles every detail of the high groin could be distinctly seen.

Not knowing what adventures we might encounter, we thought it wise to provide ourselves with a second luncheon, which we safely stowed in our breast-pockets, and taking our ice-axe and Alpine rope, we set out for the shore. It looked deceptively near, nor was it until we had marched for nearly an hour without making any marked difference in its appearance that we realized we were in for a long job.

By this time we were again crossing long undulations which increased in height as we advanced; soon from the summits of the waves we could see signs of greater disturbances ahead, and at five o'clock we found ourselves at the edge of a chasm resembling that which had prevented us from reaching the shore farther to the north. This was not an encouraging spectacle, but on the opposite side, a mile or so away, we could see that a gentle slope led to the rocks, and that once across this disturbance we should have no difficulty in proceeding. On the near side the spaces between the ice-blocks had been much drifted up with snow, so that we found no great difficulty in descending or in starting our climb amongst the ice-blocks; but as we advanced the snow became lighter and the climbing steeper. We could get no hold with our finneskoes on the harder places, and in the softer we sank knee-deep, whilst the lightly-bridged crevasses became more difficult to avoid, and once or twice we were only saved from a bad fall by the fact of being roped together. Constantly after circling a large block with difficulty we found in front of us some unclimbable place, and were obliged to retrace our steps and try in some new direction; but we now knew that we must be approaching the opposite side, and so we struggled on.

At length, however, when we thought our troubles must surely be ending, we cut steps around a sharp corner to find the opposite bank of the chasm close to us, but instead of the rough slopes by which we had descended, we found here a steep, overhanging face of ice, towering some fifty feet above us. To climb this face was obviously impossible, and we were reluctantly forced to confess that all our trouble had been in vain. It was a great disappointment, as we had confidently hoped to get some rock specimens from this far south land, and now I do not see that we shall have a chance to do so.

Before starting our homeward climb we sat down to rest, and, of course, someone mentioned the provisions – it was tomorrow's lunch that we carried – and someone else added that it would be absurd to take it back to the camp. Then the temptation became too great; though we knew it was wrong, our famished condition swept us away, and in five minutes not a remnant remained. After this we started our return climb, and at ten o'clock we reached the camp pretty well "done".

There can be little doubt, I think, that the chasm we have seen today is caused by the ice pushing out of the southern strait against the Barrier, and possibly it may end a little farther to the north, but I could not see any signs of its ending; the blocks of ice within seem to have been split off from the sloping ice-foot – in fact, we saw some in the process of being broken away – and the fact that there is so much less snow towards the land seems to show that the inner ones are of more recent origin. The ice-foot is fed by the ice-cap on the hills above, which at this part flows over in a steep cascade. I do not see that we can make another attempt to reach the land before we get back to Depot "B"; in fact, we shall have none too easy a task in doing that alone. We shall have to average more than seven miles a day, and the dogs are now practically useless; but, what is worse, I cannot help feeling that we ourselves are not so strong as we were. Our walk today has tired us more than it ought.

Tonight Shackleton upset the hoosh pot. There was an awful moment when we thought some of it was going to run away on to the snow luckily it all remained on our waterproof floorcloth, and by the time we had done scraping I do not think that any was wasted.

January 1, 1903. We have opened the new year with a march which is likely to be a sample of those which will follow for many a day to come. The state of our dog team is now quite pitiable; with a very few exceptions they cannot pretend to pull; at the start of the march some have to be lifted on to their feet and held up for a minute or two before their limbs become stiff enough to support them. Poor "Spud" fell in his tracks today; we carried him for a long way on the sledge, and then tried him once more, but he fell again, and had to be carried for the rest of the journey tucked away inside the canvas tank. Towards the end of our day's march it has always been possible to get a semblance of spirit into our poor animals by saying, "Up for supper." They learnt early what the words meant, and it has generally been "Spud" who gave the first responsive whimper. This afternoon it was most pathetic; the cheering shout for the last half-mile was raised as usual, but there was no response, until suddenly from the interior of the sledge-tank came the muffled ghost of a whimper. It was "Spud's" last effort: on halting we carried him back to his place, but in an hour he was dead.

The whole team are in a truly lamentable condition; "Gus" and "Bismarck" are tottering; "Lewis" and "Birdie" may fail any moment; "Jim" is probably the strongest – he had reserves of fat to draw on, and has been a great thief; "Nigger" is something of a mystery: he is weak, but not reduced to the same straits as the others, and seems capable of surprising efforts.

This afternoon a southerly breeze sprang up, and we improvised a sail out of our tent floorcloth; it makes an excellent spread of canvas. Some time ago I fixed up our bamboo mast as a permanency by stepping it in the runner and binding it with wire to one of the standards. On this we hosited our sail, spreading it with two bamboo ski-poles. This evening we saw the last of Mount Markham, and Mount Longstaff is already growing small in the distance.

January 3. We are not finding our homeward march so easy as we expected, and we are not clearing a large margin over the distances which are actually necessary for each day; it is plain that if there are blizzards now we must go on right through them. But today we have done rather better than before. This morning there was a hot sun, which brought the snow-surface nearly up to freezing-point, and we found the sledge drew easily. This afternoon there was a fresh breeze, when we got a great deal of help from our sail. The dogs have not pulled throughout the day – we do not expect it of them now – and this afternoon Shackleton was ahead dragging on those who could not walk. Wilson was carrying their long trace in rear to prevent it getting foul of the sledges, whilst I was employed in keeping the latter straight before the wind and in helping them over the rough places; the sail did most of the pulling. We have only two sledges left now, as we find this is sufficient to carry our much-lightened load.

To walk eight or nine miles in a day does not sound much of a task for even a tired dog, yet it is too much for ours, and they are dropping daily. Yesterday poor little "Nell" fell on the march, tried to rise, and fell again, looking round with a most pathetic expression. She was carried till the night, but this morning was as bad as ever, and at lunchtime was put out of her misery. This afternoon, shortly after starting, "Gus" fell, quite played out, and just before our halt, to our greater grief, "Kid" caved in. One could almost weep over this last case; he has pulled like a Trojan throughout, and his stout little heart bore him up till his legs failed beneath him, and he fell never to rise again.

It is useless to carry all this dog-food, so we have decided to serve it out freely, and the seven animals that remain are now lying about quite replete; at any rate, poor things, they will not die of starvation.

Save for a glimpse of the sun this morning, a high stratus cloud has hung over us all day. We see the land, but not very clearly; we are inside our course in passing down the coast, and about ten miles from the remarkable cliffs we then noticed. To the north-west we recognize well-known landmarks. In spite of our troubles we managed to keep going for seven hours today, but we feel that this is the utmost that we can do at present owing to our poor team.

January 6. This morning saw us start off in overcast weather, but with a high temperature making very wet snow, and in consequence a comparatively easy surface. By lunchtime it had commenced to snow in large flakes, and the temperature had risen to +33° by the sling thermometer; this is the first time the air-temperature has been above freezing; the snow falling on us or on the sledges immediately melted, so that the effect was precisely the same as a shower of rain; and it was ludicrous to see us trying to push things into holes and corners where they would not get sopping wet. We wore our gaberdine blouses this afternoon, and they had the appearance and the effect of mackintoshes. All this is a strangely new experience to us, and certainly one would never have dreamt that an umbrella might be a desirable thing on the Great Barrier. This wave of heat with thick foggy snow came from the south with a fairish breeze.

We have been trying once or twice lately to go on ski as the snow is very soft and we sink deeply, but we find that we cannot put the same weight on the traces as we do on foot. On the whole our ski so far have been of little value. They have saved us labour on the rare occasions on which we have not had to pull, such as when we returned for the second load at our relay work; but the labour thus saved is a doubtful compensation for the extra weight which they add to the load. Another thing to be remembered is that one gets used to plodding, even in heavy snow, and, though it is very tiring at first, one's capacity for performance on foot ought not to be judged until one is thoroughly accustomed to the work.

We have passed our old track once or twice lately; it is partly obliterated but much clearer than I expected to find it after the recent winds. We made sail again this afternoon, and the dogs, which have now become only a hindrance, were hitched on behind the sledges – a very striking example of the cart before the horse. "Boss" fell, and was put on the sledge.

January 7. We have had a very warm and uncommonly pleasant day. The temperature at noon rose to 34° and the snow surface was just on the melting-point, a condition that is excellent for the sledge-runners. We dropped all the dogs out of the traces and pulled steadily ourselves for seven hours, covering ten good miles by sledge-meter. "Boss", when we left, turned back to the old camp; later he was seen following, but he has not turned up tonight, though supper-hour is long past. The rest of the animals walked pretty steadily alongside the sledges. It is a queer ending for our team; I do not suppose they will ever go into harness again, unless it is to help them along.

But who could describe the relief this is to us? No more cheering and dragging in front, no more shouting and yelling behind, no more clearing of tangled traces, no more dismal stoppages, and no more whip. All day we have been steadily plodding on with the one purpose of covering the miles by our own unaided efforts, and one feels that one would sooner have ten such days than one with the harrowing necessity of driving a worn-out dog team. For the first time we were able to converse freely on the march, and in consequence the time passed much more rapidly.

We have seen little of the land of late, though occasionally our landmarks show up. The sun has been flickering in and out all day. Much cloud hangs above the coast; this afternoon it developed into masses of rolled cumulus which clung about the higher peaks like rolls of cotton wool. It is the first time we have seen these to the south, and they are pleasantly reminiscent of milder climates; they would certainly appear to have some connection with the wave of heat that is passing over us.

We have been arguing tonight that if we can only get to the depot in good time we can afford to have an extra feed, a sort of revival of Christmas Day; at present we have gained a day on our allowance. We are positively ravenous, but this thought is sending us to bed in a much happier frame of mind.

January 8. Truly our travelling is full of surprises. Last night we had a mild snow-storm depositing flaky crystals, but none of us guessed what the result would be. This morning the air temperature had fallen to 22°, the snow surface was 23°, and below the upper layer 26°; after breakfast the fog gradually cleared, the sun came out, and a brisk northerly breeze sprang up. We got into our harness in good time, and, lo! and behold, found we could scarcely move the sledges. We scraped the runners and tried again without any difference; somewhat alarmed, we buckled to with all our energy, and after three hours of the hardest work succeeded in advancing one mile and a quarter; then we camped to discuss the matter. It was evident that the surface had completely changed: last night we could have dragged double our present load with ease; this morning each step was a severe strain, we were constantly brought to a standstill and had to break the sledges away with a jerk. As the wind came up, the loose snow settled into little sandy heaps, and seemed actually to grip at the runners. We have decided to remain in camp until the surface changes, but the question one cannot help asking is, Will it change? I suppose it is bound to come right, but we have less than a week's provisions and are at least fifty miles from the depot. Consequently the prospect of a daily rate of one mile and a quarter does not smile on us – in fact, we are none of us very cheerful tonight; and to add to his discomfort poor Shackleton has another bad attack of snow-blindness.

We got a clear view of the land this afternoon, and I was able to get an excellent round of angles. We are opposite the high pyramidal and tabular mountains once more, and get a good idea of the general loftiness of the country.

"Birdie" remained behind at the camp this morning, but came on later; "Boss" has never rejoined – he must have sunk like the rest from sheer exhaustion, but with no one by to give him the last merciful *quietus*; "Joe" was sacrificed for the common good tonight. It is fortunate that numbers will not permit these massacres to continue much longer; yet, after all, one cannot help being struck with the extraordinary and merciful lack of intelligence that these beasts display in such tragic moments. We have had the most impressive examples of this.

When a decree has gone forth against any poor wretch, it has been our custom to lead him some way to the rear of the sledges and there, of course, to put an end to him as painlessly as possible. As the intended victim has been led away, the rest of the team have known at once what is going to happen, and as far as their feeble state has allowed they have raised the same chorus of barks as they used to do when they knew that we were going to fetch their food. Of course the cause is precisely the same; they know in some way that this means food. But the astonishing fact is that the victim himself has never known: he has always followed willingly with his tail wagging, evidently under the impression that he is going to be taken to the place where the food comes from, nor, until the last, has he ever shown the least suspicion of his end.

Thus we have seen an animal howling with joy at seeing his comrade led to the slaughter, and the next night going on the same road himself with every sign of pleasure; it has a distinctly pathetic side, but it is good to know clearly that they have not the intelligence to anticipate their fate.

I have used the pronoun "we" above, but I must confess that I personally have taken no part in the slaughter; it is a moral coward-ice of which I am heartily ashamed, and I know perfectly well that my companions hate the whole thing as much as I do. At the first this horrid duty was performed by Wilson, because it was tacitly agreed that he would be by far the most expert; and later, when I was perfectly capable of taking a share, I suppose I must have shrunk from it so obviously that he, with his usual self-sacrifice, volunteered to do the whole thing throughout. And so it has been arranged, and I occupy the somewhat unenviable position of allowing someone else to do my share of the dirty work.

January 9. Late last night I was awakened by a flapping of wings, and found a solitary skua gull hovering round the camp. One cannot guess how the creature can have spotted us, espe-cially as we had a northerly wind yesterday; but whatever has brought him, it is cheering to see a sign of life once more, as it is more than a month since we saw the last. It was anxious work trying the surface this morning, and we hurried over the break-fast to get into harness. We found the pulling hard work, but very much better than yesterday, and in the afternoon we were able to set our sail again. We have made a fairly good march, but now, unfortunately, cannot tell the exact distance covered, as this morning we found that the sledge-meter had refused duty. An examination showed that one of the cog-wheels had dropped off, so we detached the counter mechanism and abandoned the rest; it has done us good service, and we shall miss its exact record of our work.

Our four remaining dogs roam around the sledges all day, sometimes lying down for a spell, but never dropping far behind. "Nigger" and "Jim" are moderately well, but "Birdie" and "Lewis" are very weak and emaciated. Poor "Nigger" seems rather lost out of harness; he will sometimes get close to our traces and march along as though he was still doing his share of the pulling.

January 10. We started this morning at 8.25, with a moderately bright outlook and the land clear; the surface was a trifle better than yesterday, but with no helping wind we found it heavy enough until at eleven o'clock a high stratus cloud drifted up from the south and plunged us into gloom. With this the temperature rose and the surface improved as if by magic, and for the last hour before lunch we were able to step out briskly. Soon after this the wind came, and as we started our afternoon march it became evident that a blizzard was beginning. It is the first time we have marched in a blizzard, and though it has been very trying work, it has given us several extra miles.

Almost immediately after lunch the sledges began to outrun us, and soon we were obliged to reef our sail, and even with reduced canvas the mast was bending like a whip. The great difficulties were to keep the course and to run the sledges straight. At first we tried to steer by the direction of the wind, and only discovered how wildly we were going by the sail suddenly flying flat aback on either tack. The air was so thick with driving snow that one could not see more than twenty or thirty yards, and against the grey background it was impossible to see the direction in which the snow was driving. After this we tried steering by compass; Shackleton and Wilson pushed on before the wind, whilst I rested the compass in the snow, and when the needle had steadied directed them by shouting; then as they were disappearing in the gloom, I had to pick up the compass and fly after them. It can be imagined how tiring this sort of thing was to all concerned. At length I made up my mind that we could only hope to hold an approximate course, and getting Shackleton well ahead of me, I observed the manner in which the snow was drifting against his back, and for the remainder of the day I directed him according to this rough guide.

As it was evident that, although we were not steering straight, we were covering the ground quickly, we decided to go on for two hours extra and take every advantage we could from the wind. It was as much as we could do to hold out for this time, and when at length the halt was called we were all thoroughly exhausted. We had difficulty in getting our tent up in the heavy gale that was now blowing, and, as luck would have it, our wretched Primus lamp chose this occasion to refuse work, so that it was late before we could prepare our hot meal.

The march has been the most tiring we have done; we are more or less used to steady plodding, but today we have sometimes had to run, sometimes to pull forward, sometimes backward, and sometimes sideways, and always with our senses keenly on the alert and our muscles strung up for instant action. Wilson and I are very much "done", though only to the extent that needs a night's rest; but Shackleton is a good deal worse, I think, and I am not feeling happy about his condition.

We could very rarely spare our attention for the dogs today. Poor "Birdie" gave out early, and was carried on the sledge; as tonight he could not stand, we have had to give up hope of saving him, and he has breathed his last. "Nigger" and "Jim" have kept up well, but "Lewis" has only done so with great difficulty, and has sometimes dropped a long way behind.

We cannot now be far from our depot, but then we do not exactly know where we are; there is not many days' food left, and if this thick weather continues we shall possibly not be able to find it.

January 11. The surface has been truly awful today; with the wind swelling our sail and our united efforts we could scarcely budge the sledges. Nothing could be seen; not a sign of land; cold snow was driving at our backs, and it was most difficult to steer anything like a straight course. At noon the sun peeped out for a few minutes, and I got an altitude which gives the latitude as 80.44 S.; tonight, therefore, we cannot be more than ten or twelve miles from the depot.

Our loads are ridiculously light, and that we should be making such heavy weather of them is very discouraging. It may be because we are overdone, but I cannot help thinking that the surface is getting consistently worse; and with no knowledge of our climate we have certain dismal forebodings that a snowy season has set in, which may be a regular thing at this time of year. With no sight of landmarks and nothing about one but the unchanging grey it is impossible to avoid a sense of being lost; never before have we entirely lost sight of the land for more than twenty-four consecutive hours, and looking at the diminished food-bag we are obliged to realize that we are running things very close. However, it is no use meeting troubles halfway; the only thing now is to push on all we can.

We are not very comfortable in our camping equipment, as everything is wet through – clothes, sleeping-bags, and tent-gear. The canvas tanks and covers of the sledges are shrunk and sodden; the snow was melted as it drifted against one side of our sail today, and from the other hung long icicles.

"Lewis" dropped farther and farther astern this morning, and as he has not come up tonight I fear we shall not see him again.

January 12. This morning as we breakfasted there was just a glimpse of landmarks, but before we could properly recognize them the pall of cloud descended once more; we saw enough to show us that we cannot be very far from the depot. Thanks to a good southerly breeze we have done a good march, and with the help of another latitude sight I calculate the depot must be within a very few miles, but the continuance of this thick weather naturally damps our spirits.

There is no doubt we are approaching a very critical time. The depot is a very small spot on a very big ocean of snow; with luck one might see it at a mile and a half or two miles, and fortune may direct our course within this radius of it; but, on the other hand, it is impossible not to contemplate the ease with which such a small spot can be missed. In a blizzard we should certainly miss it; of course we must stop to search when we know we have passed its latitude, but the low tide in the provision-tank shows that the search cannot be prolonged for any time, though we still have the two dogs to fall back on if the worst comes to the worst. The annoying thing is that one good clear sight of the land would solve all our difficulties.

For a long time we have been discussing the possible advantage of stripping the German silver off the sledge-runners. Once off it cannot be replaced, and therefore to strip them is a serious step; the only way in which we have been able to guess the relative merits of the wood and metal runners is by contrasting the sledges and the ski, and it has always seemed to us that the latter are as likely to clog as the former, but the differing conditions of their use make the comparison difficult. However, the pulling has been so severe lately that I cannot but think that, however bad the wood may be, it cannot be worse than the German silver, and, though we may not gain by stripping our runners, we cannot very well lose; so tomorrow morning I intend to strip one of the sledges for trial, and we are looking forward with some anxiety to the result of the experiment.

January 13, noon. This morning we stripped a sledge and then started on our march. Everything was as bad as it could be. There was not a sign of the land; the whole outlook was one monotonous grey, and when we started to march we found the surface in the most trying condition. Steering could only be done by one person pulling behind, catching the shadow of the others on the light sastrugi, and constantly directing right or left; we were obliged to put every ounce of our strength on the traces, and even thus advanced at a rate which was something less than three-quarters of a mile an hour. The whole thing was heartbreaking, and after three hours of incessant labour we decided to halt. I am now writing in the tent, and, I am bound to say, in no very cheerful frame of mind. We have thought it wise to reduce our meals still further, so that luncheon has been the very poorest ray of comfort.

And so here we lie, again waiting for a favourable change. Little has been said, but I have no doubt we have all been thinking a good deal. The food-bag is a mere trifle to lift; we could finish all that remains in it at one sitting and still rise hungry; the depot cannot be far away, but where is it in this terrible expanse of grey? And with this surface, even if we pick it up, how are we to carry its extra weight when we cannot even make headway with our light sledges?

I have been staring up at the green canvas and asking myself these questions with no very cheering result.

January 13, midnight. Catching a glimpse of the sun in the tent today, I tumbled out of my sleeping-bag in hopes of getting a meridional altitude; it was one of those cases which have been common of late when observation is very difficult. Light, ragged

clouds were drifting across the face of the sun, and through the
theodolite telescope at one moment one saw its blurred, indistin-
guishable image, and at the next was blinded with the full force
of its rays. After getting the best result that I could, I casually
lowered the telescope and swept it round the horizon; suddenly
a speck seemed to flash by, and a wild hope sprang up. Slowly I
brought the telescope back; yes, there it was again; yes, and on
either side of it two smaller specks – the depot, without the
shadow of a doubt. I sprang up and shouted, "Boys, there's the
depot." We are not a demonstrative party, but I think we excused
ourselves for the wild cheer that greeted this announcement. It
could not have been more than five minutes before everything
was packed on the sledges and we were stepping out for those
distant specks. The work was as heavy as before, but we were in
a very different mood to undertake it. Throughout the morning
we had marched in dogged silence; now every tongue was clat-
tering and all minor troubles were forgotten in knowledge that
we were going to have a *fat* hoosh at last. It took us nearly two
hours to get up, and we found everything as we had left it, and
not much drifted up with snow.

We have had our *fat* hoosh, and again, after a long interval,
have a grateful sense of comfort in the inner man. After supper
we completed our experimental comparison of the two sledges,
which have respectively metal and wood runners; we equalized
the weights as nearly as possible, and started to tow the sledges
round singly; we found that there was an astonishing difference:
two of us could barely move the metalled sledge as fast as one
could drag the other. We are wholly at a loss to account for this
difference; one would have thought that if metal was ever to give
a good running surface it would be now when the temperatures
are high; but though the result puzzles us, we have of course
decided to strip the second sledge.

On the whole things stand favourably for us; we have perhaps
130 miles to cover to our next depot, but we have a full three
weeks' provisions, and it looks as though we should not have
great difficulties with our load, now that we are on wood runners. On the other hand, I am not altogether satisfied with the
state of our health. There is no doubt that we are not as fit as we
were: we are all a bit "done". In Shackleton's case especially I

feel uneasy; his scorbutic signs are increasing, and he was again terribly done up when we camped tonight. All things considered, without knowledge of what may be before us, it is safer not to increase our food allowance for the present, more especially as in going north I want to steer inwards so as to examine more closely those masses of land which we have seen only in the far distance. But in spite of all, our circumstances are very different tonight from what they were last night; the finding of the depot has lifted a load of anxiety, and I think we shall all sleep the better for it.

We are all terrible-looking ruffians now; the sun has burnt us quite black, and for many days our only bit of soap has remained untouched. It is some time, too, since we clipped our beards, and our hair has grown uncomfortably long; our faces have developed new lines and wrinkles, and look haggard and worn – in fact, our general appearance and tattered clothing have been a source of some amusement to us of late.

January 14. This morning we had a thorough medical examination, and the result was distinctly unsatisfactory. Shackleton has very angry-looking gums – swollen and dark; he is also suffering greatly from shortness of breath; his throat seems to be congested, and he gets fits of coughing, when he is obliged to spit, and once or twice today he has spat blood. I myself have distinctly red gums, and a very slight swelling in the ankles. Wilson's gums are affected in one spot, where there is a large plum-coloured lump; otherwise he seems free from symptoms. Both he and I feel quite fit and well, and as far as we are concerned I think a breakdown is very far removed.

Early this morning we reorganized our load, dropping everything that was unnecessary, overhauling mast and sail and generally putting everything ship-shape. When we got away at last we carried, besides our own belongings, a small quantity of food for our two remaining dogs, the whole amounting to a weight of 510 lbs., or 170 lbs. per man. We made a fairly good march, and to our surprise the sledges came easily; the only marring element was poor Shackleton's heavy breathing. The sky has been overcast all day, but for a short time we had a good view of the lower land and could very clearly see the leading marks on which we had placed the depot, a sight which would have meant much to us a day or two ago.

Soon after coming to camp I went to the sledges to feed the dogs, and, looking round, found that Wilson had followed me; his face was very serious, and his news still more so. He told me that he was distinctly alarmed about Shackleton's condition; he did not know that the breakdown would come at once, but he felt sure that it was not far removed. The conversation could only be conducted in the most fragmentary fashion for fear it should be overheard, but it was sufficiently impressive to make our supper a very thoughtful meal. It's a bad case, but we must make the best of it and trust to its not getting worse; now that human life is at stake all other objects must be sacrificed. It is plain that we must make a bee-line for the next depot regardless of the northern coast; it is plain also that we must travel as lightly as possible.

It went to my heart to give the order, but it had to be done, and the dogs are to be killed in the morning. I have thought of the instruments, which are a heavy item, but some of them may be needed again, and I am loath to leave any until it is absolutely necessary.

One of the difficulties we foresee with Shakleton, with his restless, energetic temperament, is to keep him idle in camp, so tonight I have talked seriously to him. He is not to do any camping work, but to allow everything to be done for him; he is not to pull on the march, but to walk as easily as possible, and he is to let us know directly he feels tired. I have tried to impress on him the folly of pretending to be stronger than he is, and have pointed out how likely he is to aggravate the evil if he does not consent to nurse himself. We have decided to increase our seal-meat allowance in another effort to drive back the scurvy.

More than this I do not see that we can do at present. Every effort must be devoted to keeping Shackleton on his legs, and we must trust to luck to bring him through. In case he should break down soon and be unable to walk, I can think of absolutely no workable scheme; we could only carry him by doing relay work, and I doubt if Wilson or I am up to covering the distance in that fashion; it is a knotty problem which is best left till the contingency arises.

It looks as though life for the next week or two is not going to be pleasant for any of us, and it is rather curious because we have always looked forward to this part of the journey as promising an easier time.

January 15. This morning "Nigger" and "Jim" were taken a short distance from the camp and killed. This was the saddest scene of all; I think we could all have wept. And so this is the last of our dog team, the finale to a tale of tragedy; I scarcely like to write of it. Through our most troublous time we always looked forward to getting some of our animals home. At first it was to have been nine, then seven, then five, and at the last we thought that surely we should be able to bring back these two.

After the completion of this sad business we got into our harness, where another shock awaited us, for we put our weights on the traces without the least effect, and it was only when we jerked the sledges sideways the least movement followed. It was evident that something was wrong, and on turning the sledges up we found the runners solidly crusted with ice. It took us twenty minutes to clear them; but afterwards we got on well and have covered nearly eight miles. As this caking of the runners is likely to happen whenever our sledges are left long in one position, we have decided to lift them off the snow every night.

In the morning march we had bright sunlight, and it cheered us all wonderfully after its long absence. We could see the northern side of the high rounded snow-cape abreast of which we left our depot, and which we have always known as "Cape A". This northern side forms the southern boundary of the great glacier which occupies the strait, and it is very steep, with high frowning cliffs. We are now crossing more directly across the mouth of the strait, and there are already indications of ice disturbances; we have been travelling over slight undulations and most confused sastrugi.

Shackleton's state last night was highly alarming; he scarcely slept at all, and had violent paroxysms of coughing, between which he was forced to gasp for breath. This morning to our relief he was better, and this evening he is rather better than last, though very fagged with the day's work. We try to make him do as little pulling as possible until the pace is settled, and he can lean steadily forward in his harness.

It is early to judge, but the double ration of seal-meat seems already to have a good effect: gums seem a trifle better. On the other hand, I have some stiffness in the right foot, which I suppose is caused by the taint, but at present I have not mentioned it, as my gums look so well that I am in hopes it will pass away.

January 16. The sledges have been running easily, and we have made a good march, but the surface is getting more uneven, and under the dark, gloomy sky we could not see the inequalities and stumbled frequently. This sort of thing is very bad for Shackleton; twice he slipped his leg down a deep crack and fell heavily, and on each occasion we had to stop several minutes for him to recover. He has been coughing and spitting up blood again, and at lunch-time was very "groggy". With his excitable temperament it is especially difficult for him to take things quietly, and at the end of each march he is panting, dizzy, and exhausted.

It is all very dreadful to watch, knowing that we can do nothing to relieve him; if at the ship, he would be sent straight to bed, but here every effort must be made to keep him on his feet during the marches. There is now no doubt that the scorbutic symptoms are diminishing; both Wilson and I have much cleaner gums, and my leg is vastly improved. Our seal-meat at the present rate will last another fifteen days, by which time we ought to be within reach of safety Six weeks ago we were very much inclined to swear at the cook, who had been careless enough to leave a good deal of blubber in our seal-meat, but now we bless his carelessness, and are only too eager to discover that our "whack" has a streak of yellow running through the dark flesh. I could not have believed it possible that I should ever have enjoyed blubber, and the fact that we do is an eloquent testimony to our famished condition.

This afternoon we have had some glimpses of the land and have got some bearings, but there are still masses of cloud over the mountains. We can see the steep cliffs on the northern side of Cape A, and similar cliffs fringing the foothills on the opposite side of the strait, but what stands behind we cannot hope to know, unless the weather clears. So far as exploring is concerned, on these overcast days one might just as well be blindfolded.

The sunlight this afternoon showed that we are crossing a very peculiar surface of hard, cracked, lateral ridges, with softish snow between, due no doubt to the pressure of the ice-mass pushing out through the strait.

January 17. . . . The continuance of our overcast weather has brought a trouble which is now becoming a serious matter, and that is the difficulty of steering. I take it on myself to do most of it now, sometimes by a cloud, sometimes by the sun, and sometimes by sastrugi, and in half an hour it often happens that each of these methods has to be employed in turn.

January 17 (continued). This morning we started with an overcast sky and an unshaded wall of grey ahead. A rapidly closing bright patch on our starboard beam was the only guide. After two hours I had to give up leading; Wilson went ahead, but by lunch his eyes had had enough, and I finished the afternoon. It is difficult to describe the trying nature of this work; for hours one plods on, ever searching for some more definite sign. Sometimes the eye picks up a shade on the surface or a cloud slightly lighter or darker than its surroundings; these may occur at any angle, and have often to be kept in the corner of the eye. Frequently there comes a minute or two of absolute confusion, when one may be going in any direction and for the time the mind seems blank. It can scarcely be imagined how tiring this is or how trying to the eyes; one's whole attention must be given to it, without relaxing for a moment the strain on the harness. At lunch today I fixed up a new device by securing a small teased-out shred of wool to the end of a light bamboo to act as a wind vane. The wind was light and shifty, but the vane relieved my eyes.

January 18. We started today on another abominable "blind" march. For half an hour I could just see some ridges and the slightest gleam in the sky to the north; for another spell, a very light easterly breeze kept my vane on the flutter. The sastrugi under foot are light and confused, and when at last the wind fell we were left with no guide at all, and were forced to camp; for the last ten minutes we had been four points off our course. Wilson says his eyes are on the point of going; mine, on which I see the party must principally depend, are not quite right, but not yet painful. The situation is startling, but we have not yet exhausted our resources. If there is no improvement after lunch, Shackleton will start on ahead with a flag, and when he has been directed for half a mile, Wilson and I propose to bring on the sledges; it promises to be slow work, but we must get on somehow.

Midnight. All was going well with our march this afternoon, when Shackleton gave out. He had a bad attack of breathlessness, and we are forced to camp in a hurry; tonight matters are serious with him again. He is very plucky about it, for he does not complain, though there is no doubt he is suffering badly.

January 19. Another long "blind" march. It is very distressing work, and the gloom does not tend to enliven our spirits; but Shackleton was better this morning and is still better tonight. We have now had overcast weather almost continuously for ten days.

January 20. At luncheon we found ourselves in latitude 79.51 S., and on coming out of the tent were rejoiced to find a sight of the land on our left, though as yet but hazy. It rapidly cleared as we resumed our march, and soon a new scene was unfolded to our view. An opportunity of this sort was not to be missed, and we camped early, since which we have been busy taking angles and sketching. The temperature has fallen to zero, so that both these tasks have been pretty "nippy". The beautiful feathery hexagonal ice-crystals are falling again, and came floating down on our books and instruments as we worked.

The land is a long way from us, but much closer than it was on the outward march; the detached appearance which it then had is still maintained to some extent, but there is now every indication that a still closer view would show a continuous coastline, and that in the gaps between the nearer high mountain ranges would be found lower and perhaps more distant hills.

Cape A is far behind us; we get a distant view up the strait on its northern side, and see only enough to show that it must penetrate deeply into the land before it rises in altitude to any extent. If, as one cannot but suppose, it contains a glacier, that glacier must be the largest yet known in the world; but with ice disturbance commencing nearly thirty miles from its mouth, one can imagine that to travel up it would not be an easy task. Through the gap of the strait we get a distant view of more mountains – in fact, at any place on this coastline one is struck with the vast numbers of peaks that are within sight at the same moment. There are far more than one could hope to fix on such a journey as ours: to plot the coastal ranges alone would be a big task, but wherever we get a view behind them it is to see a confusion of more distant hills.

Northward of the strait we again see the high flanking range end on; northward of this, again, are three distinct coastal ranges. The farthest may possibly be the Royal Society range, though of this we cannot be sure at present; but perhaps the most pleasing sight tonight is the glimpse we get of Mount Discovery; its conical peak rises just above our horizon, and the sight of that well-known landmark has seemed to bring us miles nearer to home and safety.

January 21. The clouds have drawn down on us again, shutting out the land, but we have had a brisk southerly breeze, and, setting our sail, got along at a fine rate. For a time Shackleton was carried on the sledges, but for most of the march he walked along independently, taking things as easily as possible. Our sail did most of the pulling. I, hitched to the bow of the front sledge, kept it straight, and helped it over the rough places; Wilson hitched to the back of the rear sledge, and by hauling sideways acted as a sort of rudder. We got on fast, but it was by no means easy work, being so extraordinarily jerky and irregular. Shackleton is improving, but takes his breakdown much to heart.

January 22. The southerly wind continued today; it is a godsend, and is taking us to the north faster than we ever hoped for. The masses of low heavy cumulus and stratus cloud and the higher cirro-cumulus, all hurrying to the north, have given us the most beautiful cloud effects. The sun has peeped forth occasionally, but the land is still heavily overcast. We are beginning to hope that we shall soon be able slightly to increase our food allowance.

January 23. I think the fates have decided in our favour.

Farthest South

Ernest Shackleton

Of all the Antarctic explorers from the "Heroic Age" the reputation of Shackleton has stood highest longest. Scott has been found wanting for his amateurism, Amundsen – perversely – for his clinical professionalism, but of Shackleton the only complaint is the occasional peccadillo. So high, indeed, is Shackleton's stock that he is a curriculum subject in US business schools for those wanting to learn leadership skills.

Born in 1874 in County Kildare, Shackleton was apprenticed to the Merchant Navy and became a junior officer under Robert F. Scott during the 1901–4 expedition to the South Pole. Shackleton, to his chagrin, was invalided home. In 1907 Shackleton led his own expedition to Antarctica on the whaler Nimrod. *After wintering at Cape Royds on the Ross Sea, the expedition discovered the Magnetic South Pole, climbed 12,500-foot Mount Erebus – and then, as Shackleton relates below, pushed further South than any had gone before.*

November 26. A day to remember, for we have passed the "farthest South" previously reached by man. Tonight we are in latitude 82° 18½' South, longitude 168° East, and this latitude we have been able to reach in much less time than on the last long march with Captain Scott, when we made latitude 82° 16½' our "farthest South". We started in lovely weather this morning, with the temperature plus 19°F, and it has been up to plus 20°F during the day, giving us a chance to dry our sleeping-bags. We were rather anxious at starting about Quan, who had a sharp attack of colic, the result no doubt of his morbid craving for bits of rope and other odds and ends in preference to his proper food. He soon got well enough to pull, and we got away at 7.40 a.m., the surface still very soft. There are abundant signs that the wind blows strongly from the south south-east during the winter, for the sastrugi are very marked in that direction. There are extremely large circular crystals of snow on the Barrier surface, and they seem hard and brittle. They catch the light from the sun, each one forming a reflector that dazzles the eyes as one glances at the million points of light. As each hour went on today, we found new interest to the west, where the land lies, for we opened out Shackleton Inlet, and up the inlet lies a great chain of mountains, and far into the west appear more peaks; to the west of Cape Wilson appears another chain of sharp peaks about 10,000 ft high, stretching away to the north beyond the Snow Cape, and continuing the land on which Mount A. Markham lies. To the south south-east ever appear new mountains. I trust that no land will block our path. We celebrated the breaking of the "farthest South" record with a four-ounce bottle of Curacao, sent us by a friend at home. After this had been shared out into two table-spoonfuls each, we had a smoke and a talk before turning in. One wonders what the next month will bring forth. We ought by that time to be near our goal, all being well.

NOTE. It falls to the lot of few men to view land not previously seen by human eyes, and it was with feelings of keen curiosity, not unmingled with awe, that we watched the new mountains rise from the great unknown that lay ahead of us. Mighty peaks they were, the eternal snows at their bases, and their rough-hewn forms rising high towards the sky. No man of us could tell what we would discover in our march south, what wonders might not be revealed to us, and our imaginations would take wings until a stumble in the snow, the sharp pangs of hunger, or the dull ache of physical weariness brought back our attention to the needs of the immediate present. As the days wore on, and mountain after mountain came into view, grimly majestic, the consciousness of our insignificance seemed to grow upon us. We were but tiny black specks crawling slowly and painfully across the white plain, and bending our puny strength to the task of wresting from nature secrets preserved inviolate through all the ages. Our anxiety to learn what lay beyond was nonetheless keen, however, and the long days of marching over the Barrier surface were saved from monotony by the continued appearance of new land to the south-east.

November 27. Started at 8 a.m., the ponies pulling well over a bad surface of very soft snow. The weather is fine and clear save for a strong mirage, which throws all the land up much higher than it really is. All day we have seen new mountains arise, and it is causing us some anxiety to note that they trend more and more to the eastward, for that means an alteration of our course from nearly due south. Still they are a long way off, and when we get up to them we may find some strait that will enable us to go right through them and on south. One speculates greatly as we march along, but patience is what is needed. I think that the ponies are feeling the day in, day out drudgery of pulling on this plain. Poor beasts, they cannot understand, of course, what it is all for, and the wonder of the great mountains is naught to them, though one notices them at times looking at the distant land. At lunchtime I took a photograph of our camp, with Mount Longstaff in the background. We had our sledge flags up to celebrate the breaking of the southern record. The long snow cape marked on the chart as being attached to Mount Longstaff is not really so. It is attached to a lower bluff mountain to the north of Mount Longstaff. The most northerly peak of Mount Longstaff goes sheer down into the Barrier, and all along this range of mountains are very steep glaciers, greatly crevassed. As we pass along the mountains the capes disappear, but there are several well marked ones of which we have taken angles. Still more mountains appeared above the horizon during the afternoon, and when we camped tonight some were quite clearly defined, many, many miles away. The temperature has been up to plus 22°F today, and we took the opportunity of drying our sleeping-bags, which we turned inside out and laid on the sledges. Tonight the temperature is plus 13°F. We find that raw frozen pony meat cools one on the march, and during the ten minutes' spell after an hour's march we all cut up meat for lunch or dinner; in the hot sun it thaws well. This fresh meat ought to keep away scurvy from us. Quan seems much better today, but Grisi does not appear fit at all. He seems to be snow blind. Our distance today was 16 miles 1,200 yards.

November 28. Started at 7.50 a.m. in beautiful weather, but with a truly awful surface, the ponies sinking in very deeply. The sledges ran easily, as the temperature was high, plus 17° to plus

20°F, the hot sun making the snow surface almost melt. We halted at noon for a latitude observation, and found our latitude to be 82° 38' South. The land now appears more to the east, bearing south-east by south, and some very high mountains a long way off with lower foothills, can be seen in front, quite different to the land abeam of us, which consists of huge sharp pointed mountains with crevassed glaciers moving down gullies in their sides. Marshall is making a careful survey of all the principal heights. All day we have been travelling up and down long undulations, the width from crest to crest being about one and a half miles, and the rise about 1 in 100. We can easily see the line by our tracks sometimes being cut off sharp when we are on the down gradient and appearing again a long way astern as we rise. The first indication of the undulation was the fact of the mound we had made in the morning disappearing before we had travelled a quarter of a mile. During the afternoon the weather was very hot. A cool breeze had helped us in the forenoon, but it died away later. Marshall has a touch of snow blindness, and both Grisi and Socks were also affected during the day. When we camped tonight Grisi was shot. He had fallen off during the last few days, and the snow blindness was bad for him, putting him off his feed. He was the one chosen to go at the depot we made this evening. This is Depot C, and we are leaving one week's provisions and oil, with horse meat, to carry us back to Depot B. We will go on tomorrow with 1,200 lb. weight (nine weeks' provisions), and we four will pull with the ponies, two on each sledge. It is late now, 11 p.m., and we have just turned in. We get up at 5.30 every morning. Our march for the day was 15 miles 1,500 yards statute.

November 29. Started at 8.45 a.m. with adjusted loads of 630 lb. on each sledge. We harnessed up ourselves, but found that the ponies would not pull when we did, and as the loads came away lightly, we untoggled our harness. The surface was very soft, but during the morning there were occasional patches of hard sastrugi, all pointing south south-east. This is the course we are now steering, as the land is trending about south-east by east. During the day still more great mountains appeared to the south-east, and to the west we opened up several huge peaks, 10,000 to 15,000 ft in height. The whole country seems to be made up of range after range of mountains, one behind the other. The worst feature of today's march was the terribly soft snow in the hollows of the great undulations we were passing. During the afternoon one place was so bad that the ponies sank in right up to their bellies, and we had to pull with might and main to get the sledges along at all. When we began to ascend the rise on the southern side of the undulation it got better. The ponies were played out by 5.45 p.m., especially old Quan, who nearly collapsed, not from the weight of the sledge, but from the effort of lifting his feet and limbs through the soft snow. The weather is calm and clear, but very hot, and it is trying to man and beast. We are on a short allowance of food, for we must save all we can, so as to help the advance as far as possible. Marshall has taken the angles of the new land today. He does this regularly. The hypsometer readings at 1 p.m. are very high now if there is no correction, and it is not due to weather. We must be at about sea level. The undulations run about east by south, and west by west, and are at the moment a puzzle to us. I cannot think that the feeding of the glaciers from the adjacent mountains has anything to do with their existence. There are several glaciers, but their size is inconsiderable compared to the vast extent of Barrier affected. The glaciers are greatly crevassed. There are enormous granite cliffs at the foot of the range we are passing, and they stand vertically about 4,000 to 5,000 ft without a vestige of snow upon them. The main bare rocks appear to be like the schists of the western mountains opposite our winter quarters, but we are too far away, of course, to be able to tell with any certainty. Down to the south are mountains entirely clear of snow, for their sides are vertical, and they must be not less than 8,000 to 9,000 ft in height. Altogether it is a weird and wonderful country. The only familiar thing is the broad expanse of Barrier to the east, where as yet no land appears. We did 14 miles 900 yards (statute) today, and are tired. The snow came well above our ankles, and each step became a labour. Still we are making our way south, and each mile gained reduces the unknown. We have now done over 300 miles due south in less than a month.

November 30. We started at 8 a.m. this morning. Quan very shaky and seemingly on his last legs, poor beast. Both he and Socks are snow blind, so we have improvised shades for their eyes, which we trust will help them a little. We took turns of an hour each hauling at Quan's sledge, one at each side, to help him. Socks, being faster, always gets ahead and then has a short spell, which eases him considerably. We advanced very slowly today, for the surface was as bad as ever till the afternoon, and the total distance covered was 12 miles 150 yards. Quan was quite played out, so we camped at 5.45 p.m. We give the ponies ample food, but they do not eat it all, though Quan whinnies for his every meal time. He is particularly fond of the Maujee ration, and neglects his maize for it. Again today we saw new land to the south, and unfortunately for our quick progress in that direction, we find the trend of the coast more to the eastward. A time is coming, I can see, when we will have to ascend the mountains, for the land runs round more and more in an easterly direction. Still after all we must not expect to find things cut and dried and all suited to us in such a place. We will be thankful if we can keep the ponies as far as our next depot which will be in latitude 84° South. They are at the present moment lying down in the warm sun. It is a beautifully calm clear evening; indeed as regards weather we have been wonderfully fortunate, and it has given Marshall the chance to take all the necessary angles for the survey of these new mountains and coastline. Wild is cook this week, and my week is over so I am now living in the other tent. We are all fit and well, but our appetites are increasing at an alarming rate. We noticed this tonight after the heavy pulling today. A great deal of the land we are passing seems to consist of granite in huge masses, and here and there are much crevassed glaciers pouring down between the mountains, perhaps from some inland ice sheet similar to that in the north of Victoria Land. The mountains show great similarity in outline, and there is no sign of any volcanic action at all so far. The temperature for the day has ranged between plus 16° and plus 12°F, but the hot sun has made things appear much warmer.

December 1. Started at 8 a.m. today. Quan has been growing weaker each hour, and we practically pulled the sledge. We passed over three undulations, and camped at 1 p.m. In the afternoon we only did four miles, Quan being led by Wild. He also led Socks with one sledge, whilst Adams, Marshall, and I hauled 200 lb. each on the other sledge, over a terribly soft surface. Poor old Quan was quite finished when we came to camp at 6 p.m., having done 12 miles 200 yards, so he was shot. We all felt losing him, I particularly, for he was my special horse ever since he was ill last March. I had looked after him, and in spite of all his annoying tricks he was a general favourite. He seemed so intelligent. Still it was best for him to go, and like the others he was well fed to the last. We have now only one pony left, and are in latitude 83° 16' South. Ahead of us we can see the land stretching away to the east, with a long white line in front of it that looks like a giant Barrier, and nearer a very crusted-up appearance, as though there were great pressure ridges in front of us. It seems as though the Barrier end had come, and that there is now going to be a change in some gigantic way in keeping with the vastness of the whole place. We fervently trust that we will not be delayed in our march south. We are living mainly on horsemeat now, and on the march, to cool our throats when pulling in the hot sun, we chew some raw frozen meat. There was a slight breeze for a time today, and we felt chilly, as we were pulling stripped to our shirts. We wear our goggles all the time, for the glare from the snow surface is intense and the sky is cloudless. A few wisps of fleecy cloud settle on the tops of the loftiest mountains, but that is all. The surface of the Barrier still sparkles with the million frozen crystals which stand apart from the ordinary surface snow. One or two new peaks came in sight today, so we are ever adding to the chain of wonderful mountains that we have found. At one moment our thoughts are on the grandeur of the scene, the next of what we would have to eat if only we were let loose in a good restaurant. We are very hungry these days, and we know that we are likely to be for another three months. One of the granite cliffs we are nearing is over 6,000 ft sheer, and much bare rock is showing, which must have running water on it as the hot sun plays down. The moon was visible in the sky all day and it was something familiar, yet far removed from these days of hot sunshine and wide white pathways. The temperature is now plus 16°F, and it is quite warm in the tent.

December 2. Started at 8 a.m., all four of us hauling one sledge, and Socks following behind with the other. He soon got into our regular pace, and did very well indeed. The surface during the morning was extremely bad and it was heavy work for us. The sun beat down on our heads and we perspired freely, though we were working only in shirts and pyjama trousers, whilst our feet were cold in the snow. We halted for lunch at 1 p.m., and had some of Quan cooked, but he was very tough meat, poor old beast. Socks, the only pony left now, is lonely. He whinnied all night for his lost companion. At 1 p.m. today we had got close enough to the disturbance ahead of us to see that it consisted of enormous pressure ridges, heavily crevassed and running a long way east, with not the slightest chance of our being able to get southing that way any longer on the Barrier. So after lunch we struck due south in towards the land, which is now running in a south-east direction, and at 6 p.m. we were close to the ridges off the coast. There is a red hill about 3,000 ft in height, which we hope to ascend tomorrow, so as to gain view of the surrounding country. Then we will make our way if possible, with the pony up a glacier ahead of us on to the huge ice, and on to the Pole if all goes well. It is an anxious time for us, for time is precious and food more so; we will be greatly relieved if we find a good route through the mountains. Now that we are close to the land we can see more clearly the nature of the mountains. From Mount Longstaff in a south-east direction, the land appears to be far more glaciated than further north, and since the valleys are very steep, the glaciers that they contain are heavily crevassed. These glaciers bear out in a north-east direction into the Barrier. Immediately opposite our camp the snow seems to have been blown off the steep mountain sides. The mountain ahead of us, which we are going to climb tomorrow, is undoubtedly granite, but very mildly weathered. In the distance it looked like volcanic rock, but now there can be no doubt that it consists of granite. Evidently the great ice sheet has passed over this part of the land, for the rounded forms could not have been caused by ordinary weathering. Enormous pressure ridges that run out from the south of the mountain ahead must be due to a glacier far greater in extent than any we have yet met. The glacier that comes out of Shackleton Inlet makes a disturbance in the Barrier ice, but not nearly as great as the disturbance in our immediate neigh-bourhood at the present time. The glacier at Shackleton Inlet is quite a short one. We have now closed in to the land, but before we did so we could see the rounded tops of great mountains extending in a south-easterly direction. If we are fortunate enough to reach the summit of the mountain tomorrow, we should be able to see more clearly the line of these mountains to the south-east. It would be very interesting to follow along the Barrier to the south-east, and see the trend of the mountains but that does not enter into our programme. Our way lies to the south. How one wishes for time and unlimited provisions. Then indeed we could penetrate the secrets of this great lonely continent. Regrets are vain, however, and we wonder what is in store for us beyond the mountains if we are able to get there. The closer observation of these mountains ought to give geological results of importance. We may have the good fortune to discover fossils, or at any rate to bring back specimens that will determine the geological history of the country and prove a connection between the granite boulders lying on the slopes of Erebus and Terror and the land lying to the far south. Our position tonight is latitude 83° 28' South, longitude 171° 30' East. If we can get on the mountain tomorrow, it will be the pioneer landing in the far south. We travelled 11 miles 1,450 yards (statute) today, which was not bad, seeing that we were pulling 180 lb. per man on a bad surface. We got a photograph of the wonderful red granite peaks close to us, for now we are only eight miles or so off the land. The temperature is plus 20°, with a high barometer. The same fine weather continues, but the wind is cold in the early morning, when we turn out at 5.30 a.m. for breakfast.

December 4. Unable to write yesterday owing to bad attack of snow blindness, and not much better tonight, but I must record the events of the two most remarkable days that we have experienced since leaving the winter quarters. After breakfast at 5.30 a.m. yesterday, we started off from camp, leaving all camp gear standing and a good feed by Socks to last him the whole day. We got under way at 9 a.m., taking four biscuits, four lumps of sugar, and two ounces of chocolate each for lunch. We hoped to get water at the first of the rocks when we landed. Hardly had we gone one hundred yards when we came to a crevasse, which we did not see very distinctly, for the light was bad, and the sun obscured by clouds. We roped up and went on in single file, each with his ice-pick handy. I found it very difficult to see clearly with my goggles, and so took them off, and the present attack of snow blindness is the result, for the sun came out gloriously later on. We crossed several crevasses filled with snow except at the sides, the gaps being about 2 ft wide, and the whole crevasses from 10 to 20 ft across. Then we were brought up all standing by an enormous chasm of about 80 ft wide and 300 ft deep which lay right across our route. This chasm was similar to, only larger than, the one we encountered in latitude 80° 30' South when on the southern journey with Captain Scott during the *Discovery* expedition. By making a detour to the right we found that it gradually pinched out and became filled with snow, and so we were able to cross and resume our line to the land, which very deceptively appeared quite close but was really some miles away.

Crossing several ridges of ice pressure and many more crevasses, we eventually at 12.30 p.m. reached an area of smooth blue ice in which were embedded several granite boulders, and here we obtained a drink of delicious water formed by the sun playing on the rock face and heating the ice at the base. After travelling for half a mile, we reached the base of the mountain which we hoped to climb in order to gain a view of the surrounding country. This hill is composed of granite, the red appearance being no doubt due to iron. At 1 p.m. we had a couple of biscuits and some water, and then started to make our way up the precipitous rock face. This was the most difficult part of the whole climb, for the granite was weathered and split in every direction, and some of the larger pieces seemed to be just nicely balanced on smaller pieces, so that once could almost push them over by a touch. With great difficulty we clambered up this rock face, and then ascended a gentle snow slope to another rocky bit, but not so difficult to climb. From the top of this ridge there burst upon our view an open road to the south, for there stretched before us a great glacier running almost south and north between two huge mountain ranges. As far as we could see, except towards the mouth, the glacier appeared to be smooth, yet this was not a certainty, for the distance was so great. Eagerly we clambered up the remaining ridges and over a snow slope, and found ourselves at the top of the mountain, the height being 3,350 ft according to aneroid and hypsometer. From the summit we could see the glacier stretching away south inland till at last it seemed to merge in high inland ice. Where the glacier fell into the Barrier about north-east bearing, the pressure waves were enormous, and for miles the surface of the Barrier was broken up. This was what we had seen ahead of us the last few days, and we now understood the reason of the commotion on the Barrier surface. To the south-east we could see the lofty range of mountains we had been following still stretching away in the same direction, and we can safely say that the Barrier is bounded by a chain of mountains extending in a south-easterly direction as far as the 86th parallel South. The mountains to the west appear to be more heavily glaciated than the ones to the eastward. There are some huge granite faces on the southern sides of the mountains, and these faces are joined up by cliffs of a very dark hue. To the south south-east, towards what is apparently the head of the glacier, there are several sharp cones of very black rock, eight or nine in all. Beyond these are red granite faces, with sharp, needlelike spurs, similar in appearance to the 'cathedral' rocks described by Armitage in connection with the *Discovery* expedition to the western mountains. Further on to the south the mountains have a bluff appearance, with long lines of stratification running almost horizontally. This bluff mountain range seems to break about sixty miles away, and beyond can be seen dimly other mountains. Turning to the west, the mountains on that side appeared to be rounded and covered with huge masses of ice, and glaciers showing the lines of crevasses. In the far distance there is what looked like an active volcano. There is a big mountain with a cloud on the top, bearing all the appearance of steam from an active cone. It would be very interesting to find an active volcano so far south. After taking bearings of the trend of the mountains, Barrier and glacier, we ate our frugal lunch and wished for more, and then descended. Adams had boiled the hypsometer and taken the temperature on the top, whilst Marshall, who had carried the camera on his back all the way up, took a couple of photographs. How we wished we had more plates to spare to get a record of the wonderful country we were passing through. At 4 p.m. we began to descend, and at 5 p.m. we were on the Barrier again. We were rather tired and very hungry when, at 7 p.m., we reached our camp. After a good dinner, and a cupful of Maujee ration in the hoosh as an extra, we turned in.

Today, December 4, we got under way at 8 a.m. and steered into the land, for we could see that there was no question as to the way we should go now. Though on the glacier, we might encounter crevasses and difficulties not to be met with on the Barrier, yet on the latter we could get no further than 86° South, and then would have to turn in towards the land and get over the mountains to reach the Pole. We felt that our main difficulty on the glacier route would be with the pony Socks, and we could not expect to drag the full load ourselves as yet without relay work. Adams, Marshall, and I pulled one sledge with 680 lb. weight, and Wild followed with Socks directly in our wake, so that if we came to a crevasse he would have warning. Everything went on well except that when we were close in to land, Marshall went through the snow covering of a crevasse. He managed to hold himself up by his arms. We could see no bottom to this crevasse. At 1 p.m. we were close to the snow slope up which we hoped to reach the interior of the land and thence get on to the glacier. We had lunch and then proceeded, finding, instead of a steep, short slope, a long, fairly steep gradient. All the afternoon we toiled at the sledge, Socks pulling his load easily enough, and eventually, at 5 p.m., reached the head of the pass, 2,000 ft above sea level. From that point there was a gentle descent towards the glacier, and at 6 p.m. we camped close to some blue ice with granite boulders embedded in it, around which were pools of water. This water saves a certain amount of our oil, for we have not to melt snow or ice. We turned in at 8 p.m., well satisfied with the day's work. The weather now is wonderfully fine, with not a breath of wind, and a warm sun beating down on us. The temperature was up to plus 22°F at noon, and is now plus 18°F. The pass through which we have come is flanked by great granite pillars at least 2,000 ft in height and making a magnificent entrance to the "Highway to the South". It is all so interesting and everything is on such a vast scale that one cannot describe it well. We four are seeing these great designs and the play of nature in her grandest moods for the first time, and possibly they may never be seen by man again. Poor Marshall had another four miles' walk this evening, for he found that he had lost his Jaeger jacket off the sledge. He had therefore to tramp back uphill for it, and found it two miles away on the trail. Socks is not feeding well. He seems lonely without his companions. We gave him a drink of thaw water this evening, but he did not seem to appreciate it, preferring the snow at his feet.

December 5. Broke camp sharp at 8 a.m. and proceeded south down an icy slope to the main glacier. The ice was too slippery for the pony, so Wild took him by a circuitous route to the bottom on snow. At the end of our ice slope, down which the sledge skidded rapidly, though we had put on rope brakes and hung on to it as well as we could, there was a patch of soft snow running parallel with the glacier, which here trended about south-west by south. Close ahead of us were the massed up, fantastically shaped and split masses of pressure across which it would have been impossible for us to have gone, but, fortunately, it was not necessary even to try, for close into the land was a snow slope free from all crevasses, and along this gentle rise we made our way. After a time this snow slope gave place to blue ice, with numberless cracks and small crevasses across which it was quite impossible for the pony to drag the sledge without a serious risk of a broken leg in one of the many holes, the depth of which we could not ascertain. We therefore unharnessed Socks, and Wild took him over this bit of ground very carefully, whilst we others first hauled our sledge and then the pony sledge across to a patch of snow under some gigantic granite pillars over 2,000 ft in height, and here, close to some thaw water, we made our lunch camp. I was still badly snow blind, so stayed in camp whilst Marshall and Adams went on to spy out a good route to follow after lunch was over. When they returned they informed me that there was more cracked-up blue ice ahead, and that the main pressure of the glacier came in very close to the pillar of granite that stood before us, but that beyond that there appeared to be a snow slope and good going. The most remarkable thing they reported was that as they were walking along a bird, brown in colour with a white line under each wing, flew just over their heads and disappeared to the south. It is, indeed, strange to hear of such an incident in latitude 83° 40' South. They were sure it was not a skua gull, which is the only bird I could think of that would venture down here, and the gull might have been attracted by the last dead pony, for when in latitude 80° 30' South, on my last southern trip, a skua gull arrived shortly after we had killed a dog.

After lunch we started again, and by dint of great exertions managed, at 6 p.m., to camp after getting both sledges and then the pony over another couple of miles of crevassed blue ice. We then went on and had a look ahead, and saw that we are going to have a tough time tomorrow to get along at all. I can see that it will, at least, mean relaying three or four times across nearly half a mile of terribly crevassed ice, covered in places with treacherous snow, and razor edged in other places, all of it sloping down towards the rock debris-strewn shore on the cliff side. We are camped under a wonderful pillar of granite that has been arounded by the winds into a perfectly symmetrical shape, and is banded by lines of gneiss. There is just one little patch of snow for our tents, and even that bridges some crevasses. Providence will look over us tonight, for we can do nothing more. One feels that at any moment some great piece of rock may come hurtling down, for all around us are pieces of granite, ranging from the size of a hazelnut to great boulders twenty to forty tons in weight, and on one snow slope is the fresh track of a fallen rock. Still we can do no better, for it is impossible to spread a tent on the blue ice, and we cannot get any further tonight. We are leaving a depot here. My eyes are my only trouble, for their condition makes it impossible for me to pick out the route or do much more than pull. The distance covered today was 9 miles with 4 miles relay.

December 6. Started at 8 a.m. today in fine weather to get our loads over the half mile of crevassed ice that lay between us and the snow slope to the south south-west. We divided up the load and managed to get the whole lot over in three journeys, but it was an awful job, for every step was a venture, and I, with one eye entirely blocked up because of snow blindness, felt it particularly uncomfortable work. However, by 1 p.m. all our gear was safely over, and the other three went back for Socks. Wild led him, and by 2 p.m. we were all camped on the snow again. Providence has indeed looked after us. At 3 p.m. we started south south-west up a long slope to the right of the main glacier pressure. It was very heavy going, and we camped at 5 p.m. close to a huge crevasse, the snow bridge of which we crossed. There is a wonderful view of the mountains, with new peaks and ranges to the south-east, south and south-west. There is a dark rock running in conjunction with the granite on several of the mountains. We are now over 1,700 ft up on the glacier, and can see down on to the Barrier. The cloud still hangs on the mountain ahead of us; it certainly looks as though it were a volcano cloud, but it may be due to condensation. The lower current clouds are travelling very fast from south south-east to north north-west. The weather is fine and clear, and the temperature plus 17°F.

December 7. Started at 8 a.m., Adams, Marshall and self pulling one sledge. Wild leading Socks behind. We travelled up and down slopes with very deep snow, into which Socks sank up to his belly, and we plunged in and out continuously, making it very trying work. Passed several crevasses on our right hand and could see more to the left. The light became bad at 1 p.m., when we camped for lunch, and it was hard to see the crevasses, as most were more or less snow covered. After lunch the light was better, and as we marched along we were congratulating ourselves upon it when suddenly we heard a shout of 'help' from Wild. We stopped at once and rushed to his assistance, and saw the pony sledge with the forward end down a crevasse and Wild reaching out from the side of the gulf grasping the sledge. No sign of the pony. We soon got up to Wild, and he scrambled out of the dangerous position, but poor Socks had gone. Wild had a miraculous escape. He was following up our tracks, and we had passed over a crevasse which was entirely covered with snow, but the weight of the pony broke through the snow crust and in a second all was over. Wild says he just felt a sort of rushing wind, the leading rope was snatched from his hand, and he put out his arms and just caught the further edge of the chasm. Fortunately for Wild and us, Socks' weight snapped the swingle-tree of the sledge, so it was saved, though the upper bearer is broken. We lay down on our stomachs and looked over into the gulf, but no sound or sign came to us; a black bottomless pit it seemed to be. We hitched the pony sledge to ourselves and started off again, now with a weight of 1,000 lb. for the four of us. Camped at 6.20 p.m., very tired, having to retreat from a maze of crevasses and rotten ice on to a patch where we could pitch our tents. We are indeed thankful for Wild's escape. When I think over the events of the day I realize what the loss of the sledge would have meant to us. We would have had left only two sleeping-bags for the four of us, and I doubt whether we could have got back to winter quarters with the short equipment. Our chance of reaching the Pole would have been gone. We take on the maize to eat ourselves. There is one ray of light in this bad day, and that is that, anyhow we could not have taken Socks on much further. We would have had to shoot him tonight, so that although his loss is a serious matter to us, for we had counted on the meat, still we know that for traction purposes he would have been of little further use. When we tried to camp tonight we stuck our ice-axes into the snow to see whether there were any more hidden crevasses, and everywhere the axes went through. It would have been folly to have pitched our camp in that place, as we might easily have dropped through during the night. We had to retreat a quarter of a mile to pitch the tent. It was very unpleasant to turn back, even for this short distance, but on this job one must expect reverses.

December 8. Started at 8 a.m. and immediately began dodging crevasses and pits of unknown depth. Wild and I were leading, for, thank heaven, my eyes are fit and well again. We slowly toiled up a long crevassed slope, and by lunchtime were about 1,900 ft up the glacier. We had covered 6 miles 150 yards of an uphill drag, with about 250 lb. per man to haul. After lunch we still travelled up, but came on to blue glacier ice almost free from crevasses, so did much better, the sledges running easily. We camped at 6 p.m., the day's journey having been 12 miles 150 yards. The slope we went up in the morning, was not as bad as we had anticipated, but quite bad enough for us to be thankful that we are out, at any rate for a time, from the region of hidden crevasses. The hypsometer tonight gave our height as 2,300 ft above sea level. It is beautifully fine still. We have been wonderfully fortunate in this, especially in view of the situation we are in.

December 9. Another splendid day as far as the weather is concerned, and much we needed it, for we have had one of our hardest day's work and certainly the most dangerous so far. We started at 7.45 a.m. over the blue ice, and in less than an hour were in a perfect maze of crevasses, some thinly bridged with snow and others with a thicker and therefore more deceptive covering. Marshall went through one and was only saved by his harness. He had quite disappeared down below the level of the ice, and it was one of those crevasses that open out from the top, with no bottom to be seen, and I daresay there was a drop of at least 1,000 ft. Soon after, Adams went through, then I did. The situation became momentarily more dangerous and uncertain. The sledges, skidding about, came up against the sheer, knife-like edges of some of the crevasses, and thus the bow of the second sledge, which had been strained when Socks fell, gave way. We decided to relay our gear over this portion of a glacier until we got on to safer ground, and it was well past eleven o'clock before we had got both sledges on to better ice. We camped at 11.45 a.m. to get the sun's meridian altitude, and, to save time while watching the sun's rise and fall, decided to lunch at noon. The latitude we found to be 84° 2' South, which is not so bad considering that we have been hauling our heavy load of 250 lb. per man uphill for the last two days. At noon we were nearly 2,500 ft above sea level. In the afternoon we had another heavy pull, and now are camped between two huge crevasses, but on a patch of hard snow. We pitched camp at 6 p.m., very tired and extremely hungry after dragging uphill all the afternoon for over five hours. It is 8 p.m. now, and we are nearly 3,000 ft above sea level. Low cumulus clouds are hanging to the south of us, as they have done for many days past, obscuring any view in that direction. We are anxiously hoping to find soon a level and inland ice sheet so that we can put on more speed. The distance today was 11 miles 1,450 yards plus two miles relay. The talk now is mainly about food and the things we would like to eat, and at meal times our hoosh disappears with far too great speed. We are all looking forward to Christmas Day, for then, come what may, we are going to be full of food.

December 10. Falls, bruises, cut shins, crevasses, razor edged ice, and a heavy upward pull have made up the sum of the day's trials, but there has been a measure of compensation in the wonderful scenery, the marvellous rocks and the covering of a distance of 11 miles 860 yards towards our goal. We started at 7.30 a.m. amongst crevasses, but soon got out of them and pulled up a long slope of snow. Our altitude at noon was 3,250 ft above sea level. Then we slid down a blue ice slope, after crossing crevasses. Marshall and I each went down one. We lunched at 1 p.m. and started at 2 p.m. up a long ridge by the side moraine of the glacier. It was heavy work, as the ice was split and presented knife-like edges between the cracks, and there were also some crevasses. Adams got into one. The going was terribly heavy, as the sledges brought up against the ice edges every now and then, and then there was a struggle to get them started again. We changed our foot gear, substituting ski boots for the finnesko, but nevertheless had many painful falls on the treacherous blue ice, cutting our hands and shins. We are all much bruised. We camped on a patch of snow by the land at 6 p.m. The rocks of the moraine are remarkable, being of every hue and description. I cannot describe them, but we will carry specimens back for the geologists to deal with. The main rocks of the "Cloud Maker", the mountain under which we are camped, appear to be slates, reef quartz and a very hard, dark brown rock, the name of which I do not know. The erratics of marble, conglomerate, and breccia are beautiful, showing a great mass of wonderful colours, but these rocks we cannot take away. We can only take with us small specimens of the main rocks, as weight is of importance to us, and from these small specimens the geologists must determine the character of the land. This mountain is the one we thought might be an active volcano when we saw it from the mountain at the foot of the glacier, but the cloud has blown away from its head today, and we can see definitely that it is not a volcano. It is a remarkable sight as it towers above us with the snow clinging to its sides. Tonight there is a cold north wind. I climbed about 600 ft up the mountain and got specimens of the main rocks *in situ*. The glacier is evidently moving very slowly, and not filling as much of the valley as it did at some previous date, for the old moraines lie higher up in terraces. Low cumulus clouds to the south are hiding some of the new land in that direction. We are all very hungry and tired tonight after the day's fight with glacier. Whilst I went up the mountain to spy out the land the others ground up the balance of the maize, brought for pony feed, between flat stones, in order that we may use it ourselves to eke out our supply of food. The method of preparation was primitive, but it represented the only way of getting it fit to cook without the necessity of using more oil than we can spare for lengthy boiling. The temperature was plus 12°F at noon today, and is plus 14° now at 8 p.m. We are getting south, and we hope to reach the inland ice in a couple of days; then our marching will be faster. The weather is still fine.

December 11. A heavy day. We started away at 7.40 a.m. and tried to keep alongside the land, but the ice of the glacier sloped so much that we had to go on to the ridge, where the sledges could run without side slipping. This slipping cuts the runners very badly. We crossed the medial moraine, and found rock there with what looked like plant impressions. We collected some specimens.

In the afternoon we found the surface better, as the cracks were nearly all filled up with water turned to ice. We camped for lunch on rubbly ice. After lunch we rounded some pressure ridges fairly easily, and then pulled up a long ice slope with many sharp points. All the afternoon we were passing over ice in which the cracks had been closed up, and we began to have great hopes that the end of the glacier was in sight, and that we would soon be able to put in some good marches on the plateau. At 5 p.m. we found more cracks and a mass of pressure ice ahead and land appeared as the clouds ahead lifted. I cannot tell what it means, but the position makes us anxious. The sledges will not stand much more of this ice work, and we are still 340 geographical miles away from the Pole. Thank God the weather is fine still. We camped at 6 p.m. on hard ice between two crevasses. There was no snow to pack round the tents, so we had to put the sledges and the provision bags on the snow cloths. We made the floor level inside by chipping away the points of ice with our ice-axes. We were very hungry after hoosh tonight. Awkward features about the glacier are the little pits filled with mud, of which I collected a small sample.[*] It seems to be ground down rock material, but what the action has been I cannot tell. The hot sun, beating down on this mud, makes it gradually sink into the body of the glacier, leaving a rotten ice covering through which we often break. It is like walking over a cucumber frame, and sometimes the boulders that have sunk down through the ice can be seen 3 to 4 ft below the surface. The ice that has formed above the sunken rocks is more clear than the ordinary glacier ice. We are 3,700 ft up, and made 8 miles 900 yards to the good today. We have the satisfaction of feeling that we are getting south, and perhaps tomorrow may see the end of all our difficulties. Difficulties are just things to overcome after all. Every one is very fit.

December 12. Our distance – three miles for the day – expresses more readily than I can write it the nature of the day's work. We started at 7.40 a.m. on the worst surface possible, sharp edged blue ice full of chasms and crevasses, rising to hills and descending into gullies; in fact, a surface that could not be equalled in any polar work for difficulty in travelling. Our sledges are suffering greatly, and it is a constant strain on us both to save the sledges from breaking or going down crevasses, and to save ourselves as well. We are a mass of bruises where we have fallen on the sharp ice, but, thank God, no one has even a sprain. It has been relay work today, for we could only take on one sledge at a time, two of us taking turns at pulling the sledge whilst the others steadied and held the sledge to keep it straight. Thus we would advance one mile, and then return over the crevasses and haul up the other sledge. By repeating this today for three miles we marched nine miles over a surface where many times a slip meant death. Still we have advanced three miles to the south, and tonight we are camped on a patch of névé. By using our ice-axes we made a place for the tent. The weather is still splendidly fine, though low clouds obscure our horizon to the south. We are anxiously hoping to cross the main pressure tomorrow, and trust that we will then have better travelling. Given good travelling, we will not be long in reaching our goal. Marshall is putting in the

---

[*]   These pits are known as cryoconite holes.

bearings and angles of the new mountains. They still keep appearing to the west and east. Distance 3 miles 500 yards, with relays 9 miles 1500 yards.

December 13. We made a start at 8 a.m. and once again went up hill and down dale, over crevasses and blue, ribbed ice, relaying the sledges. We had covered about a mile when we came to a place where it seemed almost impossible to proceed. However, to our right, bearing about south-west by south, there seemed to be better surface and we decided to make a detour in that direction in order, if possible, to get round the pressure. While returning for one of the sledges I fell on the ice and hurt my left knee, which was a serious matter, or rather might have been. I have had a bandage on all the afternoon while pulling, and the knee feels better now, but one realizes what it would mean if any member of our party were to be damaged under these conditions and in this place. This afternoon we came on to a better surface, and were able to pull both sledges instead of relaying. We are still gradually rising, and tonight our hypsometer gives 203.7, or 4,370 ft up. There is a cool southerly wind; indeed, more than we have had before, and as we have only a patch of névé on the glacier for our tents, we had to take the provision bags and gear off the sledges to keep the tent cloths down. The temperature is plus 19°F. New mountains are still appearing to the west south-west as we rise. We seem now to be going up a long yellow track, for the ice is not so blue, and we are evidently travelling over an old moraine, where the stones have sunk through the ice when its onward movement has been retarded. I am sure that the bulk of the glacier is growing less, but the onward movement still continues, though at a much slower pace than at some previous period. The gain for the day was five miles, and in addition we did four miles relay work.

December 14. This has been one of our hardest day's work so far. We have been steering all day about south south-west up the glacier, mainly in the bed of an ancient moraine, which is full of holes through which the stones and boulders have melted down long years ago. It has been snowing all day with a high temperature, and this has made everything very wet. We have ascended over 1,000 ft today, our altitude at 6 p.m. being 5,600 ft above sea level, so the mountains to the west must be from 10,000 to 15,000 ft in height, judging from their comparative elevation. My knee is better today. We have had a heavy pull and many falls on the slippery ice. Just before camping, Adams went through some snow, but held up over an awful chasm. Our sledges are much the worse for wear, and the one with the broken bow constantly strikes against the hard, sharp ice, pulling us up with a jerk and often flinging us down. At this high altitude the heavy pulling is very trying, especially as we slip on the snow covering the blue ice. There has evidently been an enormous glaciation here, and now it is dwindling away. Even the mountains show signs of this. Tonight our hopes are high that we are nearly at the end of the rise and that soon we will reach our longed for plateau. Then southward indeed! Food is the determining factor with us. We did 7½ miles today.

December 15. Started at 7.40 a.m. in clear weather. It was heavy going uphill on the blue ice, but gradually we rose the land ahead, and it seemed as though at last we were going to have a change, and that we would see something new. At lunchtime we were on a better surface, with patches of snow, and we could see stretching out in front of us what was apparently a long, wide plain. It looked as though now really we were coming to the level ground for which we have longed, especially as the hypsometer gave us an altitude of 7,230 ft, but this altitude at night came down to 5,830 ft so the apparent height may be due to barometric pressure and change of weather, for in the afternoon a stiff breeze from the south-west sprang up. The temperature was plus 18°F at noon, and when the wind came up it felt cold, as we were pulling in our pyjama trousers, with nothing underneath. We have been going steadily uphill all the afternoon, but on a vastly improved surface, consisting of hard névé instead of blue ice and no cracks, only covered in crevasses, which are easily seen. Ahead of us really lies the plateau. We can also see ahead of us detached mountains, piercing through the inland ice, which is the road to the south for us. Huge mountains stretch out to the east and west. After last week's toil and anxiety the change is delightful. The distance covered today was 13 miles 200 yards.

December 16. We started at 7 a.m., having had breakfast at 5.30 a.m. It was snowing slightly for the first few hours, and then the weather cleared. The surface was hard and the going good. We camped at noon and took sights for latitude, and ascertained that our position was 84° 50' South. Ahead of us we could see a long slope, icy and crevassed, but we did 13 miles 1,650 yards for the day. We camped at 5.30 p.m., and got ready our depot gear. We have decided to travel as lightly as possible, taking only the clothes we are wearing, and we will leave four days' food, which I calculate should get us back to the last depot on short ration. We have now traversed nearly one hundred miles of crevassed ice, and risen 6,000 ft on the largest glacier in the world. One more crevassed slope, and we will be on the plateau, please God. We are all fit and well. The temperature tonight is plus 15°F, and the wind is blowing freshly from the south-west. There are splendid ranges of mountains to the west south-west, and we have an extended view of glacier and mountains. Ahead of us lie three sharp peaks, connected up and forming an island in what is apparently inland ice or the head of the glacier. The peaks lie due south of us. To the eastward and westward of this island the ice bears down from the inland ice sheet, and joins the head of the glacier proper. To the westward the mountains along the side of the glacier are all of the bluff type, and the lines of stratification can be seen plainly. Still further to the westward, behind the frontal range, lie sharper peaks, some of them almost perfect cones. The trend of the land from the "Cloudmaker" is about south south-west. We are travelling up the west side of the glacier. On the other side, to the east, there is a break in the bluff mountains, and the land beyond runs away more to the south-east. The valley is filled with pressure ice, which seems to have come from the inland ice sheet. The mountains to the south-east also show lines of stratification. I hope that the photographs will be clear enough to give an idea of the character of this land. These mountains are not beautiful in the ordinary acceptance of the term, but they are magnificent in their stern and rugged grandeur. No foot has ever trod on their mighty sides, and until we reached this frozen land no human eyes had seen their forms.

December 17. We made a start at 7.20 a.m. and had an uphill pull all the morning over blue ice with patches of snow, which impeded our progress until we learned that the best way was to rush the sledges over them, for it was very difficult to keep one's footing on the smooth ice, and haul the sledges astern over the snow. By 1 p.m. we had done eight miles of this uphill work, and in the afternoon we did four more. We had worked from 7.23 a.m. until 6.40 p.m. with one hour's rest for lunch only and it seems as though twelve miles was not much, but the last two hours' going was very stiff. We had to take on one sledge at a time up the icy slope, and even then we had to cut steps with our ice-axes as we went along. The work was made more difficult by the fact that a strong southerly wind was dead in our faces. The second sledge we hauled up the rise by means of the alpine rope. We made it fast to the sledge, went on with the first sledge till the rope was stretched out to its full length, then cut a place to stand on, and by our united efforts hauled the sledge up to where we stood. We repeated this until we had managed to reach a fairly level spot with both the sledges, and we pitched our tents on a small patch of snow. There was not enough of the snow to make fast the snow cloths of the tents, and we had to take the gear off the sledges and pile that round to supplement the snow. We have burned our boats behind us now as regards warm clothing, for this afternoon we made a depot in by the rocks of the island we are passing, and there left everything except the barest necessaries. After dinner tonight Wild went up the hillside in order to have a look at the plateau. He came down with the news that the plateau is in sight at last, and that tomorrow should see us at the end of our difficulties. He also brought down with him some very interesting geological specimens, some of which certainly look like coal. The quality may be poor, but I have little doubt that the stuff is coal. If that proves to be the case, the discovery will be most interesting to the scientific world. Wild tells me that there are about six seams of this dark stuff, mingled with sandstone, and that the seams are from 4 in. to 7 or 8 ft in thickness. There are vast quantities of it lying on the hillside. We took a photograph of the sandstone, and I wish very much that we could spare time to examine the rocks more thoroughly. We may be able to do this on the way back. We have but little time for geological work, for our way is south and time is short, but we found that the main rock is sandstone and on our way back we will collect some. I expect that this will be the most southerly rock that we shall obtain, for we ought to reach the plateau tomorrow, and then there will be no more land close to us. It is gusty tonight, but beautifully clear. The altitude, according to the hypsometer, is 6,100 ft.

NOTE. When I showed the specimens to Professor David after our return to the *Nimrod*, he stated definitely that some of them were coal and others "mother of coal".

December 18. Almost up: The altitude tonight is 7,400 ft above sea level. This has been one of our hardest days, but worth it, for we are just on the plateau at last. We started at 7.30 a.m., relaying the sledges, and did 6 miles 600 yards, which means nearly 19 miles for the day of actual travelling. All the morning we worked up loose, slippery ice, hauling the sledges up one at a time by means of the alpine rope, then pulling in harness on the less stiff rises. We camped for lunch at 12.45 p.m. on the crest of a rise close to the pressure and in the midst of crevasses, into one of which I managed to fall, also Adams. Whilst lunch was preparing I got some rock from the land, quite different to the sandstone of yesterday. The mountains are all different just here. The land on our left shows beautifully clear stratified lines, and on the west side sandstone stands out, greatly weathered. All the afternoon we relayed up a long snow slope, and we were hungry and tired when we reached camp. We have been saving food to make it spin out, and that increases our hunger; each night we all dream of foods. We save two biscuits per man per day, also pemmican and sugar, eking out our food with pony maize, which we soak in water to make it less hard. All this means that we have now five weeks' food, while we are about 300 geographical miles from the Pole, with the same distance back to the last depot we left yesterday, so we must march on short food to reach our goal. The temperature is plus 16°F tonight, but a cold wind all the morning cut our faces and broken lips. We keep crevasses with us still, but I think that tomorrow will see the end of this. When we passed the main slope today, more mountains appeared to the west of south, some with sheer cliffs and others rounded off, ending in long snow slopes. I judge the southern limit of the mountains to the west to be about latitude 86° South.

December 19. Not on the plateau level yet, though we are tonight 7,888 ft up, and still there is another rise ahead of us. We got breakfast at 5 a.m. and started at 7 a.m. sharp, taking on one sledge. Soon we got to the top of a ridge, and went back for the second sledge, then hauled both together all the rest of the day. The weight was about 200 lb. per man, and we kept going until 6 p.m., with a stop of one hour for lunch. We got a meridian altitude at noon, and found that our latitude was 85° 5' South. We seem unable to get rid of the crevasses, and we have been falling into them and steering through them all day in the face of a cold southerly wind, with a temperature varying from plus 15° to plus 9°F. The work was very heavy, for we were going uphill all day, and our sledge runners, which have been suffering from the sharp ice and rough travelling, are in a bad way. Soft snow in places greatly retarded our progress, but we have covered our ten miles, and now are camped on good snow between two crevasses. I really think that tomorrow will see us on the plateau proper. This glacier must be one of the largest, if not the largest, in the world. The sastrugi seem to point mainly to the south, so we may expect head winds all the way to the Pole. Marshall has a cold job tonight, taking the angles of the new mountains to the west, some of which appeared today. After dinner we examined the sledge runners and turned one sledge end for end, for it had been badly torn while we were coming up the glacier, and in the soft snow it clogged greatly. We are still favoured with splendid weather, and that is a great comfort to us, for it would be almost impossible under other conditions to travel amongst these crevasses, which are caused by the congestion of the ice between the headlands when it was flowing from the plateau down between the mountains. Now there is comparatively little movement, and many of the crevasses have become snow-filled. Tonight we are 290 geographical miles from the Pole. We are thinking of our Christmas dinner. We will be full that day, anyhow.

December 20. Not yet up, but nearly so. We got away from camp at 7 a.m., with a strong head wind from the south, and this wind continued all day, with a temperature ranging from plus 7° to plus 5°. Our beards coated with ice. It was an uphill pull all day around pressure ice, and we reached an altitude of over 8,000 ft above sea level. The weather was clear, but there were various clouds, which were noted by Adams. Marshall took bearings and angles at noon, and we got the sun's meridian altitude, showing that we were in latitude 85° 17' South. We hope all the time that each ridge we come to will be the last, but each time another rises ahead, split up by pressure, and we begin the same toil again. It is trying work and as we have now reduced our food at breakfast to one pannikin of hoosh and one biscuit, by the time the lunch hour has arrived, after five hours' hauling in the cold wind up the slope, we are very hungry. At lunch we have a little chocolate, tea with plasmon, a pannikin of cocoa, and three biscuits. Today we did 11 miles 950 yards (statute), having to relay the sledges over the last bit, for the ridge we were on was so steep that we could not get the two sledges up together. Still, we are getting on; we have only 279 more miles to go, and then we will have reached the Pole. The land appears to run away to the south-east now, and soon we will be just a speck on this great inland waste of snow and ice. It is cold tonight. I am cook for the week, and started tonight. Every one is fit and well.

December 21. Midsummer Day, with 28° of frost! We have frost-bitten fingers and ears, and a strong blizzard wind has been blowing from the south all day, all due to the fact that we have climbed to an altitude of over 8,000 ft above sea level. From early morning we have been striving to the south, but six miles is the total distance gained, for from noon, or rather from lunch at 1 p.m., we have been hauling the sledges up, one after the other, by standing pulls across crevasses and over great pressure ridges. When we had advanced one sledge some distance, we put up a flag on a bamboo to mark its position, and then roped up and returned for the other. The wind, no doubt, has a great deal to do with the low temperature, and we feel the cold, as we are going on short commons. The altitude adds to the difficulties, but we are getting south all the time. We started away from camp at 6.45 a.m. today, and except for an hour's halt at lunch, worked on until 6 p.m. Now we are camped in a filled-up crevasse, the only place where snow to put around the tents can be obtained, for all the rest of the ground we are on is either névé or hard ice. We little thought that this particular pressure ridge was going to be such an obstacle; it looked quite ordinary, even a short way off, but we have now decided to trust nothing to eyesight, for the distances are so deceptive up here. It is a wonderful sight to look down over the glacier from the great altitude we are at, and to see the mountains stretching away east and west, some of them over 15,000 ft in height. We are very hungry now, and it seems as cold almost as the spring sledging. Our beards are masses of ice all day long. Thank God we are fit and well and have had no accident, which is a mercy, seeing that we have covered over 130 miles of crevassed ice.

December 22. As I write of today's events, I can easily imagine I am on a spring sledging journey, for the temperature is minus 5°F and a chilly south-easterly wind is blowing and finds its way through the walls of our tent, which are getting worn. All day long, from 7 a.m., except for the hour when we stopped for lunch, we have been relaying the sledges over the pressure mounds and across crevasses. Our total distance to the good for the whole day was only four miles southward, but this evening our prospects look brighter, for we must now have come to the end of the great glacier. It is flattening out, and except for crevasses there will not be much trouble in hauling the sledges tomorrow. One sledge today, when coming down with a run over a pressure ridge, turned a complete somersault, but nothing was damaged, in spite of the total weight being over 400 lb. We are now dragging 400 lb. at a time up the steep slopes and across the ridges, working with the alpine rope all day, and roping ourselves together when we go back for the second sledge, for the ground is so treacherous that many times during the day we are saved only by the rope from falling into fathomless pits. Wild describes the sensation of walking over this surface, half ice and half snow, as like walking over the glass roof of a station. The usual query when one of us falls into a crevasse is: "Have you found it?" One gets somewhat callous as regards the immediate danger, though we are always glad to meet crevasses with their coats off, that is, not hidden by the snow covering. Tonight we are camped in a filled-in crevasse. Away to the north down the glacier a thick cumulus cloud is lying, but some of the largest mountains are standing out clearly. Immediately behind us lies a broken sea of pressure ice. Please God, ahead of us there is a clear road to the Pole.

December 23. Eight thousand eight hundred and twenty feet up, and still steering upward amid great waves of pressure and ice falls, for our plateau, after a good morning's march, began to rise in higher ridges, so that it really was not the plateau after all. Today's crevasses have been far more dangerous than any others we have crossed, as the soft snow hides all trace of them until we fall through. Constantly today one or another of the party has had to be hauled out from a chasm by means of his harness, which had alone saved him from death in the icy vault below. We started at 6.40 a.m. and worked on steadily until 6 p.m., with the usual lunch hour in the middle of the day. The pony maize does not swell in the water now, as the temperature is very low and the water freezes. The result is that it swells inside after we have eaten it. We are very hungry indeed, and talk a great deal of what we would like to eat. In spite of the crevasses, we have done thirteen miles today to the south, and we are now in latitude 85° 41' South. The temperature at noon was plus 6°F and at 6 p.m. it was minus 1°F, but it is much lower at night. There was a strong south-east to south south-east wind blowing all day, and it was cutting to our noses and burst lips. Wild was frost-bitten. I do trust that tomorrow will see the end of this bad travelling, so that we can stretch out our legs for the Pole.

December 24. A much better day for us; indeed, the brightest we have had since entering our Southern Gateway. We started off at 7 a.m. across waves and undulations of ice, with someone or other of our little party falling through the thin crust of snow every now and then. At 10.30 a.m. I decided to steer more to the west, and we soon got on to a better surface, and covered 5 miles 250 yards in the forenoon. After lunch, as the surface was distinctly improving, we discarded the second sledge, and started our afternoon's march with one sledge. It has been blowing freshly from the south and drifting all day, and this, with over 40° of frost, has coated our faces with ice. We get superficial frost-bites every now and then. During the afternoon the surface improved greatly, and the cracks and crevasses disappeared, but we are still going uphill, and from the summit of one ridge saw some new land, which runs south south-east down to latitude 86° South. We camped at 6 p.m., very tired and with cold feet. We have only the clothes we stand up in now, as we depoted everything else, and this continued rise means lower temperatures than I had anticipated. Tonight we are 9,095 ft above sea level, and the way before us is still rising. I trust that it will soon level out, for it is hard work pulling at this altitude. So far there is no sign of the very hard surface that Captain Scott speaks of in connection with his journey on the Northern Plateau. There seem to be just here regular layers of snow, not much wind swept, but we will see better the surface conditions in a few days. Tomorrow will be Christmas Day, and our thoughts turn to home and all the attendant joys of the time. One longs to hear "the hansoms slurring through the London mud". Instead of that, we are lying in a little tent, isolated high on the roof of the end of the world, far, indeed, from the ways trodden of men. Still, our thoughts can fly across the wastes of ice and snow and across the oceans to those whom we are striving for and who are thinking of us now. And, thank God, we are nearing our goal. The distance covered today was 11 miles 250 yards.

December 25. Christmas Day. There has been from 45° to 48° of frost, drifting snow and a strong biting south wind, and such has been the order of the day's march from 7 a.m. to 6 p.m. up one of the steepest rises we have yet done, crevassed in places. Now, as I write, we are 9,500 ft above sea level, and our latitude at 6 p.m. was 85° 55' South. We started away after a good breakfast, and soon came to soft snow, through which our worn and torn sledge-runners dragged heavily. All morning we hauled along, and at noon had done 5 miles 250 yards. Sights gave us latitude 85° 51' South. We had lunch then, and I took a photograph of the camp with the Queen's flag flying and also our tent flags, my companions being in the picture. It was very cold, the temperature being minus 16°F, and the wind went through us. All the afternoon we worked steadily uphill, and we could see at 6 p.m. the new land plainly trending to the south-east. This land is very much glaciated. It is comparatively bare of snow, and there are well-defined glaciers on the side of the range, which seems to end up in the south-east with a large mountain like a keep. We have called it 'The Castle'. Behind these the mountains have more gentle slopes and are more rounded. They seem to fall away to the south-east, so that, as we are going south, the angle opens and we will soon miss them. When we camped at 6 p.m. the wind was decreasing. It is hard to understand this soft snow with such a persistent wind, and I can only suppose that we have not yet reached the actual plateau level, and that the snow we are travelling over just now is on the slopes, blown down by the south and south-east wind. We had a splendid dinner. First came hoosh, consisting of pony ration boiled up with pemmican and some of our emergency Oxo and biscuit. Then in the cocoa water I boiled our little plum pudding, which a friend of Wild's had given him. This, with a drop of medical brandy, was a luxury which Lucullus himself might have envied; then came cocoa, and lastly cigars and a spoonful of *crème de menthe* sent us by a friend in Scotland. We are full tonight, and this is the last time we will be for many a long day. After dinner we discussed the situation, and we have decided to still further reduce our food. We have now nearly 500 miles, geographical, to do if we are to get to the Pole and back to the spot where we are at the present moment. We have one month's food, but only three weeks' biscuit, so we are going to make each week's food last ten days. We will have one biscuit in the morning, three at midday, and two at night. It is the only thing to do. Tomorrow we will throw away everything except the most absolute necessities. Already we are, as regards clothes, down to the limit, but we must trust to the old sledge runners and dump the spare ones. One must risk this. We are very far away from all the world, and home thoughts have been much with us today, thoughts interrupted by pitching forward into a hidden crevasse more than once. Ah, well, we shall see all our own people when the work here is done. Marshall took our temperatures tonight. We are all two degrees subnormal, but as fit as can be. It is a fine open air life and we are getting south.

December 26. Got away at 7 a.m. sharp, after dumping a lot of gear. We marched steadily all day except for lunch, and we have done 14 miles 480 yards on an uphill march, with soft snow at times and a bad wind. Ridge after ridge we met, and though the surface is better and harder in places, we feel very tired at the end of ten hours' pulling. Our height tonight is 9,590 ft above sea level according to the hypsometer. The ridges we meet with are almost similar in appearance. We see the sun shining on them in the distance, and then the rise begins very gradually. The snow gets soft, and the weight of the sledge becomes more marked. As we near the top the soft snow gives place to a hard surface, and on the summit of the ridge we find small crevasses. Every time we reach the top of a ridge we say to ourselves: "Perhaps this is the last," but it never is the last; always there appears away ahead of us another ridge. I do not think that the land lies very far below the ice sheet, for the crevasses on the summits of the ridges suggest that the sheet is moving over land at no great depth. It would seem that the descent towards the glacier proper from the plateau is by a series of terraces. We lost sight of the land today, having left it all behind us, and now we have the waste of snow all around. Two more days and our maize will be finished. Then our hooshes will be more woefully thin than ever. This shortness of food is unpleasant, but if we allow ourselves what, under ordinary circumstances, would be a reasonable amount, we would have to abandon all idea of getting far south.

December 27. If a great snow plain, rising every seven miles in a steep ridge, can be called a plateau, then we are on it at last, with an altitude above the sea of 9,820 ft. We started at 7 a.m. and marched till noon, encountering at 11 a.m. a steep snow ridge which pretty well cooked us, but we got the sledge up by noon and camped. We are pulling 150 lb. per man. In the afternoon we had good going till 5 p.m. and then another ridge as difficult as the previous one, so that our backs and legs were in a bad way when we reached the top at 6 p.m., having done 14 miles 930 yards for the day. Thank heaven it has been a fine day, with little wind. The temperature is minus 9°F. This surface is most peculiar, showing layers of snow with little sastrugi all pointing south south-east. Short food make us think of plum puddings, and hard half-cooked maize gives us indigestion, but we are getting south. The latitude is 86° 19' South tonight. Our thoughts are with the people at home a great deal.

December 28. If the Barrier is a changing sea, the plateau is a changing sky. During the morning march we continued to go uphill steadily, but the surface was constantly changing. First there was soft snow in layers, then soft snow so deep that we were well over our ankles, and the temperature being well below zero, our feet were cold through sinking in. No one can say what we are going to find next, but we can go steadily ahead. We started at 6.55 a.m., and had done 7 miles 200 yards by noon, the pulling being very hard. Some of the snow is blown into hard sastrugi, some that look perfectly smooth and hard have only a thin crust through which we break when pulling; all of it is a trouble. Yesterday we passed our last crevasse, though there are a few cracks or ridges fringed with crystals shining like diamonds, warning us that the cracks are open. We are now 10,199 ft above sea level, and the plateau is gradually flattening out, but it was heavy work pulling this afternoon. The high altitude and a temperature of 48° of frost made breathing and work difficult. We are getting south – attitude 86° 31' South tonight. The last sixty miles we hope to rush, leaving everything possible, taking one tent only and using the poles of the other as marks every ten miles, for we will leave all our food sixty miles off the Pole except enough to carry us there and back. I hope with good weather to reach the Pole on January 12, and then we will try and rush it to get to Hut Point by February 28. We are so tired after each hour's pulling that we throw ourselves on our backs for a three minute spell. It took us over ten hours to do 14 miles 450 yards today, but we did it all right. It is a wonderful thing to be over 10,000 ft up, almost at the end of the world. The short food is trying, but when we have done the work we will be happy. Adams had a bad headache all yesterday, and today I had the same trouble, but it is better now. Otherwise we are all fit and well. I think the country is flattening out more and more, and hope tomorrow to make fifteen miles, at least.

December 29. Yesterday I wrote that we hoped to do fifteen miles today, but such is the variable character of this surface that one cannot prophesy with any certainty an hour ahead. A strong southerly wind, with from 44° to 49° of frost, combined with the effect of short rations, made our distance 12 miles 600 yards instead. We have reached an altitude of 10,310 ft, and an uphill gradient gave us one of the most severe pulls for ten hours that would be possible. It looks serious, for we must increase the food if we are to get on at all, and we must risk a depot at seventy miles off the Pole and dash for it then. Our sledge is badly strained, and on the abominably bad surface of soft snow is dreadfully hard to move. I have been suffering from a bad headache all day, and Adams also was worried by the cold. I think that these headaches are a form of mountain sickness, due to our high altitude. The others have bled from the nose, and that must relieve them. Physical effort is always trying at a high altitude, and we are straining at the harness all day, sometimes slipping in the soft snow that overlies the hard sastrugi. My head is very bad. The sensation is as though the nerves were being twisted up with a cork-screw and then pulled out. Marshall took our temperatures tonight, and we are all at about 94°, but in spite of this we are getting south. We are only 198 miles off our goal now. If the rise would stop the cold would not matter, but it is hard to know what is man's limit. We have only 150 lb. per man to pull, but it is more severe work than the 250 lb. per man up the glacier was. The Pole is hard to get.

December 30. We only did 4 miles 100 yards today. We started at 7 a.m., but had to camp at 11 a.m., a blizzard springing up from the south. It is more than annoying. I cannot express my feelings. We were pulling at last on a level surface, but very soft snow, when at about 10 a.m. the south wind and drift commenced to increase, and at 11 a.m. it was so bad that we had to camp. And here all day we have been lying in our sleeping-bags trying to keep warm and listening to the threshing drift on the tent side. I am in the cooking tent, and the wind comes through, it is so thin. Our precious food is going and the time also, and it is so important to us to get on. We lie here and think of how to make things better, but we cannot reduce food now, and the only thing will be to rush all possible at the end. We will do and are doing all humanly possible. It is with Providence to help us.

December 31. The last day of the old year, and the hardest day we have had almost, pushing through soft snow uphill with a strong head wind and drift all day. The temperature is minus 7°F, and our altitude is 10,477 ft above sea level. The altitude is trying. My head has been very bad all day, and we are all feeling the short food, but still we are getting south. We are in latitude 86° 54' South tonight, but we have only three weeks' food and two weeks' biscuit to do nearly 500 geographical miles. We can only do our best. Too tired to write more tonight. We all get iced up about our faces, and are on the verge of frostbite all the time. Please God the weather will be fine during the next fourteen days. Then all will be well. The distance today was eleven miles.

NOTE. If we had only known that we were going to get such cold weather as we were at this time experiencing, we would have kept a pair of scissors to trim our beards. The moisture from the condensation of one's breath accumulated on the beard and trickled down on to the Burberry blouse. Then it froze into a sheet of ice inside, and it became very painful to pull the Burberry off in camp. Little troubles of this sort would have seemed less serious to us if we had been able to get a decent feed at the end of the day's work, but we were very hungry. We thought of food most of the time. The chocolate certainly seemed better than the cheese, because the two spoonfuls of cheese per man allowed under our scale of diet would not last as long as the two sticks of chocolate. We did not have both at the same meal. We had the bad luck at this time to strike a tin in which the biscuits were thin and overbaked. Under ordinary circumstances they would probably have tasted rather better than the other biscuits, but we wanted bulk. We soaked them in our tea so that they would swell up and appear larger, but if one soaked a biscuit too much, the sensation of biting something was lost, and the food seemed to disappear much too easily.

January 1, 1909. Head too bad to write much. We did 11 miles 900 yards (statute) today, and the latitude at 6 p.m. was 87° 6½'

South, so we have beaten North and South records. Struggling uphill all day in very soft snow. Every one done up and weak from want of food. When we camped at 6 p.m. fine warm weather, thank God. Only 172½ miles from the Pole. The height above sea level, now 10,755 ft, makes all work difficult. Surface seems to be better ahead. I do trust it will be so tomorrow.

January 2. Terribly hard work today. We started at 6.45 a.m. with a fairly good surface, which soon became very soft. We were sinking in over our ankles, and our broken sledge, by running sideways, added to the drag. We have been going uphill all day, and tonight are 11,034 ft above sea level. It has taken us all day to do 10 miles 450 yards, though the weights are fairly light. A cold wind, with a temperature of minus 14°F, goes right through us now, as we are weakening from want of food, and the high altitude makes every movement an effort, especially if we stumble on the march. My head is giving me trouble all the time. Wild seems the most fit of us. God knows we are doing all we can, but the outlook is serious if this surface continues and the plateau gets higher, for we are not travelling fast enough to make our food spin out and get back to our depot in time. I cannot think of failure yet. I must look at the matter sensibly and consider the lives of those who are with me. I feel that if we go on too far it will be impossible to get back over this surface, and then all the results will be lost to the world. We can now definitely locate the South Pole on the highest plateau in the world, and our geological work and meteorology will be of the greatest use to science; but all this is not the Pole. Man can only do his best, and we have arrayed against us the strongest forces of nature. This cutting south wind with drift plays the mischief with us, and after ten hours of struggling against it one pannikin of food with two biscuits and a cup of cocoa does not warm one up much. I must think over the situation carefully tomorrow, for time is going on and food is going also.

January 3. Started at 6.55 a.m., cloudy but fairly warm. The temperature was minus 8°F at noon. We had a terrible surface all the morning, and did only 5 miles 100 yards. A meridian altitude

gave us latitude 87° 22' South at noon. The surface was better in
the afternoon, and we did six geographical miles. The temperature at 6 p.m. was minus 11°F. It was an uphill pull towards the
evening, and we camped at 6:20 p.m., the altitude being 11,220
ft above the sea. Tomorrow we must risk making a depot on the
plateau, and make a dash for it, but even then, if this surface
continues, we will be two weeks in carrying in through.

January 4. The end is in sight. We can only go for three more
days at the most, for we are weakening rapidly. Short food and a
blizzard wind from the south, with driving drift, at a temperature
of 47° of frost, have plainly told us today that we are reaching our
limit, for we were so done up at noon with cold that the clinical
thermometer failed to register the temperature of three of us at
94°. We started at 7:40 a.m., leaving a depot on this great wide
plateau, a risk that only this case justified, and one that my
comrades agreed to, as they have to every one so far, with the
same cheerfulness and regardlessness of self that have been the
means of our getting as far as we have done so far. Pathetically
small looked the bamboo, one of the tent poles, with a bit of bag
sewn on as a flag, to mark our stock of provisions, which has to
take us back to our depot, one hundred and fifty miles north. We
lost sight of it in half an hour, and are now trusting to our footprints in the snow to guide us back to each bamboo until we pick
up the depot again. I trust that the weather will keep clear. Today
we have done 12½ geographical miles, and with only 70 lb. per
man to pull it is as hard, even harder, work than the 100 odd lb.
was yesterday, and far harder than the 250 lb. were three weeks
ago, when we were climbing the glacier. This, I consider, is a
clear indication of our failing strength. The main thing against us
is the altitude of 11,200 ft and the biting wind. Our faces are cut,
and our feet and hands are always on the verge of frostbite. Our
fingers, indeed, often go, but we get them around more or less. I
have great trouble with two fingers on my left hand. They had
been badly jammed when we were getting the motor up over the
ice face at winter quarters, and the circulation is not good. Our
boots now are pretty well worn out, and we have to halt at times
to pick the snow out of the soles. Our stock of sennegrass is
nearly exhausted, so we have to use the same frozen stuff day

after day. Another trouble is that the lamp wick with which we tie the finnesko is chafed through, and we have to tie knots in it. These knots catch the snow under our feet, making a lump that has to be cleared every now and then. I am of the opinion that to sledge even in the height of summer on this plateau, we should have at least forty ounces of food a day per man, and we are on short rations of the ordinary allowance of thirty-two ounces. We depoted our extra underclothing to save weight about three weeks ago, and are now in the same clothes night and day. One suit of under-clothing, shirt and guernsey, and our thin Burberries, now all patched. When we get up in the morning, out of the wet bag, our Burberries become like a coat of mail at once, and our heads and beards get iced-up with the moisture when breathing on the march. There is half a gale blowing dead in our teeth all the time. We hope to reach within 100 geographical miles of the Pole; I am confident that the Pole lies on the great plateau we have discovered, miles and miles from any outstanding land. The temperature tonight is minus 24°F.

January 5. Today headwind and drift again, with 50° of frost, and a terrible surface. We have been marching through 8 in. of snow, covering sharp sastrugi, which plays havoc with our feet, but we have done 13⅓ geographical miles, for we increased our food, seeing that it was absolutely necessary to do this to enable us to accomplish anything. I realize that the food we have been having has not been sufficient to keep up our strength, let alone supply the wastage caused by exertion, and now we must try to keep warmth in us, though our strength is being used up. Our temperatures at 5 a.m. were 94°F. We got away at 7 a.m. sharp and marched till noon, then from 1 p.m. sharp till 6 p.m. All being in one tent makes our camp work slower, for we are so cramped for room, and we get up at 4:40 a.m. so as to get away by 7 a.m. Two of us have to stand outside the tent at night until things are squared up inside, and we find it cold work. Hunger grips us hard, and the food supply is very small. My head still gives me great trouble. I began by wishing that my worst enemy had it instead of myself, but now I don't wish even my worst enemy to have such a headache; still, it is no use talking about it. Self is a subject that most of us are fluent on. We find the

utmost difficulty in carrying through the day, and we can only
go for two or three more days. Never once has the temperature
been above zero since we got on to the plateau, though this is
the height of summer. We have done our best, and we thank
God for having allowed us to get so far.

January 6. This must be our last outward march with the sledge
and camp equipment. Tomorrow we must leave camp with some
food, and push as far south as possible, and then plant the flag.
Today's story is 57° of frost, with a strong blizzard and high drift;
yet we marched 13¼ geographical miles through soft snow,
being helped by extra food. This does not mean full rations, but
a bigger ration than we have been having lately. The pony maize
is all finished. The most trying day we have yet spent, our fingers
and faces being frost-bitten continually. Tomorrow we will rush
south with the flag. We are at 88° 7' South tonight. It is our last
outward march. Blowing hard tonight. I would fail to explain my
feelings if I tried to write them down, now that the end has come.
There is only one thing that lightens the disappointment, and
that is the feeling that we have done all we could. It is the forces
of nature that have prevented us from going right through. I
cannot write more.

January 7. A blinding, shrieking blizzard all day, with the temperature ranging from 60° to 70° of frost. It has been impossible
to leave the tent, which is snowed up on the lee side. We have
been lying in our bags all day, only warm at food time, with fine
snow making through the walls of the worn tent and covering our
bags. We are greatly cramped. Adams is suffering from cramp
every now and then. We are eating our valuable food without
marching. The wind has been blowing eighty to ninety miles an
hour. We can hardly sleep. Tomorrow I trust this will be over.
Directly the wind drops we march as far south as possible, then
plant the flag, and turn homeward. Our chief anxiety is lest our
tracks may drift up, for to them we must trust mainly to find our
depot; we have no land bearings in this great plain of snow. It is
a serious risk that we have taken, but we had to play the game to
the utmost, and Providence will look after us.

January 8. Again all day in our bags, suffering considerably physically from cold hands and feet, and from hunger, but more mentally, for we cannot get on south, and we simply lie here shivering. Every now and then one of our party's feet go, and the unfortunate beggar has to take his leg out of the sleeping-bag and have his frozen foot nursed into life again by placing it inside the shirt, against the skin of his almost equally unfortunate neighbour. We must do something more to the south, even though the food is going, and we weaken lying in the cold, for with 72° of frost the wind cuts through our thin tent, and even the drift is finding its way in and on to our bags, which are wet enough as it is. Cramp is not uncommon every now and then, and the drift all round the tent has made it so small that there is hardly room for us at all. The wind has been blowing hard all day; some of the gusts must be over seventy or eighty miles an hour. This evening it seems as though it were going to ease down, and directly it does we shall be up and away south for a rush. I feel that this march must be our limit. We are so short of food, and at this high altitude, 11,600 ft, it is hard to keep any warmth in our bodies between the scanty meals. We have nothing to read now, having depoted our little books to save weight, and it is dreary work lying in the tent with nothing to read, and too cold to write much in the diary.

January 9. Our last day outwards. We have shot our bolt, and the tale is latitude 88° 23' South, longitude 162° East. The wind eased down at 1 a.m., and at 2 a.m. we were up and had breakfast. At 4 a.m. started south, with the Queen's Union Jack, a brass cylinder containing stamps and documents to place at the furthest south point, camera, glasses, and compass. At 9 a.m. we were in 88° 23' South, half running and half walking over a surface much hardened by the recent blizzard. It was strange for us to go along without the nightmare of a sledge dragging behind us. We hoisted Her Majesty's flag and the other Union Jack afterwards, and took possession of the plateau in the name of His Majesty. While the Union Jack blew out stiffly in the icy gale that cut us to the bone, we looked south with our powerful glasses, but could see nothing but the dead white snow plain. There was no break in the plateau as it extended towards the Pole, and we feel sure that the goal we have failed to reach lies on this plain. We stayed only a few minutes, and then, taking the Queen's flag and eating our scanty meal as we went, we hurried back and reached our camp about 3 p.m. We were so dead tired that we only did two hours' march in the afternoon and camped at 5:30 p.m. The temperature was minus 19°F. Fortunately for us, our tracks were not obliterated by the blizzard; indeed, they stood up, making a trail easily followed. Homeward bound at last. Whatever regrets may be, we have done our best.

Shackleton's feat in reaching within 97 miles of the Pole earned him a knighthood. Four years later, he returned to Antarctica with the epic Endurance *expedition (see pp 274ff).*

The Ascent of Mount Erebus

T. W. Edgeworth David

The scientific officer on Shackleton's Nimrod *expedition (see p247), Professor David led the successful assault on Mount Erebus. David's account of the summiting is from* Aurora Australis, *the book the expedition produced in a hut at Camp Royd recording its exploits and the first book to be published in Antarctica.*

The angle of ascent was now steeper than ever, being 34°, that is a rise of 1 in 1½. As the hard snow slopes were mostly much too steep to climb, without resorting to the tedious expedient of cutting steps with an ice-axe, we kept as much as possible to the rocky arêtes. Occasionally, however, the arête would terminate upwards in a large snow slope, and in such cases we cut steps across the névé to any arête which seemed to persist for some length in an upward direction. Often this second arête would end upwards in a névé field, and then we had to cut steps as before.

Burdened as we were with our forty pound loads, and more or less stiff after thirty continuous hours in our sleeping-bags, and beginning besides to find respiration more difficult as the altitude increased, we felt exhausted, while we were still 800 feet below the rim of the main crater. Accordingly we halted at noon, thawed some snow with the Primus, and were soon revelling in cups of delicious tea, hot and strong, which at once reinvigourated us. Once more we tackled the ascent. When close to the top Mackay, who had become separated from the rest of the party, started cutting steps with his ice-axe up a long and very steep névé slope. The task was almost impossible for one so heavily loaded as he was, but nevertheless, he won his way unaided to the summit.

By this time we had reached the rim of the main crater. Often, while toiling up its slopes, we had tried to picture to ourselves the probable scenery at the summit, and had imagined an even plain of névé, or glacier ice, filling the extinct crater to the brim, and sloping up gradually to the active cone at its southern end: but we now found ourselves on the very brink of a massive precipice of black rock, forming the inner edge of the vast crater. This wall of dark lava is mostly vertical, while in places it overhangs: it is from 80 to 100 feet in height. The base of this cliff was separated from the snow plain beyond by a deep ditch, like a huge dry moat. The ditch was evidently not a "bergschrund", but was due chiefly to the action of the blizzards. These winds blowing fiercely from the south-east, and striking against the great inner wall of the old crater, give rise to a powerful back eddy at the base of the cliff, and it is this eddy which has scooped out the deep trench in the hard snow; the trench was from thirty to forty feet deep, and was bounded by more or less vertical sides.

Beyond the wall and trench was an extensive snowfield, with the active cone and crater at its south end, the latter emitting great volumes of steam; but what surprised us most were the extraordinary structures which rose every here and there above the surface of this snowfield. These were in the form of mounds and pinnacles of the most varied and fantastic appearance. Some resembled bee-hives, others were like huge ventilating cowls, others like isolated turrets, or bits of battlemented walls; others again in shape resembled various animals. We were wholly unable at first sight, to divine the origin of these remarkable objects, and the need for rest and refreshment cut short contemplation for the time. We hurried along the rampart of the old crater wall, in search of a suitable camping ground. It was at this time that our figures, thrown up against the skyline, were seen through a telescope by Armytage from our winter quarters at Cape Royds, over twelve miles distant. We selected for our camp, a little rocky gully on the north-west slope of the main cone, and fifty feet below the rim of the old crater. Here we had the satisfaction of being able to ease our shoulders at last from their burdens.

While some cooked the meal, Dr Marshall examined Brocklehurst's feet, as the latter stated that for some time past he had lost all feeling in them. We were all surprised and shocked, when his ski-boots and socks were taken off, to see that both his big toes were black, and had evidently been 'gone' for several hours, and that four more toes, though less severely affected, were also frost-bitten. It must have required great pluck and determination on his part to have climbed almost continuously for nine hours, up the steep and difficult track we had followed, with his feet so badly frost-bitten. Doctors Marshall and Mackay at once set to work with a will to restore circulation in the feet, by warming and chafing them. Their efforts were, under the circumstances, eminently successful, but it was clear that recovery from so severe a frost-bite would be slow and tedious. Brocklehurst's feet having been thoroughly warmed were put into dry socks, and finneskoes stuffed with sennegraes; and then we all had lunch at about 3.30 p.m.

Leaving Brocklehurst safely tucked up in the three man sleeping-bag, the remaining five of us started off to explore the floor of the old crater. Ascending to the crater rim we climbed along it, until we came to a spot where there was a practicable breach in the crater wall, and where a narrow tongue of snow bridged the névé trench at its base. As soon as we arrived on the hard snow on the far side, Mackay joined us all up with the alpine rope, and with him in the lead we advanced cautiously over the snow plain, keeping a sharp lookout for crevasses. We steered for one of the remarkable mounds which had so interested us at a distance; when we reached the nearest of them, and curious examined it, we were as far as ever from understanding how it had formed: we noticed some curious hollows, like large drains partly roofed in, running towards the mound, and at the time we supposed these to be ordinary crevasses. Pushing on slowly we reached eventually a small parasitic cone, about 1,000 feet above the level of our camp, and over a mile distant.

Here peeped from under the snow brown masses of earthy looking material, which we found to consist of lumps of lava, large felspar crystals, from one to three inches in length, and fragments of pumice; both felspar and pumice were, in many cases, coated with sulphur. We now started to return to our camp; we were no longer roped together, as we had not met with any definite crevasses on our way up. We directed our steps towards one of the ice mounds, which resembled a lion couchant. To our surprise the lion appeared now to be blowing smoke out of his mouth.

The origin of the mounds was no longer a mystery; they were the outward and visible signs of fumaroles. In ordinary climates, a fumarole, or volcanic vapour well, may be detected by the thin cloud of steam above it, like breath exhaled on a frosty day, and usually one can at once feel the warmth, by passing one's hand into the vapour column; but, in the rigour of the Antarctic climate, the fumaroles of Erebus have their vapour turned into ice as soon as it reaches the surface of the snow plain. Thus ice mounds, somewhat similar in shape to the sinter mounds formed by the geysers of New Zealand, of Iceland, and of Yellowstone Park, are built up around the orifices of the fumaroles of Erebus. When exploring one of these fumaroles, Mackay fell suddenly up to his thighs into one of its concealed conduits; he saved himself however, from falling in deeper still, with his ice-axe. Marshall had a nearly similar experience at about the same time. Eventually we all arrived safely at our camp soon after 6 p.m., and found Brocklehurst progressing as well as could be expected.

As we sat on the rocks at tea, we had a glorious view to the west. While the foothills of Erebus flushed rosy red in the sunset, a vast rolling sea of cumulus cloud covered all the land from Cape Bird to Cape Royds. McMurdo Sound, now rapidly freezing over, showed warm ochreous tints, where the floe ice had formed, with dark purplish grey streaks marking the leads of open water between. Far away the Western Mountains glowed with the purest tints of greenish purple and amethyst. That night we had nothing but hard rock rubble under our sleeping-bags, and quite anticipated another blizzard; nevertheless, "weariness can snore upon the flint", and thus we slept soundly couched on Kenyte lava.

The following morning had two surprises for us; first, when we arose at 4 a.m. there was no sign of a blizzard, and next, while we were preparing breakfast, someone exclaimed, 'Look at the great shadow of Erebus,' and a truly wonderful sight it was. All the land below the base of the main cone, and for forty miles to the west of it, across McMurdo Sound, was a rolling sea of dense cumulus cloud. Projected obliquely on this, as on a vast magic lantern screen, was the huge bulk of the giant volcano. The sun had just risen, and flung the shadow of Erebus right across the Sound, and against the foothills of the Western Mountains. Every detail of the profile of Erebus, as outlined on the clouds, could be readily recognized. There to the right was the great black fang, the relic of the first crater; far above and beyond that was to be seen the rim of the main crater, near our camp; then further to the left, and still higher, rose the active crater with its canopy of steam faithfully portrayed on the cloud screen. Still further to the left the dark shadow dipped rapidly down into the shining fields of cloud below. All within the shadow of Erebus was a soft bluish grey; all without was warm, bright and golden. Words fail to describe a scene of such transcendent majesty and beauty.

After breakfast while Marshall was attending to Brocklehurst's feet, the hypsometer which had become frozen on the way up, was thawed out with the heat of the Primus, and a boiling point determination was made. This when reduced, and combined with the mean of our aneroid levels, made the altitude of the old crater rim, just above our camp, 11,400 feet. The highest point reached by us on the preceding evening, according to our aneroid, was about 1,000 feet above the preceding level, and thus was 12,400 feet above the sea.

At 6 a.m. we left our camp, and made all speed to reach the crater summit. As soon as we had crossed the snow trench, at the foot of the cliff, we roped ourselves together in the same order as before, and stood over towards a conspicuous fumarole. This was the one which bore some resemblance to a lion; it was about 20 feet in height; Mawson* photographed this from here, and also took a view of the active crater, about one and a half miles distant. There was considerable difficulty in taking photographs on Erebus, owing to the focal plane of the camera having become frozen. Near the furthest point reached by us on the preceding afternoon, we observed that there were several patches of ice of a lemon-yellow colour, the yellow being due to sulphur. We next ascended several rather steep slopes, formed of alternating beds

---

* Douglas Mawson: British-Australian geologist, later leader of the Australasian Antarctic Expedition. See pp262ff.

of hard snow and vast quantities of large and perfect felspar crystals, mixed with pumice; all these beds dipped away from the active crater. A little further on we reached the foot of the recent cone of the active crater; here we unroped, as there was no possibility of any crevasses ahead of us.

Our progress was now painfully slow, as the altitude and cold combined to make respiration difficult.

The cone was built up chiefly of blocks of pumice, from a few inches up to three feet in diameter. Externally these were grey, or often yellow, owing to incrustations of sulphur, but internally they were of a resinous brown colour. A shout of joy and surprise broke from the leading files, when a little after 10 a.m., the edge of the active crater was at last reached. We had travelled only about two and a half miles from our camp, and had ascended just 2,000 feet, and yet this had taken us, with a few short halts, just four hours.

The scene that now suddenly burst upon us was magnificent and awe-inspiring. We stood on the verge of a vast abyss, and at first could neither see to the bottom, nor across it, on account of the huge mass of steam filling the crater, and soaring aloft in a column 500 to 1,000 feet high. After a continuous loud hissing sound, lasting for some minutes, there would come from below a big dull boom, and immediately afterwards a great globular mass of steam would rush upwards to swell the volume of the snow-white cloud which ever sways over the crater. These phenomena recurred at intervals of a few minutes during the whole of our stay at the crater. Meanwhile the whole of the air around us was extremely redolent of burning sulphur.

Presently a gentle northerly breeze fanned away the steam cloud and at once the whole crater stood revealed to us in all its vast extent and depth.

Mawson's measurements made the depth 900 feet, and the greatest width about half a mile. There were evidently at least three well-like openings at the bottom of the caldron, and it was from these that the steam explosions proceeded. Near the southwest portion of the crater, there was an immense rift in the rim perhaps 300 to 400 feet deep. The crater wall opposite to the one at the top of which we were standing, presented features of special interest. Beds of dark pumiceous lava, or pumice alternated with white zones of snow; there was no direct evidence that the snow was interbedded with the lava, though it is possible that such may have been the case. From the top of one of the thickest of the lava, or pumice beds, just where it touched a belt of snow, there rose scores of small steam jets, all in a row; they were too numerous and too close together to have been each an independent fumarole. The appearance was rather suggestive of the snow being converted into steam by the heat of the layer of rock immediately below it. While at the crater's edge we made a boiling point determination with the hypsometer, but the result was not so satisfactory as that made earlier in the morning at our camp. As the result of averaging aneroid levels, together with the hypsometer determination at our camp at the top of the old crater, calculations made by us show that the summit of Erebus is probably about 13,370 feet above sea-level.

As soon as our measurements had been made, and some photographs had been taken by Mawson, we hurried back towards our camp, as it was imperatively necessary to get Brocklehurst down to the base of the main cone that day, and this meant a descent in all, of nearly 8,000 feet. On the way back a traverse was made of the main crater, and levels taken for constructing a geological section; we also collected numerous specimens of the unique felspar crystals, and of the pumice and sulphur.

On arrival in camp we had a hasty meal, and having hurriedly packed up, shouldered our burdens once more, and started down the steep mountain slope. Brocklehurst insisted on carrying his heavy load, in spite of his frost-bitten feet. We followed a course a little to the west of the one we took when ascending. The rock was rubbly and kept slipping under our feet, so that falls were frequent. After descending a few hundreds of feet, we found that the rubbly spur of rock, down which we were floundering, ended abruptly in a long and steep névé slope.

Three courses were now open to us; either to retrace our steps to the point above us, where our rocky spur had deviated from the main arête; or to cut steps across the névé slope to this arête; or to glissade down some 500 to 600 feet to the rocky ledge below. Naturally, in our then tired state, we preferred to move in the path of least resistance offered by the glissade; accordingly we all dumped our burdens, and rearranged such as needed to be altered, so that they might all well and truly roll. We were now very thirsty, and some of us quenched our thirst, satisfactorily for the time, by gathering a little snow, squeezing it into a ball in the palm of one's hand, and then placing it on the surface of a piece of rock. Although the shade temperature was then considerably below zero, Fahr., the black rock had absorbed so much heat from the direct rays of the sun, that the snowball, when placed on it, commenced to melt almost immediately, and the thaw water started to trickle over the surface of the rock. The chill having been taken off the snowball in this way, the remainder could be safely transferred to one's mouth, and yielded a refreshing drink.

Our loads having now been modelled into the shape of sausages, we launched them down the slope, and watched them intently, as, like animated things, they bumped and bounded over the wavy ridges of the névé slope. Brocklehurst's load, consisting largely of all our cooking utensils, done up in a large bag, if not the most erratic, was certainly the noisiest, and recalled, on a small scale, Kipling's Bolivar, "clanging like a smithy shop after every roll". The battered remains of the aluminium vessels fetched up with a final big bang against the rocks below. Mackay now led the glissade, and firmly grasping his ice-axe, slid to the bottom in less than a minute; we all followed suit.

As we gathered speed on our downward course, and the chisel edge of the ice-axe bit deeper into the hard névé, it sprayed our faces and necks with a miniature shower of ice. The temperature was low, and whenever the steel of the ice-axe touched one's bare skin, it seemed to burn it like a hot iron. We all reached the bottom of the slope safely, and fired with the success of our first glissade, and finding an almost endless succession of snow slopes below us, we let ourselves go again and again, in a series of wild rushes towards the foot of the main cone. Here and there we bumped heavily against the opposing edges of hard "sastrugi", or tore our nether garments on projecting points of sharp rock. Unfortunately it was not only clothes and cookers which suffered in our wild career: a valuable aneroid was lost, and one of the hypsometer thermometers broken. It seemed as though we should never reach the bottom of the cone, but at last the slope flattened out to the gently inclined terrace, where our depot lay; altogether we had dropped down 5,000 feet in level by glissading.

South with Scott

E. R. G. R. Evans

Edward "Teddy" Evans RN sailed with Scott on the British Antarctic Expedition of 1910, the main objects of which was to reach the South Pole and carry out an ambitious scientific programme. Setting sail from Cardiff in the Terra Nova, *the expedition's passage south was beset by storms; on nearing the white continent the* Terra Nova *encountered unusually heavy pack ice.*

We sighted our first iceberg in latitude 62° on the evening of Wednesday, 7 December. Cheetham's squeaky hail came down from aloft and I went up to the crow's-nest to look at it, and from this time on we passed all kinds of icebergs, from the huge tabular variety to the little weathered water-worn bergs. Some we steamed quite close to and they seemed for all the world like great masses of sugar floating in the sea.

From latitudes 60° to 63° we saw a fair number of birds: southern fulmars, whale birds, mollymawks, sooty albatrosses, and occasionally Cape-pigeons still. Then the brown-backed petrels began to appear, sure precursors of the pack ice – it was in sight right enough the day after the brown-backs were seen. By breakfast time on 9 December, when nearly in latitude 65°, we were steaming through thin streams of broken pack with floes from six to twelve feet across. A few penguins and seals were seen, and by 10 a.m. no less than twenty-seven icebergs in sight. The newcomers to these regions were clustered in little groups on the forecastle and poop sketching and painting, hanging over the bows and gleefully watching this lighter stuff being brushed aside by our strong stem.

We were passing through pack all day, but the ice hereabouts was not close enough nor heavy enough to stop us appreciably.

The ship was usually conned by Pennell and myself from the crow's-nest, and I took the ship very near one berg for Ponting to cinematograph it. We now began to see snow petrels with black beaks and pure white bodies, rather resembling doves. Also we saw great numbers of brown-backed petrels the first day in the pack, whole flights of them resting on the icebergs. The sun was just below the horizon at midnight and we had a most glorious sunset, which was first a blazing copper changing to salmon pink and then purple. The pools of water between the floes caught the reflection, the sea was perfectly still and every berg and ice-floe caught something of the delicate colour. Wilson, of course, was up and about till long after midnight sketching and painting. The Antarctic pack ice lends itself to water-colour work far better than to oils.

When conning the ship from up in the crow's-nest one has a glorious view of this great changing ice-field. Moving through lanes of clear blue water, cannoning into this floe and splitting it with iron-bound stem, overriding that and gnawing off a twenty ton lump, gliding south, east, west, through leads of open water, then charging an innocent-looking piece which brings the ship up all-standing, astern and ahead again, screwing and working the wonderful wooden ship steadily southward until perhaps two huge floes gradually narrow the lane and hold the little lady fast in their frozen grip.

This is the time to wait and have a look round: on one side floes the size of a football field, all jammed together, with their torn up edges showing their limits and where the pressure is taken. Then three or four bergs, carved from the distant Barrier, imprisoned a mile or so away, with the evening sun's soft rays casting beautiful shadows about them and kissing their glistening cliff faces.

Glancing down from the crow's-nest the ship throws deep shadows over the ice and, while the sun is just below the southern horizon, the still pools of water show delicate blues and greens that no artist can ever do justice to. It is a scene from fairyland.

I loved this part of the voyage, for I was in my element. At odd times during the night, if one can call it night, the crow's-nest would have visitors, and hot cocoa would be sent up in covered pots by means of signal halyards. The pack ice was new to all the ship's officers except myself, but they soon got into the way of conning and working through open water leads and, as time went on, distinguished the thinner ice from the harder and more dangerous stuff.

On 10 December we stopped the ship and secured her to a heavy floe from which we took in sufficient ice to make eight tons of fresh water, and whilst doing this Rennick sounded and obtained bottom in 1,964 fathoms, fora-minifera and decomposed skeleton unicellular organs, also two pieces of black basic lava. Lillie and Nelson took plankton and water bottle samples to about 280 fathoms. A few penguins came round and a good many crabeater seals were seen. In the afternoon we got under way again and worked for about eight miles through the pack, which was gradually becoming denser. About 2.30 p.m. I saw from the crow's-nest four seals on a floe. I slid down a backstay, and whilst the officer on watch worked the ship close to them, I got two or three others with all our firearms and shot the lot from the forecastle head. We had seal liver for dinner that night; one or two rather turned up their noses at it, but, as Scott pointed out, the time would come when seal liver would be a delicacy to dream about.

Campbell did not do much conning except in the early morning, as his executive duties kept him well occupied. The Polar sledge journey had its attractions, but Campbell's party were to have interesting work and were envied by many on board. For reasons which need not here be entered into Campbell had to abandon the King Edward VII Land programme, but in these days his mob were known as the Eastern Party, to consist of the Wicked Mate, Levick, and Priestley, with three seamen, Abbott, Browning, and Dickason. Campbell had the face of an angel and the heart of a hornet. With the most refined and innocent smile he would come up to me and ask whether the Eastern Party could have a small amount of this or that luxury. Of course I would agree, and sure enough Bowers would tell me that Campbell had already appropriated a far greater share than he was ever entitled to of the commodity in question. This happened again and again, but the refined smile was irresistible and I am bound to say the Wicked Mate generally got away with it, for even Bowers, the incomparable, was bowled over by that smile.

We crossed the Antarctic Circle on the morning of the 10th, little dreaming in those happy days that the finest amongst us would never recross it again.

We took a number of deep-sea soundings, several of over 2,000 fathoms, on this first southward voyage. Rennick showed himself very expert with the deep-sea gear and got his soundings far more easily than we had done in the *Discovery* and *Morning* days.

We were rather unfortunate as regards the pack ice met with, and must have passed through 400 miles of it from north to south. On my two previous voyages we had had easier conditions altogether, and then it had not mattered, but all with these dogs and ponies cooped up and losing condition, with the *Terra Nova* eating coal and sixty hungry men scoffing enormous meals, we did not seem to be doing much or getting on with the show. It was, of course, nobody's fault, but our patience was sorely tried.

We made frequent stops in the pack ice, even letting fires out and furling sail, and sometimes the ice would be all jammed up so that not a water hole was visible – this condition would continue for days. Then, for no apparent reason, leads would appear and black water-skies would tempt us to raise steam again. Scott himself showed an admirable patience, for the rest of us had something to occupy our time with. Pennell and I, for instance, were constantly taking sights and working them out to find our position and also to get the set and drift of the current. Then there were magnetic observations to be taken on board and out on the ice away from the magnetic influence of the ship, such as it was. Simpson had heaps to busy himself with, and Ponting was here, there, and everywhere with his camera and cinematograph machine. Had it not been for our anxiety to make southward progress, the time would have passed pleasantly enough, especially in fine weather. Days came when we could get out on the floe and exercise on ski, and Gran zealously looked to all our requirements in this direction.

December 11 witnessed the extraordinary sight of our company standing bareheaded on deck whilst Captain Scott performed Divine Service. Two hymns were sung, which broke strangely the great white silence. The weather was against us this day in that we had snow, thaw, and actually rain, but we could not complain on the score of weather conditions generally.

Practically all the ship's company exercised on the floes while we remained fast frozen. Next day there was some slight loosening of the pack and we tried sailing through it and managed half a degree southward in the forty-eight hours. We got along a few miles here and there, but when ice conditions continued favourable for making any serious advance it was better to light up and push our way onward with all the power we could command. We got some heavy bumps on the 13th December and as this hammering was not doing the ship much good, since I was unable to make southing then at a greater rate than one mile an hour, we let fires right out and prepared, as Captain Scott said, "To wait till the clouds roll by." For the next few days there was not much doing nor did we experience such pleasant weather.

Constant visits were made to the crow's-nest in search of a way through. December 16 and 17 were two very grey days with fresh wind, snow, and some sleet. Affectionate memories of Captain Colbeck and the little relief ship, *Morning*, came back when the wind soughed and whistled through the rigging. This sound is most uncanny and the ice always seemed to exaggerate any noise.

I hated the overcast days in the pack. It was bitterly cold in the crow's-nest however much one put on then, and water skies often turned out to be nimbus clouds after we had laboured and cannoned towards them. The light, too, tired and strained one's eyes far more than on clear days.

When two hundred miles into the pack the ice varied surprisingly. We would be passing through ice a few inches thick and then suddenly great floes four feet above the water and twelve to fifteen feet deep would be encountered. December 18 saw us steaming through tremendous leads of open water. A very funny occurrence was witnessed in the evening when the wash of the ship turned a floe over under water and on its floating back a fish was left stranded. It was a funny little creature, nine inches in length, a species of notathenia. Several snow petrels and a skua gull made attempts to secure the fish, but the afterguard kept up such a chorus of cheers, hoots and howls that the birds were scared away till one of us secured the fish from the floe.

Early on the 19th we passed close to a large iceberg which had a shelving beach like an island. We began to make better progress to the south-westward and worked into a series of open leads. We came across our first emperor penguin, a young one, and two sea-leopards, besides crabeater seals, many penguins, some giant petrels, and a Wilson petrel. That afternoon tremendous pieces of ice were passed; they were absolutely solid and regular floes, being ten to twelve feet above water and, as far as one could judge, about 50 feet below. The water here was beautifully clear.

We had now reached latitude 68° and, as penguins were plentiful, Archer and Clissold, the cooks, made us penguin stews and "hooshes" to eke out our fresh provisions. Concerning the penguins, they frequently came and inspected the ship. One day Wilson and I chased some, but they continually kept just out of our reach; then Uncle Bill lay down on the snow, and when one, out of curiosity, came up to him he grabbed it by the leg and brought it to the ship, protesting violently, for all the world like a little old man in a dinner jacket. Atkinson and Wilson found a new kind of tapeworm in this penguin, with a head like a propeller. This worm has since been named after one of us!

We were now down to under 300 tons of coal, some of which had perforce to be landed, in addition to the 30 tons of patent fuel which were under the forward stores. I had no idea that Captain Scott could be so patient. He put the best face on everything, although he certainly was disappointed in the *Terra Nova* and her steaming capacity. He could not well have been otherwise when comparing her with his beloved *Discovery*. Whilst in the pack our leader spent his time in getting hold of the more detailed part of our scientific programme and mildly tying the scientists in knots.

We had some good views of whales in the pack. Whenever a whale was sighted Wilson was called to identify it unless it proved to belong to one of the more common species. We saw Sibbald's whale, Rorquals, and many killer whales, but no Right whales were properly identified this trip.

I very much wanted to show Scott the island we had discovered in the first Antarctic Relief Expedition and named after him, but when in its vicinity snow squalls and low visibility prevented this.

On the 22nd Bowers, Wright, Griffith Taylor and myself

chased a lot of young penguins on the ice and secured nine for our Christmas dinner. We spent a very pleasant Christmas this year, devoting great attention to food. We commenced the day with kidneys from our frozen meat store. Captain Scott conducted the Christmas church service and all hands attended since we had no steam up and were fast held in the pack. The ward-room was decorated with our sledge flags and a new blue tablecloth generally brightened up our Mess. We had fresh mutton for lunch and the seamen had their Christmas dinner at this time. The afterguard dined at 6.30 on fresh penguin, roast beef, plum pudding, mince pies, and asparagus, while we had champagne, port, and liqueurs to drink and an enormous box of Fry's fancy chocolates for dessert. This "mortal gorge" was followed by a sing-song lasting until midnight, nearly every one, even the most modest, contributing. Around the Christmas days we made but insignificant headway, only achieving thirty-one miles in the best part of the week, but on the 29th the floes became thin and the ice showed signs of recent formation, though intermingled with heavier floes of old and rotten ice. There was much diatomacea in the rotten floes. About 2.40 a.m. the ship broke through into a lead of open water six miles in length.

I spent the middle watch in the crow's-nest, Bowers being up there with me talking over the Expedition, his future and mine. He was a wonderful watch companion, especially when he got on to his favourite subject, India. He had some good tales to tell of the Persian Gulf, of days and weeks spent boat-cruising, of attacks made on gun-running dhows and kindred adventure. He told me that one dhow was boarded while he was up the Gulf, when the Arabs, waiting until most of the boat's crew of blue-jackets were on board, suddenly let go the halyards of their great sail and let it down crash over the lot, the boom breaking many heads and the sail burying our seamen, while the Arabs got to work and practically scuppered the crowd.

Soon after 4 a.m. I went below and turned in, confident that we were nearing the southern extreme of the pack. Captain Scott awoke when I went into the cabin, pleased at the prospect, but after so many adverse ice conditions he shook his head, unwilling to believe that we should get clear yet awhile. I bet him ten sardine sandwiches that we should be out of the pack by noon on

the 30th, and when I turned out at 8 o'clock I was delighted to
find the ship steaming through thin floes and passing into a series
of great open water leads. By 6 p.m. on the 29th a strong breeze
was blowing, snow was falling, and we were punching along
under steam and sail. Sure enough we got out of the pack early
on the 30th and, cracking on all our canvas, were soon doing
eight knots with a following wind.

Later in the day the wind headed us with driving snow, fine
rain, and, unfortunately, a considerable head swell. This caused
the ship to pitch so badly that the ponies began to give trouble
again. Oates asked for the speed to be reduced, but we got over
this by setting fore and aft sail and keeping the ship's head three
or four points off the wind. New Year's Eve gave us another
anxious time, for we encountered a hard blow from the SSE. It
was necessary to heave the ship to most of the day under bare
poles with the engines just jogging to keep the swell on her bow.
A thin line of pack ice was sighted in the morning and this turned
out to be quite a blessing in disguise, for I took the ship close to
the edge of it and skirted along to leeward. The ice formed a
natural breakwater and damped the swell most effectually. The
swell and sea in the open would have been too much for the
ponies as it must be remembered that they had been in their
stalls on board for five weeks.

We had now reached the Continental Shelf, the depth of water
had changed from 1,111 fathoms on the 30th to 180 fathoms
this day. The biologists took advantage of our jogging along in
the open water to trawl, but very few specimens were obtained.
At midnight the "youth of the town" made the devil of a din by
striking sixteen bells, blowing whistles on the siren, hooting with
the foghorn, cheering and singing. What children we were, but
what matter!

1911 came like the opening of a new volume of an exciting
book. This was the year in which Scott hoped to reach the Pole,
the ideal date he had given being 21 December. This was the
year that Campbell and his party were looking forward to so
eagerly – if only they could be successful in landing their gear
and equipment in King Edward VII Land – and, for the less
showy but more scientific sledgers, 1911 held a wealth of excitement in store. Griffith Taylor and Debenham knew pretty well

that next New Year's Day would see them in the midst of their Western journey with the secrets of those rugged mountains revealed perhaps. I do not know what my own feelings were, it would be impossible to describe them. I read up part of Shackleton's diary and something of what his companion Wilde had written. Just this:

12 miles, 200 yards. – 1/1/08.

"Started usual time. Quan (pony) got through the forenoon fairly well with assistance, but after lunch the poor chap broke down and we had to take him out of harness. Shackleton, Adams, and Marshall dragged his sledge, and I brought the ponies along with the other load. As soon as we camped I gave Quan the bullet, and Marshall and I cut him up. He was a tough one. I am cook this week with Marshall as my tent mate."

The more one read into Shackleton's story the more wonderful it all seemed, and with our resources failure appeared impossible – yet that telegram which Captain Scott had received at Melbourne:

"Beg leave to inform you proceeding Antarctic.
                                                    —Amundsen."

We all knew that Amundsen had no previous Antarctic sledging experience, but no one could deny that to Norwegians ice-work, and particularly skiing, was second nature, and here lay some good food for thought and discussion. Where would the *Fram* enter the pack? Where would Amundsen make his base? The answers never once suggested anything like the truth.

Actually on New Year's Day Amundsen was between 500 and 600 miles north of us, but of Roald Amundsen more anon.

How strange to be once more in open water, able to steer whatever course we chose, with broad daylight all night, and at noon only a couple of days' run from Cape Crozier. Practically no ice in sight, but a sunlit summer sea in place of the pack, with blue sky and cumulo stratus clouds, so different from the grey, hard skies that hung so much over the great ice field we had just forced. The wind came fair as the day wore on and by 10 p.m. we were under plain sail, doing a good six knots. High mountains were visible to the westward, part of the Admiralty Range, two splendid peaks to be seen towering above the remainder, which appeared to be Mounts Sabine and Herschell. Coulman Island was seen in the distance during the day.

What odd thrills the sight of the Antarctic Continent sent through most of us. Land was first sighted late on New Year's Eve and I think everybody had come on deck at the cry 'Land oh!' To me those peaks always did and always will represent silent defiance; there were times when they made me shudder, but it is good to have looked upon them and to remember them in those post-War days of general discontent, for they remind me of the four Antarctic voyages which I have made and of the unanimous goodwill that obtained in each of the little wooden ships which were our homes for so long. How infinitely distant those towering mountains seemed and how eternal their loneliness.

As we neared Cape Crozier Wilson became more and more interested. He was dreadfully keen on the beach there being selected as a base, and his enthusiasm was infectious. Certainly Scott was willing enough to try to effect a landing even apart from the advantage of having a new base. The Cape Crozier beach would probably mean a shorter journey to the Pole, for we should be spared the crevasses which radiated from White Island and necessitated a big detour being made to avoid them.

As we proceeded the distant land appeared more plainly and we were able to admire and identify the various peaks of the snow-clad mountain range. The year could not have opened more pleasantly. We had church in a warm sun, with a temperature several degrees above freezing point, and most of us spent our off-time basking in the sunshine, yarning, skylarking, and being happy in general.

We tried to get a white-bellied whale on the 2nd January, but our whale-gun did not seem to have any buck in it and the harpoon dribbled out a fraction of the distance it was expected to travel.

The same glorious weather continued on 2 January, and Oates took five of the ponies on to the upper deck and got their stables cleared out. The poor animals had had no chance of being taken from their stalls for thirty-eight days, and their boxes were between two and three feet deep with manure. The four ponies stabled on the upper deck looked fairly well but were all stiff in their legs.

Rennick took soundings every forty or fifty miles in the Ross Sea, the depth varying from 357 fathoms comparatively close up to Cape Crozier to 180 fathoms in latitude 73°.

Cape Crozier itself was sighted after breakfast on the 3rd, and the Great Ice Barrier appeared like a thin line on the southern horizon at 11.30 that morning. We were close to the Cape by lunchtime, and by 1.30 we had furled sail in order to manœuvre more freely. The *Terra Nova* steamed close up to the face of the Barrier, then along to the westward until we arrived in a little bay where the Barrier joins Cape Crozier. Quite a tide was washing past the cliff faces of the ice; it all looked very white, like chalk, while the sun was near the northern horizon, but later in the afternoon blue and green shadows were cast over the ice, giving it a softer and much more beautiful appearance. Ponting was given a chance to get some cinema films of the Barrier while we were cruising around, and then we stopped in the little bay where the Ice Barrier joins Cape Crozier, lowered a boat, and Captain Scott, Wilson, myself, and several others went inshore in a whaler. We were, however, unable to land as the swell was rather too heavy for boat work. We saw an Emperor penguin chick and a couple of adult Emperors, besides many Adélie penguins and skua gulls. We pulled along close under the great cliffs which frown over the end of the Great Ice Barrier. They contrasted strangely in their blackness with the low crystal ice cliffs of the Barrier itself. In one place we were splashed by the spray from quite a large waterfall, and one realized that the summer sun, beating down on those black foothills, must be melting enormous quantities of ice and snow. A curious ozone smell, which must have been the stench of the guano from the penguin rookeries, was noticed, but land smells of any sort were pleasant enough now for it brought home to us the fact that we should shortly embark on yet another stage of the Expedition.

Pennell conned the ship close under the cliffs and followed the boat along the coast. The *Terra Nova* was quite dwarfed by the great rocky bluffs and we realized the height of the cliffs for the first time.

Whilst we were prospecting Nelson obtained water-bottle samples and temperatures at 10, 50, 100, and 200 fathoms. The deep water apparently continued to the foot of the cliff in most places but there were two or three tiny steep beaches close to the junction of the Barrier and Ross Island.

Captain Scott being satisfied that no landing was possible, we in the boat returned to the ship and proceeded in her to the penguin rookery, a mile or so farther west. When half a mile from the shore, we found the bottom rapidly shoaling, the least depth being 9½ fathoms. Several small bergs were ashore hereabouts, but the swell breaking on the beach plainly told us that a landing was out of the question. After carefully searching the shore with glasses while the ship steamed slowly along it, all ideas of a landing were abandoned and we set course for McMurdo Sound. As soon as the ship was headed for her new destination we commenced to make a running survey of the coast to Cape Bird. This took until ten o'clock at night, and we found a great bight existed in Ross Island which quite changed its shape on the map. After 10 p.m. we ran into some fairly heavy pack ice, gave up surveying, and had a meal.

I went up to the crow's-nest in order to work the ship to the best advantage, and spent eleven hours on end there, but the excitement of getting the *Terra Nova* round Cape Bird and into McMurdo Sound made the time fly. Occasionally the ship crashed heavily as she charged her way through the ice masses which skirted the shore. Whilst I conned the ship leadsmen sounded carefully, and I was able to work her close in to the coast near Cape Bird and avoid some heavy ice which we could never have forced. At 4.30 a.m. I broke through the Cape Bird ice-field and worked the ship on as far as Cape Royds, which was passed about 6.30 a.m. Looking through our binoculars we noticed Shackleton's winter hut looking quite new and fresh.

Leaving Cape Royds we made our way up McMurdo Sound as far as Inaccessible Island, where we found the Strait frozen over from east to west. Skirting along the edge of the sea ice I found there was no way in, although I endeavoured to break into it at several points to reach what looked like open water spaces a mile or two from the ice edge. Accordingly, we stopped and I came down to report on the outlook. Captain Scott, Wilson, and I eventually went aloft to the crosstrees and had a good look round; we finally decided to land and look at a place where there appeared to be a very good beach. In *Discovery* days this spot was known as the skuary, being a favourite nesting place for skua gulls, a sort of little cape. I piloted the ship as close I could to this position, which is situate midway between Cape Bird and Cape Armitage on Ross Island. An ice anchor was laid out and then Scott, Wilson, and I landed on the sea ice and walked a mile or so over it to the little cape in question.

It appeared to be an ideal winter quarters, and was then and there selected as our base. Captain Scott named it Cape Evans, after me, for which I was very grateful. Wilson already had a Cape named after him on the Victoria Land coast in latitude 82°.

We now returned on board and immediately commenced landing motor-sledges, ponies, etc. For better working, once the various parties were landed, we adopted the standard time of meridian 180°, in other words, twelve hours fast on Greenwich Mean Time.

We now organized ourselves into three parties and I gave up the command of the *Terra Nova* to Pennell till the ship returned from New Zealand next year. The charge of the transport over the one and a half miles of sea ice which lay between the ship and shore was given to Campbell, whilst I took charge of the Base Station, erection of huts, and so forth, Captain Scott himself supervising, planning and improving.

We continued getting stuff out on the ice until late at night, and by dinner time, 7 p.m., we had put two motor-sledges, all the dogs and ponies ashore, besides most of the ordinary sledges and tents.

Next day we turned out all hands at 4.30, breakfasted at 5, started work at 6, and landed all the petrol, kerosene, and hut timber. Most of the haulage was done by motors and men, but a few runs were made with ponies. We erected a big tent on the beach at Cape Evans and in this the hut-building party and those who were stowing stores and unloading sledges on the beach got their meals and sleep. We worked continuously until 10 p.m. with only the shortest of meal intervals, and then, tired but contented, we 'flattened out' in our sleeping-bags, bunks, or hammocks.

The following day the same routine was continued and nearly the whole of the provision cases came ashore and were stacked in neat little piles under Bowers's direction. This indefatigable little worker now devoted himself entirely to the western party stores. He knew every case and all about it. Each one weighed approximately 60 lb. We had purposely arranged that this should be so when ordering stores in London to save weight and space. The cases were made of Venesta 3-ply wood. Of course, the instruments and heavier scientific gear could not stow in these handy packages, but the sixty-pound-Venesta was adhered to whenever possible. The ponies were not worked till the afternoon of the 6th, and then only the best of them with light loads.

Davis, the carpenter, had with him seaman Ford, Keohane, and Abbot. Their routine was a little different from ours: they worked at hut building from 7 a.m. till midnight usually, and their results were little short of marvellous. Odd people helped them when they could, and of these Ponting showed himself to be *facile princeps* as carpenter. I never saw anything like the speed in which he set up tongued and grooved match boarding.

Day, Nelson, and Lashly worked with the motor-sledges; the newest motor frequently towed loads of 2,500 lb. over the ice at a six mile an hour speed. The oldest hauled a ton and managed six double trips a day. Day, the motor engineer, had been down here before – both he and Priestley came from the Shackleton Expedition. The former had a decidedly comic vein which made him popular all round. From start to finish Day showed himself to be the most undefeated sportsman, and it was not his fault that the motor-sledges did badly in the end.

Perhaps my diary from 7 January 1911, to the 8th gives a good idea of the progress we were making with the base station and of the general working day here. It reads as follows:

Saturday, January 7, 1911.

All hands hard at work landing stores. Meares and Dimitri running dog teams to and fro for light gear.

Captain Scott, Dr. Wilson, Griffith Taylor, Debenham, Cherry-Garrard, and Browning leading ponies. Campbell, Levick, and Priestley hauling sledges with colossal energy and enormous loads, the majority of the ship's party unloading stores; Bowers, two seamen, Atkinson, and I unloading sledges on the beach and carrying their contents up to their assigned positions, Simpson and Wright laying the foundations for a magnetic hut, and so on. Every one happy and keen, working as incessantly as ants. I took on the job of ice inspector, and three or four times a day I go out and inspect the ice, building snow bridges over the tide cracks and thin places. The ice, excepting the floe to which the ship is fast, is several feet thick. The floe by the *Terra Nova* is very thin and rather doubtful. We, ashore, had dinner at 10 p.m. and turned in about 11.

But the following day, although included here, was by no means typical.

Sunday, January 8.

This morning a regrettable accident took place. The third and newest motor-sledge was hoisted out and, while being hauled clear on to the firm ice, it broke through and sank in deep water. Campbell and Day came in with the news, which Captain Scott took awfully well.

It was nobody's fault, as Simpson and Campbell both tested the floe first and found it quite thick and apparently good. However, there it is, in about 100 fathoms of water.

We stopped sledging for the day and those on board shifted the ship by warping, but could not get her into a satisfactory billet, so raised steam.

We spent the day working on the hut and putting chairs and benches together. Captain Scott put the sledge meters together and I helped him. These are similar to the distance meters on motorcars. They register in nautical miles (6,084 feet) and yards, to 25 yards or less by interpolation.

Took a True Bearing and found the approximate variation for Simpson (149° E).

On the following day those on board the ship shifted her to a new position alongside the fast ice, just under a mile from our beach. The transportation of stores continued and we got ashore a great

number of bales of compressed fodder, also some Crown Preserve
Patent Fuel. As there was nothing much to do on the beach my
party lent a hand with the landing of fodder, and I led the ponies
Miki, Jehu, and Blossom; the latter, having suffered greatly on
the outward voyage, was in poor condition. Still, most of the
ponies were doing well, and at night were picketed on a snow-
drift behind the hut. They occasionally got adrift, but I usually
heard them and got up to make them fast, my small sleeping-tent
being right alongside their tethering space.

Nelson continued working with me unless the requirements
of his biological work called him away. In less than a week we
had the whole of our stores and equipment landed, and from the
beginning many of us took up our quarters at Cape Evans itself.
We pitched several small tents on the beach, and it was an agree-
able change to roll up and sleep in a fur bag after the damp, cold
berths we had occupied in the ship. Teddy Nelson became my
particular friend in the shore party and shared a sledging tent
with me. The rest of the shore staff paired off and slept in the
small tents, while Captain Scott had one to himself. We called it
the "Holy of Holies", and from the privacy of this tiny dwelling
Scott issued his directions, supervised, planned, and improved
whenever improvement could be made in anything. He had a
marvellous brain and a marvellous way of getting the best possible work out of his subordinates, still he never spared himself.
One did with extraordinary little sleep, and in the sunny days it
became necessary to leave tent doors wide open, otherwise the
close-woven windproof tent cloth kept all the fresh air out and
one woke with a terrific head.

To rightly get hold of our wintering place one must imagine a
low spit of land jutting out into a fiord running, roughly north
and south and bounded on both sides by a steep-to coast line
indented with glaciers of vast size. Here and there gigantic snow-
slopes were to be seen which more gradually lowered into the
sea, and all around ice-covered mountains with black and brown
foothills. A few islands rose to heights of 300 or 400 feet in
McMurdo Sound, and these had no snow on them worth speaking of even in the winter. The visible land was of black or
chocolate-brown, being composed of volcanic tuff, basalts, and
granite. There were occasional patches of ruddy brown and

yellow which relieved the general black and white appearance of this uninhabitable land, and close to the shore on the north side of Cape Evans were small patches of even gritty sand. In the neighbourhood of our Cape hard, brittle rocks cropped up everywhere, rocks that played havoc with one's boots. Sloping up fairly steeply from Cape Evans itself we had more and more rock masses until a kind of rampart was reached, on which one could see a number of extraordinary conical piles of rock, which looked much as if they had been constructed by human hands for landmarks or surveying beacons – these were called debris cones. This part above and behind Cape Evans was christened The Ramp, and from it one merely had to step from boulders and stones on to the smooth blue ice-slope that extended almost without interruption to the summit of Erebus itself. From The Ramp one could gaze in wonder at that magnificent volcano, White Lady of the Antarctic, beautiful in her glistening gown of sparkling crystal with a stole of filmy smoke-cloud wrapped about her wonderful shoulders.

We used to gaze and gaze at that constantly changing smoke or steam which the White Lady breathes out at all seasons, and has done for thousands of years.

Those were such happy days during the first Cape Evans summer. For the most part we had hot weather and could wash in the thaw pools which formed from the melting snow, and even draw our drinking water from the cascades which bubbled over the sun-baked rock, much as they do in summer-time in Norway.

The progress made by Davis and his crew of voluntary carpenters was amazing. One week after our arrival at the Cape, Nelson, Meares, and I commenced to cut a cave out of the ice cap above our camp for stowing our fresh mutton in. When knock-off work-time came Bowers, Nelson, and I made our way over to the ship with a hundred gallons of ice from this cave to be used for drinking water, it all helped to save coal and nobody made a journey to or fro empty handed if it could be helped. Once on board we took the opportunity to bath and shave. In this country it is certainly a case of "Where I dines I sleeps", so after supper on board we coiled down in somebody's beds and slept till 5.30 next morning when we returned to camp and carried on all day, making great progress with the grotto, which was eventually lit by electric light. We had plenty of variety in the matter of work; one part of the grotto was intended for Simpson's magnetic work, and this was the illuminated section. Whenever people visited the ice caves we got them to do a bit of picking and hewing, even roping in Captain Scott, who did a healthy half-hour's work when he came along our way.

Scott and Wilson got their hands in at dog-driving now, as I did occasionally myself. Nobody could touch Meares or Dimitri at dog-team work, although later on Cherry-Garrard and Atkinson became the experts.

The hut was finished externally on 12 January and fine stables built up on its northern side. This complete, Bowers arranged an annexe on the south side from which to do the rationing and provision issues. How we blessed all this fine weather; it was hardly necessary to wear snow glasses, in spite of so much sunshine, for the glare was relieved by the dark rock and sand around us. When all the stores had been discharged from the ship she lightened up considerably, and Campbell then set to work to ballast her for Pennell. Meares amused the naval members of our party by asking, with a childlike innocence, "Had they got all the cargo out of the steamer?" There was nothing wrong in what he said, but the *Terra Nova*, Royal Yacht Squadron – and "cargo" and "steamer" – how our naval pride was hurt!

Incidentally we called the sandy strand (before the winter snow came, and covered it, and blotted it all out) Hurrah Beach; the bay to the northward of the winter quarters we christened Happy Bay. Although our work physically was of the hardest we lived in luxury for a while. Nelson provided cocoa for Captain Scott and myself at midnight just before we slept. He used to make it after supper and keep it for us in a great thermos flask. We only washed once a week and we were soon black with sun and dirt but in splendid training. In the first three weeks my shore gang, which included the lusty Canadian physicist, Wright, carried many hundreds of cases, walked miles daily, dug ice, picked, shovelled, handed ponies, cooked and danced. Outwardly we were not all prototypes of "the Sentimental Bloke", but occasionally in the stillness of the summer nights, we some of us unbent a bit, when the sun stood low in the south and all was quiet and still, and we did occasionally build castles in the air and draw home-pictures to one another, pictures of English summers, of river picnics and country life that framed those distant homes in gold and made them look to us like little bits of heaven – however, what was more important, the stores were all out of the *Terra Nova*, even to stationery, instruments, and chronometers, and we could have removed into the hut at a pinch a week before we did, or gone sledging, for that matter, had we not purposely delayed to give the ponies a chance to regain condition. It was certainly better to let the carpenter and his company straighten up first, and in our slack hours we, who were to live in the palatial hut, got the house in order, put up knick-knacks, and settled into our appointed corners with our personal gear and professional impedimenta only at the last moment, a day or two before the big depot-laying sledge journey was appointed to start. Simpson and Ponting had the best allotments in the hut, because the former had to accommodate anemometers, barometers, thermometers, motors, bells, and a diversity of scientific instruments, but yet leave room to sleep amongst them without being electrocuted, while the latter had to arrange a small-sized dark room, 8 ft by 6 ft floor dimension, for all his developing of films and plates, for stowing photographic gear and cinematograph, and for everything in connection with his important and beautiful work as camera artist to the Expedition. Ponting likewise slept where he worked, so a bed was also included in the dark room.

Before moving the chronometers ashore Pennell, Rennick, and I myself took astronomical observations to determine independently the position of the observation spot on the beach at Cape Evans. The preliminary position gave us latitude 77° 38' 23" S longitude 166° 33' 24" E, a more accurate determination was arrived at by running meridian distances from New Zealand and taking occultations during the ensuing winter, for longitude: latitudes were obtained by the mean results of stars north and south and meridian altitudes of the sun above and below pole.

Before getting busy with the preliminaries for the big depot journey, I took stock of the fresh meat in the grotto. The list of frozen flesh which I handed over to Clissold, the cook, looked luxurious enough, for it included nothing less than 700 lb of beef, 100 sheep carcasses, 2 pheasants, 3 ox-tails, and 3 tongues,

10 lb of sweetbread, 1 box of kidneys, 10 lb of suet, 82 penguins, and 11 skua gulls! The cooks' corner in the hut was very roomy, and, if my memory serves me aright, our cooking range was of similar pattern to one supplied to the Royal yacht, *Alexandra*.

On 19 January a snow road was made over to the ice foot on the south side of Cape Evans in order to save the ponies' legs and hoofs. The Siberian ponies were not shod, and this rough, volcanic rock would have shaken them considerably.

A great deal of the bay ice had broken away and drifted out of the Sound, so that by the 20th the ship was only a few hundred yards from Hurrah Beach. This day Rennick, smiling from ear to ear, came across the ice with the pianola in bits conveyed on a couple of sledges. He fixed it up with great cleverness at one end of the hut and it was quite wonderful to see how he stripped it on board, brought it through all sorts of spaces, transported it undamaged over ice and rocky beach, re-erected it, tuned it, and then played "Home, Sweet Home". What with the pianola going all out, the gramophone giving us Melba records, and the ship's company's gramophone squawking out Harry Lauder's opposition numbers, Ponting cinematographing everything of interest and worthy of pictorial record, little Anton rushing round with nosebags for the ponies, Meares and Dimitri careering with the dog teams over ice, beach, packing cases, and whatnot, sailors with coloured tam-o'-shanters bobbing around in piratical style, the hot sun beating down and brightening up everything, one might easily have imagined this to be the circus scene in the great Antarctic joyride film. Everything ran on wheels in these days, and it was difficult to imagine that in three months there would be no sun, that this sweltering beach would be encrusted with ice, and that the cold, dark winter would be upon us.

Winter Quarters

Robert F. Scott

Scott's Terra Nova *expedition spent the Antarctic winter of 1911 ensconced in the hut at Cape Evans, undertaking scientific work and preparations for the summer sledge-journey to the Pole. As ever, Scott recorded the scene in his journal.*

Sunday, 23 April: Winter Quarters. The last day of the sun and a very glorious view of its golden light over the Barne Glacier. We could not see the sun itself on account of the Glacier, the fine ice cliffs of which were in deep shadow under the rosy rays.

Impression: The long mild twilight which like a silver clasp unites today with yesterday; when morning and evening sit together hand in hand beneath the starless sky of midnight.

It blew hard last night and most of the young ice has gone as expected. Patches seem to be remaining south of the Glacier Tongue and the Island and off our own bay. In this very queer season it appears as though the final freezing is to be reached by gradual increments to the firmly established ice.

Had Divine Service. Have only seven hymn-books, those brought on shore for our first Service being very stupidly taken back to the ship.

I begin to think we are *too* comfortable in the hut and hope it will not make us slack; but it is good to see everyone in such excellent spirits – so far not a rift in the social arrangements.

Monday, 24 April: A night watchman has been instituted mainly for the purpose of observing the aurora, of which the displays have been feeble so far. The observer is to look round every hour or oftener if there is aught to be seen. He is allowed cocoa and sardines with bread and butter – the cocoa can be made over an acetylene Bunsen burner, part of Simpson's outfit. I took the first turn last night; the remainder of the afterguard follow in rotation. The long night hours give time to finish up a number of small tasks – the hut remains quite warm though the fires are out.

Simpson has been practising with balloons during our absence. This morning he sent one up for trial. The balloon is of silk and has a capacity of 1 cubic metre. It is filled with hydrogen gas, which is made in a special generator. The generation is a simple process. A vessel filled with water has an inverted vessel within it; a pipe is led to the balloon from the latter and a tube of India rubber is attached which contains calcium hydrate. By tipping the tube the amount of calcium hydrate required can be poured into the generator. As the gas is made it passes into the balloon or is collected in the inner vessel, which acts as a bell jar if the stopcock to the balloon is closed.

The arrangements for utilizing the balloon are very pretty.

An instrument weighing only 2¼ oz and recording the temperature and pressure is attached beneath a small flag and hung 10 to 15 feet below the balloon with balloon silk thread; this silk thread is of such fine quality that 5 miles of it only weighs 4 oz, whilst its breaking strain is 1¼ lb. The lower part of the instrument is again attached to the silk thread, which is cunningly wound on coned bobbins from which the balloon unwinds it without hitch or friction as it ascends.

In order to spare the silk any jerk as the balloon is released two pieces of string united with a slow match carry the strain between the instrument and the balloon until the slow match is consumed.

The balloon takes about a quarter of an hour to inflate; the slow match is then lit, and the balloon released; with a weight of 8 oz and a lifting power of 2½ lb it rises rapidly. After it is lost to ordinary vision it can be followed with glasses as mile after mile of thread runs out. Theoretically, if strain is put on the silk thread it should break between the instrument and the balloon, leaving the former free to drop, when the thread can be followed up and the instrument with its record recovered.

Today this was tried with a dummy instrument, but the thread broke close to the bobbins. In the afternoon a double thread was tried, and this acted successfully.

Today I allotted the ponies for exercise. Bowers, Cherry-Garrard, Hooper, Clissold, P.O. Evans, and Crean take animals, besides Anton and Oates. I have had to warn people that they will not necessarily lead the ponies which they now tend.

Wilson is very busy making sketches.

Tuesday, 25 April: It was comparatively calm all day yesterday and last night, and there have been light airs only from the south today. The temperature, at first comparatively high at -5°, has gradually fallen to -13°; as a result the Strait has frozen over at last and it looks as though the Hut Point party should be with us before very long. If the blizzards hold off for another three days the crossing should be perfectly safe, but I don't expect Meares to hurry.

Although we had very good sunset effects at Hut Point, Ponting and others were much disappointed with the absence of such effects at Cape Evans. This was probably due to the continual interference of frost smoke; since our return here, and especially yesterday and today, the sky and sea have been glorious in the afternoon.

Ponting has taken some coloured pictures, but the result is not very satisfactory and the plates are much spotted; Wilson is very busy with pencil and brush.

Atkinson is unpacking and setting up his sterilizers and incubators. Wright is wrestling with the electrical instruments. Evans is busy surveying the Cape and its vicinity. Oates is reorganizing the stable, making bigger stalls, etc. Cherry-Garrard is building a stone house for taxidermy and with a view to getting hints for making a shelter at Cape Crozier during the winter. Debenham and Taylor are taking advantage of the last of the light to examine the topography of the peninsula. In fact, everyone is extraordinarily busy.

I came back with the impression that we should not find our winter walks so interesting as those at Hut Point, but I'm rapidly altering my opinion; we may miss the hill climbing here, but in every direction there is abundance of interest. Today I walked round the shores of the North Bay examining the kenyte cliffs and great masses of morainic material of the Barne Glacier, then on under the huge blue ice cliffs of the Glacier itself. With the sunset lights, deep shadows, the black islands and white bergs it was all very beautiful.

Simpson and Bowers sent up a balloon today with a double thread and instrument attached; the line was checked at about 3 miles, and soon after the instrument was seen to disengage. The balloon at first went north with a light southerly breeze till it reached 300 or 400 feet, then it turned to the south, but did not travel rapidly; when 2 miles of thread had gone it seemed to be going north again or rising straight upward.

In the afternoon Simpson and Bowers went to recover their treasure, but somewhere south of Inaccessible Island they found the thread broken and the light was not good enough to continue the search.

The sides of the galley fire have caved in – there should have been cheeks to prevent this; we got some fireclay cement today and plastered up the sides. I hope this will get over the difficulty, but have some doubt.

Wednesday, 26 April: Calm. Went round Cape Evans – remarkable effects of icicles on the ice-foot, formed by spray of southerly gales.

Thursday, 27 April: The fourth day in succession without wind, but overcast. Light snow has fallen during the day – tonight the wind comes from the north.

We should have our party back soon. The temperature remains about -5° and the ice should be getting thicker with rapidity.

Went round the bergs off Cape Evans – they are very beautiful, especially one which is pierced to form a huge arch. It will be interesting to climb around these monsters as the winter proceeds.

Today I have organized a series of lectures for the winter; the people seem keen and it ought to be exceedingly interesting to discuss so many diverse subjects with experts.

We have an extraordinary diversity of talent and training in our people; it would be difficult to imagine a company composed of experiences which differed so completely. We find one hut contains an experience of every country and every clime! What an assemblage of motley knowledge!

Friday, 28 April: Another comparatively calm day – temp. -12°, clear sky. Went to ice caves on glacier S of Cape; these are really very wonderful. Ponting took some photographs with long exposure and Wright got some very fine ice crystals. The Glacier Tongue comes close around a high bluff headland of kenyte; it is much cracked and curiously composed of a broad wedge of white névé over blue ice. The faults in the dust strata in these surfaces are very mysterious and should be instructive in the explanation of certain ice problems.

It looks as though the sea had frozen over for good. If no further blizzard clears the Strait it can be said for this season that:

> The Bays froze over on 25 March
> The Strait froze over on 22 April
> The Strait dissipated on 29 April
> The Strait froze over on 30 April

Later: The Hut Point record of freezing is:

Night 24th–25th: *Ice forming midday 25th, opened with leads*
26th: *Ice all out, sound apparently open*
27th: *Strait apparently freezing*
Early 28th: *Ice over whole Strait*
29th: *All ice gone*
30th: *Freezing over*
4th May: *Broad lead opened along land to Castle Rock,* 300 *to* 400 *yards wide*
Party intended to start on 11*th, if weather fine*

Very fine display of aurora tonight, one of the brightest I have ever seen – over Erebus; it is conceded that a red tinge is seen after the movement of light.

Saturday, 29 April: Went to Inaccessible Island with Wilson. The agglomerates, kenytes, and lavas are much the same as those at Cape Evans. The Island is 540 feet high, and it is a steep climb to reach the summit over very loose sand and boulders. From the summit one has an excellent view of our surroundings and the ice in the Strait, which seemed to extend far beyond Cape Royds, but had some ominous cracks beyond the Island.

We climbed round the ice-foot after descending the hill and found it much broken up on the south side; the sea spray had washed far up on it.

It is curious to find that all the heavy seas come from the south and that it is from this direction that protection is most needed.

There is some curious weathering on the ice blocks on the N side; also the snow drifts show interesting dirt bands. The island had a good sprinkling of snow, which will all be gone, I expect, tonight. For as we reached the summit we saw a storm approaching from the south; it had blotted out the Bluff, and we watched it covering Black Island, then Hut Point and Castle Rock. By the time we started homeward it was upon us, making a harsh chatter as it struck the high rocks and sweeping along the drift on the floe.

The blow seems to have passed over tonight and the sky is clear again, but I much fear the ice has gone out in the Strait. There is an ominous black look to the westward.

Sunday, 30 April: As I feared last night, the morning light revealed the havoc made in the ice by yesterday's gale. From Wind Vane Hill (66 feet) it appeared that the Strait had not opened beyond the island, but after church I went up the Ramp with Wilson and steadily climbed over the glacier ice to a height of about 650 feet. From this elevation one could see that a broad belt of sea ice had been pushed bodily to seaward, and it was evident that last night the whole stretch of water from Hut Point to Turtle Island must have been open – so that our poor people at Hut Point are just where they were.

The only comfort is that the Strait is already frozen again; but what is to happen if every blow clears the sea like this?

Had an interesting walk. One can go at least a mile up the glacier slope before coming to crevasses, and it does not appear that these would be serious for a good way farther. The view is magnificent, and on a clear day like this one still enjoys some hours of daylight, or rather twilight, when it is possible to see everything clearly.

Have had talks of the curious cones which are such a feature of the Ramp – they are certainly partly produced by ice and partly by weathering. The ponds and various forms of ice grains interest us.

Tonight have been naming all the small land features of our vicinity.

Tuesday, 2 May: It was calm yesterday. A balloon was sent up in the morning, but only reached a mile in height before the instrument was detached (by slow match).

In the afternoon went out with Bowers and his pony to pick up instrument, which was close to the shore in the South Bay. Went on past Inaccessible Island. The ice outside the bergs has grown very thick, 14 inches or more, but there were freshly frozen pools beyond the Island.

In the evening Wilson opened the lecture series with a paper on "Antarctic Flying Birds". Considering the limits of the subject the discussion was interesting. The most attractive point raised was that of pigmentation. Does the absence of pigment suggest absence of reserve energy? Does it increase the insulating properties of the hair or feathers? Or does the animal clothed in white radiate less of his internal heat? The most interesting example of Polar colouring here is the increased proportion of albinos amongst the giant petrels found in high latitudes.

Today have had our first game of football; a harassing southerly wind sprang up, which helped my own side to the extent of three goals.

This same wind came with a clear sky and jumped up and down in force throughout the afternoon, but has died away tonight. In the afternoon I saw an ominous lead outside the Island which appeared to extend a long way south. I'm much afraid it may go across our pony track from Hut Point. I am getting anxious to have the hut party back, and begin to wonder if the ice to the south will ever hold in permanently now that the Glacier Tongue has gone.

Wednesday, 3 May: Another calm day, very beautiful and clear. Wilson and Bowers took our few dogs for a run in a sledge. Walked myself out over ice in North Bay – there are a good many cracks and pressures with varying thickness of ice, showing how tide and wind shift the thin sheets – the newest leads held young ice of 4 inches.

The temperature remains high, the lowest yesterday -13°; it should be much lower with such calm weather and clear skies. A strange fact is now very commonly noticed: in calm weather there is usually a difference of 4° or 5° between the temperature at the hut and that on Wind Vane Hill (64 feet), the latter being the higher. This shows an inverted temperature.

As I returned from my walk the southern sky seemed to grow darker, and later stratus cloud was undoubtedly spreading up from that direction – this at about 5 p.m. About 7 a moderate north wind sprang up. This seemed to indicate a southerly blow, and at about 9 the wind shifted to that quarter and blew gustily, 25 to 35 mph. One cannot see the result on the Strait, but I fear it means that the ice has gone out again in places. The wind dropped as suddenly as it had arisen soon after midnight.

In the evening Simpson gave us his first meteorological lecture – the subject, "Coronas, Halos, Rainbows, and Auroras". He has a remarkable power of exposition and taught me more of these phenomena in the hour than I had learnt by all previous interested inquiries concerning them.

I note one or two points concerning each phenomenon.

Corona: White to brown inside ring called Aureola – outside are sometimes seen two or three rings of prismatic light in addition. Caused by diffraction of light round drops of water or ice crystals; diameter of rings inversely proportionate to size of drops or crystals – mixed sizes of ditto causes aureola without rings.

Halos: Caused by refraction and reflection through and from ice crystals. In this connection the hexagonal, tetrahedonal type of crystallization is first to be noted; then the infinite number of forms in which this can be modified together with result of fractures: two forms predominate, the plate and the needle; these forms falling through air assume definite position – the plate falls horizontally swaying to and fro, the needle turns rapidly about its longer axis, which remains horizontal. Simpson showed excellent experiments to illustrate; consideration of these facts and refraction of light striking crystals clearly leads to explanation of various complicated halo phenomena such as recorded and such as seen by us on the Great Barrier, and draws attention to the critical refraction angles of 32° and 46°, the radius of inner and outer rings, the position of mock suns, contra suns, zenith circles, etc.

Further measurements are needed; for instance, of streamers from mock suns and examination of ice crystals. (Record of ice crystals seen on Barrier Surface.)

Rainbows: Caused by reflection and refraction from and through *drops of water* – colours vary with size of drops, the smaller the drop the lighter the colours and nearer to the violet end of the spectrum – hence white rainbow as seen on the Barrier, very small drops.

Double Bows – diameters must be 84° and 100° – again from laws of refraction – colours: inner, red outside; outer, red inside – i.e. reds come together.

Wanted to see more rainbows on Barrier. In this connection a good rainbow was seen to NW in February from winter quarters. Reports should note colours and relative widths of bands of colour.

Iridescent Clouds: Not yet understood; observations required, especially angular distance from the sun.

Auroras: Clearly most frequent and intense in years of maximum sun spots; this argues connection with the sun.

Points noticed requiring confirmation:

Arch: centre of arch in magnetic meridian.

Shafts: take direction of dipping needle.

Bands and Curtains with convolutions – not understood.

Corona: shafts meeting to form.

Notes required on movement and direction of movement – colours seen – supposed red and possibly green rays preceding or accompanying movement. Auroras are sometimes accompanied by magnetic storms, but not always, and *vice versa* – in general significant signs of some connection – possible common dependants on a third factor. The phenomenon further connects itself in form with lines of magnetic force about the earth.

(Curious apparent connection between spectrum of aurora and that of a heavy gas, "argon". May be coincidence.)

Two theories enunciated:

Arrhenius: Bombardments of minute charged particles from the sun gathered into the magnetic field of the earth.

Birkeland: Bombardment of free negative electrons gathered into the magnetic field of the earth.

It is experimentally shown that minute drops of water are deflected by light.

It is experimentally shown that ions are given off by dried calcium, which the sun contains.

Professor Störmer has collected much material showing connection of the phenomenon with lines of magnetic force.

Thursday, 4 May: From the small height of Wind Vane Hill (64 feet) it was impossible to say if the ice in the Strait had been out after yesterday's wind. The sea was frozen, but after twelve hours' calm it would be in any case. The dark appearance of the ice is noticeable, but this has been the case of late since the light is poor; little snow has fallen or drifted and the ice flowers are very sparse and scattered.

We had an excellent game of football again today – the exercise is delightful and we get very warm. Atkinson is by far the best player, but Hooper, P.O. Evans, and Crean are also quite good. It has been calm all day again.

Went over the sea ice beyond the Arch berg; the ice half a mile beyond is only 4 inches. I think this must have been formed since the blow of yesterday, that is, in sixteen hours or less.

Such rapid freezing is a hopeful sign, but the prompt dissipation of the floe under a southerly wind is distinctly the reverse.

I am anxious to get our people back from Hut Point, mainly on account of the two ponies; with so much calm weather there should have been no difficulty for the party in keeping up its supply of blubber; an absence of which is the only circumstance likely to discomfort it.

The new ice over which I walked is extraordinarily slippery and free from efflorescence. I think this must be a further sign of rapid formation.

Friday, 5 May: Another calm day following a quiet night. Once or twice in the night a light northerly wind, soon dying away. The temperature down to -12°. What is the meaning of this comparative warmth? As usual in calms, the Wind Vane Hill temperature is 3° or 4° higher. It is delightful to contemplate the amount of work which is being done at the station. No one is idle – all hands are full, and one cannot doubt that the labour will be productive of remarkable result.

I do not think there can be any life quite so demonstrative of character as that which we had on these expeditions. One sees a remarkable reassortment of values. Under ordinary conditions it is so easy to carry a point with a little bounce; self-assertion is a mask which covers many a weakness. As a rule we have neither the time nor the desire to look beneath it, and so it is that commonly we accept people on their own valuation. Here the outward show is nothing; it is the inward purpose that counts. So the "gods" dwindle and the humble supplant them. Pretence is useless.

One sees Wilson busy with pencil and colour box, rapidly and steadily adding to his portfolio of charming sketches and at intervals filling the gaps in his zoological work of *Discovery* times; withal ready and willing to give advice and assistance to others at all times; his sound judgement appreciated and therefore a constant referee.

Simpson, master of his craft, untiringly attentive to the working of his numerous self-recording instruments, observing all changes with scientific acumen, doing the work of two observers at least and yet ever seeking to correlate an expanded scope. So the current meteorological and magnetic observations are taken as never before by Polar expeditions.

Wright, good-hearted, strong, keen, striving to saturate his mind with the ice problems of this wonderful region. He has taken the electrical work in hand with all its modern interest of association with radio-activity.

Evans, with a clear-minded zeal in his own work, does it with all the success of result which comes from the taking of pains. Therefrom we derive a singularly exact preservation of time – an important consideration to all, but especially necessary for the physical work. Therefrom also, and including more labour, we have an accurate survey of our immediate surroundings and can trust to possess the correctly mapped results of all surveying data obtained. He has Gran for assistant.

Taylor's intellect is omnivorous and versatile – his mind is unceasingly active, his grasp wide. Whatever he writes will be of interest – his pen flows well.

Debenham's is clearer. Here we have a well-trained, sturdy worker, with a quiet meaning that carries conviction; he realizes the conceptions of thoroughness and conscientiousness.

To Bowers's practical genius is owed much of the smooth working of our station. He has a natural method in line with which all arrangements fall, so that expenditure is easily and exactly adjusted to supply, and I have the inestimable advantage of knowing the length of time which each of our possessions will last us and the assurance that there can be no waste. Active mind and active body were never more happily blended. It is a restless activity, admitting no idle moments and ever budding into new forms.

So we see the balloon ascending under his guidance and anon he is away over the floe tracking the silk thread which held it. Such a task completed, he is away to exercise his pony, and later out again with the dogs, the last typically self-suggested, because for the moment there is no one else to care for these animals. Now in a similar manner he is spreading thermometer screens to get comparative readings with the home station. He is for the open air, seemingly incapable of realizing any discomfort from it, and yet his hours within doors spent with equal profit. For he is intent on tracking the problems of sledging food and clothing to their innermost bearings and is becoming an authority on past records. This will be no small help to me and one which others never could have given.

Adjacent to the physicists' corner of the hut Atkinson is quietly pursuing the subject of parasites. Already he is in a new world. The laying out of the fish trap was his action and the catches are his field of labour. Constantly he comes to ask if I would like to see some new form, and I am taken to see some protozoon or ascidian isolated on the slide plate of his microscope. The fishes themselves are compartively new to science; it is strange that their parasites should have been under investigation so soon.

Atkinson's bench, with its array of microscopes, test-tubes, spirit lamps, etc, is next to the dark room in which Ponting spends the greater part of his life. I would describe him as sustained by artistic enthusiasm. This world of ours is a different one to him than it is to the rest of us – he gauges it by its picturesqueness – his joy is to reproduce its pictures artistically, his grief to fail to do so. No attitude could be happier for the work which he has undertaken, and one cannot doubt its productiveness. I would not imply that he is out of sympathy with the works of others, which is far from being the case, but that his energies centre devotedly on the minutiae of his business.

Cherry-Garrard is another of the open-air, self-effacing, quiet workers; his whole heart is in the life, with profound eagerness to help everyone. Indoors he is editing our Polar journal, out of doors he is busy making trial stone huts and blubber stoves, primarily with a view to the winter journey to Cape Crozier, but incidentally these are instructive experiments for any party which may get into difficult by being cut off from the home station. It is very well to know how best to use the scant resources that Nature provides in these regions. In this connection I have been study-ing our Arctic library to get details concerning snow-hut building and the implements used for it.

Oates's whole heart is in the ponies. He is really devoted to their care, and I believe will produce them in the best possible form for the sledging season. Opening out the stores, installing a blubber stove, etc, has kept *him* busy, whilst his satellite, Anton, is ever at work in the stables – an excellent little man.

P.O. Evans and Crean are repairing sleeping-bags, covering felt boots, and generally working on sledging kit. In fact, there is no one idle, and no one who has the least prospect of idleness.

Saturday, 6 May: Two more days of calm, interrupted with occa-sional gusts.

Yesterday, Friday evening, Taylor gave an introductory lecture on his remarkably fascinating subject – modern physiography.

These modern physiographers set out to explain the forms of land erosion on broad common-sense lines, heedless of geologi-cal support. They must, in consequence, have their special language. River courses, they say, are not temporary – in the main they are archaic. In conjunction with land elevations they have worked through *geographical cycles*, perhaps many. In each geographical cycle they have advanced from *infantile* V-shaped forms; the courses broaden and deepen, the bank slopes reduce in angle as maturer stages are reached until the level of sea surface is more and more nearly approximated. In *senile* stages the river is a broad sluggish stream flowing over a plain with little inequality of level. The cycle has formed a *Peneplain*. Subsequently, with fresh elevation, a new cycle is commenced. So much for the simple case, but in fact nearly all cases are modified by unequal elevations due to landslips, by variation in hardness of rock, etc. Hence modification in positions of river courses and the fact of different parts of a single river being in different stages of cycle.

Taylor illustrated his explanations with examples: the Red River, Canada – plain flat though elevated, water lies in pools, river flows in "V" "infantile" form.

The Rhine Valley – The gorgeous scenery from Mainz down due to infantile form in recently elevated region.

The Russian Plains – examples of "sensility".

Greater complexity in the Blue Mountains – these are undoubted earth folds; the Nepean River flows through an offshoot of a fold, the valley being made as the fold was elevated – curious valleys made by erosion of hard rock overlying soft.

River *piracy – domestic*, the short-circuiting of a *meander*, such as at Coo in the Ardennes; *foreign*, such as Shoalhaven River, Australia – stream has captured river.

Landslips have caused the isolation of Lake George and altered the watershed of the whole country to the south.

Later on Taylor will deal with the effects of ice and lead us to the formation of the scenery of our own region, and so we shall have much to discuss.

Sunday, 7 May: Daylight now is very short. One wonders why the Hut Point party does not come. Bowers and Cherry-Garrard have set up a thermometer screen containing maximum thermometers and thermographs on the sea floe about ¾' NW of the hut. Another smaller one is to go on top of the Ramp. They took the screen out on one of Day's bicycle-wheel carriages and found it ran very easily over the salty ice where the sledges give so much trouble. This vehicle is not easily turned, but may be very useful before there is much snowfall.

Yesterday a balloon was sent up and reached a very good height (probably 2 to 3 miles) before the instrument disengaged; the balloon went almost straight up and the silk fell in festoons over the rocky part of the Cape, affording a very difficult clue to follow; but whilst Bowers was following it, Atkinson observed the instrument fall a few hundred yards out on the Bay – it was recovered and gives the first important record of upper-air temperature.

Atkinson and Crean put out the fish trap in about 3 fathoms of water off the west beach; both yesterday morning and yesterday evening when the trap was raised it contained over forty fish, whilst this morning and this evening the catches in the same spot have been from twenty to twenty-five. We had fish for breakfast this morning, but an even more satisfactory result of the catches has been revealed by Atkinson's microscope. He had discovered quite a number of new parasites and found work to last quite a long time.

Last night it came to my turn to do night watchman again, so that I shall be glad to have a good sleep tonight.

Yesterday we had a game of football; it is pleasant to mess about, but the light is failing.

Clissold is still producing food novelties; tonight we had galantine of seal – it was *excellent*.

Monday, 8 May – Tuesday, 9 May: As one of the series of lectures I gave an outline of my plans for next season on Monday evening. Everyone was interested, naturally. I could not but hint that in my opinion the problem of reaching the Pole can best be solved by relying on the ponies and man haulage. With this sentiment the whole company appeared to be in sympathy. Everyone seems to distrust the dogs when it comes to glacier and summit. I have asked everyone to give thought to the problem, to freely discuss it, and bring suggestions to my notice. It's going to be a tough job; that is better realized the more one dives into it.

Today (Tuesday) Debenham has been showing me his photographs taken west. With Wright's and Taylor's these will make an extremely interesting series – the ice forms especially in the region of the Koettlitz glacier are unique.

The Strait has been frozen over a week. I cannot understand

why the Hut Point party doesn't return. The weather continues wonderfully calm, though now looking a little unsettled. Perhaps the unsettled look stops the party, or perhaps it waits for the moon, which will be bright in a day or two.

Anyway, I wish it would return, and shall not be free from anxiety till it does.

Cherry-Garrard is experimenting in stone huts and with blubber fires – all with a view to prolonging the stay at Cape Crozier.

Bowers has placed one thermometer screen on the floe about ¾' out, and another smaller one above the Ramp. Oddly, the floe temperature seems to agree with that on Wind Vane Hill, whilst the hut temperature is always 4° or 5° colder in calm weather. To complete the records a thermometer is to be placed in South Bay.

Science – the rock foundation of all effort!

Wednesday, 10 May: It has been blowing from the south 12 to 20 miles per hour since last night; the ice remains fast. The temperature -12° to -19°. The party does not come. I went well beyond Inaccessible Island till Hut Point and Castle Rock appeared beyond Tent Island – that is, well out on the space which was last seen as open water. The ice is 9 inches thick – not much for eight or nine days' freezing; but it is very solid – the surface wet but very slippery. I suppose Meares waits for 12 inches in thickness, or fears the floe is too slippery for the ponies.

Yet I wish he would come.

I took a thermometer on my walk today; the temperature was -12° inside Inaccessible Island, but only -8° on the sea ice outside – the wind seemed less outside. Coming in under lee of Island and bergs I was reminded of the difficulty of finding shelter in these regions. The weather side of hills seems to afford better shelter than the lee side, as I have remarked elsewhere. May it be in part because all lee sides tend to be filled by drift snow, blown and weathered rock debris? There was a good lee under one of the bergs; in one corner the ice sloped out over me and on either side, forming a sort of grotto; here the air was absolutely still.

Ponting gave us an interesting lecture on Burmah, illustrated with fine slides. His descriptive language is florid, but shows the artistic temperament. Bowers and Simpson were able to give personal reminiscences of this land of pagodas, and the discussion led to interesting statements on the religion, art, and education of its people, their philosophic idleness, etc. Our lectures are a real success.

Friday, 12 May: Yesterday morning was quiet. Played football in the morning; wind got up in the afternoon and evening.

All day it has been blowing hard, 30 to 60 miles an hour; it has never looked very dark overhead, but a watery cirrus has been in evidence for some time, causing well marked paraselene.

I have not been far from the hut, but had a great fear on one occasion that the ice had gone out in the Strait.

The wind is dropping this evening, and I have been up to Wind Vane Hill. I now think the ice has remained fast.

There has been astonishingly little drift with the wind, probably due to the fact that there has been so very little snowfall of late.

Atkinson is pretty certain that he has isolated a very motile bacterium in the snow. It is probably air borne, and though no bacteria have been found in the air, this may be carried in upper currents and brought down by the snow. If correct it is an interesting discovery.

Tonight Debenham gave a geological lecture. It was elementary. He gave little more than the rough origin and classification of rocks with a view to making his further lectures better understood.

Saturday, 13 May: The wind dropped about 10 last night. This morning it was calm and clear save for a light misty veil of ice crystals through which the moon shone with scarce clouded brilliancy, surrounded with bright cruciform halo and white paraselene. Mock moons with prismatic patches of colour appeared in the radiant ring, echoes of the main source of light. Wilson has a charming sketch of the phenomenon.

I went to Inaccessible Island, and climbing some way up the steep western face, reassured myself concerning the ice. It was evident that there had been no movement in consequence of yesterday's blow.

In climbing I had to scramble up some pretty steep rock faces and screens, and held on only in anticipation of gaining the top of the Island and an easy descent. Instead of this I came to an impossible overhanging cliff of lava, and was forced to descend as I had come up. It was no easy task, and I was glad to get down with only one slip, when I brought myself up with my ice-axe in the nick of time to prevent a fall over a cliff. This Island is very steep on all sides. There is only one known place of ascent; it will be interesting to try and find others.

After tea Atkinson came in with the glad tidings that the dog team were returning from Hut Point. We were soon on the floe to welcome the last remnant of our wintering party. Meares reported everything well and the ponies not far behind.

The dogs were unharnessed and tied up to the chains; they are all looking remarkably fit – apparently they have given no trouble at all of late; there have not even been any fights.

Half an hour later Day, Lashly, Nelson, Forde, and Keohane arrived with the two ponies – men and animals in good form.

It is a great comfort to have the men and dogs back, and a greater to contemplate all the ten ponies comfortably stabled for the winter. Everything seems to depend on these animals.

I have not seen the meteorological record brought back, but it appears that the party had had very fine calm weather since we left them, except during the last three days, when wind has been very strong. It is curious that we should only have got one day with wind.

I am promised the sea-freezing record tomorrow. Four seals were got on 22 April, the day after we left, and others have been killed since, so that there is a plentiful supply of blubber and seal-meat at the hut – the rest of the supplies seem to have been pretty well run out. Some more forage had been fetched in from the depot. A young sea leopard had been killed on the sea ice near Castle Rock three days ago, this being the second only found in the Sound.

It is a strange fact that none of the returning party seem to greatly appreciate the food luxuries they have had since their return. It would have been the same with us had we not had a day or two in tents before our return. It seems more and more certain that a very simple fare is all that is needed here – plenty of seal-meat, flour, and fat, with tea, cocoa, and sugar; these are the only real requirements for comfortable existence.

The temperatures at Hut Point have not been as low as I expected. There seems to have been an extraordinary heat wave during the spell of calm recorded since we left – the thermometer registering little below zero until the wind came, when it fell to -20°. Thus as an exception we have had a fall instead of a rise of temperature with wind.

Sunday, 14 May: Grey and dull in the morning.

Exercised the ponies and held the usual service. This morning I gave Wright some notes containing speculations on the amount of ice on the Antarctic continent and on the effects of winter movements in the sea ice. I want to get into his head the larger bearing of the problems which our physical investigations involve. He needs two years here to fully realize these things, and with all his intelligence and energy will produce little unless he has that extended experience.

The sky cleared at noon, and this afternoon I walked over the North Bay to the ice cliffs – such a very beautiful afternoon and evening – the scene bathed in moonlight, so bright and pure as to be almost golden, a very wonderful scene. At such times the Bay seems strangely homely, especially when the eye rests on our camp with the hut and lighted windows.

I am very much impressed with the extraordinary and general cordiality of the relations which exist amongst our people. I do not suppose that a statement of the real truth, namely, that there is no friction at all, will be credited – it is so generally thought that the many rubs of such a life as this are quietly and purposely sunk in oblivion. With me there is no need to draw a veil; there is nothing to cover. There are no strained relations in this hut, and nothing more emphatically evident than the universally amicable spirit which is shown on all occasions.

Such a state of affairs would be delightfully surprising under any conditions, but it is much more so when one remembers the diverse assortment of our company.

This theme is worthy of expansion. Tonight Oates, captain in a smart cavalry regiment, has been "scrapping" over chairs and tables with Debenham, a young Australian student.

It is a triumph to have collected such men.

The temperature has been down to -23°, the lowest yet

recorded here – doubtless we shall soon get lower, for I find an extraordinary difference between this season as far as it has gone and those of 1902–3.

Monday, 15 May: The wind has been strong from the north all day – about 30 miles an hour. A bank of stratus cloud about 6,000 or 7,000 feet (measured by Erebus) has been passing rapidly overhead *towards* the north; it is nothing new to find the overlying layers of air moving in opposite directions, but it is strange that the phenomenon is so persistent. Simpson has frequently remarked as a great feature of weather conditions here the seeming reluctance of the air to "mix" – the fact seems to be the explanation of many curious fluctuations of temperature.

Went for a short walk, but it was not pleasant. Wilson gave an interesting lecture on penguins. He explained the primitive characteristics in the arrangement of feathers on wings and body, the absence of primaries and secondaries or bare tracts; the modification of the muscles of the wings and in the structure of the feet (the metatarsal joint). He pointed out (and the subsequent discussion seemed to support him) that these birds probably branched at a very early stage of bird life – coming pretty directly from the lizard bird Archaeopteryx of the Jurassic age. Fossils of giant penguins of Eocene and Miocene ages show that there has been extremely little development since.

He passed on to the classification and habitat of different genera, nest-making habits, eggs, etc. Then to a brief account of the habits of the Emperors and Adélies, which was, of course, less novel ground for the old hands.

Of special points of interest I recall his explanation of the desirability of embryonic study of the Emperor to throw further light on the development of the species in the loss of teeth, etc; and Ponting's contribution and observation of adult Adélies teaching their young to swim – this point has been obscure. It has been said that the old birds push the young into the water, and, *per contra*, that they leave them deserted in the rookery – both statements seemed unlikely. It would not be strange if the young Adélie had to learn to swim (it is a well-known requirement of the Northern fur seal – sea bear), but it will be interesting to see in how far the adult birds lay themselves out to instruct their progeny.

During our trip to the ice and sledge journey one of our dogs, Vaida, was especially distinguished for his savage temper and generally uncouth manners. He became a bad wreck with his poor coat at Hut Point, and in this condition I used to massage him; at first the operation was mistrusted and only continued to the accompaniment of much growling, but later he evidently grew to like the warming effect and sidled up to me whenever I came out of the hut, though still with some suspicion. On returning here he seemed to know me at once, and now comes and buries his head in my legs whenever I go out of doors; he allows me to rub him and push him about without the slightest protest and scampers about me as I walk abroad. He is a strange beast – I imagine so unused to kindness that it took him time to appreciate it.

Tuesday, 16 May: The north wind continued all night, but dropped this forenoon. Conveniently it became calm at noon and we had a capital game of football. The light is good enough, but not much more than good enough, for this game.

Had some instruction from Wright this morning on the electrical instruments.

Later went into our carbide expenditure with Day: am glad to find it sufficient for two years, but am not making this generally known, as there are few things in which economy is less studied than light if regulations allow of waste.

For measuring the ordinary potential gradient we have two self-recording quadrant electrometers. The principle of this instrument is the same as that of the old Kelvin instrument; the clockwork attached to it unrolls a strip of paper wound on a roller; at intervals the needle of the instrument is depressed by an electromagnet and makes a dot on the moving paper. The relative position of these dots forms the record. One of our instruments is adjusted to give only $1/10^{th}$ the refinement of measurement of the other by means of reduction in the length of the quartz fibre. The object of this is to continue the record in snowstorms, etc, when the potential difference of air and earth is very great. The instruments are kept charged with batteries of small Daniels cells. The clocks are controlled by a master clock.

The instrument available for radio-activity measurements is a modified type of the old gold-leaf electroscope. The measurement is made by the mutual repulsion of quartz fibres acting against a spring – the extent of the repulsion is very clearly shown against a scale magnified by a telescope.

The measurements to be made with instrument are various:

The *ionization of the air*. A length of wire charged with 2,000 volts (negative) is exposed to the air for several hours. It is then coiled on a frame and its rate of discharge measured by the electroscope.

The *radio-activity of the various rocks* of our neighbourhood; this by direct measurement of the rock.

The *conductivity of the air*, that is, the relative movement of ions in the air; by movement of air past charged surface. Rate of absorption of + and – ions is measured, the negative ion travelling faster than the positive.

Wednesday, 17 May: For the first time this season we have a rise of temperature with a southerly wind. The wind force has been about 30 since yesterday evening; the air is fairly full of snow and the temperature has risen to -6° from -18°.

I heard one of the dogs barking in the middle of the night, and on inquiry learned that it was one of the "Serais", that he seemed to have something wrong with his hind leg, and that he had been put under shelter. This morning the poor brute was found dead.

I'm afraid we can place but little reliance on our dog teams and reflect ruefully on the misplaced confidence with which I regarded the provision of our transport. Well, one must suffer for errors of judgement.

This afternoon Wilson held a post-mortem on the dog; he could find no sufficient cause of death. This is the third animal that has died at winter quarters without apparent cause. Wilson, who is nettled, proposes to examine the brain of this animal tomorrow.

Went up the Ramp this morning. There was light enough to see our camp, and it looked homely, as it does from all sides. Somehow we loom larger here than at Cape Armitage. We seem to be more significant. It must be from contrast of size; the larger hills tend to dwarf the petty human element.

Tonight the wind has gone back to the north and is now blow-ing fresh.

This sudden and continued complete change of direction is new to our experience.

Oates has just given us an excellent little lecture on the management of horses.

He explained his plan of feeding our animals "soft" during the winter, and hardening them up during the spring. He pointed out that the horse's natural food being grass and hay, he would naturally employ a great number of hours in the day filling a stomach of small capacity with food from which he could derive only a small percentage of nutriment.

Hence it is desirable to feed horses often and light. His present routine is as follows:

Morning: *Chaff.*

Noon, after exercise: *Snow. Chaff and either oats or oil-cake alternate days.*

Evening, 5 p.m.: *Snow. Hot bran mash with oil-cake or boiled oats and chaff; finally a small quantity of hay.*

This sort of food should be causing the animals to put on flesh, but is not preparing them for work. In October he proposes to give "hard" food, all cold, and to increase the exercising hours.

As concerning the food we possess he thinks:

The *chaff* made of young wheat and hay is doubtful; there does not seem to be any grain with it – and would farmers cut young wheat? There does not seem to be any "fat" in this food, but it is very well for ordinary winter purposes.

NB: It seems to me this ought to be inquired into. *Bran* much discussed, but good because it causes horses to chew the oats with which mixed.

Oil-cake, greasy, producing energy – excellent for horses to work on.

Oats, of which we have two qualities, also very good working food – our white quality much better than the brown.

Our trainer went on to explain the value of training horses, of getting them "balanced" to pull with less effort. He owns it is very difficult when one is walking horses only for exercise, but thinks something can be done by walking them fast and occasionally making them step backwards.

Oates referred to the deeds that had been done with horses by foreigners in shows and with polo ponies by Englishmen when the animals were trained; it is, he said, a sort of gymnastic training.

The discussion was very instructive and I have only noted the salient points.

Thursday, 18 May: The wind dropped in the night; today it is calm, with slight snowfall. We have had an excellent football match – the only outdoor game possible in this light.

I think our winter routine very good. I suppose every leader of a party has thought that, since he has the power of altering it. On the other hand, routine in this connection must take into consideration the facilities of work and play afforded by the preliminary preparations for the expedition. The winter occupations of most of our party depend on the instruments and implements, the clothing and sledging outfit, provided by forethought, and the routine is adapted to these occupations.

The busy winter routine of our party may therefore be excusably held as a subject for self-congratulation.

Friday, 19 May: Wind from the north in the morning, temperature comparatively high (about -6°). We played football during the noon hour – the game gets better as we improve our football condition and skill.

In the afternoon the wind came from the north, dying away again late at night.

In the evening Wright lectured on "Ice Problems". He had a difficult subject and was nervous. He is young and has never done original work; is only beginning to see the importance of his task.

He started on the crystallization of ice, and explained with very good illustrations the various forms of crystals, the manner of their growth under different conditions and different temperatures. This was instructive. Passing to the freezing of salt water, he was not very clear. Then on to glaciers and their movements, theories for same and observations in these regions.

There was a good deal of disconnected information – silt

bands, crevasses were mentioned. Finally he put the problems of larger aspect.

The upshot of the discussion was a decision to devote another evening to the larger problems such as the Great Ice Barrier and the interior ice sheet. I think I will write the paper to be discussed on this occasion.

I note with much satisfaction that the talks on ice problems and the interest shown in them has had the effect of making Wright devote the whole of his time to them. That may mean a great deal, for he is a hard and conscientious worker.

Atkinson has a new hole for his fish trap in 15 fathoms; yesterday morning he got a record catch of forty-three fish, but oddly enough yesterday evening there were only two caught.

Saturday, 20 May: Blowing hard from the south, with some snow and very cold. Few of us went far; Wilson and Bowers went to the top of the Ramp and found the wind there force 6 to 7, temperature -24°; as a consequence they got frost-bitten. There was lively cheering when they reappeared in this condition, such is the sympathy which is here displayed for affliction; but with Wilson much of the amusement arises from his peculiarly scant headgear and the confessed jealousy of those of us who cannot face the weather with so little face protection.

The wind dropped at night.

Sunday, 21 May: Observed as usual. It blew from the north in the morning. Had an idea to go to Cape Royds this evening, but it was reported that the open water reached to the Barne Glacier, and last night my own observation seemed to confirm this.

This afternoon I started out for the open water. I found the ice solid off the Barne Glacier tongue, but always ahead of me a dark horizon as though I was within a very short distance of its edge. I held on with this appearance still holding up to C. Barne itself and then past that Cape and halfway between it and C. Royds. This was far enough to make it evident that the ice was continuous to C. Royds, and has been so for a long time. Under these circumstances the continual appearance of open water to the north is most extraordinary and quite inexplicable.

Have had some very interesting discussion with Wilson,

Wright, and Taylor on the ice formations to the west. How to account for the marine organisms found on the weathered glacier ice north of the Koettlitz Glacier? We have been elabourating a theory under which this ice had once a negative buoyancy due to the morainic material on top and in the lower layers of the ice mass, and had subsequently floated when the greater amount of this material had weathered out.

Have arranged to go to C. Royds tomorrow.

The temperatures have sunk very steadily this year; for a long time they hung about zero, then for a considerable interval remained about -10°; now they are down in the -20s, with signs of falling (today -24°).

Bowers's meteorological stations have been amusingly named Archibald, Bertram, Clarence – they are entered by the initial letter, but spoken of by full title.

Tonight we had a glorious auroral display – quite the most brilliant I have seen. At one time the sky from NNW to SSE as high as the zenith was massed with arches, band, and curtains, always in rapid movement. The waving curtains were especially fascinating – a wave of bright light would start at one end and run along to the other, or a patch of brighter light would spread as if to reinforce the failing light of the curtain.

The auroral light is of a palish green colour, but we now see distinctly a red flush preceding the motion of any bright part.

The green ghostly light seems suddenly to spring to life with rosy blushes. There is infinite suggestion in this phenomenon, and in that lies its charm; the suggestion of life, form, colour, and movement never less than evanescent, mysterious – no reality. It is the language of mystic signs and portents – the inspiration of the gods – wholly spiritual – divine signalling. Remindful of superstition, provocative of imagination. Might not the inhabitants of some other world (Mars) controlling mighty forces thus surround our globe with fiery symbols, a golden writing which we have not the key to decipher?

There is argument on the confession of Ponting's inability to obtain photographs of the aurora. Professor Störmer of Norway seems to have been successful. Simpson made notes of his method, which seems to depend merely on the rapidity of lens and plate.

Ponting claims to have greater rapidity in both, yet gets no result even with long exposure. It is not only a question of aurora; the stars are equally reluctant to show themselves on Ponting's plate. Even with five seconds' exposure the stars become short lines of light on the plate of a fixed camera. Störmer's stars are points and therefore his exposure must have been short, yet there is detail in some of his pictures which it seems impossible could have been got with a short exposure. It is all very puzzling.

Monday, 22 May: Wilson, Bowers, Atkinson, Evans (P.O.), Clissold, and self went to C. Royds with a "go cart" carrying our sleeping-bags, a cooker, and a small quantity of provision.

The "go cart" consists of a framework of steel tubing supported on four bicycle wheels.

The surface of the floes carries 1 to 2 inches of snow, barely covering the salt ice flowers, and for this condition this vehicle of Day's is excellent. The advantage is that it meets the case where the salt crystals form a heavy frictional surface for wood runners. I'm inclined to think that there are great numbers of cases when wheels would be more efficient than runners on the sea ice.

We reached Cape Royds in 2½ hours, killing an Emperor penguin in the bay beyond C. Barne. This bird was in splendid plumage, the breast reflecting the dim northern light like a mirror.

It was fairly dark when we stumbled over the rocks and dropped on to Shackleton's Hut. Clissold started the cooking-range, Wilson and I walked over to the Black Beach and round back by Blue Lake.

The temperature was down at -31° and the interior of the hut was very cold.

Tuesday, 23 May: We spent the morning mustering the stores within and without the hut, after a cold night which we passed very comfortably in our bags.

We found a good quantity of flour and Danish butter and a fair amount of paraffin, with smaller supplies of assorted articles – the whole sufficient to afford provision for such a party as ours for about six or eight months if well administered. In case of necessity this would undoubtedly be a very useful reserve to fall back upon. These stores are somewhat scattered, and the hut has a dilapidated, comfortless appearance due to its tenantless condition; but even so it seemed to me much less inviting than our old *Discovery* Hut at C. Armitage.

After a cup of cocoa there was nothing to detain us, and we started back, the only useful articles added to our weights being a scrap or two of leather and *five hymn-books*. Hitherto we have been only able to muster seven copies; this increase will improve our Sunday Services.

Wednesday, 24 May: A quiet day with northerly wind; the temperature rose gradually to zero. Having the night duty, did not go out. The moon has gone and there is little to attract one out of doors.

Atkinson gave us an interesting little discourse on parasitology, with a brief account of the life history of some ecto- and some endo-parasites – Nematodes, Trematodes. He pointed out how that in nearly every case there was a secondary host, how in some cases disease was caused, and in others the presence of the parasite was even helpful. He acknowledged the small progress that had been made in this study. He mentioned ankylostomiasis, blood-sucking worms, Bilhartsia (Trematode) attacking bladder (Egypt), Filaria (round tapeworm), Guinea worm, Trichina (pork), and others, pointing to disease caused.

From worms he went to Protozoa – Trypanosomes, sleeping sickness, host tsetse-fly – showed life history comparatively, propagated in secondary host or encysting in primary host – similarly malarial germs spread by Anopheles mosquitoes – all very interesting.

In the discussion following Wilson gave some account of the grouse disease worm, and especially of the interest in finding free living species almost identical; also part of the life of disease worm is free living. Here we approached a point pressed by Nelson concerning the degeneration consequent on adoption of the parasitic habit. All parasites seem to have descended from free living beasts. One asks "what is degeneration?" without receiving a very satisfactory answer. After all, such terms must be empirical.

Thursday, 25 May: It has been blowing from south with heavy gusts and snow, temperature extraordinarily high, -6°. This has been a heavy gale. The weather conditions are certainly very interesting; Simpson has again called attention to the wind in February, March, and April at Cape Evans – the record shows an extraordinarily large percentage of gales. It is quite certain that we scarcely got a fraction of the wind on the Barrier and doubtful if we got as much as Hut Point.

Friday, 26 May: A calm and clear day – a nice change from recent weather. It makes an enormous difference to the enjoyment of this life if one is able to get out and stretch one's legs every day. This morning I went up the Ramp. No sign of open water, so that my fears for a broken highway in the coming season are now at rest. In future gales can only be a temporary annoyance – anxiety as to their result is finally allayed.

This afternoon I searched out ski and ski sticks and went for a short run over the floe. The surface is quite good since the recent snowfall and wind. This is satisfactory, as sledging can now be conducted on ordinary lines, and if convenient our parties can pull on ski. The young ice troubles of April and May have passed away. It is curious that circumstances caused us to miss them altogether during our stay in the *Discovery*.

We are living extraordinarily well. At dinner last night we had some excellent thick seal soup, very much like thick hare soup; this was followed by an equally tasty seal steak and kidney pie and a fruit jelly. The smell of frying greeted us on awakening this morning, and at breakfast each of us had two of our nutty little *Notothenia* fish after our bowl of porridge. These little fish have an extraordinarily sweet taste – bread and butter and marmalade finished the meal. At the midday meal we had bread and butter, cheese, and cake, and tonight I smell mutton in the preparation. Under the circumstances it would be difficult to conceive more appetising repasts or a regime which is less likely to produce scorbutic symptoms. I cannot think we shall get scurvy.

Nelson lectured to us tonight, giving a very able little elementary sketch of the objects of the biologist. A fact struck one in his explanation of the rates of elimination. Two of the offspring of two parents alone survive, speaking broadly; this the same of the human species or the "ling", with 24,000,000 eggs in the roe of each female! He talked much of evolution, adaptation, etc. Mendelism became the most debated point of the discussion; the transmission of characters has a wonderful fascination for the human mind. There was also a point striking deep in the debate on Professor Loeb's experiments with sea urchins; how far had he succeeded in reproducing the species without the male spermatozoa? Not very far, it seemed, when all was said.

A theme for a pen would be the expansion of interest in Polar affairs; compare the interests of a winter spent by the old Arctic voyagers with our own, and look into the causes. The aspect of everything changes as our knowledge expands.

The expansion of human interest in rude surroundings may perhaps best be illustrated by comparisons. It will serve to recall such a simple case as the fact that our ancestors applied the terms horrid, frightful, to mountain crags which in our own day are more justly admired as lofty, grand, and beautiful.

The poetic conception of this natural phenomenon has followed not so much an inherent change of sentiment as the intimacy of wider knowledge and the death of superstitious influence. One is much struck by the importance of realizing limits.

Saturday, 27 May: A very unpleasant, cold, windy day. Annoyed with the conditions, so did not go out.

In the evening Bowers gave his lecture on sledging diets. He has shown great courage in undertaking the task, great perseverance in unearthing facts from books, and a considerable practical skill in stringing these together. It is a thankless task to search Polar literature for dietary facts and still more difficult to attach due weight to varying statements. Some authors omit discussion of this important item altogether, others fail to note alterations made in practice or additions afforded by circumstances, others again forget to describe the nature of various foodstuffs.

Our lecturer was both entertaining and instructive when he dealt with old-time rations; but he naturally grew weak in approaching the physiological aspect of the question. He went through with it manfully and with a touch of humour much appreciated; whereas, for instance, he deduced facts from "the equivalent of Mr Joule, a gentleman whose statements he had no reason to doubt".

Wilson was the mainstay of the subsequent discussion and put all doubtful matters in a clearer light. "Increase your fats (carbohydrate)" is what science seems to say, and practice with conservativism is inclined to step cautiously in response to this urgency. I shall, of course, go into the whole question as thoroughly as available information and experience permits. Meanwhile it is useful to have had a discussion which aired the popular opinions.

Feeling went deepest on the subject of tea versus cocoa; admitting all that can be said concerning stimulation and reaction, I am inclined to see much in favour of tea. Why should not one be mildly stimulated during the marching hours if one can cope with reaction by profounder rest during the hours of inaction?

Sunday, 28 May: Quite an excitement last night. One of the ponies (the grey which I led last year and salved from the floe) either fell or tried to lie down in his stall, his head being lashed up to the stanchions on either side. In this condition he struggled and kicked till his body was twisted right round and his attitude extremely uncomfortable. Very luckily his struggles were heard almost at once, and his head ropes being cut, Oates got him on his feet again. He looked a good deal distressed at the time, but is now quite well again and has been out for his usual exercise.

Held Service as usual.

This afternoon went on ski around the bay and back across. Little or no wind; sky clear, temperature -25°. It was wonderfully mild considering the temperature – this sounds paradoxical, but the sensation of cold does not conform to the thermometer – it is obviously dependent on the wind and less obviously on the humidity of the air and the ice crystals floating in it. I cannot very clearly account for this effect, but as a matter of fact I have certainly felt colder in still air at -10° than I did today when the thermometer was down to -25°, other conditions apparently equal.

The amazing circumstance is that by no means can we measure the humidity, or indeed the precipitation or evaporation. I have just been discussing with Simpson the insuperable difficulties that stand in the way of experiment in this direction, since cold air can only hold the smallest quantities of moisture, and saturation covers an extremely small range of temperature.

Monday, 29 May: Another beautiful calm day. Went out both before and after the midday meal. This morning with Wilson and Bowers towards the thermometer off Inaccessible Island. On the way my companionable dog was heard barking and dimly seen – we went towards him and found that he was worrying a young sea leopard. This is the second found in the Strait this season. We had to secure it as a specimen, but it was sad to have to kill. The long lithe body of this seal makes it almost beautiful in comparison with our stout, bloated Weddells. This poor beast turned swiftly from side to side as we strove to stun it with a blow on the nose. As it turned it gaped its jaws wide, but oddly enough not a sound came forth, not even a hiss.

After lunch a sledge was taken out to secure the prize, which had been photographed by flashlight.

Ponting has been making great advances in flashlight work, and has opened up quite a new field in which artistic results can be obtained in the winter.

Lecture – Japan. Tonight Ponting gave us a charming lecture on Japan with wonderful illustrations of his own. He is happiest in his descriptions of the artistic side of the people, with which he is in fullest sympathy. So he took us to see the flower pageants. The joyful festivals of the cherry blossom, the wistaria, the iris and chrysanthemum, the sombre colours of the beech blossom and the paths about the lotus gardens, where mankind meditated in solemn mood. We had pictures, too, of Nikko and its beauties, of Temples and great Buddhas. Then in more touristy strain of volcanoes and their craters, waterfalls and river gorges, tiny tree-clad islets, that feature of Japan – baths and their bathers, Ainos, and so on. His descriptions were well given and we all of us thoroughly enjoyed our evening.

Tuesday, 30 May: Am busy with my physiological investigations. Atkinson reported a sea leopard at the tide crack; it proved to be a crabeater, young and very active. In curious contrast to the sea leopard of yesterday, in snapping round it uttered considerable noise, a gasping throaty growl.

Went to the outer berg, where there was quite a collection of people, mostly in connection with Ponting, who had brought camera and flashlight.

It was beautifully calm and comparatively warm. It was good to hear the gay chatter and laughter, and see ponies and their leaders come up out of the gloom to add liveliness to the scene. The sky was extraordinarily clear at noon and to the north very bright.

We have had an exceptionally large tidal range during the last three days – it has upset the tide gauge arrangements and brought a little doubt on the method. Day is going into the question, which we thoroughly discussed today. Tidal measurements will be worse than useless unless we can be sure of the accuracy of our methods. Pools of salt water have formed over the beach floes in consequence of the high tide, and in the chase of the crabeater today very brilliant flashes of phosphorescent light appeared in these pools. We think it due to a small copepod. I have just found a reference to the same phenomenon in Nordenskiöld's "Vega". He, and apparently Bellot before him, noted the phenomenon. An interesting instance of bi-polarity.

Another interesting phenomenon observed today was a cirrus cloud lit by sunlight. It was seen by Wilson and Bowers 5° above the northern horizon – the sun is 9° below our horizon, and without refraction we calculate a cloud could be seen which was 12 miles high. Allowing refraction the phenomenon appears very possible.

Wednesday, 31 May: The sky was overcast this morning and the temperature up to -13°. Went out after lunch to "Land's End". The surface of snow was sticky for ski, except where drifts were deep. There was an oppressive feel in the air and I got very hot, coming in with head and hands bare.

At 5, from dead calm the wind suddenly sprang up from the south, force 40 miles per hour, and since that it has been blowing a blizzard; wind very gusty, from 20 to 60 miles. I have never known a storm come on so suddenly, and it shows what possibility there is of individuals becoming lost even if they only go a short way from the hut.

Tonight Wilson has given us a very interesting lecture on sketching. He started by explaining his methods of rough sketch and written colour record, and explained its suitability to this climate as opposed to coloured chalks, etc – a very practical method for cold fingers and one that becomes more accurate with practice in observation. His theme then became the extreme importance of accuracy, his mode of expression and explanation frankly Ruskinesque. Don't put in meaningless lines – every line should be from observation. So with contrast of light and shade – fine shading, subtle distinction, everything – impossible without care, patience, and trained attention.

He raised a smile by generalizing failures in sketches of others of our party which had been brought to him for criticizm. He pointed out how much had been put in from preconceived notion. "He will draw a berg faithfully as it is now and he studies it, but he leaves sea and sky to be put in afterwards, as he thinks they must be like sea and sky everywhere else, and he is content to try and remember how these *should* be done." Nature's harmonies cannot be guessed at.

He quoted much from Ruskin, leading on a little deeper to "Composition", paying a hearty tribute to Ponting.

The lecture was delivered in the author's usual modest strain, but unconsciously it was expressive of himself and his whole-hearted thoroughness. He stands very high in the scale of human beings – how high I scarcely knew till the experience of the past few months.

There is no member of our party so universally esteemed; only tonight I realize how patiently and consistently he has given time and attention to help the efforts of the other sketchers, and so it is all through; he has had a hand in almost every lecture given, and has been consulted in almost every effort which has been made towards the solution of the practical or theoretical problems of our Polar world.

The achievement of a great result by patient work is the best possible object-lesson for struggling humanity, for the results of genius, however admirable, can rarely be instructive. The chief of the Scientific Staff sets an example which is more potent than any other factor in maintaining that bond of good fellowship which is the marked and beneficent characteristic of our community.

Thursday, 1 June: The wind blew hard all night, gusts arising to 72 mph; the anemometer choked five times – temperature +9°. It is still blowing this morning. Incidentally we have found that these heavy winds react very conveniently on our ventilating system. A fire is always a good ventilator, ensuring the circulation of inside air and the indraught of fresh air; its defect as a ventilator lies in the low level at which it extracts inside air. Our ventilating system utilizes the normal fire draught, but also by suitable holes in the funnelling causes the same draught to extract foul air at higher levels. I think this is the first time such a system has been used. It is a bold step to make holes in the funnelling, as obviously any uncertainty of draught might fill the hut with smoke. Since this does not happen with us it follows that there is always strong suction through our stove-pipes, and this is achieved by the exceptionally large dimensions and by the length of the outer chimney pipe.

With wind this draught is greatly increased and with high winds the draught would be too great for the stoves if it were not for the relief of the ventilating holes.

In these circumstances, therefore, the rate of extraction of air automatically rises, and since high wind is usually accompanied with marked rise of temperature, the rise occurs at the most convenient season, when the interior of the hut would otherwise tend to become oppressively warm. The practical result of the system is that in spite of the numbers of people living in the hut, the cooking, and the smoking, the inside air is nearly always warm, sweet, and fresh.

There is usually a drawback to the best of arrangements, and I have said "nearly" always. The exceptions in this connection occur when the outside air is calm and warm and the galley fire, as in the early morning, needs to be worked up; it is necessary under these conditions to temporarily close the ventilating holes, and if at this time the cook is intent on preparing our breakfast with a frying-pan we are quickly made aware of his intentions. A combination of this sort is rare and lasts only for a very short time, for directly the fire is aglow the ventilator can be opened again and the relief is almost instantaneous.

This very satisfactory condition of inside air must be a highly important factor in the preservation of health.

I have today regularized the pony "nicknames"; I must leave it to Drake to pull out the relation to the "proper" names according to our school contracts!*

The nicknames are as follows:

James Pigg	*Keohane*
Bones	*Crean*
Michael	*Clissold*
Snatcher	*Evans (P.O.)*
Jehu	
China	
Christopher	*Hooper*
Victor	*Bowers*
Snippets (windsucker)	
Nobby	*Lashly*

Friday, 2 June: The wind still high. The drift ceased at an early hour yesterday; it is difficult to account for the fact. At night the sky cleared; then and this morning we had a fair display of aurora streamers to the N and a faint arch east. Curiously enough the temperature still remains high, about +7°.

The meteorological conditions are very puzzling.

Saturday, 3 June: The wind dropped last night, but at 4 a.m. suddenly sprang up from a dead calm to 30 miles an hour. Almost instantaneously, certainly within the space of one minute, there was a temperature rise of nine degrees. It is the most extraordinary and interesting example of a rise of temperature with a southerly wind that I can remember. It is certainly difficult to account for unless we imagine that during the calm the surface layer of cold air is extremely thin and that there is a steep inverted gradient. When the wind arose the sky overhead was clearer than I ever remember to have seen it, the constellations brilliant, and the Milky Way like a bright auroral streamer.

The wind has continued all day, making it unpleasant out of doors. I went for a walk over the land; it was dark, the rock very black, very little snow lying; old footprints in the soft, sandy soil

---

*   Many schools had subscribed for the purchase of ponies

were filled with snow, showing quite white on a black ground.
Have been digging away at food statistics.

Simpson has just given us a discourse, in the ordinary lectures
series, on his instruments. Having already described these instruments, there is little to comment upon; he is excellently lucid in
his explanations.

As an analogy to the attempt to make a scientific observation
when the condition under consideration is affected by the means
employed, he rather quaintly cited the impossibility of discover-
ing the length of trousers by bending over to see!

Simpson is admirable as a worker, admirable as a scientist,
and admirable as a lecturer.

Sunday, 4 June: A calm and beautiful day. The account of this, a
typical Sunday, would run as follows: Breakfast. A half-hour or
so selecting hymns and preparing for Service whilst the hut is
being cleared up. The Service: a hymn; Morning Prayer to the
Psalms; another hymn; prayers from Communion Service and
Litany; a final hymn and our special prayer. Wilson strikes the
note on which the hymn is to start and I try to hit it after with
doubtful success! After church the men go out with their ponies.

Today Wilson, Bowers, Cherry-Garrard, Lashly, and I went
to start the building of our first "igloo". There is a good deal of
difference of opinion as to the best implement with which to cut
snow blocks. Cherry-Garrard had a knife which I designed and
Lashly made, Wilson a saw, and Bowers a large trowel. I'm
inclined to think the knife will prove most effective, but the
others don't acknowledge it *yet*. As far as one can see at present
this knife should have a longer handle and much coarser teeth in
the saw edge – perhaps also the blade should be thinner.

We must go on with this hut building till we get good at it. I'm
sure it's going to be a useful art.

We only did three courses of blocks when tea-time arrived,
and light was not good enough to proceed after tea.

Sunday afternoon for the men means a "stretch off the land".

I went over the floe on ski. The best possible surface after the
late winds as far as Inaccessible Island. Here, and doubtless in
most places along the shore, this, the first week of June, may be
noted as the date by which the wet, sticky salt crystals become

covered and the surface possible for wood runners. Beyond the island the snow is still very thin, barely covering the ice flowers, and the surface is still bad.

There has been quite a small landslide on the S side of the Island; seven or eight blocks of rock, one or two tons in weight, have dropped on to the floe, an interesting instance of the possibility of transport by sea ice.

Ponting has been out to the bergs photographing by flashlight. As I passed south of the Island with its whole mass between myself and the photographer I saw the flashes of magnesium light, having all the appearance of lightning. The light illuminated the sky and apparently objects at a great distance from the camera. It is evident that there may be very great possibilities in the use of this light for signalling purposes, and I propose to have some experiments.

NB: Magnesium flashlight as signalling apparatus in the summer.

Another crabeater seal was secured today; he had come up by the bergs.

Monday, 5 June: The wind has been S all day, sky overcast and air misty with snow crystals. The temperature has gone steadily up and tonight rose to +16°. Everything seems to threaten a blizzard which cometh not. But what is to be made of this extraordinary high temperature heaven only knows. Went for a walk over the rocks and found it very warm and muggy.

Taylor gave us a paper on the Beardmore Glacier. He has taken pains to work up available information; on the ice side he showed the very gradual gradient as compared with the Ferrar. If crevasses are as plentiful as reported, the motion of glacier must be very considerable. There seem to be three badly crevassed parts where the glacier is constricted and the fall is heavier.

Geologically he explained the rocks found and the problems unsolved. The basement rocks, as to the north, appear to be reddish and grey granites and altered slate (possibly bearing fossils). The Cloudmaker appears to be diorite; Mt Buckley sedimentary. The suggested formation is of several layers of coal with sandstone above and below; interesting to find if it is so, and investigate coal. Wood fossil conifer appears to have come from this – better to get leaves – wrap fossils up for protection.

Mt Dawson described as pinkish limestone, with a wedge of dark rock; this very doubtful! Limestone is of great interest owing to chance of finding Cambrian fossils (Archeocyathus).

He mentioned the interest of finding here, as in Dry Valley, volcanic cones of recent date (later than the recession of the ice).

Debenham in discussion mentioned usefulness of small chips of rock – many chips from several places are more valuable than few larger specimens.

We had an interesting little discussion.

I must enter a protest against the use made of the word "glaciated" by geologists and physiographers.

To them a "glaciated land" is one which appears to have been shaped by former ice action.

The meaning I attach to the phrase, and one which I believe is more commonly current, is that it describes a land at present wholly or partly covered with ice and snow.

I hold the latter is the obvious meaning and the former results from a piracy committed in very recent times.

The alternative terms descriptive of the different meanings are ice covered and ice eroded.

Today I have been helping the Soldier to design pony rugs; the great thing, I think, is to get something which will completely cover the hindquarters.

Tuesday, 6 June: The temperature has been as high as +19° today; the south wind persisted until the evening with clear sky except for fine effects of torn cloud round about the mountain. Tonight the moon has emerged from behind the mountain and sails across the cloudless northern sky; the wind has fallen and the scene is glorious.

It is my birthday, a fact I might easily have forgotten, but my kind people did not. At lunch an immense birthday cake made its appearance and we were photographed assembled about it. Clissold had decorated its sugared top with various devices in chocolate and crystallized fruit, flags and photographs of myself.

After my walk I discovered that great preparations were in progress for a special dinner, and when the hour for that meal arrived we sat down to a sumptuous spread with our sledge banners hung about us. Clissold's especially excellent seal soup, roast mutton and red currant jelly, fruit salad, asparagus and chocolate – such was our menu. For drink we had cider cup, a mystery not yet fathomed, some sherry and a liqueur.

After this luxurious meal everyone was very festive and amiably argumentative. As I write there is a group in the dark room discussing political progress with large discussions – another at one corner of the dinner-table airing its views on the origin of matter and the probability of its ultimate discovery, and yet another debating military problems. The scraps that reach me from the various groups sometimes piece together in ludicrous fashion. Perhaps these arguments are practically unprofitable, but they give a great deal of pleasure to the participants. It's delightful to hear the ring of triumph in some voice when the owner imagines he has delivered himself of a well-rounded period or a clinching statement concerning the point under discussion. They are boys, all of them, but such excellent good-natured ones; there has been no sign of sharpness or anger, no jarring note, in all these wordy contests; all end with a laugh.

Nelson has offered Taylor a pair of socks to teach him some geology! This lulls me to sleep!

Wednesday, 7 June: A very beautiful day. In the afternoon went well out over the floe to the south, looking up Nelson at his ice hole and picking up Bowers at his thermometer. The surface was polished and beautifully smooth for ski, the scene brightly illuminated with moonlight, the air still and crisp, and the thermometer at -10°. Perfect conditions for a winter walk.

In the evening I read a paper on "The Ice Barrier and Inland Ice". I have strung together a good many new points and the interest taken in the discussion was very genuine – so keen, in fact, that we did not break up till close on midnight. I am keeping this paper, which makes a very good basis for all future work on these subjects.

My night on duty. The silent hours passed rapidly and comfortably. To bed 7 a.m.

Thursday, 8 June: Did not turn out till 1 p.m, then with a bad head, an inevitable sequel to a night of vigil. Walked out to and around the bergs, bright moonlight, but clouds rapidly spreading up from south.

Tried the snow knife, which is developing. Debenham and Gran went off to Hut Point this morning; they should return tomorrow.

Friday, 9 June: No wind came with the clouds of yesterday, but the sky has not been clear since they spread over it except for about two hours in the middle of the night when the moonlight was so bright that one might have imagined the day returned.

Otherwise the web of stratus which hangs over us thickens and thins, rises and falls with very bewildering uncertainty. We want theories for these mysterious weather conditions; meanwhile it is annoying to lose the advantages of the moonlight.

This morning had some discussion with Nelson and Wright regarding the action of sea water in melting barrier and sea ice. The discussion was useful to me in drawing attention to the equilibrium of layers of sea water.

In the afternoon I went round the Razor Back Islands on ski, a run of 5 or 6 miles; the surface was good but in places still irregular with the pressures formed when the ice was "young".

The snow is astonishingly soft on the south side of both islands. It is clear that in the heaviest blizzard one could escape the wind altogether by camping to windward of the larger island. One sees more and more clearly what shelter is afforded on the weather side of steep-sided objects.

Passed three seals asleep on the ice. Two others were killed near the bergs.

Saturday, 10 June: The impending blizzard has come; the wind came with a burst at 9.30 this morning.

Atkinson has found a trypanosome in the fish – it has been stained, photographed and drawn – an interesting discovery having regard to the few species that have been found. A trypanosome is the cause of "sleeping sickness".

The blizzard has continued all day with a good deal of drift. I went for a walk, but the conditions were not inviting.

We have begun to consider details of next season's travelling equipment. The crampons, repair of finnesko with sealskin, and an idea for a double tent have been discussed today. P.O. Evans and Lashly are delightfully intelligent in carrying out instructions.

Sunday, 11 June: A fine clear morning, the moon now revolving well aloft and with full face.

For exercise a run on ski to the South Bay in the morning and a dash up the Ramp before dinner. Wind and drift arose in the middle of the day, but it is now nearly calm again.

At our morning service Cherry-Garrard, good fellow, vamped the accompaniment of two hymns; he received encouraging thanks and will cope with all three hymns next Sunday.

Day by day news grows scant in this midwinter season; all events seem to compress into a small record, yet a little reflection shows that this is not the case. For instance, I have had at least three important discussions on weather and ice conditions today, concerning which many notes might be made, and quite a number of small arrangements have been made.

If a diary can be so inadequate here, how difficult must be the task of making a faithful record of a day's events in ordinary civilized life! I think this is why I have found it so difficult to keep a diary at home.

Monday, 12 June: The weather is not kind to us. There has not been much wind today, but the moon has been hid behind stratus cloud. One feels horribly cheated in losing the pleasure of its light. I scarcely know what the Crozier party can do if they don't get better luck next month.

Debenham and Gran have not yet returned; this is their fifth day of absence.

Bowers and Cherry-Garrard went to Cape Royds this afternoon to stay the night. Taylor and Wright walked there and back after breakfast this morning. They returned shortly after lunch.

Went for a short spin on ski this morning and again this afternoon. This evening Evans has given us a lecture on surveying. He was shy and slow, but very painstaking, taking a deal of trouble in preparing pictures, etc.

I took the opportunity to note hurriedly the few points to which I want attention especially directed. No doubt others will occur to me presently. I think I now understand very well how and why the old surveyors (like Belcher) failed in the early Arctic work.

1. Every officer who takes part in the Southern Journey ought to have in his memory the approximate variation of the compass at various stages of the journey and to know how to apply it to obtain a true course from the compass. The variation changes very slowly so that no great effort of memory is required.
2. He ought to know what the true course is to reach one depot from another.
3. He should be able to take an observation with the theodolite.
4. He should be able to work out a meridian altitude observation.
5. He could advantageously add to his knowledge the ability to work out a longitude observation or an ex-meridian altitude.
6. He should know how to read the sledge-meter.
7. He should note and remember the error of the watch he carries and the rate which is ascertained for it from time to time.
8. He should assist the surveyor by noting the coincidences of objects, the opening out of valleys, the observation of new peaks, etc.

Tuesday, 13 June: A very beautiful day. We revelled in the calm clear moonlight; the temperature has fallen to -26°. The surface of the floe perfect for ski – had a run to South Bay in forenoon and was away on a long circuit around Inaccessible Island in the afternoon. In such weather the cold splendour of the scene is beyond description; everything is satisfying, from the deep purple of the starry sky to the gleaming bergs and the sparkle of the crystals under foot.

Some very brilliant patches of aurora over the southern shoulder of the mountain. Observed an exceedingly bright meteor shoot across the sky to the northward.

On my return found Debenham and Gran back from Cape Armitage. They had intended to start back on Sunday, but were prevented by bad weather; they seemed to have had stronger winds than we.

On arrival at the hut they found poor little "Mukáka" coiled up outside the door, looking pitifully thin and weak, but with enough energy to bark at them.

This dog was run over and dragged for a long way under the sledge runners whilst we were landing stores in January (the 7th). He has never been worth much since, but remained lively in spite of all the hardships of sledging work. At Hut Point he looked a miserable object, as the hair refused to grow on his hindquarters. It seemed as though he could scarcely continue in such a condition, and when the party came back to Cape Evans he was allowed to run free alongside the sledge.

On the arrival of the party I especially asked after the little animal and was told by Demetri that he had returned, but later it transpired that this was a mistake – that he had been missed on the journey and had not turned up again later as was supposed.

I learned this fact only a few days ago and had quite given up the hope of ever seeing the poor little beast again. It is extraordinary to realize that this poor, lame, half-clad animal has lived for a whole month by himself. He had blood on his mouth when found, implying the capture of a seal, but how he managed to kill it and then get through its skin is beyond comprehension. Hunger drives hard.

Wednesday, 14 June: Storms are giving us little rest. We found a thin stratus over the sky this morning, foreboding ill. The wind came, as usual with a rush, just after lunch. At first there was much drift – now the drift has gone but the gusts run up to 65 mph.

Had a comfortless stroll around the hut; how rapidly things change when one thinks of the delights of yesterday! Paid a visit to Wright's ice cave; the pendulum is installed and will soon be ready for observation. Wright anticipates the possibility of difficulty with ice crystals on the agate planes.

He tells me that he has seen some remarkably interesting examples of the growth of ice crystals on the walls of the cave and has observed the same unaccountable confusion of the size of grains in the ice, showing how little history can be gathered from the structure of ice.

This evening Nelson gave us his second biological lecture, starting with a brief reference to the scientific classification of the organism into Kingdom, Phylum, Group, Class, Order, Genus, Species; he stated the justification of a biologist in such an expedition, as being "To determine the condition under which organic substances exist in the sea".

He proceeded to draw divisions between the bottom organisms without power of motion, benthon, the nekton motile life in mid-water, and the plankton or floating life. Then he led very prettily on to the importance of the tiny vegetable organisms as the basis of all life.

In the killer whale may be found a seal, in the seal a fish, in the fish a smaller fish, in the smaller fish a copepod, and in the copepod a diatom. If this be regular feeding throughout, the diatom or vegetable is essentially the base of all.

Light is the essential of vegetable growth or metabolism, and light quickly vanishes in depth of water, so that all ocean life must ultimately depend on the phyto-plankton. To discover the conditions of this life is therefore to go to the root of matters.

At this point came an interlude – descriptive of the various biological implements in use in the ship and on shore. The otter trawl, the Agassiz trawl, the "D" net, and the ordinary dredger.

A word or two on the using of "D" nets and then explanation of sieves for classifying the bottom, its nature causing variation in the organisms living on it.

From this he took us amongst the tow-nets with their beautiful silk fabrics, meshes running 180 to the inch and materials costing 2 guineas the yard – to the German tow-nets for quantitative measurements, the object of the latter and its doubtful accuracy, young fish trawls.

From this to the chemical composition of sea water, the total salt about 3.5 per cent, but variable: the proportions of the various salts do not appear to differ, thus the chlorine test detects the salinity quantitatively. Physically plankton life must depend on this salinity and also on temperature, pressure, light, and movement.

(If plankton only inhabits surface waters, then density, temperatures, etc, of surface waters must be the important factors. Why should biologists strive for deeper layers? Why should not deep-sea life be maintained by dead vegetable matter?)

Here again the lecturer branched off into descriptions of water bottles, deep-sea thermometers, and current-meters, the which I think have already received some notice in this Diary. To what depth light may extend is the difficult problem, and we had some speculation, especially in the debate on this question. Simpson suggested that labouratory experiment should easily determine. Atkinson suggested growth of bacteria on a scratched plate. The idea seems to be that vegetable life cannot exist without red rays, which probably do not extend beyond 7 feet or so. Against this is an extraordinary recovery of *Holosphera Viridis* by German expedition from 2,000 fathoms; this seems to have been confirmed. Bowers caused much amusement by demanding to know "if the pycnogs (pycnogonids) were more nearly related to the arachnids (spiders) or crustaceans". As a matter of fact a very sensible question, but it caused amusement because of its sudden display of long names. Nelson is an exceedingly capable lecturer; he makes his subject very clear and is never too technical.

Thursday, 15 June: Keen cold wind overcast sky till 5.30 p.m. Spent an idle day.

Jimmy Pigg had an attack of colic in the stable this afternoon. He was taken out and doctored on the floe, which seemed to improve matters, but on return to the stable he was off his feed.

This evening the Soldier tells me he has eaten his food, so I hope all will be well again.

Friday, 16 June: Overcast again – little wind but also little moonlight. Jimmy Pigg quite recovered.

Went round the bergs in the afternoon. A great deal of ice has fallen from the irregular ones, showing that a great deal of weathering of bergs goes on during the winter and hence that the life of a berg is very limited, even if it remains in the high latitudes.

Tonight Debenham lectured on volcanoes. His matter is very good, but his voice a little monotonous, so that there were signs of slumber in the audience, but all woke up for a warm and amusing discussion succeeding the lecture.

The lecturer first showed a world chart showing distribution of volcanoes, showing general tendency of eruptive explosions to occur in lines. After following these lines in other parts of the world he showed difficulty of finding symmetrical linear distribution near McMurdo Sound. He pointed out incidentally the important inference which could be drawn from the discovery of altered sandstone in the Erebus region. He went to the shapes of volcanoes:

The massive type formed by very fluid lavas – Mauna Loa (Hawaii), Vesuvius, examples.

The more perfect cones formed by ash talus – Fujiama, Discovery.

The explosive type with parasitic cones – Erebus, Morning, Etna.

Fissure eruption – historic only in Iceland, but best prehistoric examples Deccan (India) and Oregon (US).

There is small ground for supposing relation between adjacent volcanoes – activity in one is rarely accompanied by activity in the other. It seems most likely that vent tubes are entirely separate.

Products of volcanoes: The lecturer mentioned the escape of quantities of free hydrogen – there was some discussion on this point afterwards; that water is broken up is easily understood, but what becomes of the oxygen? Simpson suggests the presence of much oxidizable material.

CO_2 as a noxious gas also mentioned and discussed – causes mythical "upas" tree – sulphurous fumes attend final stages.

Practically little or no heat escapes through sides of a volcano.

There was argument over physical conditions influencing explosions – especially as to barometric influence. There was a good deal of disjointed information on lavas, ropy or rapid flowing and viscous – also on spatter cones and caverns.

In all cases lavas cool slowly – heat has been found close to the surface after eighty-seven years. On Etna there is lava over ice. The lecturer finally reviewed the volcanicity of our own neighbourhood. He described various vents of Erebus, thinks Castle Rock a "plug" – here some discussion – Observation Hill part of old volcano, nothing in common with Crater Hill. Inaccessible Island seems to have no connection with Erebus.

Finally we had a few words on the origin of volcanicity and afterwards some discussion on an old point – the relation to the sea. Why are volcanoes close to sea? Debenham thinks not cause and effect, but two effects resulting from same cause.

Great argument as to whether effect of barometric changes on

Erebus vapour can be observed. Not much was said about the theory of volcanoes, but Debenham touched on American theories – the melting out from internal magma.

There was nothing much to catch hold of throughout, but discussion of such a subject sorts one's ideas.

Saturday, 17 June: Northerly wind, temperature changeable, dropping to -16°.

Wind doubtful in the afternoon. Moon still obscured – it is very trying. Feeling dull in spirit today.

Sunday, 18 June: Another blizzard – the weather is distressing. It ought to settle down soon, but unfortunately the moon is passing.

Held the usual Morning Service. Hymns not quite successful today.

Tonight Atkinson has taken the usual monthly measurement. I don't think there has been much change.

Monday, 19 June: A pleasant change to find the air calm and the sky clear – temperature down to -28°. At 1.30 the moon vanished behind the western mountains, after which, in spite of the clear sky, it was very dark on the floe. Went out on ski across the bay, then round about the cape, and so home, facing a keen northerly wind on return.

Atkinson is making a new fish-trap hole; from one cause and another, the breaking of the trap, and the freezing of the hole, no catch has been made for some time. I don't think we shall get good catches during the dark season, but Atkinson's own requirements are small, and the fish, though nice enough, are not such a luxury as to be greatly missed from our "menu".

Our daily routine has possessed a settled regularity for a long time. Clissold is up about 7 a.m. to start the breakfast. At 7.30 Hooper starts sweeping the floor and setting the table. Between 8 and 8.30 the men are out and about, fetching ice for melting, etc. Anton is off to feed the ponies, Demetri to see the dogs; Hooper bursts on the slumberers with repeated announcements of the time, usually a quarter of an hour ahead of the clock. There is a stretching of limbs and an interchange of morning greetings, garnished with sleepy humour. Wilson and Bowers meet in a state of nature beside a washing basin filled with snow and proceed to rub glistening limbs with this chilling substance. A little later with less hardihood some others may be seen making the most of a meagre allowance of water. Soon after 8.30 I manage to drag myself from a very comfortable bed and make my toilet with a bare pint of water. By about 10 minutes to 9 my clothes are on, my bed is made, and I sit down to my bowl of porridge; most of the others are gathered about the table by this time, but there are a few laggards who run the 9 o'clock rule very close. The rule is instituted to prevent delay in the day's work, and it has needed a little pressure to keep one or two up to its observance. By 9.20 breakfast is finished, and before the half-hour has struck the table has been cleared. From 9.30 to 1.30 the men are steadily employed on a programme of preparation for sledging, which seems likely to occupy the greater part of the winter. The repair of sleeping-bags and the alteration of tents have already been done, but there are many other tasks uncompleted or not yet begun, such as the manufacture of provision bags, crampons, sealskin soles, pony clothes, etc.

Hooper has another good sweep up the hut after breakfast, washes the mess traps, and generally tidies things. I think it a good thing that in these matters the officers need not wait on themselves; it gives long unbroken days of scientific work and must, therefore, be an economy of brain in the long run.

We meet for our midday meal at 1.30 or 1.45, and spend a very cheerful half-hour over it. Afterwards the ponies are exercised, weather permitting; this employs all the men and a few of the officers for an hour or more – the rest of us generally take exercise in some form at the same time. After this the officers go on steadily with their work, whilst the men do odd jobs to while away the time. The evening meal, our dinner, comes at 6.30, and is finished within the hour. Afterwards people read, write, or play games, or occasionally finish some piece of work. The gramophone is usually started by some kindly disposed person, and on three nights of the week the lectures to which I have referred are given. These lectures still command full audiences and lively discussions.

At 11 p.m. the acetylene lights are put out, and those who wish to remain up or to read in bed must depend on candle-light. The majority of candles are extinguished by midnight, and the night watchman alone remains awake to keep his vigil by the light of an oil lamp.

Day after day passes in this fashion. It is not a very active life perhaps, but certainly not an idle one. Few of us sleep more than eight hours out of the twenty-four.

On Saturday afternoon or Sunday morning some extra bathing takes place; chins are shaven, and perhaps clean garments donned. Such signs, with the regular Service on Sunday, mark the passage of the weeks.

Tonight Day has given us a lecture on his motor-sledge. He seems very hopeful of success, but I fear is rather more sanguine in temperament than his sledge is reliable in action. I wish I could have more confidence in his preparations, as he is certainly a delightful companion.

Tuesday, 20 June: Last night the temperature fell to -36°, the lowest we have had this year. On the Ramp the minimum was -31°, not the first indication of a reversed temperature gradient. We have had a calm day, as is usual with a low thermometer.

It was very beautiful out of doors this morning; as the crescent moon was sinking in the west, Erebus showed a heavy vapour cloud, showing that the quantity is affected by temperature rather than pressure.

I'm glad to have had a good run on ski.

The Cape Crozier Party are preparing for departure, and heads have been put together to provide as much comfort as the strenuous circumstances will permit. I came across a hint as to the value of a double tent in Sverdrup's book, "New Land", and (P.O.) Evans has made a lining for one of the tents; it is secured on the inner side of the poles and provides an air space inside the tent. I think it is going to be a great success, and that it will go far to obviate the necessity of considering the question of snow huts – though we shall continue our efforts in this direction also.

Another new departure is the decision to carry eiderdown sleeping-bags inside the reindeer ones.

With such an arrangement the early part of the journey is bound to be comfortable, but when the bags get iced difficulties are pretty certain to arise.

Day has been devoting his energies to the creation of a blubber stove, much assisted, of course, by the experience gained at Hut Point.

This stove was got going this morning in five minutes in the outer temperature with the blubber hard frozen. It will make a great difference to the Crozier Party if they can manage to build a hut, and the experience gained will be everything for the Western Party in the summer. With a satisfactory blubber stove it would never be necessary to carry fuel on a coast journey, and we shall deserve well of posterity if we can perfect one.

The Crozier journey is to be made to serve a good many trial ends. As I have already mentioned, each man is to go on a different food scale, with a view to determining the desirable proportion of fats and carbohydrates. Wilson is also to try the effect of a double windproof suit instead of extra woollen clothing.

If two suits of windproof will keep one as warm in the spring as a single suit does in the summer, it is evident that we can face the summit of Victoria Land with a very slight increase of weight.

I think the new crampons, which will also be tried on this journey, are going to be a great success. We have returned to the last *Discovery* type with improvements; the magnalium sole plates of our own crampons are retained but shod with ½-inch steel spikes; these plates are riveted through canvas to an inner leather sole, and the canvas is brought up on all sides to form a covering to the "finnesko" over which it is laced – they are less than half the weight of an ordinary ski boot, go on very easily, and secure very neatly.

Midwinter Day, the turn of the season, is very close; it will be good to have light for the more active preparations for the coming year.

Wednesday, 21 June: The temperature low again, falling to -36°. A curious hazy look in the sky, very little wind. The cold is bringing some minor troubles with the clockwork instruments in the open and with the acetylene gas plant – no insuperable difficulties. Went for a ski run round the bergs; found it very dark and uninteresting.

The temperature remained low during night and Taylor reported a very fine display of Aurora.

Thursday, 22 June: MIDWINTER. The sun reached its maximum depression at about 2.30 p.m. on the 22nd, Greenwich Mean Time: this is 2.30 a.m. on the 23rd according to the local time of the 180th meridian which we are keeping. Dinner tonight is therefore the meal which is nearest the sun's critical change of course, and has been observed with all the festivity customary at Xmas at home.

At tea we broached an enormous Buszard cake, with much gratitude to its provider, Cherry-Garrard. In preparation for the evening our "Union Jacks" and sledge flags were hung about the large table, which itself was laid with glass and a plentiful supply of champagne bottles instead of the customary mugs and enamel limejuice jugs. At seven o'clock we sat down to an extravagant bill of fare as compared with our usual simple diet.

Beginning on seal soup, by common consent the best decoction that our cook produces, we went on to roast beef with Yorkshire pudding, fried potatoes and Brussels sprouts. Then followed a flaming plum-pudding and excellent mince pies, and thereafter a dainty savoury of anchovy and cod's roe. A wondrous attractive meal even in so far as judged by our simple lights, but with its garnishments a positive feast, for withal the table was strewn with dishes of burnt almonds, crystallized fruits, chocolates and such toothsome kickshaws, whilst the unstinted stupply of champagne which accompanied the courses was succeeded by a noble array of liqueur bottles from which choice could be made in the drinking of toasts.

I screwed myself up to a little speech which drew attention to the nature of the celebration as a halfway mark not only in our winter but in the plans of the Expedition as originally published. (I fear there are some who don't realize how rapidly time passes and who have barely begun work which by this time ought to be in full swing.)

We had come through a summer season and half a winter, and had before us half a winter and a second summer. We ought to know how we stood in every respect; we did know how we stood in regard to stores and transport, and I especially thanked the officer in charge of stores and the custodians of the animals. I said that as regards the future, chance must play a part, but that experiences showed me that it would have been impossible to have chosen people more fitted to support me in the enterprise to the South than those who were to start in that direction in the spring. I thanked them all for having put their shoulders to the wheel and given me this confidence.

We drank to the Success of the Expedition.

Then everyone was called on to speak, starting on my left and working round the table; the result was very characteristic of the various individuals – one seemed to know so well the style of utterance to which each would commit himself.

Needless to say, all were entirely modest and brief; unexpectedly, all had exceedingly kind things to say of me – in fact, I was obliged to request the omission of compliments at an early stage. Nevertheless it was gratifying to have a really genuine recognition of my attitude towards the scientific workers of the Expedition, and I felt very warmly towards all these kind, good fellows for expressing it.

If goodwill and happy fellowship count towards success, very surely shall we deserve to succeed. It was matter for comment, much applauded, that there had not been a single disagreement between any two members of our party from the beginning. By the end of dinner a very cheerful spirit prevailed, and the room was cleared for Ponting and his lantern, whilst the gramophone gave forth its most lively airs.

When the table was upended, its legs removed, and chairs arranged in rows, we had quite a roomy lecture hall. Ponting had cleverly chosen this opportunity to display a series of slides made from his own local negatives. I have never so fully realized his work as on seeing these beautiful pictures; they so easily outclass anything of their kind previously taken in these regions. Our audience cheered vociferously.

After this show the table was restored for snapdragon, and a brew of milk punch was prepared in which we drank the health of Campbell's Party and of our good friends in the *Terra Nova*. Then the table was again removed and a set of lancers formed.

By this time the effect of stimulating liquid refreshment on men so long accustomed to a simple life became apparent. Our biologist had retired to bed, the silent Soldier bubbled with humour and insisted on dancing with Anton. Evans, P.O., was imparting confidences in heavy whispers. "Pat" Keohane had grown intensely Irish and desirous of political argument, whilst Clissold sat with a constant expansive smile and punctuated the babble of conversation with an occasional "Whoop" of delight or disjointed witticism. Other bright-eyed individuals merely reached the capacity to enjoy that which under ordinary circumstances might have passed without evoking a smile.

In the midst of the revelry Bowers suddenly appeared, followed by some satellites bearing an enormous Christmas Tree whose branches bore flaming candles, gaudy crackers, and little presents for all. The presents, I learnt, had been prepared with kindly thought by Miss Souper (Mrs Wilson's sister) and the tree had been made by Bowers of pieces of stick and string with coloured paper to clothe its branches; the whole erection was remarkably creditable and the distribution of the presents caused much amusement.

Whilst revelry was the order of the day within our hut, the elements without seemed desirous of celebrating the occasion with equal emphasis and greater decorum. The eastern sky was massed with swaying auroral light, the most vivid and beautiful display that I had ever seen – fold on fold the arches and curtains of vibrating luminosity rose and spread across the sky, to slowly fade and yet again spring to glowing life.

The brighter light seemed to flow, now to mass itself in wreathing folds in one quarter, from which lustrous streamers shot upward, and anon to run in waves through the system of some dimmer figure as if to infuse new life within it.

It is impossible to witness such a beautiful phenomenon without a sense of awe, and yet this sentiment is not inspired by its brilliancy but rather by its delicacy in light and colour, its transparency, and above all by its tremulous evanescence of form. There is no glittering splendour to dazzle the eye, as has been too often described; rather the appeal is to the imagination by the suggestion of something wholly spiritual, something instinct with a fluttering ethereal life, serenely confident yet restlessly mobile.

One wonders why history does not tell us of "aurora" worshippers, so easily could the phenomenon be considered the manifestation of "god" or "demon". To the little silent group which stood at gaze before such enchantment it seemed profane to return to the mental and physical atmosphere of our house.

Finally when I stepped within, I was glad to find that there had been a general movement bedwards, and in the next half-hour the last of the roysterers had succumbed to slumber.

Thus, except for a few bad heads in the morning, ended the High Festival of Midwinter.

There is little to be said for the artificial uplifting of animal spirits, yet few could take great exception to so rare an outburst in a long run of quiet days.

After all, we celebrated the birth of a season which for weal or woe must be numbered amongst the greatest in our lives.

The Winter Journey

Apsley Cherry-Garrard

Cherry-Garrard was the second youngest member of Scott's epochal
Terra Nova *expedition to Antarctica. Everything "Cherry" did there-*
after – and he lived until 1959 – was an anti-climax, even service in the
First World War: "Talk of ex-soldiers," he later wrote, "give me
ex-Antarcticists, unsoured and with their ideals intact: they could sweep
the world." Cherry-Garrard paid homage to his fellow "Antarcticists"
in his only book, The Worst Journey in the World, *1922. The title was*
perhaps misleading, for the eponymous trek was not Scott's bid for 90
South but Cherry-Garrard's own Winter Journey of June–July 1911
overland to Cape Crozier in search of the nesting place of the Emperor
penguin. No humans had ever made the journey before, no scientist had
ever retrieved the Emperor's eggs. It was, as "Cherry" said, "the weirdest
bird-nesting expedition that has been or ever will be". Accompanying the
slight, bespectacled 25-year-old Cherry-Garrard was Dr Wilson, the
expedition's scientific officer, and Lieutenant "Birdie" Bowers.

Cape Evans to Cape Crozier

The horror of the nineteen days it took us to travel from Cape
Evans to Cape Crozier would have to be re-experienced to be
appreciated; and any one would be a fool who went again: it is
not possible to describe it. The weeks which followed them were
comparative bliss, not because later our conditions were better
– they were far worse – but because we were callous. I for one
had come to that point of suffering at which I did not really care
if only I could die without much pain. They talk of the heroism
of the dying – they little know – it would be so easy to die, a
dose of morphia, a friendly crevasse, and blissful sleep. The
trouble is to go on . . .

It was the darkness that did it. I don't believe minus seventy temperatures would be bad in daylight, not comparatively bad, when you could see where you were going, where you were stepping, where the sledge straps were, the cooker, the Primus, the food; could see your footsteps lately trodden deep into the soft snow that you might find your way back to the rest of your load; could see the lashings of the food bags; could read a compass without striking three or four different boxes to find one dry match; could read your watch to see if the blissful moment of getting out of your bag was come without groping in the snow all about; when it would not take you five minutes to lash up the door of the tent, and five hours to get started in the morning . . .

But in these days we were never less than four hours from the moment when Bill cried "Time to get up" to the time when we got into our harness. It took two men to get one man into his harness, and was all they could do, for the canvas was frozen and our clothes were frozen until sometimes not even two men could bend them into the required shape.

The trouble is sweat and breath. I never knew before how much of the body's waste comes out through the pores of the skin. On the most bitter days, when we had to camp before we had done a four-hour march in order to nurse back our frozen feet, it seemed that we must be sweating. And all this sweat, instead of passing away through the porous wool of our clothing and gradually drying off us, froze and accumulated. It passed just away from our flesh and then became ice: we shook plenty of snow and ice down from inside our trousers every time we changed our foot-gear, and we could have shaken it from our vests and from between our vests and shirts, but of course we could not strip to this extent. But when we got into our sleeping-bags, if we were fortunate, we became warm enough during the night to thaw this ice: part remained in our clothes, part passed into the skins of our sleeping-bags, and soon both were sheets of armourplate.

As for our breath – in the daytime it did nothing worse than cover the lower parts of our faces with ice and solder our balaclavas tightly to our heads. It was no good trying to get your balaclava off until you had had the Primus going quite a long time, and then you could throw your breath about if you wished.

The trouble really began in your sleeping-bag, for it was far too cold to keep a hole open through which to breathe. So all night long our breath froze into the skins, and our respiration became quicker and quicker as the air in our bags got fouler and fouler: it was never possible to make a match strike or burn inside our bags!

Of course we were not iced up all at once: it took several days of this kind of thing before we really got into big difficulties on this score. It was not until I got out of the tent one morning fully ready to pack the sledge that I realized the possibilities ahead. We had had our breakfast, struggled into our foot-gear, and squared up inside the tent, which was comparatively warm. Once outside, I raised my head to look round and found I could not move it back. My clothing had frozen hard as I stood – perhaps fifteen seconds. For four hours I had to pull with my head stuck up, and from that time we all took care to bend down into a pulling position before being frozen in.

By now we had realized that we must reverse the usual sledging routine and do everything slowly, wearing when possible the fur mitts which fitted over our woollen mitts, and always stopping whatever we were doing, directly we felt that any part of us was getting frozen, until the circulation was restored. Henceforward it was common for one or other of us to leave the other two to continue the camp work while he stamped about in the snow, beat his arms, or nursed some exposed part. But we could not restore the circulation of our feet like this – the only way then was to camp and get some hot water into ourselves before we took our foot-gear off. The difficulty was to know whether our feet were frozen or not, for the only thing we knew for certain was that we had lost all feeling in them. Wilson's knowledge as a doctor came in here: many a time he had to decide from our descriptions of our feet whether to camp or to go on for another hour. A wrong decision meant disaster, for if one of us had been crippled the whole party would have been placed in great difficulties. Probably we should all have died.

On 29 June the temperature was -50° all day and there was sometimes a light breeze which was inclined to frost-bite our faces and hands. Owing to the weight of our two sledges and the bad surface our pace was not more than a slow and very heavy plod: at our lunch camp Wilson had the heel and sole of one foot frost-bitten, and I had two big toes. Bowers was never worried by frost-bitten feet.

That night was very cold, the temperature falling to -66°, and it was -55° at breakfast on 30 June. We had not shipped the eider-down linings to our sleeping-bags, in order to keep them dry as long as possible. My own fur bag was too big for me, and throughout this journey was more difficult to thaw out than the other two: on the other hand, it never split, as did Bill's.

We were now getting into that cold bay which lies between the Hut Point Peninsula and Terror Point. It was known from old *Discovery* days that the Barrier winds are deflected from this area, pouring out into McMurdo Sound behind us, and into the Ross Sea at Cape Crozier in front. In consequence of the lack of high winds the surface of the snow is never swept and hardened and polished as elsewhere: it was now a mass of the hardest and smallest snow crystals, to pull through which in cold temperatures was just like pulling through sand. I have spoken elsewhere of Barrier surfaces, and how, when the cold is very great, sledge runners cannot melt the crystal points but only advance by rolling them over and over upon one another. That was the surface we met on this journey, and in soft snow the effect is accentuated. Our feet were sinking deep at every step.

And so when we tried to start on 30 June we found we could not move both sledges together. There was nothing for it but to take one on at a time and come back for the other. This has often been done in daylight when the only risks run are those of blizzards which may spring up suddenly and obliterate tracks. Now in darkness it was more complicated. From 11 a.m. to 3 p.m. there was enough light to see the big holes made by our feet, and we took on one sledge, trudged back in our tracks, and brought on the second. Bowers used to toggle and untoggle our harnesses when we changed sledges. Of course in this relay work we covered three miles in distance for every one mile forward, and even the single sledges were very hard pulling. When we lunched the temperature was -61°. After lunch the little light had gone, and we carried a naked lighted candle back with us when we went to find our second sledge. It was the weirdest kind of procession, three frozen men and a little pool of light. Generally we steered by Jupiter, and I never see him now without recalling his friendship in those days.

We were very silent, it was not very easy to talk: but sledging is always a silent business. I remember a long discussion which began just now about cold snaps – was this the normal condition of the Barrier, or was it a cold snap? – what constituted a cold snap? The discussion lasted about a week. Do things slowly, always slowly, that was the burden of Wilson's leadership: and every now and then the question, Shall we go on? and the answer Yes. "I think we are all right as long as our appetites are good," said Bill. Always patient, self-possessed, unruffled, he was the only man on earth, as I believe, who could have led this journey.

That day we made 3¼ miles, and travelled 10 miles to do it. The temperature was -66° when we camped, and we were already pretty badly iced up. That was the last night I lay (I had written slept) in my big reindeer bag without the lining of eider-down which we each carried. For me it was a very bad night: a succession of shivering fits which I was quite unable to stop, and which took possession of my body for many minutes at a time until I thought my back would break, such was the strain placed upon it. They talk of chattering teeth: but when your body chatters you may call yourself cold. I can only compare the strain to that which I have been unfortunate enough to see in a case of lock-jaw. One of my big toes was frost-bitten, but I do not know for how long. Wilson was fairly comfortable in his smaller bag, and Bowers was snoring loudly. The minimum temperature that night as taken under the sledge was -69°; and as taken on the sledge was -75°. That is a hundred and seven degrees of frost.

We did the same relay work on 1 July, but found the pulling harder still; and it was all that we could do to move the one sledge forward. From now onwards Wilson and I, but not to the same extent as Bowers, experienced a curious optical delusion when returning in our tracks for the second sledge. I have said that we found our way back by the light of a candle, and we found it necessary to go back in our same footprints. These holes became to our tired brains not depressions but elevations: hummocks over which we stepped, raising our feet painfully and draggingly. And then we remembered, and said what fools we were, and for a while we compelled ourselves to walk through these phantom hills. But it was no lasting good, and as the days passed we realized that we must suffer this absurdity, for we could not do anything else. But of course it took it out of us.

During these days the blisters on my fingers were very painful. Long before my hands were frost-bitten, or indeed anything but cold, which was of course a normal thing, the matter inside these big blisters, which rose all down my fingers with only a skin between them, was frozen into ice. To handle the cooking gear or the food bags was agony; to start the Primus was worse; and when, one day, I was able to prick six or seven of the blisters after supper and let the liquid matter out, the relief was very great. Every night after that I treated such others as were ready in the same way until they gradually disappeared. Sometimes it was difficult not to howl.

I *did* want to howl many times every hour of these days and nights, but I invented a formula instead, which I repeated to myself continually. Especially, I remember, it came in useful when at the end of the march with my feet frost-bitten, my heart beating slowly, my vitality at its lowest ebb, my body solid with cold, I used to seize the shovel and go on digging snow on to the tent skirting while the cook inside was trying to light the Primus. "You've got it in the neck – stick it – stick it – you've got it in the neck," was the refrain, and I wanted every little bit of encouragement it would give me: then I would find myself repeating "Stick it – stick it – stick it – stick it," and then "You've got it in the neck." One of the joys of summer sledging is that you can let your mind wander thousands of miles away for weeks and weeks. Oates used to provision his little yacht (there was a pickled herring he was going to have): I invented the compactest little revolving bookcase which was going to hold not books, but pemmican and chocolate and biscuit and cocoa and sugar, and have a cooker on the top, and was going to stand always ready to quench my hunger when I got home: and we visited restaurants and theatres and grouse moors, and we thought of a pretty girl, or girls, and . . . But now that was all impossible. Our conditions forced themselves upon us without pause: it was not possible to think of anything else. We got no respite. I found it best to refuse to let myself think of the past or the future – to live only for the job of the moment, and to compel myself to think only how to do it most efficiently. Once you let yourself imagine . . .

The Emperors

We roped up, and started to worry along under the cliffs, which had now changed from ice to rock, and rose 800 feet above us. The turmult of pressure which climbed against them showed no order here. Four hundred miles of moving ice behind it had just tossed and twisted those giant ridges until Job himself would have lacked words to reproach their Maker. We scrambled over and under, hanging on with our axes, and cutting steps where we could not find a foothold with our crampons. And always we got towards the Emperor penguins, and it really began to look as if we were going to do it this time, when we came up against a wall of ice which a single glance told us we could never cross. One of the largest pressure ridges had been thrown, end on, against the cliff. We seemed to be stopped, when Bill found a black hole, something like a fox's earth, disappearing into the bowels of the ice. We looked at it: "Well, here goes!" he said, and put his head in, and disappeared. Bowers likewise. It was a longish way, but quite possible to wriggle along, and presently I found myself looking out of the other side with a deep gully below me, the rock face on one hand and the ice on the other. "Put your back against the ice and your feet against the rock and lever yourself along," said Bill, who was already standing on firm ice at the far end in a snow pit. We cut some fifteen steps to get out of that hole. Excited by now, and thoroughly enjoying ourselves, we found the way ahead easier, until the penguins' call reached us again and we stood, three crystallized ragamuffins, above the Emperors' home. They were there all right, and we were going to reach them, but where were all the thousands of which we had heard?

We stood on an ice-foot which was really a dwarf cliff some twelve feet high, and the sea-ice, with a good many ice-blocks strewn upon it, lay below. The cliff dropped straight, with a bit of an overhang and no snow-drift. This may have been because the sea had only frozen recently; whatever the reason may have been it meant that we should have a lot of difficulty in getting up again without help. It was decided that someone must stop on the top with the Alpine rope, and clearly that one should be I, for with short sight and fogged spectacles which I could not wear I was much the least useful of the party for the job immediately ahead. Had we had the sledge we could have used it as a ladder, but of course we had left this at the beginning of the moraine miles back.

We saw the Emperors standing all together huddled under the Barrier cliff some hundreds of yards away. The little light was going fast: we were much more excited about the approach of complete darkness and the look of wind in the south than we were about our triumph. After indescribable effort and hardship we were witnessing a marvel of the natural world, and we were the first and only men who had ever done so; we had within our grasp material which might prove of the utmost importance to science; we were turning theories into facts with every observation we made – and we had but a moment to give.

The disturbed Emperors made a tremendous row, trumpeting with their curious metallic voices. There was no doubt they had eggs, for they tried to shuffle along the ground without losing them off their feet. But when they were hustled a good many eggs were dropped and left lying on the ice, and some of these were quickly picked up by eggless Emperors who had probably been waiting a long time for the opportunity. In these poor birds the maternal side seems to have necessarily swamped the other functions of life. Such is the struggle for existence that they can only live by a glut of maternity, and it would be interesting to know whether such a life leads to happiness or satisfaction.

After securing several Emperor eggs, the three expeditionaries then set off on the return. The temperature dropped to -49° and seventy miles from home a blizzard blew their tent away.

The Loss of the Tent

I do not know what time it was when I woke up. It was calm, with that absolute silence which can be so soothing or so terrible as circumstances dictate. Then there came a sob of wind, and all was still again. Ten minutes and it was blowing as though the world was having a fit of hysterics. The earth was torn in pieces: the indescribable fury and roar of it all cannot be imagined.

"Bill, Bill, the tent has gone," was the next I remember – from Bowers shouting at us again and again through the door. It is always these early morning shocks which hit one hardest: our slow minds suggested that this might mean a peculiarly lingering form of death. Journey after journey Birdie and I fought our way across the few yards which had separated the tent from the igloo door. I have never understood why so much of our gear which was in the tent remained, even in the lee of the igloo. The place where the tent had been was littered with gear, and when we came to reckon up afterwards we had everything except the bottom piece of the cooker, and the top of the outer cooker. We never saw these again. The most wonderful thing of all was that our finnesko were lying where they were left, which happened to be on the ground in the part of the tent which was under the lee of the igloo. Also Birdie's bag of personal gear was there, and a tin of sweets.

Birdie brought two tins of sweets away with him. One we had to celebrate our arrival at the Knoll: this was the second, of which we knew nothing, and which was for Bill's birthday, the next day. We started eating them on Saturday, however, and the tin came in useful to Bill afterwards.

To get that gear in we fought against solid walls of black snow which flowed past us and tried to hurl us down the slope. Once started nothing could have stopped us. I saw Birdie knocked over once, but he clawed his way back just in time. Having passed everything we could find in to Bill, we got back into the igloo, and started to collect things together, including our very dishevelled minds.

There was no doubt that we were in the devil of a mess, and it was not altogether our fault. We had had to put our igloo more or less where we could get rocks with which to build it. Very naturally we had given both our tent and igloo all the shelter we could from the full force of the wind, and now it seemed we were in danger not because they were in the wind, but because they were not sufficiently in it. The main force of the hurricane, deflected by the ridge behind, fled over our heads and appeared to form by suction a vacuum below. Our tent had either been sucked upwards into this, or had been blown away because some of it was in the wind while some of it was not. The roof of our igloo was being wrenched upwards and then dropped back with great crashes: the drift was spouting in, not it seemed because it was blown in from outside, but because it was sucked in from within: the lee, not the weather, wall was the worst. Already everything was six or eight inches under snow.

Very soon we began to be alarmed about the igloo. For some time the heavy snow blocks we had heaved up on to the canvas roof kept it weighted down. But it seemed that they were being gradually moved off by the hurricane. The tension became well-nigh unendurable: the waiting in all that welter of noise was maddening. Minute after minute, hour after hour – those snow blocks were off now anyway, and the roof was smashed up and down – no canvas ever made could stand it indefinitely.

We got a meal that Saturday morning, our last for a very long time as it happened. Oil being of such importance to us we tried to use the blubber stove, but after several preliminary spasms it came to pieces in our hands, some solder having melted; and a very good thing too, I thought, for it was more dangerous than useful. We finished cooking our meal on the Primus. Two bits of the cooker having been blown away we had to balance it on the primus as best we could. We then settled that in view of the shortage of oil we would not have another meal for as long as possible. As a matter of fact God settled that for us.

We did all we could to stop up the places where the drift was coming in, plugging the holes with our socks, mitts and other clothing. But it was no real good. Our igloo was a vacuum which was filling itself up as soon as possible; and when snow was not coming in a fine black moraine dust took its place, covering us and everything. For twenty-four hours we waited for the roof to go: things were so bad now that we dare not unlash the door.

Many hours ago Bill had told us that if the roof went he considered that our best chance would be to roll over in our sleeping-bags until we were lying on the openings, and get frozen and drifted in.

Gradually the situation got more desperate. The distance between the taut-sucked canvas and the sledge on which it should have been resting became greater, and this must have been due to the stretching of the canvas itself and the loss of the snow blocks on the top: it was not drawing out of the walls. The crashes as it dropped and banged out again were louder. There was more snow coming through the walls, though all our loose mitts, socks and smaller clothing were stuffed into the worst places: our pyjama jackets were stuffed between the roof and the rocks over the door. The rocks were lifting and shaking here till we thought they would fall.

We talked by shouting, and long before this one of us proposed to try and get the Alpine rope lashed down over the roof from outside. But Bowers said it was an absolute impossibility in that wind. "You could never ask men at sea to try such a thing," he said. He was up and out of his bag continually, stopping up holes, pressing against bits of roof to try and prevent the flapping and so forth. He was magnificent.

And then it went.

Birdie was over by the door, where the canvas which was bent over the lintel board was working worse than anywhere else. Bill was practically out of his bag pressing against some part with a long stick of some kind. I don't know what I was doing but I was half out of and half in my bag.

The top of the door opened in little slits and that green Willesden canvas flapped into hundreds of little fragments in fewer seconds than it takes to read this. The uproar of it all was indescribable. Even above the savage thunder of that great wind on the mountain came the lash of the canvas as it was whipped to little tiny strips. The highest rocks which we had built into our walls fell upon us, and a sheet of drift came in.

Birdie dived for his sleeping-bag and eventually got in, together with a terrible lot of drift. Bill also – but he was better off: I was already half into mine and all right, so I turned to help Bill. "Get into your own," he shouted, and when I continued to try and help him, he leaned over until his mouth was against my ear. "*Please*, Cherry," he said, and his voice was terribly anxious. I know he felt responsible: feared it was he who had brought us to this ghastly end.

The next I knew was Bowers's head across Bill's body. "We're all right," he yelled, and we answered in the affirmative. Despite the fact that we knew we only said so because we knew we were all wrong, this statement was helpful. Then we turned our bags over as far as possible, so that the bottom of the bag was uppermost and the flaps were more or less beneath us. And we lay and thought, and sometimes we sang.

I suppose, wrote Wilson, we were all revolving plans to get back without a tent: and the one thing we had left was the floor-cloth upon which we were actually lying. Of course we could not speak at present, but later after the blizzard had stopped we discussed the possibility of digging a hole in the snow each night and covering it over with the floor-cloth. I do not think we had any idea that we could really get back in those temperatures in our present state of ice by such means, but no one ever hinted at such a thing. Birdie and Bill sang quite a lot of songs and hymns, snatches of which reached me every now and then, and I chimed in, somewhat feebly I suspect. Of course we were getting pretty badly drifted up. "I was resolved to keep warm," wrote Bowers, "and beneath my debris covering I paddled my feet and sang all the songs and hymns I knew to pass the time. I could occasionally thump Bill, and as he still moved I knew he was alive all right – what a birthday for him!" Birdie was more drifted up than we, but at times we all had to hummock ourselves up to heave the snow off our bags. By opening the flaps of our bags we could get small pinches of soft drift which we pressed together and put into our mouths to melt. When our hands warmed up again we got some more; so we did not get very thirsty. A few ribbons of canvas still remained in the wall over our heads, and these produced volleys of cracks like pistol shots hour after hour. The canvas never drew out from the walls, not an inch. The wind made just the same noise as an express train running fast through a tunnel if you have both the windows down.

I can well believe that neither of my companions gave up hope for an instant. They must have been frightened, but they were never disturbed. As for me I never had any hope at all; and when the roof went I felt that this was the end. What else could I think? We had spent days in reaching this place through the darkness in cold such as had never been experienced by human beings. We had been out for four weeks under conditions in which no man had existed previously for more than a few days, if that. During this time we had seldom slept except from sheer physical exhaustion, as men sleep on the rack; and every minute of it we had been fighting for the bed-rock necessaries of bare existence, and always in the dark. We had kept ourselves going by enormous care of our feet and hands and bodies, by burning oil, and by having plenty of hot fatty food. Now we had no tent, one tin of oil left out of six, and only part of our cooker. When we were lucky and not too cold we could almost wring water from our clothes, and directly we got out of our sleeping-bags we were frozen into solid sheets of armoured ice. In cold temperatures with all the advantages of a tent over our heads we were already taking more than an hour of fierce struggling and cramp to get into our sleeping-bags – so frozen were they and so long did it take us to thaw our way in. No! Without the tent we were dead men.

And there seemed not one chance in a million that we should ever see our tent again. We were 900 feet up on the mountain side, and the wind blew about as hard as a wind can blow straight out to sea. First there was a steep slope, so hard that a pick made little impression upon it, so slippery that if you started down in finnesko you never could stop: this ended in a great ice-cliff some hundreds of feet high, and then came miles of pressure ridges, crevassed and tumbled, in which you might as well look for a daisy as a tent: and after that the open sea. The chances, however, were that the tent had just been taken up into the air and dropped somewhere in this sea well on the way to New Zealand. Obviously the tent was gone.

Face to face with real death one does not think of the things that torment the bad people in the tracts, and fill the good people with bliss. I might have speculated on my chances of going to Heaven; but candidly I did not care. I could not have wept if I had tried. I had no wish to review the evils of my past. But the past did seem to have been a bit wasted. The road to Hell may be paved with good intentions: the road to Heaven is paved with lost opportunities.

I wanted those years over again. What fun I would have with them: what glorious fun! It was a pity. Well has the Persian said that when we come to die we, remembering that God is merciful, will gnaw our elbows with remorse for thinking of the things we have not done for fear of the Day of Judgement.

And I wanted peaches and syrup – badly. We had them at the hut, sweeter and more luscious than you can imagine. And we have been without sugar for a month. Yes – especially the syrup.

Thus impiously I set out to die, making up my mind that I was not going to try and keep warm, that it might not take too long, and thinking I would try and get some morphia from the medical case if it got very bad. Not a bit heroic, and entirely true! Yes! comfortable, warm reader. Men do not fear death, they fear the pain of dying.

And then quite naturally and no doubt disappointingly to those who would like to read of my last agonies (for who would not give pleasure by his death?) I fell asleep. I expect the temperature was pretty high during this great blizzard, and anything near zero was very high to us. That and the snow which drifted over us made a pleasant wet kind of snipe marsh inside our sleeping-bags, and I am sure we all dozed a good bit. There was so much to worry about that there was not the least use in worrying: and we were so *very* tired. We were hungry, for the last meal we had had was in the morning of the day before, but hunger was not very pressing.

And so we lay, wet and quite fairly warm, hour after hour while the wind roared round us, blowing storm force continually and rising in the gusts to something indescribable. Storm force is force 11, and force 12 is the biggest wind which can be logged: Bowers logged it force 11, but he was always so afraid of overestimating that he was inclined to underrate. I think it was blowing a full hurricane. Sometimes awake, sometimes dozing, we had not a very uncomfortable time so far as I can remember. I knew that parties which had come to Cape Crozier in the spring had experienced blizzards which lasted eight or ten days. But this did not worry us as much as I think it did Bill: I was numb. I vaguely called to mind that Peary had survived a blizzard in the open: but wasn't that in the summer?

It was in the early morning of Saturday (22 July) that we discovered the loss of the tent. Some time during that morning we had had our last meal. The roof went about noon on Sunday and we had had no meal in the interval because our supply of oil was so low; nor could we move out of our bags except as a last necessity. By Sunday night we had been without a meal for some thirty-six hours.

The rocks which fell upon us when the roof went did no damage, and though we could not get out of our bags to move them, we could fit ourselves into them without difficulty. More serious was the drift which began to pile up all round and over us. It helped to keep us warm of course, but at the same time in these comparatively high temperatures it saturated our bags even worse than they were before. If we did not find the tent (and its recovery would be a miracle) these bags and the floor-cloth of the tent on which we were lying were all we had in that fight back across the Barrier which could, I suppose, have only had one end.

Meanwhile we had to wait. It was nearly 70 miles home and it had taken us the best part of three weeks to come. In our less miserable moments we tried to think out ways of getting back, but I do not remember very much about that time. Sunday morning faded into Sunday afternoon, – into Sunday night, – into Monday morning. Till then the blizzard had raged with monstrous fury; the winds of the world were there, and they had all gone mad. We had bad winds at Cape Evans this year, and we had far worse the next winter when the open water was at our doors. But I have never heard or felt or seen a wind like this. I wondered why it did not carry away the earth.

In the early hours of Monday there was an occasional hint of a lull. Ordinarily in a big winter blizzard, when you have lived for several days and nights with that turmoil in your ears, the lulls are more trying than the noise: "the feel of not to feel it"* I do not remember noticing that now. Seven or eight more hours passed, and though it was still blowing we could make ourselves heard to one another without great difficulty. It was two days and two nights since we had had a meal.

We decided to get out of our bags and make a search for the tent. We did so, bitterly cold and utterly miserable, though I do not think any of us showed it. In the darkness we could see very little, and no trace whatever of the tent. We returned against the wind, nursing our faces and hands, and settled that we must try and cook a meal somehow. We managed about the weirdest meal eaten north or south. We got the floor-cloth wedged under our bags, then got

---

* Keats

into our bags and drew the floor-cloth over our heads. Between us we got the Primus alight somehow, and by hand we balanced the cooker on top of it, minus the two members which had been blown away. The flame flickered in the draughts. Very slowly the snow in the cooker melted, we threw in a plentiful supply of pemmican, and the smell of it was better than anything on earth. In time we got both tea and pemmican, which was full of hairs from our bags, penguin feathers, dirt and debris, but delicious. The blubber left in the cooker got burnt and gave the tea a burnt taste. None of us ever forgot that meal: I enjoyed it as much as such a meal could be enjoyed, and that burnt taste will always bring back the memory.

It was still dark and we lay down in our bags again, but soon a little glow of light began to come up, and we turned out to have a further search for the tent. Birdie went off before Bill and me. Clumsily I dragged my eider-down out of my bag on my feet, all sopping wet: it was impossible to get it back and I let it freeze: it was soon just like a rock. The sky to the south was as black and sinister as it could possibly be. It looked as though the blizzard would be on us again in a moment.

I followed Bill down the slope. We could find nothing. But, as we searched, we heard a shout somewhere below and to the right. We got on a slope, slipped, and went sliding down quite unable to stop ourselves, and came upon Birdie with the tent, the outer lining still on the bamboos. Our lives had been taken away and given back to us.

We were so thankful we said nothing.

The End of the Worst Journey

We are looked upon as beings who have come from another world. This afternoon I had a shave after soaking my face in a hot sponge, and then a bath. Lashly had already cut my hair. Bill looks very thin and we are all very blear-eyed from want of sleep. I have not much appetite, my mouth is very dry and throat sore with a troublesome hacking cough which I have had all the journey. My taste is gone. We are getting badly spoiled, but our beds are the height of all our pleasures.

Another very happy day doing nothing. After falling asleep two or three times I went to bed, read *Kim*, and slept. About two

hours after each meal we all want another, and after a tremendous supper last night we had another meal before turning in. I
have my taste back but all our fingers are impossible, they might
be so many pieces of lead except for the pins and needles feeling
in them which we have also got in our feet. My toes are very
bulbous and some toenails are coming off. My left heel is one big
burst blister. Going straight out of a warm bed into a strong wind
outside nearly bowled me over. I felt quite faint, and pulled
myself together thinking it was all nerves; but it began to come
on again and I had to make for the hut as quickly as possible.
Birdie is now full of schemes for doing the trip again next year.
Bill says it is too great a risk in the darkness, and he will not
consider it, though he thinks that to go in August might be
possible.

*Bowers and Wilson never did make another journey to the Emperors.
Instead, they joined Scott's doomed attempt on the South Pole. Cherry-
Garrard was among the search party which found their corpses.*

Pole Position

Roald Amundsen

It was Amundsen's intention to be the first to the North Pole but, on finding that Peary had beaten him to it, the Norwegian explorer secretly switched his efforts to 90° South. Landing in Antarctica, he outflanked the British expedition of R. F. Scott in a highly efficient eight-week sprint to the Pole by ski and dog-pulled sledge. Amundsen did not bother to dress up his explorations in the pretence of science or gentlemanly sport; he simply wanted to be first. And Amundsen was first to the Pole, reaching it a month before Scott, just as he had been the first to navigate the North-west Passage.

In lat. 87° S. – according to dead reckoning – we saw the last of the land to the north-east. The atmosphere was then apparently as clear as could be, and we felt certain that our view covered all the land there was to be seen from that spot. We were deceived again on this occasion, as will be seen later. Our distance that day (4 December) was close upon twenty-five miles; height above the sea, 10,100 feet.

The weather did not continue fine for long. Next day (5 December) there was a gale from the north, and once more the whole plain was a mass of drifting snow. In addition to this there was thick falling snow, which blinded us and made things worse, but a feeling of security had come over us and helped us to advance rapidly and without hesitation, although we could see nothing. That day we encountered new surface conditions – big, hard snow-waves (sastrugi). These were anything but pleasant to work among, especially when one could not see them. It was of no use for us "forerunners" to think of going in advance under these circumstances, as it was impossible to keep on one's feet. Three or four paces was often the most we managed to do before falling down. The sastrugi were very high, and often abrupt; if one came on them unexpectedly, one required to be more than an acrobat to keep on one's feet. The plan we found to work best in these conditions was to let Hanssen's dogs go first; this was an unpleasant job for Hanssen, and for his dogs too, but it succeeded, and succeeded well. An upset here and there was, of course, unavoidable, but with a little patience the sledge was always righted again. The drivers had as much as they could do to support their sledges among these sastrugi, but while supporting the sledges, they had at the same time a support for themselves. It was worse for us who had no sledges, but by keeping in the wake of them we could see where the irregularities lay, and thus get over them. Hanssen deserves a special word of praise for his driving on this surface in such weather. It is a difficult matter to drive Eskimo dogs forward when they cannot see; but Hanssen managed it well, both getting the dogs on and steering his course by compass. One would not think it possible to keep an approximately right course when the uneven ground gives such violent shocks that the needle flies several times round the compass, and is no sooner still again than it recommences the same dance; but when at last we got an observation, it turned out that Hanssen had steered to a hair, for the observations and dead reckoning agreed to a mile. In spite of all hindrances, and of being able to see nothing, the sledge-meters showed nearly twenty-five miles. The hypsometer showed 11,070 feet above the sea; we had therefore reached a greater altitude than the Butcher's.

6 December brought the same weather: thick snow, sky and plain all one, nothing to be seen. Nevertheless we made splendid progress. The sastrugi gradually became levelled out, until the surface was perfectly smooth; it was a relief to have even ground to go upon once more. These irregularities that one was constantly falling over were a nuisance; if we had met with them in our usual surroundings it would not have mattered so much; but up here on the high ground, where we had to stand and gasp for breath every time we rolled over, it was certainly not pleasant.

That day we passed 88° S, and camped in 88° 9' S. A great surprise awaited us in the tent that evening. I expected to find, as on the previous evening, that the boiling-point had fallen somewhat; in other words, that it would show a continued rise of the ground, but to our astonishment this was not so. The water boiled at exactly the same temperature as on the preceding day. I tried it several times, to convince myself that there was nothing wrong, each time with the same result. There was great rejoicing among us all when I was able to announce that we had arrived on the top of the plateau.

7 December began like the 6th, with absolutely thick weather, but, as they say, you never know what the day is like before sunset. Possibly I might have chosen a better expression than this last – one more in agreement with the natural conditions – but I will let it stand. Though for several weeks now the sun had not set, my readers will not be so critical as to reproach me with inaccuracy. With a light wind from the north-east, we now went southward at a good speed over the perfectly level plain, with excellent going. The uphill work had taken it out of our dogs, though not to any serious extent. They had turned greedy – there is no denying that – and the half kilo of pemmican they got each day was not enough to fill their stomachs. Early and late they were looking for something – no matter what – to devour. To begin with they contented themselves with such loose objects as ski-bindings, whips, boots, and the like; but as we came to know their proclivities, we took such care of everything that they found no extra meals lying about. But that was not the end of the matter. They then went for the fixed lashings of the sledges, and – if we had allowed it – would very quickly have resolved the various sledges into their component parts. But we found a way of stopping that: every evening, on halting, the sledges were buried in the snow, so as to hide all the lashings. That was successful; curiously enough, they never tried to force the "snow rampart". I may mention as a curious thing that these ravenous animals, that devoured everything they came across, even to the ebonite points of our ski-sticks, never made any attempt to break into the provision cases. They lay there and went about among the sledges with their noses just on a level with the split cases, seeing and scenting the pemmican, without once making a sign of taking any. But if one raised a lid, they were not long in showing themselves. Then they all came in a great hurry and flocked about the sledges in the hope of getting a little extra bit. I am at a loss to

explain this behaviour; that bashfulness was not at the root of it, I am tolerably certain.

During the forenoon the thick, grey curtain of cloud began to grow thinner on the horizon, and for the first time for three days we could see a few miles about us. The feeling was something like that one has on waking from a good nap, rubbing one's eyes and looking around. We had become so accustomed to the grey twilight that this positively dazzled us. Meanwhile, the upper layer of air seemed obstinately to remain the same and to be doing its best to prevent the sun from showing itself. We badly wanted to get a meridian altitude, so that we could determine our latitude. Since 86° 47' S. we had had no observation, and it was not easy to say when we should get one. Hitherto, the weather conditions on the high ground had not been particularly favourable. Although the prospects were not very promising, we halted at 11 a.m. and made ready to catch the sun if it should be kind enough to look out. Hassel and Wisting used one sextant and artificial horizon, Hanssen and I the other set.

I don't know that I have ever stood and absolutely pulled at the sun to get it out as I did that time. If we got an observation here which agreed with our reckoning, then it would be possible, if the worst came to the worst, to go to the Pole on dead reckoning; but if we got none now, it was a question whether our claim to the Pole would be admitted on the dead reckoning we should be able to produce. Whether my pulling helped or not, it is certain that the sun appeared. It was not very brilliant to begin with, but, practised as we now were in availing ourselves of even the poorest chances, it was good enough. Down it came, was checked by all, and the altitude written down. The curtain of cloud was rent more and more, and before we had finished our work – that is to say, caught the sun at its highest, and convinced ourselves that it was descending again – it was shining in all its glory. We had put away our instruments and were sitting on the sledges, engaged in the calculations. I can safely say that we were excited. What would the result be, after marching blindly for so long and over such impossible ground, as we had been doing? We added and subtracted, and at last there was the result. We looked at each other in sheer incredulity: the result was as astonishing as the most consummate conjuring trick – 88° 16' S, precisely to a minute the same as our reckoning, 88° 16' S. If we were forced to go to the Pole on dead reckoning, then surely the most exacting would admit our right to do so. We put away our observation books, ate one or two biscuits, and went at it again.

We had a great piece of work before us that day nothing less than carrying our flag farther south than the foot of man had trod. We had our silk flag ready; it was made fast to two ski-sticks and laid on Hanssen's sledge. I had given him orders that as soon as we had covered the distance to 88°S, which was Shackleton's farthest south, the flag was to be hoisted on his sledge. It was my turn as forerunner, and I pushed on. There was no longer any difficulty in holding one's course; I had the grandest cloud-formations to steer by, and everything now went like a machine. First came the forerunner for the time being, then Hanssen, then Wisting, and finally Bjaaland. The forerunner who was not on duty went where he liked; as a rule he accompanied one or other of the sledges. I had long ago fallen into a reverie – far removed from the scene in which I was moving; what I thought about I do not remember now, but I was so preoccupied that I had entirely forgotten my surroundings. Then suddenly I was roused from my dreaming by a jubilant shout, followed by ringing cheers. I turned round quickly to discover the reason of this unwonted occurrence, and stood speechless and overcome.

I find it impossible to express the feelings that possessed me at this moment. All the sledges had stopped, and from the foremost of them the Norwegian flag was flying. It shook itself out, waved and flapped so that the silk rustled; it looked wonderfully well in the pure, clear air and the shining white surroundings. 88° 23' was past; we were farther south than any human being had been. No other moment of the whole trip affected me like this. The tears forced their way to my eyes; by no effort of will could I keep them back. It was the flag yonder that conquered me and my will. Luckily I was some way in advance of the others, so that I had time to pull myself together and master my feelings before reaching my comrades. We all shook hands, with mutual congratulations; we had won our way far by holding together, and we would go farther yet – to the end.

We did not pass that spot without according our highest tribute of admiration to the man, who – together with his gallant

companions – had planted his country's flag so infinitely nearer
to the goal than any of his precursors. Sir Ernest Shackleton's
name will always be written in the annals of Antarctic exploration in letters of fire. Pluck and grit can work wonders, and I
know of no better example of this than what that man has
accomplished.

The cameras of course had to come out, and we got an excellent photograph of the scene which none of us will ever forget.
We went on a couple of miles more, to 88° 25', and then camped.
The weather had improved, and kept on improving all the time.
It was now almost perfectly calm, radiantly clear, and, under the
circumstances, quite summer-like: -0.4° F. Inside the tent it was
quite sultry. This was more than we had expected.

After much consideration and discussion we had come to the
conclusion that we ought to lay down a depot – the last one – at
this spot. The advantages of lightening our sledges were so great
that we should have to risk it. Nor would there be any great risk
attached to it, after all, since we should adopt a system of marks
that would lead even a blind man back to the place. We had
determined to mark it not only at right angles to our course –
that is, from east to west – but by snow beacons at every two
geographical miles to the south.

We stayed here on the following day to arrange this depot.
Hanssen's dogs were real marvels, all of them; nothing seemed to
have any effect on them. They had grown rather thinner, of
course, but they were still as strong as ever. It was therefore
decided not to lighten Hanssen's sledge, but only the two others;
both Wisting's and Bjaaland's teams had suffered, especially the
latter's. The reduction in weight that was effected was considerable – nearly 110 pounds on each of the two sledges; there was
thus about 220 pounds in the depot. The snow here was ill-
adapted for building, but we put up quite a respectable monument
all the same. It was dogs' pemmican and biscuits that were left
behind; we carried with us on the sledges provisions for about a
month. If, therefore, contrary to expectation, we should be so
unlucky as to miss this depot, we should nevertheless be fairly
sure of reaching our depot in 86° 21' before supplies ran short.
The cross-marking of the depot was done with sixty splinters of
black packing-case on each side, with 100 paces between each.

Every other one had a shred of black cloth on the top. The splinters on the east side were all marked, so that on seeing them we should know instantly that we were to the east of the depot. Those on the west had no marks.

The warmth of the past few days seemed to have matured our frost-sores, and we presented an awful appearance. It was Wisting, Hanssen, and I who had suffered the worst damage in the last south-east blizzard; the left side of our faces was one mass of sore, bathed in matter and serum. We looked like the worst type of tramps and ruffians, and would probably not have been recognized by our nearest relations. These sores were a great trouble to us during the latter part of the journey. The slightest gust of wind produced a sensation as if one's face were being cut backwards and forwards with a blunt knife. They lasted a long time, too; I can remember Hanssen removing the last scab when we were coming into Hobart – three months later. We were very lucky in the weather during this depot work; the sun came out all at once, and we had an excellent opportunity of taking some good azimuth observations, the last of any use that we got on the journey.

9 December arrived with the same fine weather and sunshine. True, we felt our frost-sores rather sharply that day, with -18.4°F. and a little breeze dead against us, but that could not be helped. We at once began to put up beacons – a work which was continued with great regularity right up to the Pole. These beacons were not so big as those we had built down on the Barrier; we could see that they would be quite large enough with a height of about 3 feet, as it was, very easy to see the slightest irregularity on this perfectly flat surface. While thus engaged we had an opportunity of becoming thoroughly acquainted with the nature of the snow. Often – very often indeed – on this part of the plateau, to the south of 88° 25', we had difficulty in getting snow good enough – that is, solid enough for cutting blocks. The snow up here seemed to have fallen very quietly, in light breezes or calms. We could thrust the tent-pole, which was 6 feet long, right down without meeting resistance, which showed that there was no hard layer of snow. The surface was also perfectly level; there was not a sign of sastrugi in any direction.

Every step we now took in advance brought us rapidly nearer

the goal; we could feel fairly certain of reaching it on the after-noon of the 14th. It was very natural that our conversation should be chiefly concerned with the time of arrival. None of us would admit that he was nervous, but I am inclined to think that we all had a little touch of that malady. What should we see when we got there? A vast, endless plain, that no eye had yet seen and no foot yet trodden; or – No, it was an impossibility; with the speed at which we had travelled, we must reach the goal first, there could be no doubt about that. And yet – and yet – Wherever there is the smallest loophole, doubt creeps in and gnaws and gnaws and never leaves a poor wretch in peace. "What on earth is Uroa scenting?" It was Bjaaland who made this remark, on one of these last days, when I was going by the side of his sledge and talking to him. "And the strange thing is that he's scenting to the south. It can never be—" Mylius, Ring, and Suggen, showed the same interest in the southerly direction; it was quite extraordinary to see how they raised their heads, with every sign of curiosity, put their noses in the air, and sniffed due south. One would really have thought there was something remarkable to be found there.

From 88° 25' S. the barometer and hypsometer indicated slowly but surely that the plateau was beginning to descend towards the other side. This was a pleasant surprise to us; we had thus not only found the very summit of the plateau, but also the slope down on the far side. This would have a very important bearing for obtaining an idea of the construction of the whole plateau. On 9 December observations and dead reckoning agreed within a mile. The same result again on the 10th: obser-vation 2 kilometres behind reckoning. The weather and going remained about the same as on the preceding days: light south-easterly breeze, temperature -18.4°F. The snow surface was loose, but ski and sledges glided over it well. On the 11th, the same weather conditions. Temperature -13° F. Observation and reckoning again agreed exactly. Our latitude was 89° 15' S. On the 12th we reached 89° 30', reckoning 1 kilometre behind observation. Going and surface as good as ever. Weather splen-did – calm with sunshine. The noon observation on the 13th gave 89° 37' S. Reckoning 89° 38.5' S. We halted in the after-noon, after going eight geographical miles, and camped in 89° 45', according to reckoning.

The weather during the forenoon had been just as fine as before, in the afternoon we had some snow-showers from the south-east. It was like the eve of some great festival that night in the tent. One could feel that a great event was at hand. Our flag was taken out again and lashed to the same two ski-sticks as before. Then it was rolled up and laid aside, to be ready when the time came. I was awake several times during the night, and had the same feeling that I can remember as a little boy on the night before Christmas Eve – an intense expectation of what was going to happen. Otherwise I think we slept just as well that night as any other.

On the morning of 14 December the weather was of the finest, just as if it had been made for arriving at the Pole. I am not quite sure, but I believe we despatched our breakfast rather more quickly than usual and were out of the tent sooner, though I must admit that we always accomplished this with all reasonable haste. We went in the usual order – the forerunner, Hanssen, Wisting, Bjaaland, and the reserve forerunner. By noon we had reached 89° 53' by dead reckoning, and made ready to take the rest in one stage. At 10 a.m. a light breeze had sprung up from the south-east, and it had clouded over, so that we got no noon altitude; but the clouds were not thick, and from time to time we had a glimpse of the sun through them. The going on that day was rather different from what it had been; sometimes the ski went over it well, but at others it was pretty bad. We advanced that day in the same mechanical way as before; not much was said, but eyes were used all the more. Hanssen's neck grew twice as long as before in his endeavour to see a few inches farther. I had asked him before we started to spy out ahead for all he was worth, and he did so with a vengeance. But, however keenly he stared, he could not descry anything but the endless flat plain ahead of us. The dogs had dropped their scenting, and appeared to have lost their interest in the regions about the earth's axis.

At three in the afternoon a simultaneous "Halt!" rang out from the drivers. They had carefully examined their sledge-meters, and they all showed the full distance – our Pole by reckoning. The goal was reached, the journey ended. I cannot say – though I know it would sound much more effective – that the object of my life was attained. That would be romancing rather too bare-facedly. I had better be honest and admit straight out that I have never known any man to be placed in such a diametrically opposite position to the goal of his desires as I was at that moment. The regions around the North Pole – well, yes, the North Pole itself – had attracted me from childhood, and here I was at the South Pole. Can anything more topsy-turvy be imagined?

We reckoned now that we were at the Pole. Of course, every one of us knew that we were not standing on the absolute spot; it would be an impossibility with the time and the instruments at our disposal to ascertain that exact spot. But we were so near it that the few miles which possibly separated us from it could not be of the slightest importance. It was our intention to make a circle round this camp, with a radius of twelve and a half miles (20 kilometres), and to be satisfied with that. After we had halted we collected and congratulated each other. We had good grounds for mutual respect in what had been achieved, and I think that was just the feeling that was expressed in the firm and powerful grasps of the fist that were exchanged. After this we proceeded to the greatest and most solemn act of the whole journey – the planting of our flag. Pride and affection shone in the five pairs of eyes that gazed upon the flag, as it unfurled itself with a sharp crack, and waved over the Pole. I had determined that the act of planting it – the historic event – should be equally divided among us all. It was not for one man to do this; it was for all who had staked their lives in the struggle, and held together through thick and thin. This was the only way in which I could show my gratitude to my comrades in this desolate spot. I could see that they understood and accepted it in the spirit in which it was offered. Five weather-beaten, frost-bitten fists they were that grasped the pole, raised the waving flag in the air, and planted it as the first at the geographical South Pole. "Thus we plant thee, beloved flag, at the South Pole, and give to the plain on which it lies the name of King Haakon VII's Plateau." That moment will certainly be remembered by all of us who stood there.

One gets out of the way of protracted ceremonies in those regions – the shorter they are the better. Everyday life began again at once. When we had got the tent up, Hanssen set about slaughtering Helge, and it was hard for him to have to part from his best friend. Helge had been an uncommonly useful and good-natured dog; without making any fuss he had pulled from morning to night, and had been a shining example to the team. But during the last week he had quite fallen away, and on our arrival at the Pole there was only a shadow of the old Helge left. He was only a drag on the others, and did absolutely no work. One blow on the skull, and Helge had ceased to live. "What is death to one is food to another" is a saying that can scarcely find a better application than these dog meals. Helge was portioned out on the spot, and within a couple of hours there was nothing left of him but his teeth and the tuft at the end of his tail. This was the second of our eighteen dogs that we had lost. The Major, one of Wisting's fine dogs, left us in 88 deg 25' S., and never returned. He was fearfully worn out, and must have gone away to die. We now had sixteen dogs left, and these we intended to divide into two equal teams, leaving Bjaaland's sledge behind.

Of course, there was a festivity in the tent that evening – not that champagne corks were popping and wine flowing – no, we contented ourselves with a little piece of seal-meat each, and it tasted well and did us good. There was no other sign of festival indoors. Outside we heard the flag flapping in the breeze. Conversation was lively in the tent that evening, and we talked of many things. Perhaps, too, our thoughts sent messages home of what we had done.

Everything we had with us had now to be marked with the words "South Pole" and the date, to serve afterwards as souvenirs. Wisting proved to be a first-class engraver, and many were the articles he had to mark. Tobacco – in the form of smoke – had hitherto never made its appearance in the tent. From time to time I had seen one or two of the others take a quid, but now these things were to be altered. I had brought with me an old briar pipe, which bore inscriptions from many places in the Arctic regions, and now I wanted it marked "South Pole". When I produced my pipe and was about to mark it, I received an unexpected gift: Wisting offered me tobacco for the rest of the journey. He had some cakes of plug in his kit-bag, which he would prefer to see me smoke. Can anyone grasp what such an offer meant at such a spot, made to a man who, to tell the truth, is very fond of a smoke after meals? There are not many who can understand it fully. I accepted the offer, jumping with joy, and on the way home I had a pipe of fresh, fine-cut plug every evening. Ah! that Wisting, he spoiled me entirely. Not only did he give me tobacco, but every evening – and I must confess I yielded to the temptation after a while, and had a morning smoke as well – he undertook the disagreeable work of cutting the plug and filling my pipe in all kinds of weather.

But we did not let our talk make us forget other things. As we had got no noon altitude, we should have to try and take one at midnight. The weather had brightened again, and it looked as if midnight would be a good time for the observation. We therefore crept into our bags to get a little nap in the intervening hours. In good time – soon after 11 p.m. – we were out again, and ready to catch the sun; the weather was of the best, and the opportunity excellent. We four navigators all had a share in it, as usual, and stood watching the course of the sun. This was a labour of patience, as the difference of altitude was now very slight. The result at which we finally arrived was of great interest, as it clearly shows how unreliable and valueless a single observation like this is in these regions. At 12.30 a.m. we put our instruments away, well satisfied with our work, and quite convinced that it was the midnight altitude that we had observed. The calculations which were carried out immediately afterwards gave us 89° 56' S. We were all well pleased with this result.

The arrangement now was that we should encircle this camp with a radius of about twelve and a half miles. By encircling I do not, of course, mean that we should go round in a circle with this radius; that would have taken us days, and was not to be thought of. The encircling was accomplished in this way: Three men went out in three different directions, two at right angles to the course we had been steering, and one in continuation of that course. To carry out this work I had chosen Wisting, Hassel, and Bjaaland. Having concluded our observations, we put the kettle on to give ourselves a drop of chocolate; the pleasure of standing out there in rather light attire had not exactly put warmth into our bodies. As we were engaged in swallowing the scalding drink, Bjaaland suddenly observed: "I'd like to tackle this encircling straight away. We shall have lots of time to sleep when we get back." Hassel and Wisting were quite of the same opinion, and it was agreed that they should start the work immediately. Here we have yet another example of the good spirit that prevailed in our little community. We had only lately come in from our day's work – a march of about eighteen and a half miles – and now they were asking to be allowed to go on another twenty-five miles. It seemed as if these fellows could never be tired. We therefore turned this meal into a little breakfast – that is to say, each man ate what he wanted of his bread ration, and then they began to get ready for the work. First, three small bags of light windproof stuff were made, and in each of these was placed a paper, giving the position of our camp. In addition, each of them carried a large square flag of the same dark brown material, which could be easily seen at a distance. As flag-poles we elected to use our spare sledge-runners, which were both long – 12 feet – and strong, and which we were going to take off here in any case, to lighten the sledges as much as possible for the return journey.

Thus equipped, and with thirty biscuits as an extra ration, the three men started off in the directions laid down. Their march was by no means free from danger, and does great honour to those who undertook it, not merely without raising the smallest objection, but with the greatest keenness. Let us consider for a moment the risk they ran. Our tent on the boundless plain, without marks of any kind, may very well be compared with a needle in a haystack. From this the three men were to steer out for a distance of twelve and a half miles. Compasses would have been good things to take on such a walk, but our sledge-compasses were too heavy and unsuitable for carrying. They therefore had to go without. They had the sun to go by, certainly, when they started, but who could say how long it would last? The weather was then fine enough, but it was impossible to guarantee that no sudden change would take place. If by bad luck the sun should be hidden, then their own tracks might help them. But to trust to tracks in these regions is a dangerous thing. Before you know where you are the whole plain may be one mass of driving snow, obliterating all tracks as soon as they are made. With the rapid changes of weather we had so often experienced, such a thing was not impossible. That these three risked their lives that morning, when they left the tent at 2.30, there can be no doubt at all, and they all three knew it very well. But if anyone thinks that on this account they took a solemn farewell of us who stayed behind, he is much mistaken. Not a bit; they all vanished in their different directions amid laughter and chaff.

The first thing we did – Hanssen and I – was to set about arranging a lot of trifling matters; there was something to be done here, something there, and above all we had to be ready for the series of observations we were to carry out together, so as to get as accurate a determination of our position as possible. The first observation told us at once how necessary this was. For it turned out that this, instead of giving us a greater altitude than the midnight observation, gave us a smaller one, and it was then clear that we had gone out of the meridian we thought we were following. Now the first thing to be done was to get our north and south line and latitude determined, so that we could find our position once more. Luckily for us, the weather looked as if it would hold. We measured the sun's altitude at every hour from 6 a.m. to 7 p.m., and from these observations found, with some degree of certainty, our latitude and the direction of the meridian.

By nine in the morning we began to expect the return of our comrades; according to our calculation they should then have covered the distance – twenty-five miles. It was not till ten o'clock that Hanssen made out the first black dot on the horizon, and not long after the second and third appeared. We both gave a sigh of relief as they came on; almost simultaneously the three arrived at the tent. We told them the result of our observations up to that time; it looked as if our camp was in about 89° 54' 30" S., and that with our encircling we had therefore included the actual Pole. With this result we might very well have been content, but as the weather was so good and gave the impression that it would continue so, and our store of provisions proved on examination to be very ample, we decided to go on for the remaining ten kilometres (five and a half geographical miles), and get our position determined as near to the Pole as possible. Meanwhile the three wanderers turned in – not so much because they were tired, as because it was the right thing to do – and Hanssen and I continued the series of observations.

In the afternoon we again went very carefully through our

provision supply before discussing the future. The result was that we had food enough for ourselves and the dogs for eighteen days. The surviving sixteen dogs were divided into two teams of eight each, and the contents of Bjaaland's sledge were shared between Hanssen's and Wisting's. The abandoned sledge was set upright in the snow, and proved to be a splendid mark. The sledge-meter was screwed to the sledge, and we left it there; our other two were quite sufficient for the return journey; they had all shown themselves very accurate. A couple of empty provision cases were also left behind. I wrote in pencil on a piece of case the information that our tent – "Polheim" – would be found five and a half geographical miles north-west quarter west by compass from the sledge. Having put all these things in order the same day, we turned in, very well satisfied.

Early next morning, 16 December, we were on our feet again. Bjaaland, who had now left the company of the drivers and been received with jubilation into that of the forerunners, was immediately entrusted with the honourable task of leading the expedition forward to the Pole itself. I assigned this duty, which we all regarded as a distinction, to him as a mark of gratitude to the gallant Telemarkers for their pre-eminent work in the advancement of ski spot. The leader that day had to keep as straight as a line, and if possible to follow the direction of our meridian. A little way after Bjaaland came Hassel, then Hanssen, then Wisting, and I followed a good way behind. I could thus check the direction of the march very accurately, and see that no great deviation was made. Bjaaland on this occasion showed himself a matchless forerunner; he went perfectly straight the whole time. Not once did he incline to one side or the other, and when we arrived at the end of the distance, we could still clearly see the sledge we had set up and take its bearing. This showed it to be absolutely in the right direction.

It was 11 a.m. when we reached our destination. While some of us were putting up the tent, others began to get everything ready for the coming observations. A solid snow pedestal was put up, on which the artificial horizon was to be placed, and a smaller one to rest the sextant on when it was not in use. At 11.30 a.m. the first observation was taken. We divided ourselves into two parties – Hanssen and I in one, Hassel and Wisting in the other.

While one party slept, the other took the observations, and the watches were of six hours each. The weather was altogether grand, though the sky was not perfectly bright the whole time. A very light, fine, vaporous curtain would spread across the sky from time to time, and then quickly disappear again. This film of cloud was not thick enough to hide the sun, which we could see the whole time, but the atmosphere seemed to be disturbed. The effect of this was that the sun appeared not to change its altitude for several hours, until it suddenly made a jump.

Observations were now taken every hour through the whole twenty-four. It was very strange to turn in at 6 p.m., and then on turning out again at midnight to find the sun apparently still at the same altitude, and then once more at 6 a.m. to see it still no higher. The altitude had changed, of course, but so slightly that it was imperceptible with the naked eye. To us it appeared as though the sun made the circuit of the heavens at exactly the same altitude. The times of day that I have given here are calculated according to the meridian of Framheim; we continued to reckon our time from this. The observations soon told us that we were not on the absolute Pole, but as close to it as we could hope to get with our instruments.

On 17 December at noon we had completed our observations, and it is certain that we had done all that could be done. In order if possible to come a few inches nearer to the actual Pole, Hanssen and Bjaaland went out four geographical miles (seven kilometres) in the direction of the newly found meridian.

Bjaaland astonished me at dinner that day. Speeches had not hitherto been a feature of this journey, but now Bjaaland evidently thought the time had come, and surprised us all with a really fine oration. My amazement reached its culmination when, at the conclusion of his speech, he produced a cigar-case full of cigars and offered it round. A cigar at the Pole! What do you say to that? But it did not end there. When the cigars had gone round, there were still four left. I was quite touched when he handed the case and cigars to me with the words: "Keep this to remind you of the Pole." I have taken good care of the case, and shall preserve it as one of the many happy signs of my comrades' devotion on this journey. The cigars I shared out afterwards, on Christmas Eve, and they gave us a visible mark of that occasion.

When this festival dinner at the Pole was ended, we began our preparations for departure. First we set up the little tent we had brought with us in case we should be compelled to divide into two parties. It had been made by our able sailmaker, Rönne, and was of very thin windproof gabardine. Its drab colour made it easily visible against the white surface. Another pole was lashed to the tent-pole, making its total height about 13 feet. On the top of this a little Norwegian flag was lashed fast, and underneath it a pennant, on which "Fram" was painted. The tent was well secured with guy-ropes on all sides. Inside the tent, in a little bag, I left a letter, addressed to H.M. the King, giving information of what we had accomplished. The way home was a long one, and so many things might happen to make it impossible for us to give an account of our expedition. Besides this letter, I wrote a short epistle to Captain Scott, who, I assumed, would be the first to find the tent. Other things we left there were a sextant with a glass horizon, a hypsometer case, three reindeer-skin foot-bags, some kamiks and mitts.

When everything had been laid inside, we went into the tent, one by one, to write our names on a tablet we had fastened to the tent-pole. On this occasion we received the congratulations of our companions on the successful result, for the following messages were written on a couple of strips of leather, sewed to the tent: "Good luck", and "Welcome to 90°". These good wishes, which we suddenly discovered, put us in very good spirits. They were signed by Beck and Rönne. They had good faith in us. When we had finished this we came out, and the tent-door was securely laced together, so that there was no danger of the wind getting a hold on that side.

And so goodbye to Polheim. It was a solemn moment when we bared our heads and bade farewell to our home and our flag. And then the travelling tent was taken down and the sledges packed. Now the homeward journey was to begin – homeward, step by step, mile after mile, until the whole distance was accomplished. We drove at once into our old tracks and followed them. Many were the times we turned to send a last look to Polheim. The vaporous, white air set in again, and it was not long before the last of Polheim, our little flag, disappeared from view.

Forestalled

Robert F. Scott

In November 1911 Scott and his men began the 950-mile march to the South Pole from Cape Evans. On reaching the Beardmore Glacier, the dogs were sent back and the surviving ponies killed for food. The expeditionaries then trudged along the 140-mile glacier, following Shackleton's "Farthest South" route, until they reached the Antarctic plateau.

Friday, 22 December: Camp 44, about 7,100 feet. T.-1°. Bar. 22·3. This, the third stage of our journey, is opening with good promise. We made our depot this morning, then said an affecting farewell to the returning party, who have taken things very well, dear good fellows as they are.

Then we started with our heavy loads about 9.20, I in some trepidation – quickly dissipated as we went off and up a slope at a smart pace. The second sledge came close behind us, showing that we have weeded the weak spots and made the proper choice for the returning party.

We came along very easily and lunched at 1, when the sledge-meter had to be repaired, and we didn't get off again till 3.20, camping at 6.45. Thus with 7 hours' marching we covered 10½ miles (geo.) (12 stat.).

Obs: Lat 85°13½'; Long 161°55'; Var. 175°46'E.

Tomorrow we march longer hours, about 9, I hope. Every day the loads will lighten, and so we ought to make the requisite progress. I think we have climbed about 250 feet today, but thought it more on the march. We look down on huge pressure ridges to the south and SE, and in fact all round except in the direction in which we go, SW. We seem to be travelling more or less parallel to a ridge which extends from Mt Darwin. Ahead of

us tonight is a stiffish incline and it looks as though there might
be pressure behind it. It is very difficult to judge how matters
stand, however, in such a confusion of elevations and depressions. This course doesn't work wonders in change of latitude,
but I think it is the right track to clear the pressures – at any rate
I shall hold it for the present.

We passed over one or two very broad (30 feet) bridged
crevasses with the usual gaping sides; they were running pretty
well in N and S direction. The weather has been beautifully fine
all day, as it was last night. (Night Temp. -9°). This morning
there was an hour or so of haze due to clouds from the N. Now
it is perfectly clear, and we get a fine view of the mountains
behind which Wilson has just been sketching.

Saturday, 23 December: Lunch. Bar. 22·01. Rise 370? Started
at 8, steering SW. Seemed to be rising, and went on well for
about 3 hours, then got amongst bad crevasses and hard
waves. We pushed on to SW, but things went from bad to
worse, and we had to haul out to the north, then west. West
looks clear for the present, but it is not a very satisfactory
direction. We have done 8½' (geo.), a good march. (T. -3°.
Southerly wind, force 2.) The comfort is that we are rising.
On one slope we got a good view of the land and the pressure
ridges to the SE. They seem to be disposed "en échelon" and
gave me the idea of shearing cracks. They seemed to lessen as
we ascend. It is rather trying having to march so far to the
west, but if we keep rising we must come to the end of the
obstacles some time.

Saturday night: Camp 45. T. -3°. Bar.21·61. ? Rise. Height
about 7,750. Great vicissitudes of fortune in the afternoon march.
Started west up a slope – about the fifth we have mounted in the
last two days. On top, another pressure appeared on the left, but
less lofty and more snow-covered than that which had troubled
us in the morning. There was temptation to try it, and I had been
gradually turning in its direction. But I stuck to my principle and
turned west up yet another slope. On top of this we got on the
most extraordinary surface – narrow crevasses ran in all directions. They were quite invisible, being covered with a thin crust
of hardened névé without a sign of a crack in it. We all fell in one

after another and sometimes two together. We have had many unexpected falls before, but usually through being unable to mark the run of the surface appearances of cracks, or where such cracks are covered with soft snow. How a hardened crust can form over a crack is a real puzzle – it seems to argue extremely slow movement.

Dead reckoning, 85°22'1"S, 159°31'E.

In the broader crevasses this morning we noticed that it was the lower edge of the bridge which was rotten, whereas in all the glacier the upper edge was open.

Near the narrow crevasses this afternoon we got about 10 minutes on snow which had a hard crust and loose crystals below. It was like breaking through a glass house at each step, but quite suddenly at 5 p.m. everything changed. The hard surface gave place to regular sastrugi and our horizon levelled in every direction. I hung on to the SW till 6 p.m., and then camped with a delightful feeling of security that we had at length reached the summit proper. I am feeling very cheerful about everything tonight. We marched 15 miles (geo.) (over 17 stat.) today, mounting nearly 800 feet and all in about 8½ hours. My determination to keep mounting irrespective of course is fully justified and I shall be indeed surprised if we have any further difficulties with crevasses or steep slopes. To me for the first time our goal seems really in sight. We can pull our loads and pull them much faster and farther than I expected in my most hopeful moments. I only pray for a fair share of good weather. There is a cold wind now as expected, but with good clothes and well fed as we are, we can stick a lot worse than we are getting. I trust this may prove the turning-point in our fortunes for which we have waited so patiently.

Sunday, 24 December: Lunch. Bar. 21·48. ? Rise 160 feet. Christmas Eve. 7½ miles geo. due south, and a rise, I think, more than shown by barometer. This in five hours, on the surface which ought to be a sample of what we shall have in the future. With our present loads it is a fairly heavy plod, but we get over the ground, which is a great thing. A high-pressure ridge has appeared on the "port bow". It seems isolated, but I shall be glad to lose sight of such disturbances. The wind is continuous from the SSE, very searching. We are now marching in our wind blouses and with somewhat more protection on the head.

Bar. 21·41. Camp 46. Rise for day? about 250 feet or 300 feet. Hypsometer, 8,000 feet.

The first two hours of the afternoon march went very well. Then the sledges hung a bit, and we plodded on and covered something over 14 miles (geo.) in the day. We lost sight of the big pressure ridge, but tonight another smaller one shows fine on the "port bow", and the surface is alternately very hard and fairly soft; dips and rises all round. It is evident we are skirting more disturbances, and I sincerely hope it will not mean altering course more to the west. 14 miles in 4 hours is not so bad considering the circumstances. The southerly wind is continuous and not at all pleasant in camp, but on the march it keeps us cool. (T. -3°). The only inconvenience is the extent to which our faces get iced up. The temperature hovers about zero.

We have not struck a crevasse all day, which is a good sign. The sun continues to shine in a cloudless sky, the wind rises and falls, and about us is a scene of the wildest desolation, but we are a very cheerful party and tomorrow is Christmas Day, with something extra in the hoosh.

Monday, 25 December: Christmas. Lunch. Bar. 21·14. Rise 240 feet. The wind was strong last night and this morning; a light snowfall in the night; a good deal of drift, subsiding when we started, but still about a foot high. I thought it might have spoilt the surface, but for the first hour and a half we went along in fine style. Then we started up a rise, and to our annoyance found ourselves amongst crevasses one more – very hard, smooth névé between high ridges at the edge of crevasses, and therefore very difficult to get foothold to pull the sledges. Got our ski sticks out, which improved matters, but we had to tack a good deal and several of us went half down. After half an hour of this I looked round and found the second sledge halted some way in rear – evidently someone had gone into a crevasse. We saw the rescue work going on, but had to wait half an hour for the party to come up, and got mighty cold. It appears that Lashly went down very suddenly, nearly dragging the crew with him. The sledge ran on

and jammed the span so that the Alpine rope had to be got out
and used to pull Lashly to the surface again. Lashly says the
crevasse was 50 feet deep and 8 feet across, in form U, showing
that the word "unfathomable" can rarely be applied. Lashly is 44
today and as hard as nails. His fall has not even disturbed his
equanimity.

After topping the crevasse ridge we got on a better surface and
came along fairly well, completing over 7 miles (geo.) just before
1 o'clock. We have risen nearly 250 feet this morning; the wind
was strong and therefore trying, mainly because it held the
sledge; it is a little lighter now.

Night Camp 47. Bar. 21·18. T. -7°. I am so replete that I can
scarcely write. After sundry luxuries, such as chocolate and
raisins at lunch, we started off well, but soon got amongst
crevasses, huge snow-filled roadways running almost in our
direction, and across hidden cracks into which we frequently fell.
Passing for 2 miles or so along between two roadways, we came
on a huge pit with raised sides. Is this a submerged mountain
peak or a swirl in the stream? Getting clear of crevasses and on a
slightly down grade, we came along at a swinging pace – splendid. I marched on till nearly 7.30, when we had covered 15 miles
(geo.) (17¼ stat.). I knew that supper was to be a "tightener",
and indeed it has been – so much that I must leave description
till the morning.

Dead reckoning, Lat 85°50' S; Long 159°8'2" E. Bar. 21·22.

Towards the end of the march we seemed to get into better
condition; about us the surface rises and falls on the long slopes
of vast mounds or undulations – no very definite system in their
disposition. We camped halfway up a long slope.

In the middle of the afternoon we got another fine view of the
land. The Dominion Range ends abruptly as observed, then
come two straits and two other masses of land. Similarly north of
the wild mountains is another strait and another mass of land.
The various straits are undoubtedly overflows, and the masses of
land mark the inner fringe of the exposed coastal mountains, the
general direction of which seems about SSE, from which it
appears that one could be much closer to the Pole on the Barrier
by continuing on it to the SSE. We ought to know more of this
when Evans's observations are plotted.

I must write a word of our supper last night. We had four courses. The first, pemmican, full whack, with slices of horse meat flavoured with onion and curry powder and thickened with biscuit; then an arrowroot, cocoa and biscuit hoosh sweetened; then a plum-pudding; then cocoa with raisins, and finally a dessert of caramels and ginger. After the feast it was difficult to move. Wilson and I couldn't finish our share of plum-pudding. We have all slept splendidly and feel thoroughly warm – such is the effect of full feeding.

Tuesday, 26 December: Lunch. Bar. 21·11. Four and three-quarter hours, 6¾ miles (geo.). Perhaps a little slow after plum-pudding, but I think we are getting on to the surface which is likely to continue the rest of the way. There are still mild differences of elevation, but generally speaking the plain is flattening out; no doubt we are rising slowly.

Camp 48. Bar. 21·02. The first two hours of the afternoon march went well; then we got on a rough rise and the sledge came badly. Camped at 6.30, sledge coming easier again at the end.

It seems astonishing to be disappointed with a march of 15 (stat.) miles, when I had contemplated doing little more than 10 with full loads.

We are on the 86th parallel. Obs: 86°2' S; 160°26' E; Var. 179°41' W. The temperature has been pretty consistent of late, -10° to -12° at night, -3° in the day. The wind has seemed milder today – it blows anywhere from SE to South. I had thought to have done with pressures, but tonight a crevassed slope appears on our right. We shall pass well clear of it, but there may be others. The undulating character of the plain causes a great variety of surface, owing, of course, to the varying angles at which the wind strikes the slopes. We were half an hour late starting this morning, which accounts for some loss of distance, though I should be content to keep up an average of 13' (geo.).

Wednesday, 27 December: Lunch. Bar. 21·02. The wind light this morning and the pulling heavy. Everyone sweated; especially the second team, which had great difficulty in keeping up. We have

been going up and down, the up grades very tiring, especially
when we get amongst sastrugi which jerk the sledge about, but
we have done 7¼ miles (geo.). A very bad accident this morning.
Bowers broke the only hypsometer thermometer. We have nothing to check our two aneroids.

Night Camp 49. Bar. 20·82. T. -6·3°. We marched off well
after lunch on a soft, snowy surface, then came to slippery
hard sastrugi and kept a good pace; but I felt this meant something wrong, and on topping a short rise we were once more in
the midst of crevasses and disturbances. For an hour it was
dreadfully trying – had to pick a road, tumbled into crevasses,
and got jerked about abominably. At the summit of the ridge
we came into another "pit" or "whirl", which seemed the
centre of the trouble – is it a submerged mountain peak?
During the last hour and a quarter we pulled out on to soft
snow again and moved well. Camped at 6.45, having covered
13⅓ miles (geo.). Steering the party is no light task. One
cannot allow one's thoughts to wander as others do, and when,
as this afternoon, one gets amongst disturbances, I find it is
very worrying and tiring. I do trust we shall have no more of
them. We have not lost sight of the sun since we came on the
summit; we should get an extraordinary record of sunshine. It
is monotonous work this; the sledge-meter and theodolite
govern the situation.

Thursday, 28 December: Lunch. Bar. 20·77. I start cooking
again tomorrow morning. We have had a troublesome day, but
have completed our 13 miles (geo.). My unit pulled away easy
this morning and stretched out for 2 hours as the second unit
made heavy weather. I changed with Evans and found the
second sledge heavy – could keep up, but the team was not
swinging with me as my own team swings. Then I changed
P.O. Evans for Lashly. We seemed to get on better, but at the
moment the surface changed and we came up over a rise with
hard sastrugi. At the top we camped for lunch. What was the
difficulty? One theory was that some members of the second
party were stale. Another that all was due to the bad stepping
and want of swing; another that the sledge pulled heavy. In the
afternoon we exchanged sledges, and at first went off well, but

getting into soft snow, we found a terrible drag, the second party coming quite easily with our sledge. So the sledge is the cause of the trouble, and talking it out, I found that all is due to want of care. The runners ran excellently, but the structure has been distorted by bad strapping, bad loading, etc. The party are not done, and I have told them plainly that they must wrestle with the trouble and get it right for themselves. There is no possible reason why they should not get along as easily as we do.

Night Camp 50. T. -6°. Bar. 20·66. Obs: 86°27'2" S; 161°1'15" E; Var. 179°33' E. Bar. 20·64.

Friday, 29 December: Bar. 20·52. Lunch. Height 9,050 about. The worst surface we have struck, very heavy pulling; but we came 6½ miles (geo.). It will be a strain to keep up distances if we get surfaces like this. We seem to be steadily but slowly rising. The satisfactory thing is that the second party now keeps up, as the faults have been discovered; they were due partly to the rigid loading of the sledge and partly to the bad pacing.

Night Camp 51. Bar. 20·49. T. -6°. Had another struggle this afternoon and only managed to get 12 miles (geo.). The very hard pulling has occurred on two rises. It appears that the loose snow is blown over the rises and rests in heaps on the north-facing slopes. It is these heaps that cause our worst troubles. The weather looks a little doubtful, a good deal of cirrus cloud in motion over us, radiating E and W. The wind shifts from SE to SSW, rising and falling at intervals; it is annoying to the march as it retards the sledges, but it must help the surface, I think, and so hope for better things tomorrow. The marches are terribly monotonous. One's thoughts wander occasionally to pleasanter scenes and places, but the necessity to keep the course, or some hitch in the surface, quickly brings them back. There have been some hours of very steady plodding today; these are the best part of the business, they mean forgetfulness and advance.

Saturday, 30 December: Bar. 20·42. Lunch. Night Camp 52. Bar. 20·36. Rise about 150. A very trying, tiring march, and only 11 miles (geo.) covered. Wind from the south to SE, not quite so strong as usual; the usual clear sky. Altitudes by aneroids 9,126 feet–8,970 feet.

We camped on a rise last night, and it was some time before we reached the top this morning. This took it out of us at the start and the second party dropped. I went on 6½ miles (when the second party was some way astern) and lunched. We came on in the afternoon, the other party still dropping, camped at 6.30 – they at 7.15. We came up another rise with the usual gritty snow towards the end of the march. For us the interval between the two rises, some 8 miles, was steady plodding work which one might keep up for some time. Tomorrow I'm going to march half a day, make a depot and build the 10-ft sledges. The second party is certainly tiring; it remains to be seen how they will manage with the smaller sledge and lighter load. The surface is certainly much worse than it was 50 miles back. (T. -10°.) We have caught up Shackleton's dates. Everything would be cheerful if I could persuade myself that the second party were quite fit to go forward.

Sunday, 31 December: New Year's Eve. 20·17. Height about 9,126. T. -10°. (Camp 53.) Corrected aneroid. The second party depoted its ski and some other weights equivalent to about 100 lb. I sent them off first; they marched, but not very fast. We followed and did not catch them before they camped by direction at 1.30. By this time we had covered exactly 7 miles (geo.), and we must have risen a good deal. We rose on one steep incline at the beginning of the march, and topped another at the end, showing a distance of about 5 miles between these wretched slopes which give us the hardest pulling, but as a matter of fact, we have been rising all day.

We had a good full brew of tea and then set to work stripping the sledges. That didn't take long, but the process of building up the 10-ft sledges now in operation in the other tent is a long job. Evans (P.O.) and Crean are tackling it, and it is a very remarkable piece of work. Certainly P.O. Evans is the most invaluable asset to our party. To build a sledge under these conditions is a fact for special record. Evans (Lieut.) has just found the latitude -86°56' S, so that we are pretty near the 87th parallel aimed at for tonight. We lose half a day, but I hope to make that up by going forward at much better speed.

This is to be called the "3 Degree Depot", and it holds a week's provision for both units.

There is extraordinarily little mirage up here and the refraction is very small. Except for the seamen we are all sitting in a double tent – the first time we have put up the inner lining to the tent; it seems to make us much snugger.

10 p.m. The job of rebuilding is taking longer than I expected, but is now almost done. The 10-ft sledges look very handy. We had an extra drink of tea and are now turned into our bags in the double tent (five of us) as warm as toast, and just enough light to write or work with. Did not get to bed till 2 am.

Obs: 86°55'47" S; 165°5'48" E; Var. 175°40' E. Morning Bar. 20·08.

Monday, 1 January 1912: New Year's Day. Lunch. Bar. 20·04. Roused hands about 7.30 and got away 9.30, Evans's party going ahead on foot. We followed on ski. Very stupidly we had not seen to our ski shoes beforehand, and it took a good half-hour to get them right; Wilson especially had trouble. When we did get away, to our surprise the sledge pulled very easily, and we made fine progress, rapidly gaining on the foot-haulers.

Night Camp 54. Bar. 19·98. Risen about 150 feet. Height about 9,600 above Barrier. They camped for lunch at 5½ miles and went on easily, completing 11.3 (geo.) by 7.30. We were delayed again at lunch camp, P.O. Evans repairing the tent, and I the cooker. We caught the other party more easily in the afternoon and kept alongside them the last quarter of an hour. It was surprising how easily the sledge pulled; we have scarcely exerted ourselves all day.

We have been rising again all day, but the slopes are less accentuated. I had expected trouble with ski and hard patches, but we found none at all. (T. -14°.) The temperature is steadily falling, but it seems to fall with the wind. We are *very* comfortable in our double tent. Stick of chocolate to celebrate the New Year. The supporting party not in very high spirits; they have not managed matters well for themselves. Prospects seem to get brighter – only 170 miles to go and plenty of food left.

Tuesday, 2 January: T. -17°, Camp 55. Height about 9,980. At lunch my aneroid reading over scale 12,250, shifted hand to read 10,250. Proposed to enter heights in future with correction as calculated at end of book (minus 340 feet). The foot party went off early, before 8, and marched till 1. Again from 2.35 to 6.30. We started more than half an hour later on each march and caught the others easy. It's been a plod for the foot people and pretty easy going for us, and we have covered 13 miles (geo.).

T. -11°: Obs 87°20'8" S; 160°40'53" E; Var. 180°. The sky is slightly overcast for the first time since we left the glacier; the sun can be seen already through the veil of stratus, and blue sky round the horizon. The sastrugi have all been from the SE today, and likewise the wind, which has been pretty light. I hope the clouds do not mean wind or bad surface. The latter became poor towards the end of the afternoon. We have not risen much today, and the plain seems to be flattening out. Irregularities are best seen by sastrugi. A skua gull visited us on the march this afternoon – it was evidently curious, kept alighting on the snow ahead, and fluttering a few yards as we approached. It seemed to have had little food – an extraordinary visitor considering our distance from the sea.

Wednesday, 3 January: Height: Lunch, 10,110; Night, 10,180. (Camp 56.) T. -17°. Minimum -18·5°. Within 150 miles of our goal. Last night I decided to reorganize, and this morning told off Teddy Evans, Lashly, and Crean to return. They are disappointed, but take it well. Bowers is to come into our tent, and we proceed as a five-man unit tomorrow. We have 5½ units of food – practically over a month's allowance for five people – it ought to see us through. We came along well on ski today, but the foot-haulers were slow, and so we only got a trifle over 12 miles (geo.). Very anxious to see how we shall manage tomorrow; if we can march well with the full load we shall be practically safe, I take it. The surface was very bad in patches today and the wind strong.

Thursday, 4 January: T. -17°, Lunch T. -16·5°. We were naturally late getting away this morning, the sledge having to be packed and arrangements completed for separation of parties. It is wonderful to see how neatly everything stows on a little sledge, thanks to P.O. Evans. I was anxious to see how we could pull it, and glad to find we went easy enough. Bowers on foot* pulls between, but behind, Wilson and myself; he has to keep his own pace and luckily does not throw us out at all.

The second party had followed us in case of accident, but as soon as I was certain we could get along we stopped and said farewell. Teddy Evans is terribly disappointed, but has taken it very well and behaved like a man. Poor old Crean wept and even Lashly was affected. I was glad to find their sledge is a mere nothing to them, and thus, no doubt, they will make a quick journey back. Since leaving them we have marched on till 1.15 and covered 6·2 miles (geo.). With full marching days we ought to have no difficulty in keeping up our average.

Night Camp 57. T. -16°. Height 10,280. We started well on the afternoon march, going a good speed for 1½ hours; then we came on a surface covered with loose sandy snow, and the pulling became very heavy. We managed to get off 12½ miles (geo.) by 7 p.m., but it was very heavy work.

In the afternoon the wind died away, and tonight it is flat calm; the sun so warm that in spite of the temperature we can stand about outside in the greatest comfort. It is amusing to stand thus and remember the constant horrors of our situation as they were painted for us: the sun is melting the snow on the ski, etc. The plateau is now very flat, but we are still ascending slowly. The sastrugi are getting more confused, predominant from the SE. I wonder what is in store for us. At present everything seems to be going with extraordinary smoothness, and one can scarcely believe that obstacles will not present themselves to make our task more difficult. Perhaps the surface will be the element to trouble us.

Friday, 5 January: Camp 58. Height: morning, 10,430; night, 10,320. T. -14·8°. Obs: 87°57', 159°13'. Minimum T. -23.5°; T. -21°. A dreadfully trying day. Light wind from the NNW

---

* Bowers had depoted his ski on 31 December, when it was assumed he would return with the last support party. He was without ski until 31 January.

bringing detached cloud and constant fall of ice crystals. The surface, in consequence, as bad as could be after the first hour. We started at 8.15, marched solidly till 1.15, covering 7·4 miles (geo.), and again in the afternoon we plugged on; by 7 p.m. we had done 12½ miles (geo.), the hardest we have yet done on the plateau. The sastrugi seemed to increase as we advanced and they have changed direction from SW to S by W. In the afternoon a good deal of confusing cross sastrugi, and tonight a very rough surface with evidences of hard southerly wind. Luckily the sledge shows no signs of capsizing yet. We sigh for a breeze to sweep the hard snow, but tonight the outlook is not promising better things. However, we are very close to the 88th parallel, little more than 120 miles from the Pole, only a march from Shackleton's final camp, and in a general way "getting on".

We go little over a mile and a quarter an hour now – it is a big strain as the shadows creep slowly round from our right through ahead to our left. What lots of things we think of on these monotonous marches! What castles one builds now hopefully that the Pole is ours. Bowers took sights today and will take them every third day. We feel the cold very little, the great comfort of our situation is the excellent drying effect of the sun. Our socks and finnesko are almost dry each morning. Cooking for five takes a seriously longer time than cooking for four; perhaps half an hour on the whole day. It is an item I had not considered when reorganizing.

Saturday, 6 January: Height 10,470. T. -22·3°. Obstacles arising – last night we got amongst sastrugi – they increased in height this morning and now we are in the midst of a sea of fish-hook waves well remembered from our Northern experience. We took off our ski after the first 1½ hours and pulled on foot. It is terribly heavy in places, and, to add to our trouble, every sastrugus is covered with a beard of sharp branching crystals. We have covered 6½ miles, but we cannot keep up our average if this sort of surface continues. There is no wind.

Camp 59. Lat 88°7'. Height 10,430–10,510. Rise of barometer? T. -22·5°. Minimum -25.8°. Morning. Fearfully hard pull again, and when we had marched about an hour we discovered that a sleeping-bag had fallen off the sledge. We had to go back and carry it on. It cost us over an hour and disorganized our party. We have only covered 10½ miles (geo), and it's been about the hardest pull we've had. We think of leaving our ski here, mainly because of risk of breakage. Over the sastrugi it is all up and down hill, and the covering of ice crystals prevents the sledge from gliding even on the down grade. The sastrugi, I fear, have come to stay, and we must be prepared for heavy marching, but in two days I hope to lighten loads with a depot. We are south of Shackleton's last camp, so, I suppose, have made the most southerly camp.

Sunday, 7 January: Height 10,560. Lunch. Temp. -21·3°. The vicissitudes of this work are bewildering. Last night we decided to leave our ski on account of the sastrugi. This morning we marched out a mile in 40 min. and the sastrugi gradually disappeared. I kept debating the ski question and at this point stopped, and after discussion we went back and fetched the ski; it cost us 1½ hours nearly. Marching again, I found to my horror we could scarcely move the sledge on ski; the first hour was awful owing to the wretched coating of loose sandy snow. However, we persisted, and towards the latter end of our tiring march we began to make better progress, but the work is still awfully heavy. I must stick to the ski after this.

Very heavy pulling still, but did 5 miles (geo.) in over 4 hours. Afternoon. Camp 60. T. -23°. Height 10,570. Obs: Lat 88°18'40" S; Long 157°21' E; Var. 179°15' W.

This is the shortest march we have made on the summit, but there is excuse. Still, there is no doubt if things remained as they are we could not keep up the strain of such marching for long. Things, however, luckily will not remain as they are. Tomorrow we depot a week's provision, lightening altogether about 100 lb. This afternoon the welcome southerly wind returned and is now blowing force 2 to 3. I cannot but think it will improve the surface.

The sastrugi are very much diminished, and those from the South seem to be overpowering those from the SE. Cloud travelled rapidly over from the South this afternoon, and the surface was covered with sandy crystals; these were not so bad as the "bearded" sastrugi, and oddly enough the wind and drift only gradually ablate these spiky formations. We have scarcely risen at all today, and the plain looks very flat. It doesn't look as though there were more rises ahead, and one could not wish for a better surface if only the crystal deposit would disappear or harden up. I am awfully glad we have hung on to the ski; hard as the marching is, it is far less tiring on ski. Bowers has a heavy time on foot, but nothing seems to tire him. Evans has a nasty cut on his hand (sledge-making). I hope it won't give trouble. Our food continues to amply satisfy. What luck to have hit on such an excellent ration! We really are an excellently found party.

Monday, 8 January: Camp 60. Noon. T. -19·8°. Min. for night -25°. Our first summit blizzard. We might just have started after breakfast, but the wind seemed obviously on the increase, and so it has proved. The sun has not been obscured, but snow is evidently falling as well as drifting. The sun seems to be getting a little brighter as the wind increases. The whole phenomenon is very like a Barrier blizzard, only there is much less snow, as one would expect, and at present less wind, which is somewhat of a surprise.

Evans's hand was dressed this morning, and the rest ought to be good for it. I am not sure it will not do us all good as we lie so very comfortably, warmly clothed in our comfortable bags, within our double-walled tent. However, we do not want more than a day's delay at most, both on account of lost time and food and the slow accumulation of ice. (Night T. -13·5°.) It has grown much thicker during the day, from time to time obscuring the sun for the first time. The temperature is low for a blizzard, but we are very comfortable in our double tent and the cold snow is not sticky and not easily carried into the tent, so that the sleeping-bags remain in good condition. (T. -3°.) The glass is rising slightly. I hope we shall be able to start in the morning, but fear that a disturbance of this sort may last longer than our local storms.

It is quite impossible to speak too highly of my companions. Each fulfils his office to the party; Wilson, first as doctor, ever on the lookout to alleviate the small pains and troubles incidental to the work; now as cook, quick, careful and dexterous, ever thinking of some fresh expedient to help the camp life; tough as steel on the traces, never wavering from start to finish.

Evans, a giant worker with a really remarkable headpiece. It is only now I realize how much has been due to him. Our ski-shoes and crampons have been absolutely indispensable, and if the original ideas were not his, the details of manufacture and design and the good workmanship are his alone. He is responsible for every sledge, every sledge fitting, tents, sleeping-bags, harness, and when one cannot recall a single expression of dissatisfaction with any one of these items, it shows what an invaluable assistant he has been. Now, besides superintending the putting up of the tent, he thinks out and arranges the packing of the sledge; it is extraordinary how neatly and handily everything is stowed, and how much study has been given to preserving the suppleness and good running qualities of the machine. On the Barrier, before the ponies were killed, he was ever roaming round, correcting faults of stowage.

Little Bowers remains a marvel – he is thoroughly enjoying himself. I leave all the provision arrangements in his hands, and at all times he knows exactly how we stand, or how each returning party should fare. It has been a complicated business to redistribute stores at various stages of reorganization, but not one single mistake has been made. In addition to the stores, he keeps the most thorough and conscientious meteorological record, and to this he now adds the duty of observer and photographer. Nothing comes amiss to him, and no work is too hard. It is a difficulty to get him into the tent; he seems quite oblivious of the cold, and he lies coiled in his bag writing and working out sights long after the others are asleep.

Of these three it is a matter for thought and congratulation that each is specially suited for his own work, but would not be capable of doing that of the others as well as it is done. Each is invaluable. Oates had his invaluable period with the ponies; now he is a foot slogger and goes hard the whole time, does his share of camp work, and stands the hardship as well as any of us. I would not like to be without him either. So our five people are perhaps as happily selected as it is possible to imagine.

Tuesday, 9 January: Camp 61. Record. Lat 88°25'. Height 10,270 feet. Bar. risen I think. T. -4°. Still blowing, and drifting when we got to breakfast, but signs of taking off. The wind had gradually shifted from South to ESE. After lunch we were able to break camp in a bad light, but on a good surface. We made a very steady afternoon march, covering 6½ miles (geo.). This should place us in Lat 88°25', beyond the record of Shackleton's walk. All is new ahead. The barometer has risen since the blizzard, and it looks as though we were on a level plateau, not to rise much further.

Obs: Long 159°17'45" E; Var. 179°55' W; Min. Temp. -7·2°.

More curiously the temperature continued to rise after the blow and now, at -4°, it seems quite warm. The sun has only shown very indistinctly all the afternoon, although brighter now. Clouds are still drifting over from the east. The marching is growing terribly monotonous, but one cannot grumble as long as the distance can be kept up. It can, I think, if we leave a depot, but a very annoying thing has happened. Bowers's watch has suddenly dropped 26 minutes; it may have stopped from being frozen outside his pocket, or he may have inadvertently touched the hands. Anyway it makes one more chary of leaving stores on this great plain, especially as the blizzard tended to drift up our tracks. We could only just see the back track when we started, but the light was extremely poor.

Wednesday, 10 January: Camp 62. T. -11°. Last depot 88°29' S; 159°33' E; Var. 180°. Terrible hard march in the morning; only covered 5·1 miles (geo.). Decided to leave depot at lunch camp. Built cairn and left one week's food together with sundry articles of clothing. We are down as close as we can go in the latter. We go forward with eighteen days' food. Yesterday I should have said certain to see us through, but now the surface is beyond words, and if it continues we shall have the greatest difficulty to keep our march long enough. The surface is quite covered with sandy snow, and when the sun shines it is terrible. During the early part of the afternoon it was overcast, and we started our lightened sledge with a good swing, but during the last two hours the sun cast shadows again, and the work was distressingly hard. We have covered only 10·8 miles (geo.).

Only 85 miles (geo.) from the Pole, but it's going to be a stiff pull *both ways* apparently; still we do make progress, which is something. Tonight the sky is overcast, the temperature (-11°) much higher than I anticipated; it is very difficult to imagine what is happening to the weather. The sastrugi grow more and more confused, running from S to E. Very difficult steering in uncertain light and with rapidly moving clouds. The clouds don't seem to come from anywhere, form and disperse without visible reason. The surface seems to be growing softer. The meteorological conditions seem to point to an area of variable light winds, and that plot will thicken as we advance.

Thursday, 11 January: Lunch. Height 10,540. T. -15°8'. It was heavy pulling from the beginning today, but for the first 2½ hours we could keep the sledge moving; then the sun came out (it had been overcast and snowing with light south-easterly breeze) and the rest of the forenoon was agonizing. I never had such pulling; all the time the sledge rasps and creaks. We have covered 6 miles, but at fearful cost to ourselves.

Night camp 63. Height 10,530. Temp. -16·3°. Minimum -25·8°. Another hard grind in the afternoon and 5 miles added. About 74 miles from the Pole – can we keep this up for seven days? It takes it out of us like anything. None of us ever had such hard work before. Cloud has been coming and going overhead all day, drifting from the SE, but continually altering shape. Snow crystals falling all the time; a very light S breeze at start soon dying away. The sun so bright and warm tonight that it is almost impossible to imagine a minus temperature. The snow seems to get softer as we advance; the sastrugi, though sometimes high and undercut, are not hard – no crusts, except yesterday the surface subsided once, as on the Barrier. It seems pretty certain there is no steady wind here. Our chance still holds good if we can put the work in, but it's a terribly trying time.

Friday, 12 January: Camp 64. T. -17·5°, Lat 88°57'. Another heavy march with snow getting softer all the time. Sun very bright, calm at start; first 2 hours terribly slow. Lunch, 4¾ hours, 5·6 miles geo.; Sight Lat 88°52'. Afternoon, 4 hours, 5·1 miles – total 10·7.

In the afternoon we seemed to be going better; clouds spread over from the west with light chill wind and for a few brief minutes we tasted the delight of having the sledge following free. Alas! in a few minutes it was worse than ever, in spite of the sun's eclipse. However, the short experience was salutary. I had got to fear that we were weakening badly in our pulling; those few minutes showed me that we only want a good surface to get along as merrily as of old. With the surface as it is, one gets horribly sick of the monotony and can easily imagine oneself getting played out, were it not that at the lunch and night camps one so quickly forgets all one's troubles and bucks up for a fresh effort. It is an effort to keep up the double figures, but if we can do so for another four marches we ought to get through. It is going to be a close thing.

At camping tonight everyone was chilled and we guessed a cold snap, but to our surprise the actual temperature was higher than last night, when we could dawdle in the sun. It is most unaccountable why we should suddenly feel the cold in this manner; partly the exhaustion of the march, but partly some damp quality in the air, I think. Little Bowers is wonderful; in spite of my protest he *would* take sights after we had camped tonight, after marching in the soft snow all day where we have been comparatively restful on ski.

Night position: Lat 88°57'25" S; Long 160°21' E; Var. 179°49' W. Minimum T. -23·5°.

Only 63 miles (geo.) from the Pole tonight. We ought to do the trick, but oh! for a better surface. It is quite evident this is a comparatively windless area. The sastrugi are few and far between, and all soft. I should imagine occasional blizzards sweep up from the SE, but none with violence. We have deep tracks in the snow, which is soft as deep as you like to dig down.

Saturday, 13 January: Lunch. Height 10,390. Barometer low? lunch Lat 89°3'18". Started on some soft snow, very heavy dragging and went slow. We could have supposed nothing but that such conditions would last from now onward, but to our surprise, after 2 hours we came on a sea of sastrugi, all lying from S to E, predominant ESE. Have had a cold little wind from SE and SSE, where the sky is overcast. Have done 5·6 miles and are now over the 89th parallel.

Night camp 65. Height 10,270. T. -22·5°, Minimum -23·5°. Lat 89°9' S very nearly. We started very well in the afternoon. Thought we were going to make a real good march, but after the first 2 hours surface crystals became as sandy as ever. Still we did 5·6 miles (geo.), giving over 11 for the day. Well, another day with double figures and a bit over. The chance holds.

It looks as though we were descending slightly; sastrugi remain as in forenoon. It is wearisome work this tugging and straining to advance a light sledge. Still, we get along. I did manage to get my thoughts off the work for a time today, which is very restful. We should be in a poor way without our ski, though Bowers manages to struggle through the soft snow without tiring his short legs.

Only 51 miles from the Pole tonight. If we don't get to it we shall be d——d close. There is a little southerly breeze tonight; I devoutly hope it may increase in force. The alternation of soft snow and sastrugi seem to suggest that the coastal mountains are not so very far away.

Sunday, 14 January: Camp 66. Lunch T. -18°, Night T. -15°. Sun showing mistily through overcast sky all day. Light southerly wind with very low drift. In consequence the surface was a little better, and we came along very steadily 6·3 miles in the morning and 5·5 in the afternoon, but the steering was awfully difficult and trying; very often I could see nothing, and Bowers in my shadows directed me. Under such circumstances it is an immense help to be pulling on ski. Tonight it is looking very thick. The sun can barely be distinguished, the temperature has risen, and there are serious indications of a blizzard. I trust they will not come to anything; there are practically no signs of heavy wind here, so that even if it blows a little we may be able to march. Meanwhile we are less than 40 miles from the Pole.

Again we noticed the cold; at lunch today (Obs: Lat 89°20'53" S) all our feet were cold, but this was mainly due to the bald state of our finnesko. I put some grease under the bare skin and found it made all the difference. Oates seems to be feeling the cold and fatigue more than the rest of us, but we are all very fit. It is a critical time, but we ought to pull through. The barometer has fallen very considerably and we cannot tell whether due to ascent of plateau or change of weather. Oh! for a few fine days! So close it seems and only the weather to balk us.

Monday, 15 January: Lunch camp, Height 9,950. Last depot. During the night the air cleared entirely and the sun shone in a perfectly clear sky. The light wind had dropped and the temperature fallen to -25°, minimum -27°. I guessed this meant a hard pull, and guessed right. The surface was terrible, but for 4¾ hours yielded 6 miles (geo.). We were all pretty well done at camping, and here we leave our last depot – only 4 days' food and a sundry or two. The load is now very light, but I fear that the friction will not be greatly reduced.

Night, 15 January: Height 9,920. T. -25°. The sledge came surprisingly lightly after lunch – something from loss of weight, something, I think, from stowage, and, most of all perhaps, as a result of tea. Anyhow, we made a capital afternoon march of 6·3 miles, bringing the total for the day to over 12 (12·3). The sastrugi again very confused, but mostly SE quadrant; the heaviest now almost East, so that the sledge continually bumps over ridges. The wind is from the WNW and chilly, but the weather remains fine and there are no sastrugi from that direction.

Camp 67. Lunch obs: Lat 89°26'57"; Lat dead reckoning, 89°33'15"S; Long 160°56'45"E; Var. 179° E.

It is wonderful to think that two long marches would land us at the Pole. We left our depot today with 9 days' provisions, so that it ought to be a certain thing now, and the only appalling possibility the sight of the Norwegian flag forestalling ours. Little Bowers continues his indefatigable efforts to get good sights, and it is wonderful how he works them up in his sleeping-bag in our congested tent. (Minimum for night -27·5°.) Only 27 miles from the Pole. We *ought* to do it now.

Tuesday, 16 January: Camp 68. Height 9,760, T. -23.5°. The worst has happened, or nearly the worst. We marched well in the morning and covered 7½ miles. Noon sight showed us in Lat. 89° 42' S, and we started off in high spirits in the afternoon, feeling that tomorrow would see us at our destination. About the second hour of the march Bowers's sharp eyes detected what he thought was a cairn; he was uneasy about it, but argued that it must be a sastrugus. Half an hour later he detected a black speck ahead. Soon we knew that this could not be a natural snow feature. We marched on, found that it was a black flag tied to a sledge bearer; near by the remains of a camp; sledge tracks and ski tracks going and coming and the clear trace of dogs' paws – many dogs. This told us the whole story. The Norwegians have forestalled us and are first at the Pole. It is a terrible disappointment, and I am very sorry for my loyal companions. Many thoughts come and much discussion have we had. Tomorrow we must march on to the Pole and then hasten home with all the speed we can compass. All the daydreams must go; it will be a wearisome return. Certainly we are descending in altitude – certainly also the Norwegians found an easy way up.

Wednesday 17 January: Camp 69. T. -22° at start. Night -21°. The Pole. Yes, but under very different circumstances from those expected. We have had a horrible day – add to our disappointment a head wind 4 to 5,* with a temperature -22°, and companions labouring on with cold feet and hands.

We started at 7.30, none of us having slept much after the shock of our discovery. We followed the Norwegian sledge tracks for some way; as far as we make out there are only two men. In about three miles we passed two small cairns. Then the weather overcast, and the tracks being increasingly drifted up and obviously going too far to the west, we decided to make straight for the Pole according to our calculations. At 12.30 Evans had such cold hands we camped for lunch – an excellent "weekend" one. We had marched 7.4 miles. Lat. sight gave 89° 53' 37". We started out and did 6½ miles due south. Tonight little Bowers is laying himself out to get sights in terrible difficult circumstances; the wind is blowing hard, T. -21°, and there is that curious damp, cold feeling in the air which chills one to the bone in no time. We have been descending again, I

---

* Half a gale. The velocity of wind is denoted by numbers (1–10).

think, but there looks to be a rise ahead; otherwise there is very little that is different from the awful monotony of past days. Great God! this is an awful place and terrible enough for us to have laboured to it without the reward of priority. Well, it is something to have got here, and the wind may be our friend tomorrow. We have had a fat Polar hoosh in spite of our chagrin, and feel comfortable inside – added a small stick of chocolate and the queer taste of a cigarette brought by Wilson. Now for the run home and a desperate struggle. I wonder if we can do it.

Thursday morning, 18 January: Decided after summing up all observations that we were 3.5 miles away from the Pole – one mile beyond it and 3 to the right. More or less in this direction Bowers saw a cairn or tent.

We have just arrived at this tent, 2 miles from our camp, therefore about 1½ miles from the Pole. In the tent we find a record of five Norwegians having been here, as follows:

> Roald Amundsen
> Olav Olavson Bjaaland
> Hilmer Hanssen
> Sverre H. Hassel
> Oscar Wisting.
> 16 Dec. 1911.

The tent is fine – a small compact affair supported by a single bamboo. A note from Amundsen, which I keep, asks me to forward a letter to King Haakon!

The following articles have been left in the tent: 3 half bags of reindeer containing a miscellaneous assortment of mitts and sleeping socks, very various in description, a sextant, a Norwegian artificial horizon and a hypsometer without boiling-point thermometers, a sextant and hypsometer of English make.

Left a note to say I had visited the tent with companions; Bowers photographing and Wilson sketching. Since lunch we have marched 6.2 miles SSE by compass (i.e. northwards).

Sights at lunch gave us ½ to ¾ of a mile from the Pole, so we call it the Pole Camp. (Temp. Lunch -21°.) We built a cairn, put up our poor slighted Union Jack, and photographed ourselves – mighty cold work all of it – less than ½ a mile south we saw stuck up an old underrunner of a sledge. This we commandeered as a yard for a floorcloth sail. I imagine it was intended to mark the exact spot of the Pole as near as the Norwegians could fix it. (Height 9,500.) A note attached talked of the tent as being 2 miles from the Pole. Wilson keeps the note. There is no doubt that our predecessors have made thoroughly sure of their mark and fully carried out their programme. I think the Pole is about 9,500 feet in height; this is remarkable, considering that in Lat. 88° we were about 10,500.

We carried the Union Jack about ¾ of a mile north with us and left it on a piece of stick as near as we could fix it. I fancy the Norwegians arrived at the pole on the 15th Dec. and left on the 17th, ahead of a date quoted by me in London as ideal, viz. 22 Dec. It looks as though the Norwegian party expected colder weather on the summit than they got; it could scarcely be otherwise from Shackleton's account. Well, we have turned our back now on the goal of our ambition and must face our 800 miles of solid dragging – and goodbye to most of the daydreams!

Friday, 19 January: Lunch 8.1, T. -22.6 deg. Early in the march we picked up a Norwegian cairn and our outward tracks. We followed these to the ominous black flag which had first apprised us of our predecessors' success. We have picked this flag up, using the staff for our sail, and are now camped about 1½ miles further back on our tracks. So that is the last of the Norwegians for the present. The surface undulates considerably about this latitude; it was more evident today than when we were outward bound.

Night camp R. 2. Height 9,700. T. -18.5 deg., Minimum -25.6 deg. Came along well this afternoon for three hours, then a rather dreary finish for the last 1½. Weather very curious, snow clouds, looking very dense and spoiling the light, pass overhead

from the S, dropping very minute crystals; between showers the
sun shows and the wind goes to the SW. The fine crystals absolutely spoil the surface; we had heavy dragging during the last
hour in spite of the light load and a full sail. Our old tracks are
drifted up, deep in places, and toothed sastrugi have formed
over them. It looks as though this sandy snow was drifted about
like sand from place to place. How account for the present state
of our three day old tracks and the month old ones of the
Norwegians?

It is warmer and pleasanter marching with the wind, but I'm
not sure we don't feel the cold more when we stop and camp
than we did on the outward march. We pick up our cairns easily,
and ought to do so right through, I think; but, of course, one will
be a bit anxious till the Three Degree Depot is reached. I'm
afraid the return journey is going to be dreadfully tiring and
monotonous.

Saturday, 20 January: Lunch camp, 9,810. We have come along
very well this morning, although the surface was terrible bad –
9.3 miles in 5 hours 20 m. This has brought us to our Southern
Depot, and we pick up 4 days' food. We carry on 7 days from
tonight with 55 miles to go to the Half Degree Depot made on
10 January. The same sort of weather and a little more wind, sail
drawing well.

Night camp R. 3. 9,860. Temp. -18 deg. It was blowing quite
hard and drifting when we started our afternoon march. At
first with full sail we went along at a great rate; then we got on
to an extraordinary surface, the drifting snow lying in heaps;
it clung to the ski, which could only be pushed forward with
an effort. The pulling was really awful, but we went steadily
on and camped a short way beyond our cairn of the 14th. I'm
afraid we are in for a bad pull again tomorrow, luckily the
wind holds. I shall be very glad when Bowers gets his ski; I'm
afraid he must find these long marches very trying with short
legs, but he is an undefeated little sportsman. I think Oates is
feeling the cold and fatigue more than most of us. It is blowing pretty hard tonight, but with a good march we have earned
one good hoosh and are very comfortable in the tent. It is

everything now to keep up a good marching pace; I trust we shall be able to do so and catch the ship. Total march, 18½ miles.

Sunday, January 21: R. 4. 10,010. Temp, blizzard, -18 deg. to -11 deg., to -14 deg. now. Awoke to a stiff blizzard; air very thick with snow and sun very dim. We decided not to march owing to likelihood of losing track; expected at least a day of lay up, but whilst at lunch there was a sudden clearance and wind dropped to light breeze. We got ready to march, but gear was so iced up we did not get away till 3.45. Marched till 7.40 – a terribly weary four-hour drag; even with helping wind we only did 5½ miles (6¼ statute). The surface bad, horribly bad on new sastrugi, and decidedly rising again in elevation.

We are going to have a pretty hard time this next 100 miles I expect. If it was difficult to drag downhill over this belt, it will probably be a good deal more difficult to drag up. Luckily the cracks are fairly distinct, though we only see our cairns when less than a mile away; 45 miles to the next depot and 6 days' food in hand – then pick up 7 days' food (T. -22 deg.) and 90 miles to go to the "Three Degree" Depot. Once there we ought to be safe, but we ought to have a day or two in hand on arrival and may have difficulty with following the tracks. However, if we can get a rating sight for our watches tomorrow we shall be independent of the tracks at a pinch.

Monday, 22 January: 10,000. Temp. -21 deg. I think about the most tiring march we have had; solid pulling the whole way, in spite of the light sledge and some little helping wind at first. Then in the last part of the afternoon the sun came out, and almost immediately we had the whole surface covered with soft snow.

We got away sharp at 8 and marched a solid 9 hours, and thus we have covered 14.5 miles (geo.) but, by Jove! it has been a grind. We are just about on the 89th parallel. Tonight Bowers got a rating sight. I'm afraid we have passed out of the wind area. We are within 2½ miles of the 64th camp cairn, 30 miles from our depot, and with 5 days' food in hand. Ski boots are beginning to show signs of wear; I trust we shall have no giving out of ski or boots, since there are yet so many miles to go. I thought we were climbing today, but the barometer gives no change.

Tuesday, 23 January: Lowest Minimum last night -30 deg., Temp, at start -28 deg. Lunch height 10,100. Temp, with wind 6 to 7, -19 deg. Little wind and heavy marching at start. Then wind increased and we did 8.7 miles by lunch, when it was practically blowing a blizzard. The old tracks show so remarkably well that we can follow them without much difficulty – a great piece of luck.

In the afternoon we had to reorganize. Could carry a whole sail. Bowers hung on to the sledge, Evans and Oates had to lengthen out. We came along at a great rate and should have got within an easy march of our depot had not Wilson suddenly discovered that Evans's nose was frost-bitten – it was white and hard. We thought it best to camp at 6.45. Got the tent up with some difficulty, and now pretty cosy after good hoosh.

There is no doubt Evans is a good deal run down – his fingers are badly blistered and his nose is rather seriously congested with frequent frost-bites. He is very much annoyed with himself, which is not a good sign. I think Wilson, Bowers and I are as fit as possible under the circumstances. Oates gets cold feet. One way and another, I shall be glad to get off the summit! We are only about 13 miles from our "Degree and half" Depot and should get there tomorrow. The weather seems to be breaking up. Pray God we have something of a track to follow to the Three Degree Depot – once we pick that up we ought to be right.

Wednesday, 24 January: Lunch Temp. -8 deg. Things beginning to look a little serious. A strong wind at the start has developed into a full blizzard at lunch, and we have had to get into our sleeping-bags. It was a bad march, but we covered 7 miles. At first Evans, and then Wilson went ahead to scout for tracks. Bowers guided the sledge alone for the first hour, then both Oates and he remained alongside it; they had a fearful time trying to make the pace between the soft patches. At 12.30 the sun coming ahead made it impossible to see the tracks further, and we had to stop.

By this time the gale was at its height and we had the dickens of a time getting up the tent, cold fingers all round. We are only 7 miles from our depot, but I made sure we should be there tonight. This is the second full gale since we left the Pole. I don't like the look of it. Is the weather breaking up? If so, God help us, with the tremendous summit journey and scant food. Wilson and Bowers are my standby. I don't like the easy way in which Oates and Evans get frost-bitten.

Thursday, 25 January: Temp. Lunch -11 deg., Temp. night -16 deg. Thank God we found our Half Degree Depot. After lying in our bags yesterday afternoon and all night, we debated breakfast; decided to have it later and go without lunch. At the time the gale seemed as bad as ever, but during breakfast the sun showed and there was light enough to see the old track. It was a long and terribly cold job digging out our sledge and breaking camp, but we got through and on the march without sail, all pulling. This was about 11, and at about 2.30, to our joy, we saw the red depot flag. We had lunch and left with 9½ days' provisions, still following the track – marched till 8 and covered over 5 miles, over 12 in the day. Only 89 miles (geogr.) to the next depot, but it's time we cleared off this plateau. We are not without ailments: Oates suffers from a very cold foot; Evans's fingers and nose are in a bad state, and tonight Wilson is suffering tortures from his eyes. Bowers and I are the only members of the party without troubles just at present. The weather still looks unsettled, and I fear a succession of blizzards at this time of year; the wind is strong from the south, and this afternoon has been very helpful with the full sail. Needless to say I shall sleep much better with our provision bag full again. The only real anxiety now is the finding of the Three Degree Depot. The tracks seem as good as ever so far, sometimes for 30 or 40 yards we lose them under drifts, but then they reappear quite clearly raised above the surface. If the light is good there is not the least difficulty in following. Blizzards are our bugbear, not only stopping our marches, but the cold damp air takes it out of us. Bowers got another rating sight tonight – it was wonderful how he managed to observe in such a horribly cold wind. He has been on ski today whilst Wilson walked by the sledge or pulled ahead of it.

Friday, 26 January: Temp. -17 deg. Height 9,700, must be high barometer. Started late, 8.50 – for no reason, as I called the hands rather early. We must have fewer delays. There was a good stiff breeze and plenty of drift, but the tracks held. To our old blizzard camp of the 7th we got on well, 7 miles. But beyond the camp we found the tracks completely wiped out. We searched for some time, then marched on a short way and lunched, the weather gradually clearing, though the wind holding. Knowing there were two cairns at four mile intervals, we had little anxiety till we picked up the first far on our right, then steering right by a stroke of fortune, and Bowers's sharp eyes caught a glimpse of the second far on the left. Evidently we made a bad course outward at this part. There is not a sign of our tracks between these cairns, but the last, marking our night camp of the 6th, No. 59, is in the belt of hard sastrugi, and I was comforted to see signs of the track reappearing as we camped. I hope to goodness we can follow it tomorrow. We marched 16 miles (geo.) today, but made good only 15.4.

Saturday, 27 January: R. 10. Temp. -16 deg. (lunch), -14.3 deg. (evening). Minimum – 19 deg. Height 9,900. Barometer low? Called the hands half an hour late, but we got away in good time. The forenoon march was over the belt of storm-tossed sastrugi; it looked like a rough sea. Wilson and I pulled in front on ski, the remainder on foot. It was very tricky work following the track, which pretty constantly disappeared, and in fact only showed itself by faint signs anywhere – a foot or two of raised sledge-track, a dozen yards of the trail of the sledge-meter wheel, or a spatter of hard snow-flicks where feet had trodden. Sometimes none of these were distinct, but one got an impression of lines which guided. The trouble was that on the outward track one had to shape course constantly to avoid the heaviest mounds, and consequently there were many zig-zags. We lost a good deal over a mile by these halts, in which we unharnessed and went on the search for signs. However, by hook or crook, we managed to stick on the old track. Came on the cairn quite suddenly, marched past it, and camped for lunch at 7 miles. In the afternoon the sastrugi gradually diminished in size and now we are on fairly level ground today, the obstruction practically at an end, and, to our joy, the tracks showing up much plainer again. For the last two hours we had no difficulty at all in following them. There has been a nice helpful southerly breeze all day, a clear sky and comparatively warm temperature. The air is dry again, so that tents and equipment are gradually losing their icy condition imposed by the blizzard conditions of the past week.

Our sleeping-bags are slowly but surely getting wetter and I'm afraid it will take a lot of this weather to put them right. However, we all sleep well enough in them, the hours allowed being now on the short side. We are slowly getting more hungry, and it would be an advantage to have a little more food, especially for lunch. If we get to the next depot in a few marches (it is now less than 60 miles and we have a full week's food) we ought to be able to open out a little, but we can't look for a real feed till we get to the pony food depot. A long way to go, and, by Jove, this is tremendous labour.

Sunday, 28 January: Lunch, -20 deg. Height, night, 10,130. R. 11. Supper Temp. -18 deg. Little wind and heavy going in forenoon. We just ran out 8 miles in 5 hours and added another 8 in 3 hours 40 mins. in the afternoon with a good wind and better surface. It is very difficult to say if we are going up or down hill; the barometer is quite different from outward readings. We are 43 miles from the depot, with six days' food in hand. We are camped opposite our lunch cairn of the 4th, only half a day's march from the point at which the last supporting party left us.

Three articles were dropped on our outward march – Oates's pipe, Bowers's fur mitts, and Evans's night boots. We picked up the boots and mitts on the track, and tonight we found the pipe lying placidly in sight on the snow. The sledge tracks were very easy to follow today; they are becoming more and more raised, giving a good line shadow often visible half a mile ahead. If this goes on and the weather holds we shall get our depot without trouble. I shall indeed be glad to get it on the sledge. We are getting more hungry, there is no doubt. The lunch meal is beginning to seem inadequate. We are pretty thin, especially Evans, but none of us are feeling worked out. I doubt if we could drag heavy loads, but we can keep going well with our light one. We talk of food a good deal more, and shall be glad to open out on it.

Monday, 29 January: R. 12. Lunch Temp. -23 deg. Supper Temp. -25 deg. Height 10,000. Excellent march of 19½ miles, 10.5 before lunch. Wind helping greatly, considerable drift; tracks for the most part very plain. Some time before lunch we picked up the return track of the supporting party, so that there are now three distinct sledge impressions. We are only 24 miles from our depot – an easy day and a half. Given a fine day tomorrow we ought to get it without difficulty. The wind and sastrugi are SSE and SE. If the weather holds we ought to do the rest of the inland ice journey in little over a week. The surface is very much altered since we passed out. The loose snow has been swept into heaps, hard and wind-tossed. The rest has a glazed appearance, the loose drifting snow no doubt acting on it, polishing it like a sand blast. The sledge with our good wind behind runs splendidly on it; it is all soft and sandy beneath the glaze. We are certainly getting hungrier every day. The day after tomorrow we should be able to increase allowances. It is monotonous work, but, thank God, the miles are coming fast at last. We ought not to be delayed much now with the down-grade in front of us.

Tuesday, 30 January: R. 13. 9,860. Lunch Temp. -25 deg. Supper Temp. -24.5 deg. Thank the Lord, another fine march – 19 miles. We have passed the last cairn before the depot, the track is clear ahead, the weather fair, the wind helpful, the gradient down – with any luck we should pick up our depot in the middle of the morning march. This is the bright side; the reverse of the medal is serious. Wilson has strained a tendon in his leg; it has given pain all day and is swollen tonight. Of course, he is full of pluck over it, but I don't like the idea of such an accident here. To add to the trouble Evans has dislodged two fingernails tonight; his hands are really bad, and to my surprise he shows signs of losing heart over it. He hasn't been cheerful since the accident. The wind shifted from SE to S and back again all day, but luckily it keeps strong. We can get along with bad fingers, but it (will be) a mighty serious thing if Wilson's leg doesn't improve.

Wednesday, 31 January: 9,800. Lunch Temp. -20 deg. Supper Temp. -20 deg. The day opened fine with a fair breeze; we marched on the depot, [39] picked it up, and lunched an hour later. In the afternoon the surface became fearfully bad, the wind dropped to light southerly air. Ill luck that this should happen just when we have only four men to pull. Wilson rested his leg as much as possible by walking quietly beside the sledge; the result has been good, and tonight there is much less inflammation. I hope he will be all right again soon, but it is trying to have an injured limb in the party. I see we had a very heavy surface here on our outward march. There is no doubt we are travelling over undulations, but the inequality of level does not make a great difference to our pace; it is the sandy crystals that hold us up. There has been very great alteration of the surface since we were last here – the sledge tracks stand high. This afternoon we picked up Bowers's ski – the last thing we have to find on the summit, thank Heaven! Now we have only to go north and so shall welcome strong winds.

Thursday, 1 February: R. 15. 9,778. Lunch Temp. -20 deg. Supper Temp. -19.8 deg. Heavy collar work most of the day. Wind light. Did 8 miles, 4¾ hours. Started well in the afternoon and came down a steep slope in quick time; then the surface turned real bad – sandy drifts – very heavy pulling. Working on past 8 p.m. we just fetched a lunch cairn of 29 December, when we were only a week out from the depot. It ought to be easy to get in with a margin, having 8 days' food in hand (full feeding). We have opened out on the ¹/₇th increase and it makes a lot of difference. Wilson's leg much better. Evans's fingers now very bad, two nails coming off, blisters burst.

Friday, 2 February: 9,340. R. 16. Temp. Lunch -19 deg. Supper -17 deg. We started well on a strong southerly wind. Soon got to a steep grade, when the sledge overran and upset us one

after another. We got off our ski, and pulling on foot reeled off
9 miles by lunch at 1.30. Started in the afternoon on foot,
going very strong. We noticed a curious circumstance towards
the end of the forenoon. The tracks were drifted over, but the
drifts formed a sort of causeway along which we pulled. In the
afternoon we soon came to a steep slope – the same on which
we exchanged sledges on 28 December. All went well till, in
trying to keep the track at the same time as my feet, on a very
slippery surface, I came an awful "purler" on my shoulder. It
is horribly sore tonight and another sick person added to our
tent – three out of five injured, and the most troublesome
surfaces to come. We shall be lucky if we get through without
serious injury. Wilson's leg is better, but might easily get bad
again, and Evans's fingers.

At the bottom of the slope this afternoon we came on a
confused sea of sastrugi. We lost the track. Later, on soft snow,
we picked up E. Evans's return track, which we are now following. We have managed to get off 17 miles. The extra food is
certainly helping us, but we are getting pretty hungry. The
weather is already a trifle warmer and the altitude lower, and
only 80 miles or so to Mount Darwin. It is time we were off the
summit – Pray God another four days will see us pretty well clear
of it. Our bags are getting very wet and we ought to have more
sleep.

Saturday, 3 February: R. 17. Temp. Lunch -20 deg.; Supper -20
deg. Height 9,040 feet. Started pretty well on foot; came to
steep slope with crevasses (few). I went on ski to avoid another
fall, and we took the slope gently with our sail, constantly
losing the track, but picked up a much weathered cairn on our
right. Vexatious delays, searching for tracks, &c., reduced
morning march to 8.1 miles. Afternoon, came along a little
better, but again lost tracks on hard slope. Tonight we are near
camp of 26 December, but cannot see cairn. Have decided it is
waste of time looking for tracks and cairn, and shall push on
due north as fast as we can.

The surface is greatly changed since we passed outward, in
most places polished smooth, but with heaps of new toothed
sastrugi which are disagreeable obstacles. Evans's fingers are

going on as well as can be expected, but it will be long before he will be able to help properly with the work. Wilson's leg much better, and my shoulder also, though it gives bad twinges. The extra food is doing us all good, but we ought to have more sleep. Very few more days on the plateau I hope.

Sunday, 4 February: R. 18. 8,620 feet. Temp. Lunch -22 deg.; Supper -23 deg. Pulled on foot in the morning over good hard surface and covered 9.7 miles. Just before lunch unexpectedly fell into crevasses, Evans and I together – a second fall for Evans, and I camped. After lunch saw disturbance ahead, and what I took for disturbance (land) to the right. We went on ski over hard shiny descending surface. Did very well, especially towards end of march, covering in all 18.1. We have come down some hundreds of feet. Halfway in the march the land showed up splendidly, and I decided to make straight for Mt Darwin, which we are rounding. Every sign points to getting away off this platcau. The temperature is 20 deg. lower than when we were here before; the party is not improving in condition, especially Evans, who is becoming rather dull and incapable. Thank the Lord we have good food at each meal, but we get hungrier in spite of it. Bowers is splendid, full of energy and bustle all the time. I hope we are not going to have trouble with ice-falls.

Monday, 5 February: R. 19. Lunch, 8,320 ft, Temp. -17 deg.; Supper, 8,120 ft, Temp -17.2 deg. A good forenoon, few crevasses; we covered 10.2 miles. In the afternoon we soon got into difficulties. We saw the land very clearly, but the difficulty is to get at it. An hour after starting we came on huge pressures and great street crevasses partly open. We had to steer more and more to the west, so that our course was very erratic. Late in the march we turned more to the north and again encountered open crevasses across our track. It is very difficult manoeuvring amongst these and I should not like to do it without ski.

We are camped in a very disturbed region, but the wind has fallen very light here, and our camp is comfortable for the first time for many weeks. We may be anything from 25 to 30 miles from our depot, but I wish to goodness we could see a way through the disturbances ahead. Our faces are much cut up by all the winds we have had, mine least of all; the others tell me they feel their noses more going with than against the wind. Evans's nose is almost as bad as his fingers. He is a good deal crocked up.

Tuesday, 6 February: Lunch 7,900; Supper 7,210. Temp. -15 deg. We've had a horrid day and not covered good mileage. On turning out found sky overcast; a beastly position amidst crevasses. Luckily it cleared just before we started. We went straight for Mt Darwin, but in half an hour found ourselves amongst huge open chasms, unbridged, but not very deep, I think. We turned to the north between two, but to our chagrin they converged into chaotic disturbance. We had to retrace our steps for a mile or so, then struck to the west and got on to a confused sea of sastrugi, pulling very hard; we put up the sail, Evans's nose suffered, Wilson very cold, everything horrid. Camped for lunch in the sastrugi; the only comfort, things looked clearer to the west and we were obviously going downhill. In the afternoon we struggled on, got out of sastrugi and turned over on glazed surface, crossing many crevasses – very easy work on ski. Towards the end of the march we realized the certainty of maintaining a more or less straight course to the depot, and estimate distance 10 to 15 miles.

Food is low and weather uncertain, so that many hours of the day were anxious; but this evening, though we are not as far advanced as I expected, the outlook is much more promising. Evans is the chief anxiety now; his cuts and wounds suppurate, his nose looks very bad, and altogether he shows considerable signs of being played out. Things may mend for him on the glacier, and his wounds get some respite under warmer conditions. I am indeed glad to think we shall so soon have done with plateau conditions. It took us 27 days to reach the Pole and 21 days back – in all 48 days – nearly 7 weeks in low temperature with almost incessant wind.

Sunday, 11 February: R. 25. Lunch Temp. +6.5°; Supper + 3.5°. The worst day we have had during the trip and greatly owing to our own fault. We started on a wretched surface with light SW wind, sail set, and pulling on ski – in a horrible light, which made everything look fantastic. As we went on the light got worse, and suddenly we found ourselves in pressure. Then came the fatal decision to steer east. We went on for 6 hours, hoping to do a good distance, which in fact I suppose we did, but for the last hour or two we pressed on into a regular trap. Getting on to a good surface we did not reduce our lunch meal, and thought all going well, but half an hour after lunch we got into the worst ice mess I have ever been in. For three hours we plunged on on ski, first thinking we were too much to the right, then too much to the left; meanwhile the disturbance got worse and my spirits received a very rude shock. There were times when it seemed almost impossible to find a way out of the awful turmoil in which we found ourselves. At length, arguing that there must be a way on our left, we plunged in that direction. It got worse, harder, more icy and crevassed. We could not manage our ski and pulled on foot, falling into crevasses every minute – most luckily with no bad accident. At length we saw a smoother slope towards the land, pushed for it, but knew it was a woefully long way from us. The turmoil changed in character, irregular crevassed surface giving way to huge chasms, closely packed and most difficult to cross. It was very heavy work, but we had grown desperate. We won through at 10 p.m. and I write after 12 hours on the march. I *think* we are on or about the right track now, but we are still a good number of miles from the depot, so we reduced rations tonight. We had three pemmican meals left and decided to make them into four. Tomorrow's lunch must serve for two if we do not make big progress. It was a test of our endurance on the march and our fitness with small supper. We have come through well. A good wind has come down the glacier which is clearing the sky and surface. Pray God the wind holds tomorrow.

Wednesday, 14 February: There is no getting away from the fact that we are not pulling strong: probably none of us. Wilson's leg still troubles him and he doesn't like to trust himself on ski; but the worst case is Evans, who is giving us serious anxiety. This morning he suddenly disclosed a huge blister on his foot.

It delayed us on the march, when he had to have his crampon readjusted. Sometimes I fear he is going from bad to worse, but I trust he will pick up again when we come to steady work on ski like this afternoon. He is hungry and so is Wilson. We can't risk opening out our food again, and as cook at present I am serving something under full allowance. We are inclined to get slack and slow with our camping arrangements, and small delays increase. I have talked of the matter tonight and hope for improvement. We cannot do distance without the hours. The next depot some 30 miles away and nearly 3 days' food in hand.

Saturday, 17 February: A very terrible day. Evans looked a little better after a good sleep, and declared, as he always did, that he was quite well. He started in his place on the traces, but half an hour later worked his ski shoes adrift, and had to leave the sledge. The surface was awful, the soft recently fallen snow clogging the ski and runners at every step, the sledge groaning, the sky overcast, and the land hazy. We stopped after about one hour, and Evans came up again, but very slowly. Half an hour later he dropped out again on the same plea. He asked Bowers to lend him a piece of string. I cautioned him to come on as quickly as he could, and he answered cheerfully as I thought. We had to push on, and the remainder of us were forced to pull very hard, sweating heavily. Abreast the Monument Rock we stopped, and seeing Evans a long way astern, I camped for lunch. There was no alarm at first, and we prepared tea and our own meal, consuming the latter. After lunch, and Evans still not appearing, we looked out, to see him still afar off. By this time we were alarmed, and all four started back on ski. I was first to reach the poor man and shocked at his appearance; he was on his knees with clothing disarranged, hands uncovered and frost-bitten, and a wild look in his eyes. Asked what was the matter, he replied with a slow speech that he didn't know, but thought he must have fainted. We got him on his feet, but after two or three steps he sank down again. He showed every sign of complete collapse. Wilson, Bowers, and I went back for the sledge, whilst Oates remained with him. When we returned he was practically

unconscious, and when we got him into the tent quite coma-
tose. He died quietly at 12.30 a.m. On discussing the
symptoms we think he began to get weaker just before we
reached the Pole, and that his downward path was accelerated
first by the shock of his frost-bitten fingers, and later by falls
during rough travelling on the glacier, further by his loss of all
confidence in himself. Wilson thinks it certain he must have
injured his brain by a fall. It is a terrible thing to lose a
companion in this way, but calm reflection shows that there
could not have been a better ending to the terrible anxieties of
the past week. Discussion of the situation at lunch yesterday
shows us what a desperate pass we were in with a sick man on
our hands so far from home . . .

Friday 2, March: Lunch. Misfortunes rarely come singly. We
marched to the [Middle Barrier] depot fairly easily yesterday
afternoon, and since that have suffered three distinct blows
which have placed us in a bad position. First we found a
shortage of oil; with most rigid economy it can scarce carry us
to the next depot on this surface [71 miles away]. Second,
Titus Oates disclosed his feet, the toes showing very bad
indeed, evidently bitten by the late temperatures. The third
blow came in the night, when the wind, which we had hailed
with some joy, brought dark overcast weather. It fell below
-40° in the night, and this morning it took 1½ hours to get
our foot-gear on, but we got away before eight. We lost cairn
and tracks together and made as steady as we could N by W,
but have seen nothing. Worse was to come – the surface is
simply awful. In spite of strong wind and full sail we have
only done 5½ miles. We are in a *very* queer street, since there
is no doubt we cannot do the extra marches and feel the cold
horribly.

Monday, 5 March: Lunch. Regret to say going from bad to
worse. We got a slant of wind yesterday afternoon, and going on
5 hours we converted our wretched morning run of 3½ miles
into something over 9. We went to bed on a cup of cocoa and
pemmican solid with the chill off. (R. 47.) The result is telling
on all, but mainly on Oates, whose feet are in a wretched

condition. One swelled up tremendously last night and he is very lame this morning. We started march on tea and pemmican as last night – we pretend to prefer the pemmican this way. Marched for 5 hours this morning over a slightly better surface covered with high moundy sastrugi. Sledge capsized twice; we pulled on foot, covering about 5½ miles. We are two pony marches and 4 miles about from our depot. Our fuel dreadfully low and the poor Soldier nearly done. It is pathetic enough because we can do nothing for him; more hot food might do a little, but only a little, I fear. We none of us expected these terribly low temperatures, and of the rest of us Wilson is feeling them most; mainly, I fear, from his self-sacrificing devotion in doctoring Oates's feet. We cannot help each other, each has enough to do to take care of himself. We get cold on the march when the trudging is heavy, and the wind pierces our worn garments. The others, all of them, are unendingly cheerful when in the tent. We mean to see the game through with a proper spirit, but it's tough work to be pulling harder than we ever pulled in our lives for long hours, and to feel that the progress is so slow. One can only say "God help us!" and plod on our weary way, cold and very miserable, though outwardly cheerful. We talk of all sorts of subjects in the tent, not much of food now, since we decided to take the risk of running a full ration. We simply couldn't go hungry at this time.

Saturday, 10 March: Things steadily downhill. Oates's foot worse. He has rare pluck and must know that he can never get through. He asked Wilson if he had a chance this morning, and of course Bill had to say he didn't know. In point of fact he has none. Apart from him, if he went under now, I doubt whether we could get through. With great care we might have a dog's chance, but no more. The weather conditions are awful, and our gear gets steadily more icy and difficult to manage. At the same time, of course, poor Titus is the greatest handicap. He keeps us waiting in the morning until we have partly lost the warming effect of our good breakfast, when the only wise policy is to be up and away at once; again at lunch. Poor chap! it is too pathetic to watch him; one cannot but try to cheer him up.

Yesterday we marched up the depot, Mt Hooper. Cold comfort. Shortage on our allowance all round . . .

Sunday, 11 March: Titus Oates is very near the end, one feels. What we or he will do, God only knows. We discussed the matter after breakfast; he is a brave fine fellow and understands the situation, but he practically asked for advice. Nothing could be said but to urge him to march as long as he could. One satisfactory result to the discussion; I practically ordered Wilson to hand over the means of ending our troubles to us, so that any one of us may know how to do so. Wilson had no choice between doing so and our ransacking the medicine case. We have 30 opium tabloids apiece and he is left with a tube of morphine. So far the tragical side of our story.

The sky was completely overcast when we started this morning. We could see nothing, lost the tracks, and doubtless have been swaying a good deal since − 3.1 miles for the forenoon − terribly heavy dragging − expected it. Know that 6 miles is about the limit of our endurance now, if we get no help from wind or surfaces. We have 7 days' food and should be about 55 miles from One Ton Camp tonight, 6 × 7 = 42, leaving us 13 miles short of our distance, even if things get no worse. Meanwhile the season rapidly advances . . .

Wednesday, 14 March: No doubt about the going downhill, but everything going wrong for us. Yesterday we woke to a strong northerly wind with temp. -37°. Couldn't face it, so remained in camp till 2, then did 5¼ miles. Wanted to march later, but party feeling the cold badly as the breeze (N) never took off entirely, and as the sun sank the temp. fell. Long time getting supper in dark.

This morning started with southerly breeze, set sail and passed another cairn at good speed; halfway, however, the wind shifted to W by S or WSW, blew through our wind clothes and into our mitts. Poor Wilson horribly cold, could [not] get off ski for some time. Bowers and I practically made camp, and when we got into the tent at last we were all deadly cold. Then temp. now midday down -13° and the wind strong. We *must* go on, but now the making of every camp must be more difficult and dangerous. It must be near the end, but a pretty merciful end.

Poor Oates got it again in the foot. I shudder to think what it will be like tomorrow. It is only with greatest pains rest of us keep off frost-bites. No idea there could be temperatures like this at this time of year with such winds. Truly awful outside the tent. Must fight it out to the last biscuit, but can't reduce rations.

Friday, 16 March or Saturday, 17: Lost track of dates, but think the last correct. Tragedy all along the line. At lunch, the day before yesterday, poor Titus Oates said he couldn't go on; he proposed we should leave him in his sleeping-bag. That we could not do, and we induced him to come on, on the afternoon march. In spite of its awful nature for him he struggled on and we made a few miles. At night he was worse and we knew the end had come.

Should this be found I want these facts recorded. Oates's last thoughts were of his mother, but immediately before he took pride in thinking that his regiment would be pleased with the bold way in which he met his death. We can testify to his bravery. He has borne intense suffering for weeks without complaint, and to the very last was able and willing to discuss outside subjects. He did not – would not – give up hope till the very end. He was a brave soul. This was the end. He slept through the night before last, hoping not to wake; but he woke in the morning – yesterday. It was blowing a blizzard. He said, "I am just going outside and may be some time." He went out into the blizzard and we have not seen him since.

I take this opportunity of saying that we have stuck to our sick companions to the last. In case of Edgar Evans, when absolutely out of food and he lay insensible, the safety of the remainder seemed to demand his abandonment, but Providence mercifully removed him at this critical moment. He died a natural death, and we did not leave him till two hours after his death. We knew that poor Oates was walking to his death, but though we tried to dissuade him, we knew it was the act of a brave man and an English gentleman. We all hope to meet the end with a similar spirit, and assuredly the end is not far.

I can only write at lunch and then only occasionally. The cold is intense, -40° at midday. My companions are unendingly cheerful, but we are all on the verge of serious frost-bites, and though we constantly talk of fetching through, I don't think any one of us believes it in his heart.

We are cold on the march now, and at all times except meals. Yesterday we had to lie up for a blizzard and today we move dreadfully slowly. We are at No. 14 pony camp, only two pony marches from One Ton Depot. We leave here our theodolite, a camera, and Oates's sleeping-bags. Diaries, etc., and geological specimens carried at Wilson's special request, will be found with us or on our sledge.

Sunday, 18 March: Today, lunch, we are 21 miles from the depot. Ill fortune presses, but better may come. We have had more wind and drift from ahead yesterday; had to stop marching; wind NW, force 4, temp. -35°. No human being could face it, and we are worn out *nearly*.

My right foot has gone, nearly all the toes – two days ago I was proud possessor of best feet. These are the steps of my downfall. Like an ass I mixed a small spoonful of curry powder with my melted pemmican – it gave me violent indigestion. I lay awake and in pain all night; woke and felt done on the march; foot went and I didn't know it. A very small measure of neglect and I have a foot which is not pleasant to contemplate. Bowers takes first place in condition, but there is not much to choose after all. The others are still confident of getting through – or pretend to be – I don't know! We have the last *half* fill of oil in our Primus and a very small quantity of spirit – this alone between us and thirst. The wind is fair for the moment, and that is perhaps a fact to help. The mileage would have seemed ridiculously small on our outward journey.

Monday, 19 March: Lunch. We camped with difficulty last night and were dreadfully cold till after our supper of cold pemmican and biscuit and a half a pannikin of cocoa cooked over the spirit. Then, contrary to expectation, we got warm and all slept well. Today we started in the usual dragging manner. Sledge dreadfully heavy. We are 15½ miles from the depot and ought to get there in three days. What progress! We have two days' food, but barely a

day's fuel. All our feet are getting bad – Wilson's best, my right foot
worse, left all right. There is no chance to nurse one's feet till we
can get hot food into us. Amputation is the least I can hope for
now, but will the trouble spread? That is the serious question. The
weather doesn't give us a chance – the wind from N to NW and
-40° temp today.

Wednesday, 21 March: Got within 11 miles of depot Monday
night; had to lie up all yesterday in severe blizzard. Today forlorn
hope, Wilson and Bowers going to depot for fuel.

22 and 23: Blizzard bad as ever – Wilson and Bowers unable to
start – tomorrow last chance – no fuel and only one or two
[rations] of food left – must be near the end. Have decided it
shall be natural – we shall march for the depot with or without
our effects and die in our tracks.

[Thursday], 29 March: Since the 21st we have had a continuous
gale from WSW and SW. We had fuel to make two cups of tea
apiece and bare food for two days on the 20th. Every day we
have been ready to start for our depot 11 *miles* away, but outside
the door of the tent it remains a scene of whirling drift. I do not
think we can hope for any better things now. We shall stick it out
to the end, but we are getting weaker, of course, and the end
cannot be far.

It seems a pity, but I do not think I can write more.

                                                        R. Scott.

Last entry.
For God's sake look after our people.

*The bodies of Scott and his companions were found on 12 November
1912. Among the search party was Lieutenant Atkinson:*

Eight months afterwards we found the tent. It was an object
partially snowed up and looking like a cairn. Before it were the
ski sticks and in front of them a bamboo which probably was the
mast of the sledge. The tent was practically on the line of cairns
which we had built in the previous season. It was within a

quarter of a mile of the remains of the cairn, which showed as a small hummock beneath the snow.

Inside the tent were the bodies of Captain Scott, Doctor Wilson, and Lieutenant Bowers. Wilson and Bowers were found in the attitude of sleep, their sleeping-bags closed over their heads as they would naturally close them.

Scott died later. He had thrown back the flaps of his sleeping-bag and opened his coat. The little wallet containing the three notebooks was under his shoulders, and his arm was flung across Wilson. They had pitched their tent well, and it had withstood all the blizzards of an exceptionally hard winter. Each man of the Expedition recognized the bodies. From Captain Scott's diary* I found his reasons for this disaster. When the men had been assembled I read to them these reasons, the place of death of Petty Officer Evans, and the story of Captain Oates's heroic end.

We recovered all their gear and dug out the sledge with their belongings on it. Amongst these were 35 lbs of very important geological specimens which had been collected on the moraines of the Beardmore Glacier; at Doctor Wilson's request they had stuck to these up to the very end, even when disaster stared them in the face and they knew that the specimens were so much weight added to what they had to pull.

When everything had been gathered up, we covered them with the outer tent and read the Burial Service. From this time until well into the next day we started to build a mighty cairn above them. This cairn was finished the next morning, and upon it a rough cross was placed, made from the greater portion of two skis, and on either side were up-ended two sledges, and they were fixed firmly in the snow, to be an added mark. Between the eastern sledge and the cairn a bamboo was placed, containing a metal cylinder, and in this the following record was left:

12 November 1912, lat. 79 degrees, 50 mins. South. This cross and cairn are erected over the bodies of Captain Scott, C.V.O., R.N., Doctor E. A. Wilson, M.B., B. C. Cantab., and

---

* Atkinson found, as well as Scott's diary, his farewell letters. See Appendix I

Lieutenant H. R. Bowers, Royal Indian Marine – a slight token to perpetuate their successful and gallant attempt to reach the Pole. This they did on 17 January 1912, after the Norwegian Expedition had already done so. Inclement weather with lack of fuel as the cause of their death. Also to commemorate their two gallant comrades, Captain L. E. G. Oates of the Inniskilling Dragoons, who walked to his death in a blizzard to save his comrades about eighteen miles south of this position; also of Seaman Edgar Evans, who died at the foot of the Beardmore Glacier. "The Lord gave and the Lord taketh away; blessed be the name of the Lord."

This was signed by all the members of the party. I decided then to march twenty miles south with the whole of the Expedition and try to find the body of Captain Oates.

For half that day we proceeded south, as far as possible along the line of the previous season's march. On one of the old pony walls, which was simply marked by a ridge of the surface of the snow, we found Oates's sleeping-bag, which they had brought along with them after he had left.

The next day we proceeded thirteen more miles south, hoping and searching to find his body. When we arrived at the place where he had left them, we saw that there was no chance of doing so. The kindly snow had covered his body, giving him a fitting burial. Here, again, as near to the site of the death as we could judge, we built another cairn to his memory, and placed thereon a small cross and the following record:

Hereabouts died a very gallant gentleman, Captain L. E. G. Oates of the Inniskilling Dragoons. In March 1912, returning from the Pole, he walked willingly to his death in a blizzard, to try and save his comrades, beset by hardships. This note is left by the Relief Expedition of 1912.

It was signed by Cherry-Garrard and myself.

On the second day we came again to the resting-place of the three and bade them a final farewell. There alone in their greatness they will lie without change or bodily decay, with the most fitting tomb in the world above them.

Atkinson, Cherry-Garrard and the search party then turned away, but the gaze of the world has found it hard to leave the tragic scenes of Scott's last journey. Some see the responsible frailties of Scott's leadership, some seek the epitome of human bravery.

Both, perhaps, lie there in the snow and ice, eleven miles from One Ton Depot.

Last Man Walking

Douglas Mawson

A British-Australian geologist, Mawson was introduced to Antarctica by Shackleton's "Farthest South" expedition of 1907–9, during which he co-discovered the South Magnetic Pole. Two years later, Mawson was appointed to the great white road again, this time as leader of the Australasian Antarctic Expedition. Mawson entitled his memoirs of the expedition Home of the Blizzard *on account of the 300-kilometre-an-hour winds which blew in the base camp region. In November 1912 Mawson, accompanied by Dr Xavier Mertz, a Swiss mountaineer, and Lieutenant B. E. S. Ninnis set out to explore George V Land.*

December 2, 1912. When next I looked back, it was in response to the anxious gaze of Mertz who had turned round and halted in his tracks. Behind me nothing met the eye except my own sledge tracks running back in the distance. Where were Ninnis and his sledge?

I hastened back along the trail thinking that a rise in the ground obscured the view. There was no such good fortune, however, for I came to a gaping hole in the surface about eleven feet wide. The lid of the crevasse that had caused me so little thought had broken in; two sledge tracks led up to it on the far side – only one continued beyond.

Frantically waving to Mertz to bring up my sledge, upon which there was some alpine rope, I leaned over and shouted into the dark depths below. No sound came back but the moaning of a dog, caught on a shelf just visible 150 feet below. The poor creature appeared to have a broken back, for it was attempting to sit up with the front part of its body, while the hinder portion lay limp. Another dog lay motionless by its side. Close by was what appeared in the gloom to be the remains of the tent and a canvas foodtank containing a fortnight's supply.

We broke back the edge of the hard snow lid and, secured by a rope, took turns leaning over, calling into the darkness in the hope that our companion might be still alive. For three hours we called unceasingly but no answering sound came back. The dog had ceased to moan and lay without a movement. A chill draught rose out of the abyss. We felt that there was no hope.

It was difficult to realize that Ninnis, who was a young giant in build, so jovial and so real but a few minutes before, should thus have vanished without even a sound. It seemed so incredible that we half expected, on turning round, to find him standing there.

Why had the first sledge escaped? It seemed that I had been fortunate, as my sledge had crossed diagonally, with a greater chance of breaking the lid. The sledges were within thirty pounds of the same weight. The explanation appeared to be that Ninnis had walked by the side of his sledge, whereas I had crossed it sitting on the sledge. The whole weight of a man's body bearing on his foot is a formidable load, and no doubt was sufficient to smash the arch of the roof.

By means of a fishing line we ascertained that it was 150 feet sheer to the ledge upon which the remains were seen; on either side the crevasse descended into blackness. It seemed so very far down there and the dogs looked so small that we got out the field-glass to complete the scrutiny of the depths.

All our available rope was tied together but the total length was insufficient to reach the ledge, and any idea of going below to investigate and to secure some of the food had to be abandoned.

Later in the afternoon Mertz and I went on to a higher point in order to obtain a better view of our surroundings and to see if anything helpful lay ahead. In that direction, however, the prospect of reaching the sea, where lay chances of obtaining seal and penguin meat, was hopeless on account of the appalling manner in which the coastal slopes were shattered. At a point 2,400 feet above sea-level and 315¾ miles eastward from the Hut, a complete set of observations was taken.

We returned to the crevasse to consider what was to be done

and prepare for the future. At regular intervals we called down
into those dark depths in case our companion might not have
been killed outright, and, in the meantime, have become unconscious. There was no reply.

A weight was lowered on the fishing line as far as the dog
which had earlier shown some signs of life, but there was no
response. All were dead, swallowed up in an instant . . .

At 9 p.m. we stood by the side of the crevasse and I read the
burial service. Then Mertz shook me by the hand with a short
"Thank you!" and we turned away to harness up the dogs . . .

The night of 6 January [1913] was long and wearisome as I
tossed about sleeplessly, mindful that for both of us our chances
of reaching succour were now slipping silently and relentlessly
away. I was aching to get on, but there could be no question of
abandoning my companion whose condition now set the pace.

The morning of 7 January opened with better weather, for
there was little wind and no snow falling; even the sun appeared
gleaming through the clouds.

In view of the seriousness of the position it had been agreed
overnight that at all costs we would go on in the morning, sledge-
sailing with Mertz in his bag strapped on the sledge. It was
therefore a doubly sad blow that morning to find that my
companion was again touched with dysentery and so weak as to
be quite helpless. After tucking him into the bag again, I slid into
my own in order to kill time and keep warm, for the cold had a
new sting about it in those days of want.

At 10 a.m. hearing a rustle from my companion's bag I rose to
find him in a fit. Shortly afterwards he became normal and
exchanged a few words, but did not appear to realize that
anything out of the way had happened.

The information that this incident conveyed fell upon me like
a thunderbolt, for it was certain that my companion was in a very
serious state with little hope of any alleviation, for he was already
unable to assimilate the meagre foods available.

There was no prospect of proceeding so I settled myself to
stand by my stricken comrade and ease his sufferings as far as
possible. It would require a miracle to bring him round to a fit
travelling condition, but I prayed that it might be granted.

After noon he improved and drank some thick cocoa and soup.

Later in the afternoon he had several more fits and then, becoming delirious, talked incoherently until midnight. Most of that time his strength returned and he struggled to climb out of the sleeping-bag, keeping me very busy tucking him in again. About midnight he appeared to doze off to sleep and with a feeling of relief I slid down into my own bag, not to sleep, though weary enough, but to get warm again and to think matters over. After a couple of hours, having felt no movement, I stretched out my arm and found that my comrade was stiff in death. He had been accepted into "the peace that passeth all understanding".

It was unutterably sad that he should have perished thus, after the splendid work he had accomplished not only on that particular sledging journey but throughout the expedition. No one could have done better. Favoured with a generous and lovable character, he had been a general favourite amongst all the members of the expedition. Now all was over, he had done his duty and passed on. All that remained was his mortal frame which, toggled up in his sleeping-bag, still offered some sense of companionship as I threw myself down for the remainder of the night, revolving in my mind all that lay behind and the chances of the future.

Outside the bowl of chaos was brimming with drift-snow and as I lay in the sleeping-bag beside my dead companion I wondered how, in such conditions, I would manage to break and pitch camp single-handed. There appeared to be little hope of reaching the Hut, still 100 miles away. It was easy to sleep in the bag, and the weather was cruel outside. But inaction is hard to bear and I braced myself together determined to put up a good fight.

Failing to reach the Hut it would be something done if I managed to get to some prominent point likely to catch the eye of a search-party, where a cairn might be erected and our diaries cached. So I commenced to modify the sledge and camping gear to meet fresh requirements.

The sky remained clouded, but the wind fell off to a calm which lasted several hours. I took the opportunity to set to work on the sledge, sawing it in halves with a pocket tool and discarding the rear section. A mast was made out of one of the rails no longer required, and a spar was cut from the other. Finally, the load was cut down to a minimum by the elimination of all but the barest necessities, the abandoned articles including, sad to relate, all that remained of the exposed photographic films.

Late that evening, the 8th, I took the body of Mertz, still toggled up in his bag, outside the tent, piled snow blocks around it and raised a rough cross made of the two discarded halves of the sledge runners.

On 9 January the weather was overcast and fairly thick drift was flying in a gale of wind, reaching about fifty miles an hour. As certain matters still required attention and my chances of re-erecting the tent were rather doubtful . . . the start was delayed.

Part of the time that day was occupied with cutting up a waterproof clothes-bag and Mertz's burberry jacket and sewing them together to form a sail. Before retiring to rest in the evening I read through the burial service and put the finishing touches on the grave.

10 January arrived in a turmoil of wind and thick drift. The start was still further delayed. I spent part of the time in reckoning up the food remaining and in cooking the rest of the dog meat, this latter operation serving the good object of lightening the load, in that the kerosene for the purpose was consumed there and then and had not to be dragged forward for subsequent use. Late in the afternoon the wind fell and the sun peered amongst the clouds just as I was in the middle of a long job riveting and lashing the broken shovel.

The next day, 11 January, a beautiful, calm day of sunshine, I set out over a good surface with a slight down grade.

From the start my feet felt curiously lumpy and sore. They had become so painful after a mile of walking that I decided to examine them on the spot, sitting in the lee of the sledge in brilliant sunshine. I had not had my socks off for some days for, while lying in camp, it had not seemed necessary. On taking off the third and inner pair of socks the sight of my feet gave me quite a shock, for the thickened skin of the soles had separated in each case as a complete layer, and abundant watery fluid had escaped, saturating the sock. The new skin beneath was very much abraded and raw. Several of my toes had commenced to blacken and fester near the tips and the nails were puffed and loose.

I began to wonder if there was ever to be a day without some special disappointment. However, there was nothing to be done but make the best of it. I smeared the new skin and the raw surfaces with lanoline, of which there was fortunately a good store, and then with the aid of bandages bound the old skin casts back in place, for these were comfortable and soft in contact with the abraded surface. Over the bandages were slipped six pairs of thick woollen socks, then fur boots and finally crampon over-shoes. The latter, having large stiff soles, spread the weight nicely and saved my feet from the jagged ice encountered shortly afterwards.

So glorious was it to feel the sun on one's skin after being without it for so long that I next removed most of my clothing and bathed my body in the rays until my flesh fairly tingled – a wonderful sensation which spread throughout my whole person, and made me feel stronger and happier . . .

[17 January] A start was made at 8 a.m. and the pulling proved more easy than on the previous day. Some two miles had been negotiated in safety when an event occurred which, but for a miracle, would have terminated the story then and there. Never have I come so near to an end; never has anyone more miraculously escaped.

I was hauling the sledge through deep snow up a fairly steep sloop when my feet broke through into a crevasse. Fortunately as I fell I caught my weight with my arms on the edge and did not plunge in further than the thighs. The outline of the crevasse did not show through the blanket of snow on the surface, but an idea of the trend was obtained with a stick. I decided to try a crossing about fifty yards further along, hoping that there it would be better bridged. Alas! it took an unexpected turn catching me unawares. This time I shot through the centre of the bridge in a flash, but the latter part of the fall was decelerated by the friction of the harness ropes which, as the sledge ran up, sawed back into the thick compact snow forming the margin of the lid. Having seen my comrades perish in diverse ways and having lost hope of ever reaching the Hut, I had already many times speculated on what the end would be like. So it happened that as I fell through into the crevasse the thought "so this is the end" blazed up in my mind, for it was to be expected that the next moment the sledge would follow through, crash on my head and all go to the unseen bottom. But the unexpected happened and the sledge held, the deep snow acting as a brake.

In the moment that elapsed before the rope ceased to descend, delaying the issue, a great regret swept through my mind, namely, that after having stinted myself so assiduously in order to save food, I should pass on now to eternity without the satisfaction of what remained – to such an extent does food take possession of one under such circumstances. Realizing that the sledge was holding I began to look around. The crevasse was somewhat over six feet wide and sheer-walled, descending into blue depths below. My clothes, which, with a view to ventilation, had been but loosely secured, were now stuffed with snow broken from the roof, and very chilly it was. Above at the other end of the fourteen-foot rope, was the daylight seen through the hole in the lid.

In my weak condition, the prospect of climbing out seemed very poor indeed, but in a few moments the struggle was begun. A great effort brought a knot in the rope within my grasp, and, after a moment's rest, I was able to draw myself up and reach another, and, at length, hauled my body on to the overhanging snow-lid. Then, when all appeared to be well and before I could get to quite solid ground, a further section of the lid gave way, precipitating me once more to the full length of the rope.

There, exhausted, weak and chilled, hanging freely in space and slowly turning round as the rope twisted one way and the other, I felt that I had done my utmost and failed, that I had no more strength to try again and that all was over except the passing. It was to be a miserable and slow end and I reflected with disappointment that there was in my pocket no antidote to speed matters; but there always remained the alternative of slipping from the harness. There on the brink of the great Beyond I well remember how I looked forward to the peace of the great release – how almost excited I was at the prospect of the unknown to be unveiled. From those flights of mind I came back to earth, and remembering how Providence had miraculously brought me so far, felt that nothing was impossible and determined to act up to Service's lines:

> Just have one more try – it's dead easy to die,
> It's the keeping-on-living that's hard.

My strength was fast ebbing; in a few minutes it would be too late. It was the occasion for a supreme attempt. Fired by the passion that burns the blood in the act of strife, new power seemed to come as I applied myself to one last tremendous effort. The struggle occupied some time, but I slowly worked upward to the surface. This time emerging feet first, still clinging to the rope, I pushed myself out extended at full length on the lid and then shuffled safely on to the solid ground at the side. Then came the reaction from the great nerve strain and lying there alongside the sledge my mind faded into a blank.

When consciousness returned it was a full hour or two later, for I was partly covered with newly fallen snow and numb with the cold. I took at least three hours to erect the tent, get things snugly inside and clear the snow from my clothes. Between each movement, almost, I had to rest. Then reclining in luxury in the sleeping-bag I ate a little food and thought matters over. It was a time when the mood of the Persian philosopher appealed to me:

> Unborn Tomorrow and dead Yesterday,
> Why fret about them if Today be sweet?

I was confronted with this problem: whether it was better to enjoy life for a few days, sleeping and eating my fill until the provisions gave out, or to "plug on" again in hunger with the prospect of plunging at any moment into eternity without the supreme satisfaction and pleasure of the food. While thus cogitating an idea presented itself which greatly improved the prospects and clinched the decision to go ahead. It was to construct a ladder from a length of alpine rope that remained; one end was to be secured to the bow of the sledge and the other carried over my left shoulder and loosely attached to the sledge harness. Thus if I fell into a crevasse again, provided the sledge was not also engulfed, it would be easy for me, even though weakened by starvation, to scramble out by the ladder.

Notwithstanding the possibilities of the rope-ladder, I could not sleep properly, for my nerves had been overtaxed. All night long considerable wind and drift continued.

On the 19th it was overcast and light snow falling; very dispiriting conditions after the experience of the day before, but I resolved to go ahead and leave the rest to Providence . . .

[29 January] I was travelling along on an even down grade and was wondering how long the two pounds of food which remained would last, when something dark loomed through the haze of the drift a short distance away to the right. All sorts of possibilities raced through my mind as I headed the sledge for it. The unexpected had happened – in thick weather I had run fairly into a cairn of snow blocks erected by McLean, Hodgeman and Hurley, who had been out searching for my party. On the top of the mound, outlined in black bunting, was a bag of food, left on the chance that it might be picked up by us. In a tin was a note stating the bearing and distance of the mound from Aladdin's Cave (E 30° S, distance 23 miles), and mentioning that the ship had arrived at the Hut and was waiting, and had brought the news that Amundsen had reached the Pole, and that Scott was remaining another year in Antarctica.

It certainly was remarkably good fortune that I had come upon the depot of food; a few hundred yards to either side and it would have been lost to sight in the drift. On reading the note carefully I found that I had just missed by six hours what would have been crowning good luck, for it appeared that the search party had left the mound at 8 a.m. that very day . . . It was about 2 p.m. when I reached it. Thus, during the night of the 28th our camps had been only some five miles apart.

Hauling down the bag of food I tore it open in the lee of the cairn and in my greed scattered the contents about on the ground. Having partaken heartily of frozen pemmican, I stuffed my pocket, bundled the rest into a bag on the sledge and started off in high glee, stimulated in body and mind. As I left the depot there appeared to be nothing on earth that could prevent me reaching the Hut within a couple of days, but a fresh obstacle with which I had not reckoned was to arise and cause further delay, leading to far-reaching results.

It happened that after several hours' march the surface changed from snow to polished névé and then to slippery ice. I could scarcely keep on my feet at all, falling every few moments and bruising my emaciated self until I expected to see my bones burst through the clothes. How I regretted having abandoned those crampons after crossing the Mertz Glacier; shod with them, all would be easy.

With nothing but finnesko on the feet, to walk over such a sloping surface would have been difficult enough in the wind without any other hindrance; with the sledge sidling down the slope and tugging at one, it was quite impossible. I found that I had made too far to the east and to reach Aladdin's Cave had unfortunately to strike across the wind.

Before giving up, I even tried crawling on my hands and knees.

However, the day's run, fourteen miles, was by no means a poor one.

Having erected the tent I set to work to improvise crampons. With this object in view the theodolite case was cut up, providing two flat pieces of wood into which were stuck as many screws and nails as could be procured by dismantling the sledge-meter and the theodolite itself. In the repair-bag there were still a few ice-nails which at this time were of great use.

Late the next day, the wind which had risen in the night fell off and a start was made westwards over the ice slopes with the pieces of nail-studded wood lashed to my feet. A glorious expanse of sea lay to the north and several recognizable points on the coast were clearly in view to east and west.

The crampons were not a complete success for they gradually broke up, lasting only a distance of six miles . . .

A blizzard was in full career on 31 January and I spent all day and most of the night on the crampons. On 1 February the wind and drift had subsided late in the afternoon, and I got under way expecting great things from the new crampons. The beacon marking Aladdin's Cave was clearly visible as a black dot on the ice slopes to the west.

At 7 p.m. that haven within the ice was attained. It took but a few moments to dig away the snow and throw back the canvas flap scaling the entrance. A moment later I slid down inside, arriving amidst familiar surroundings. Something unusual in one corner caught the eye – three oranges and a pineapple – circumstantial evidence of the arrival of the *Aurora*.

The improvised crampons had given way and were squeezing my feet painfully. I rummaged about amongst a pile of food-bags, hoping to find some crampons or leather boots, but was disappointed, so there was nothing left but to repair the damaged ones. That done and a drink of hot milk having been prepared, I packed up to make a start for the Hut. On climbing out of the cave imagine my disappointment at finding a strong wind and drift had risen. To have attempted the descent of the five and a half miles of steep ice slope to the Hut with such inadequate and fragile crampons, weak as I still was, would have been only as a last resort. So I camped in the comfortable cave and hoped for better weather next day.

But the blizzard droned on night and day for over a week with never a break. Think of my feelings as I sat within the cave, so near and yet so far from the Hut, impatient and anxious, ready to spring out and take the trail at a moment's notice. Improvements to the crampons kept me busy for a time; then, as there was a couple of old boxes lying about, I set to work and constructed a second emergency pair in case the others should break up during the descent. I tried the makeshift crampons on the ice outside, but was disappointed to find that they had not sufficient grip to face the wind, so had to abandon the idea of attempting the descent during the continuance of the blizzard. Nevertheless, by 8 February my anxiety as to what was happening at the Hut reached such a pitch that I resolved to try the passage in spite of everything, having worked out a plan whereby I was to sit on the sledge and sail down as far as possible.

Whilst these preparations were in progress the wind slackened. At last the longed-for event was to be realized. I snatched a hasty meal and set off. Before a couple of miles had been covered the wind had fallen off altogether, and after that it was gloriously calm and clear.

I had reached within one and a half miles of the Hut and there was no sign of the *Aurora* lying in the offing. I was comforted with the thought that she might still be at the anchorage and have swung inshore so as to be hidden under the ice cliffs. But even as I gazed about seeking for a clue, a speck on the north-west horizon caught my eye and my hopes went down. It looked like a distant ship – Was it the *Aurora*? Well, what matter! the long journey was at an end – a terrible chapter of my life was concluded!

Then the rocks around winter quarters began to come into view; part of the basin of the Boat Harbour appeared, and lo! there were human figures! They almost seemed unreal – was it all a dream? No, indeed, for after a brief moment one of them observed me and waved an arm – I replied – there was a commotion and they all ran towards the Hut. Then they were lost, hidden by the crest of the first steep slope. It almost seemed to me that they had run away to hide.

Minutes passed as I slowly descended trailing the sledge. Then a head rose over the brow of the hill and there was Bickerton, breathless after a long run uphill. I expect for a while he wondered which of us it was. Soon we had shaken hands and he knew all in a few brief words, I for my part learning that the ship had left earlier that very day.

On his eventual return home Mawson was given a knighthood. In addition to its discovery of George V Land, Mawson's expedition had found Queen Mary Land and garnered a huge amount of scientific data. Of the "Heroic Age" missions South, the Australasian Antarctic Expedition was to be counted amongst the most successful.

The Loss of the *Endurance*

Ernest Shackleton

After failing to reach the Pole in 1908, Shackleton returned South in 1914; his intention, now that the Pole had been achieved by both Amundsen and Scott, was to cross the entire mass of Antarctica. Things went wrong from the start. The expedition's ship, the Endurance, *froze firm in the Weddell Sea.*

The pressure-ridges, massive and threatening, testified to the overwhelming nature of the forces that were at work. Huge blocks of ice, weighing many tons, were lifted into the air and tossed aside as other masses rose beneath them. We were helpless intruders in a strange world, our lives dependent upon the play of grim elementary forces that made a mock of our puny efforts. I scarcely dared hope now that the *Endurance* would live, and throughout that anxious day I reviewed again the plans made long before for the sledging journey that we must make in the event of our having to take to the ice. We were ready, as far as forethought could make us, for every contingency. Stores, dogs, sledges, and equipment were ready to be moved from the ship at a moment's notice.

The following day brought bright clear weather, with a blue sky. The sunshine was inspiriting. The roar of pressure could be heard all around us. New ridges were rising, and I could see as the day wore on that the lines of major disturbance were drawing nearer to the ship. The *Endurance* suffered some strains at intervals. Listening below, I could hear the creaking and groaning of her timbers, the pistol-like cracks that told of the starting of a trenail or plank, and the faint, indefinable whispers of our ship's distress. Overhead the sun shone serenely; occasional fleecy clouds drifted before the southerly breeze, and the light glinted and sparkled on the million facets of the new pressure-ridges. The day passed slowly. At 7 p.m. very heavy pressure developed, with twisting strains that racked the ship fore and aft. The butts of planking were opened four and five inches on the starboard side, and at the same time we could see from the bridge that the ship was bending like a bow under titanic pressure. Almost like a living creature, she resisted the forces that would crush her; but it was a one-sided battle. Millions of tons of ice pressed inexorably upon the little ship that had dared the challenge of the Antarctic. The *Endurance* was now leaking badly, and at 9 p.m. I gave the order to lower boats, gear, provisions, and sledges to the floe, and move them to the flat ice a little way from the ship. The working of the ice closed he leaks slightly at midnight, but all hands were pumping all night. A strange occurrence was the sudden appearance of eight emperor penguins from a crack 100 yds away at the moment when the pressure upon the ship was at its climax. They walked a little way towards us, halted, and after a few ordinary calls proceeded to utter weird cries that sounded like a dirge for the ship. None of us had ever before heard the emperors utter any other than the most simple calls or cries, and the effect of this concerted effort was almost startling.

Then came a fateful day – Wednesday, October 27 [1915]. The position was lat. 69° 5' S, long. 51° 30' W. The temperature was -8.5° Fahr., a gentle southerly breeze was blowing and the sun shone in a clear sky.

*After long months of ceaseless anxiety and strain, after times when hope beat high and times when the outlook was black indeed, the end of the *Endurance* has come. But though we have been compelled to abandon the ship, which is crushed beyond all hope of ever being righted, we are alive and well, and we have stores and equipment for the task that lies before us. The task is to reach land with all the members of the Expedition. It is hard to write what I feel. To a sailor his ship is more than a floating home, and in the *Endurance* I had centred ambitions, hopes, and desires. Now, straining and groaning, her timbers cracking and her wounds gaping, she is slowly giving up her sentient life at the very outset of her career. She is crushed and abandoned after

---

* From the diary.

drifting more than 570 miles in a north-westerly direction during the 281 days since she became locked in the ice. The distance from the point where she became beset to the place where she now rests mortally hurt in the grip of the floes is 573 miles, but the total drift through all observed positions has been 1,186 miles, and probably we actually covered more than 1500 miles. We are now 346 miles from Paulet Island, the nearest point where there is any possibility of finding food and shelter. A small hut built there by the Swedish expedition in 1902 is filled with stores left by the Argentine relief ship. I know all about those stores, for I purchased them in London on behalf of the Argentine Government when they asked me to equip the relief expedition. The distance to the nearest barrier west of us is about 180 miles, but a party going there would still be about 360 miles from Paulet Island and there would be no means of sustaining life on the Barrier. We could not take from here food enough for the whole journey; the weight would be too great.

This morning, our last on the ship, the weather was clear, with a gentle south-south-easterly to south-south-westerly breeze. From the crow's-nest there was no sign of land of any sort. The pressure was increasing steadily, and the passing hours brought no relief or respite for the ship. The attack of the ice reached its climax at 4 p.m. The ship was hove stern up by the pressure, and the driving floe, moving laterally across the stern, split the rudder and tore out the rudder-post and stern-post. Then, while we watched, the ice loosened and the *Endurance* sank a little. The decks were breaking upwards and the water was pouring in below. Again the pressure began, and at 5 p.m. I ordered all hands on to the ice. The twisting, grinding floes were working their will at last on the ship. It was a sickening sensation to feel the decks breaking up under one's feet, the great beams bending and then snapping with a noise like heavy gun-fire. The water was overmastering the pumps, and to avoid an explosion when it reached the boilers I had to give orders for the fires to be drawn and the steam let down. The plans for abandoning the ship in case of emergency had been made well in advance, and men and dogs descended to the floe and made their way to the compara- tive safety of an unbroken portion of the floe without a hitch. Just before leaving, I looked down the engine-room skylight as I stood on the quivering deck, and saw the engines dropping sideways as the stays and bed-plates gave way. I cannot describe the impression of relentless destruction that was forced upon me as I looked down and around. The floes, with the force of millions of tons of moving ice behind them, were simply annihilating the ship . . .

Tonight the temperature has dropped to -16° Fahr., and most of the men are cold and uncomfortable. After the tents had been pitched I mustered all hands and explained the position to them briefly and, I hope, clearly. I have told them the distance to the Barrier and the distance to Paulet Island, and have stated that I propose to try to march with equipment across the ice in the direction of Paulet Island. I thanked the men for the steadiness and good *morale* they have shown in these trying circumstances, and told them I had no doubt that, provided they continued to work their utmost and to trust me, we will all reach safety in the end. Then we had supper, which the cook had prepared at the big blubber stove, and after a watch had been set all hands except the watch turned in.

For myself, I could not sleep. The destruction and abandonment of the ship was no sudden shock. The disaster had been looming ahead for many months, and I had studied my plans for all contingencies a hundred times. But the thoughts that came to me as I walked up and down in the darkness were not particularly cheerful. The task now was to secure the safety of the party, and to that I must bend my energies and mental power and apply every bit of knowledge that experience of the Antarctic had given me. The task was likely to be long and strenuous, and an ordered mind and a clear programme were essential if we were to come through without loss of life. A man must shape himself to a new mark directly the old one goes to ground.

At midnight I was pacing the ice, listening to the grinding floe and to the groans and crashes that told of the death-agony of the *Endurance*, when I noticed suddenly a crack running across our floe right through the camp. The alarm-whistle brought all hands tumbling out, and we moved the tents and stores lying on what was now the smaller portion of the floe to the larger portion. Nothing more could be done at that moment, and the men turned in again; but there was little sleep. Each time I came to the end of my beat on the floe I could just see in the darkness the uprearing piles of pressure-ice, which toppled over and narrowed still further the little floating island we occupied. I did not notice at the time that my tent, which had been on the wrong side of the crack, had not been erected again. Hudson and James had managed to squeeze themselves into other tents, and Hurley had wrapped himself in the canvas of No. 1 tent. I discovered this about 5 a.m. All night long the electric light gleamed from the stern of the dying *Endurance*. Hussey had left this light switched on when he took a last observation, and, like a lamp in a cottage window, it braved the night until in the early morning the *Endurance* received a particularly violent squeeze. There was a sound of rending beams and the light disappeared. The connexion had been cut.

Morning came in chill and cheerless. All hands were stiff and weary after their first disturbed night on the floe. Just at daybreak I went over to the *Endurance* with Wild and Hurley, in order to retrieve some tins of petrol that could be used to boil up milk for the rest of the men. The ship presented a painful spectacle of chaos and wreck. The jib-boom and bowsprit had snapped off during the night and now lay at right angles to the ship, with the chains, martingale, and bobstay dragging them as the vessel quivered and moved in the grinding pack. The ice had driven over the forecastle and she was well down by the head. We secured two tins of petrol with some difficulty, and postponed the further examination of the ship until after breakfast. Jumping across cracks with the tins, we soon reached camp, and built a fireplace out of the triangular watertight tanks we had ripped from the lifeboat. This we had done in order to make more room. Then we pierced a petrol-tin in half a dozen places with an ice-axe and set fire to it. The petrol blazed fiercely under the five-gallon drum we used as a cooker, and the hot milk was ready in quick time. Then we three ministering angels went round the tents with the life-giving drink, and were surprised and a trifle chagrined at the matter-of-fact manner in which some of the men accepted this contribution to their comfort. They did not quite understand what work we had done for them in the early dawn, and I heard Wild say, "If any of you gentlemen would like your boots cleaned just put them outside!" This was his gentle way of reminding them that a little thanks will go a long way on such occasions.

The cook prepared breakfast, which consisted of biscuit and hoosh, at 8 a.m., and I then went over to the *Endurance* again and made a fuller examination of the wreck. Only six of the cabins had not been pierced by floes and blocks of ice. Every one of the starboard cabins had been crushed. The whole of the after part of the ship had been crushed concertina fashion. The forecastle and the Ritz were submerged, and the wardroom was three-quarters full of ice. The starboard side of the wardroom had come away. The motor-engine forward had been driven through the galley. Petrol-cases that had been stacked on the foredeck had been driven by the floe through the wall into the wardroom and had carried before them a large picture. Curiously enough, the glass of this picture had not been cracked, whereas in the immediate neighbourhood I saw heavy iron davits that had been twisted and bent like the ironwork of a wrecked train. The ship was being crushed remorselessly.

Under a dull, overcast sky I returned to camp and examined our situation. The floe occupied by the camp was still subject to pressure, and I thought it wise to move to a larger and apparently stronger floe about 200 yds away, off the starboard bow of the ship. This camp was to become known as Dump Camp, owing to the amount of stuff that was thrown away there. We could not afford to carry unnecessary gear, and a drastic sorting of equipment took place. I decided to issue a complete new set of Burberrys and underclothing to each man, and also a supply of new socks. The camp was transferred to the larger floe quickly, and I began there to direct the preparations for the long journey across the floes to Paulet Island or Snow Hill.

Hurley meanwhile had rigged his kinematograph-camera and was getting pictures of the *Endurance* in her death-throes. While he was engaged thus, the ice, driving against the standing rigging and the fore-, main- and mizzen-masts, snapped the shrouds. The foretop and topgallant-mast came down with a run and hung in wreckage on the fore-mast with the foreyard vertical. The mainmast followed immediately, snapping off about 10 ft above the main deck. The crow's-nest fell within 10 ft of where Hurley stood turning the handle of his camera, but he did not stop the machine, and so secured a unique, though sad, picture.

The issue of clothing was quickly accomplished. Sleeping-bags were required also. We had eighteen fur bags, and it was necessary, therefore, to issue ten of the Jaeger woollen bags in order to provide for the twenty-eight men of the party. The woollen bags were lighter and less warm than the reindeer bags, and so each man who received one of them was allowed also a reindeer-skin to lie upon. It seemed fair to distribute the fur bags by lot, but some of us older hands did not join in the lottery. We thought we could do quite as well with the Jaegers as with the furs. With quick dispatch the clothing was apportioned, and then we turned one of the boats on its side and supported it with two broken oars to make a lee for the galley. The cook got the blubber-stove going, and a little later, when I was sitting round the corner of the stove, I heard one man say, "Cook, I like my tea strong." Another joined in, "Cook, I like mine weak." It was pleasant to know that their minds were untroubled, but I thought the time opportune to mention that the tea would be the same for all hands and that we would be fortunate if two months later we had any tea at all. It occurred to me at the time that the incident had psychological interest. Here were men, their home crushed, the camp pitched on the unstable floes, and their chance of reaching safety apparently remote, calmly attending to the details of existence and giving their attention to such trifles as the strength of a brew of tea.

During the afternoon the work continued. Every now and then we heard a noise like heavy guns or distant thunder, caused by the floes grinding together. The pressure caused by the congestion in this area of the pack is producing a scene of absolute chaos. The floes grind stupendously, throw up great ridges, and shatter one another mercilessly. The ridges, or hedge-rows, marking the pressure-lines that border the fast-diminishing pieces of smooth floe-ice, are enormous. The ice moves majestically, irresistibly. Human effort is not futile, but man fights against the giant forces of Nature in a spirit of humility. One has a sense of dependence on the Higher Power. Today two seals, a Weddell and a crabeater, came close to the camp and were shot. Four others were chased back into the water, for their presence disturbed the dog teams, and this meant floggings and trouble with the harness. The arrangement of the tents has been completed and their internal management settled. Each tent has a mess orderly, the duty being taken in turn on an alphabetical rota. The orderly takes the hoosh-pots of his tent to the galley, gets all the hoosh he is allowed, and, after the meal, cleans the vessels with snow and stores them in sledge or boat ready for a possible move.

[October 29]. We passed a quiet night, although the pressure was grinding around us. Our floe is a heavy one and it withstood the blows it received . . . The ship is still afloat, with the spurs of the pack driven through her and holding her up. The forecastle-head is under water, the decks are burst up by the pressure, the wreckage lies around in dismal confusion, but over all the blue ensign flies still.

Escape from the Ice

Ernest Shackleton

After the sinking of the Endurance *in October 1915 in the Weddell Sea, Shackleton's expedition camped on the ice, which steadily drifted north, shrinking and cracking all the while, until the floe beneath the men measured only 200 feet by 100 feet.*

The swell increased that night and the movement of the ice became more pronounced. Occasionally a neighbouring floe would hammer against the ice on which we were camped, and the lesson of these blows was plain to read. We must get solid ground under our feet quickly. When the vibration ceased after a heavy surge, my thoughts flew round to the problem ahead. If the party had not numbered more than six men a solution would not have been so hard to find; but obviously the transportation of the whole party to a place of safety, with the limited means at our disposal, was going to be a matter of extreme difficulty. There were twenty-eight men on our floating cake of ice, which was steadily dwindling under the influence of wind, weather, charging floes, and heavy swell. I confess that I felt the burden of responsibility sit heavily on my shoulders; but, on the other hand, I was stimulated and cheered by the attitude of the men. Loneliness is the penalty of leadership, but the man who has to make the decisions is assisted greatly if he feels that there is no uncertainty in the minds of those who follow him, and that his orders will be carried out confidently and in expectation of success.

The sun was shining in the blue sky on the following morning (8 April). Clarence Island showed clearly on the horizon, and Elephant Island could also be distinguished. The single snow-clad peak of Clarence Island stood up as a beacon of safety, though the most optimistic imagination could not make an easy path of the ice and ocean that separated us from that giant, white and austere. "The pack was much looser this morning, and the long rolling swell from the north-east is more pronounced than it was yesterday. The floes rise and fall with the surge of the sea. We evidently are drifting with the surface current, for all the heavier masses of floe, bergs, and hummocks are being left behind. There has been some discussion in the camp as to the advisability of making one of the bergs our home for the time being and drifting with it to the west. The idea is not sound. I cannot be sure that the berg would drift in the right direction. If it did move west and carried us into the open water, what would be our fate when we tried to launch the boats down the steep sides of the berg in the sea swell after the surrounding floes had left us? One must reckon, too, the chance of the berg splitting or even overturning during our stay. It is not possible to gauge the condition of a big mass of ice by surface appearance. The ice may have a fault, and when the wind, current, and swell set up strains and tensions, the line of weakness may reveal itself suddenly and disastrously. No, I do not like the idea of drifting on a berg. We must stay on our floe till conditions improve and then make another attempt to advance towards the land."

At 6:30 p.m. a particularly heavy shock went through our floe. The watchman and other members of the party made an immediate inspection and found a crack right under the *James Caird* and between the other two boats and the main camp. Within five minutes the boats were over the crack and close to the tents. The trouble was not caused by a blow from another floe. We could see that the piece of ice we occupied had slewed and now presented its long axis towards the oncoming swell. The floe, therefore, was pitching in the manner of a ship, and it had cracked across when the swell lifted the centre, leaving the two ends comparatively unsupported. We were now on a triangular raft of ice, the three sides measuring, roughly, 90, 100, and 120 yds. Night came down dull and overcast, and before midnight the wind had freshened from the west. We could see that the pack was opening under the influence of wind, wave, and current, and I felt that the time for launching the boats was near at hand. Indeed, it was obvious that even if the conditions were unfavourable for a start during the coming day, we could not safely stay on the floe many hours longer. The movement of the ice in the swell was increasing, and the floe might split right under our camp. We had made preparations for quick action if anything of the kind occurred. Our case would be desperate if the ice broke into small pieces not large enough to support our party and not loose enough to permit the use of the boats.

The following day was Sunday (9 April), but it proved no day of rest for us. Many of the important events of our Expedition occurred on Sundays, and this particular day was to see our forced departure from the floe on which we had lived for nearly six months, and the start of our journeyings in the boats. "This has been an eventful day. The morning was fine, though somewhat overcast by stratus and cumulus clouds; moderate south-south-westerly and south-easterly breezes. We hoped that with this wind the ice would drift nearer to Clarence Island. At 7 a.m. lanes of water and leads could be seen on the horizon to the west. The ice separating us from the lanes was loose, but did not appear to be workable for the boats. The long swell from the north-west was coming in more freely than on the previous day and was driving the floes together in the utmost confusion. The loose brash between the masses of ice was being churned to mudlike consistency, and no boat could have lived in the channels that opened and closed around us. Our own floe was suffering in the general disturbance, and after breakfast I ordered the tents to be struck and everything prepared for an immediate start when the boats could be launched." I had decided to take the *James Caird* myself, with Wild and eleven men. This was the largest of our boats, and in addition to her human complement she carried the major portion of the stores. Worsley had charge of the *Dudley Docker* with nine men, and Hudson and Crean were the senior men on the *Stancomb Wills*.

Soon after breakfast the ice closed again. We were standing by, with our preparations as complete as they could be made, when at 11 a.m. our floe suddenly split right across under the boats. We rushed our gear on to the larger of the two pieces and watched with strained attention for the next development. The crack had cut through the site of my tent. I stood on the edge of the new fracture, and, looking across the widening channel of water, could see the spot where for many months my head and shoulders had rested when I was in my sleeping-bag. The depression formed by my body and legs was on our side of the crack. The ice had sunk under my weight during the months of waiting in the tent, and I had many times put snow under the bag to fill the hollow. The lines of stratification showed clearly the different layers of snow. How fragile and precarious had been our resting place! Yet usage had dulled our sense of danger. The floe had become our home, and during the early months of the drift we had almost ceased to realize that it was but a sheet of ice floating on unfathomed seas. Now our home was being shattered under our feet, and we had a sense of loss and incompleteness hard to describe.

The fragments of our floe came together again a little later, and we had our lunch of seal-meat, all hands eating their fill. I thought that a good meal would be the best possible preparation for the journey that now seemed imminent, and as we would not be able to take all our meat with us when we finally moved, we could regard every pound eaten as a pound rescued. The call to action came at 1 p.m. The pack opened well and the channels became navigable. The conditions were not all one could have desired, but it was best not to wait any longer. The *Dudley Docker* and the *Stancomb Wills* were launched quickly. Stores were thrown in, and the two boats were pulled clear of the immediate floes towards a pool of open water three miles broad, in which floated a lone and mighty berg. The *James Caird* was the last boat to leave, heavily loaded with stores and odds and ends of camp equipment. Many things regarded by us as essentials at that time were to be discarded a little later as the pressure of the primitive became more severe. Man can sustain life with very scanty means. The trappings of civilization are soon cast aside in the face of stern realities, and given the barest opportunity of winning food and shelter, man can live and even find his laughter ringing true.

The three boats were a mile away from our floe home at 2 p.m. We had made our way through the channels and had entered the big pool when we saw a rush of foam-clad water and tossing ice approaching us, like the tidal bore of a river. The pack was being impelled to the east by a tide-rip, and two huge masses of ice were driving down upon us on converging courses. The *James Caird* was leading. Starboarding the helm and bending strongly to the oars, we managed to get clear. The two other boats followed us, though from their position astern at first they had not realized the immediate danger. The *Stancomb Wills* was the last boat and she was very nearly caught, but by great exertion she was kept just ahead of the driving ice. It was an unusual and startling experience. The effect of tidal action on ice is not often as marked as it was that day. The advancing ice, accompanied by a large wave, appeared to be travelling at about three knots, and if we had not succeeded in pulling clear we would certainly have been swamped.

We pulled hard for an hour to windward of the berg that lay in the open water. The swell was crashing on its perpendicular sides and throwing spray to a height of sixty feet. Evidently there was an ice foot at the east end, for the swell broke before it reached the berg face and flung its white spray on to the blue ice wall. We might have paused to have admired the spectacle under other conditions; but night was coming on apace, and we needed a camping place. As we steered north-west, still amid the ice floes, the *Dudley Docker* got jammed between two masses while attempting to make a short cut. The old adage about a short cut being the longest way round is often as true in the Antarctic as it is in the peaceful countryside. The *James Caird* got a line aboard the *Dudley Docker*, and after some hauling the boat was brought clear of the ice again. We hastened forward in the twilight in search of a flat, old floe, and presently found a fairly large piece rocking in the swell. It was not an ideal camping place by any means, but darkness had overtaken us. We hauled the boats up, and by 8 p.m. had the tents pitched and the blubber stove burning cheerily. Soon all hands were well fed and happy in their tents, and snatches of song came to me as I wrote up my log.

Some intangible feeling of uneasiness made me leave my tent about 11 p.m. that night and glance around the quiet camp. The stars between the snow flurries showed that the floe had swung round and was end on to the swell, a position exposing it to sudden strains. I started to walk across the floe in order to warn the watchman to look carefully for cracks, and as I was passing the men's tent the floe lifted on the crest of a swell and cracked right under my feet. The men were in one of the dome-shaped tents, and it began to stretch apart as the ice opened. A muffled sound, suggestive of suffocation, came from beneath the stretching tent. I rushed forward, helped some emerging men from under the canvas, and called out, "Are you all right?" "There are two in the water," somebody answered. The crack had widened to about four feet, and as I threw myself down at the edge, I saw a whitish object floating in the water. It was a sleeping-bag with a man inside. I was able to grasp it, and with a heave lifted man and bag on to the floe. A few seconds later the ice edges came together again with tremendous force. Fortunately, there had been but one man in the water, or the incident might have been a tragedy. The rescued bag contained Holness, who was wet down to the waist but otherwise unscathed. The crack was now opening again. The *James Caird* and my tent were on one side of the opening and the remaining two boats and the rest of the camp on the other side. With two or three men to help me I struck my tent; then all hands manned the painter and rushed the *James Caird* across the opening crack. We held to the rope while, one by one, the men left on our side of the floe jumped the channel or scrambled over by means of the boat. Finally I was left alone. The night had swallowed all the others and the rapid movement of the ice forced me to let go the painter. For a moment I felt that my piece of rocking floe was the loneliest place in the world. Peering into the darkness, I could just see the dark figures on the other floe. I hailed Wild, ordering him to launch the *Stancomb Wills*, but I need not have troubled. His quick brain had anticipated the order and already the boat was being manned and hauled to the ice edge. Two or three minutes later she reached me, and I was ferried across to the camp.

We were now on a piece of flat ice about 200 ft long and 100 ft wide. There was no more sleep for any of us that night. The killers were blowing in the lanes around, and we waited for daylight and watched for signs of another crack in the ice. The hours passed with laggard feet as we stood huddled together or walked to and fro in the effort to keep some warmth in our bodies. We lit the blubber stove at 3 a.m., and with pipes going and a cup of hot milk for each man, we were able to discover some bright spots in our outlook. At any rate, we were on the move at last, and if dangers and difficulties loomed ahead we could meet and overcome them. No longer were we drifting helplessly at the mercy of wind and current.

The first glimmerings of dawn came at 6 a.m., and I waited anxiously for the full daylight. The swell was growing, and at times our ice was surrounded closely by similar pieces. At 6:30 a.m. we had hot hoosh, and then stood by waiting for the pack to open. Our chance came at 8, when we launched the boats, loaded them, and started to make our way through the lanes in a northerly direction. The *James Caird* was in the lead, with the *Stancomb Wills* next and the *Dudley Docker* bringing up the rear. In order to make the boats more seaworthy we had left some of our shovels, picks, and dried vegetables on the floe, and for a long time we could see the abandoned stores forming a dark spot on the ice. The boats were still heavily loaded. We got out of the lanes and entered a stretch of open water at 11 a.m. A strong easterly breeze was blowing, but the fringe of pack lying outside protected us from the full force of the swell, just as the coral reef of a tropical island checks the rollers of the Pacific. Our way was across the open sea, and soon after noon we swung round the north end of the pack and laid a course to the westward, the *James Caird* still in the lead. Immediately our deeply laden boats began to make heavy weather. They shipped sprays, which, freezing as they fell, covered men and gear with ice, and soon it was clear that we could not safely proceed. I put the *James Caird* round and ran for the shelter of the pack again, the other boats following. Back inside the outer line of ice the sea was not breaking. This was at 3 p.m., and all hands were tired and cold. A big floeberg resting peacefully ahead caught my eye, and half an hour later we had hauled up the boats and pitched camp for the night. It was a fine, big, blue berg with an attractively solid appearance, and from our camp we could get a good view of the surrounding sea and ice. The highest point was about 15 ft above sea level. After a hot meal all hands, except the watchman, turned in. Every one was in need of rest after the troubles of the previous night and the unaccustomed strain of the last thirty-six hours at the oars. The berg appeared well able to withstand the battering of the sea, and too deep and massive to be seriously affected by the swell; but it was not as safe as it looked. About midnight the watchman called me and showed me that the heavy north-westerly swell was undermining the ice. A great piece had broken off within eight feet of my tent. We made what inspection was possible in the darkness, and found that on the westward side of the berg the thick snow covering was yielding rapidly to the attack of the sea. An ice foot had formed just under the surface of the water. I decided that there was no immediate danger and did not call the men. The north-westerly wind strengthened during the night.

The morning of 11 April was overcast and misty. There was a haze on the horizon, and daylight showed that the pack had closed round our berg, making it impossible in the heavy swell to launch the boats. We could see no sign of the water. Numerous whales and killers were blowing between the floes, and Cape pigeons, petrels, and fulmars were circling round our berg. The scene from our camp as the daylight brightened was magnificent beyond description, though I must admit that we viewed it with anxiety. Heaving hills of pack and floe were sweeping towards us in long undulations, later to be broken here and there by the dark lines that indicated open water. As each swell lifted around our rapidly dissolving berg it drove floe ice on to the ice foot, shearing off more of the top snow covering and reducing the size of our camp. When the floes retreated to attack again the water swirled over the ice foot, which was rapidly increasing in width. The launching of the boats under such conditions would be difficult. Time after time, so often that a track was formed, Worsley, Wild, and I climbed to the highest point of the berg and stared out to the horizon in search of a break in the pack. After long hours had dragged past, far away on the lift of the swell there appeared a dark break in the tossing field of ice. Aeons seemed to pass, so slowly it approached. I noticed enviously the calm, peaceful attitudes of two seals which lolled lazily on a rocking floe. They were at home and had no reason for worry or cause for fear. If they thought at all, I suppose they counted it an ideal day for a joyous journey on the tumbling ice. To us it was a day that seemed likely to lead to no more days. I do not think I had ever before felt the anxiety that belongs to leadership quite so keenly. When I looked down at the camp to rest my eyes from the strain of watching the wide white expanse broken by that one black

ribbon of open water, I could see that my companions were waiting with more than ordinary interest to learn what I thought
about it all. After one particularly heavy collision somebody
shouted sharply, "She has cracked in the middle." I jumped off
the lookout station and ran to the place the men were examining.
There was a crack, but investigation showed it to be a mere
surface break in the snow with no indication of a split in the berg
itself. The carpenter mentioned calmly that earlier in the day he
had actually gone adrift on a fragment of ice. He was standing
near the edge of our camping ground when the ice under his feet
parted from the parent mass. A quick jump over the widening
gap saved him.

The hours dragged on. One of the anxieties in my mind was
the possibility that we would be driven by the current through
the eighty-mile gap between Clarence Island and Prince George
Island into the open Atlantic; but slowly the open water came
nearer, and at noon it had almost reached us. A long lane, narrow
but navigable, stretched out to the south-west horizon. Our
chance came a little later. We rushed our boats over the edge of
the reeling berg and swung them clear of the ice foot as it rose
beneath them. The *James Caird* was nearly capsized by a blow
from below as the berg rolled away, but she got into deep water.
We flung stores and gear aboard and within a few minutes were
away. The *James Caird* and *Dudley Docker* had good sails and
with a favourable breeze could make progress along the lane, with
the rolling fields of ice on either side. The swell was heavy and
spray was breaking over the ice floes. An attempt to set a little rag
of sail on the *Stancomb Wills* resulted in serious delay. The area
of sail was too small to be of much assistance, and while the men
were engaged in this work the boat drifted down towards the ice
floe, where her position was likely to be perilous. Seeing her
plight, I sent the *Dudley Docker* back for her and tied the *James
Caird* up to a piece of ice. The *Dudley Docker* had to tow the
Stancomb Wills, and the delay cost us two hours of valuable
daylight. When I had the three boats together again we continued down the lane, and soon saw a wider stretch of water to the
west; it appeared to offer us release from the grip of the pack. At
the head of an ice tongue that nearly closed the gap through
which we might enter the open space was a wave-worn berg

shaped like some curious antediluvian monster, an icy Cerberus guarding the way. It had head and eyes and rolled so heavily that it almost overturned. Its sides dipped deep in the sea, and as it rose again the water seemed to be streaming from its eyes, as though it were weeping at our escape from the clutch of the floes. This may seem fanciful to the reader, but the impression was real to us at the time. People living under civilized conditions, surrounded by Nature's varied forms of life and by all the familiar work of their own hands, may scarcely realize how quickly the mind, influenced by the eyes, responds to the unusual and weaves about it curious imaginings like the firelight fancies of our childhood days. We had lived long amid the ice, and we half-unconsciously strove to see resemblances to human faces and living forms in the fantastic contours and massively uncouth shapes of berg and floe.

At dusk we made fast to a heavy floe, each boat having its painter fastened to a separate hummock in order to avoid collisions in the swell. We landed the blubber stove, boiled some water in order to provide hot milk, and served cold rations. I also landed the dome tents and stripped the coverings from the hoops. Our experience of the previous day in the open sea had shown us that the tents must be packed tightly. The spray had dashed over the bows and turned to ice on the cloth, which had soon grown dangerously heavy. Other articles of our scanty equipment had to go that night. We were carrying only the things that had seemed essential, but we stripped now to the barest limit of safety. We had hoped for a quiet night, but presently we were forced to cast off, since pieces of loose ice began to work round the floe. Drift ice is always attracted to the lee side of a heavy floe, where it bumps and presses under the influence of the current. I had determined not to risk a repetition of the last night's experience and so had not pulled the boats up. We spent the hours of darkness keeping an offing from the main line of pack under the lee of the smaller pieces. Constant rain and snow squalls blotted out the stars and soaked us through, and at times it was only by shouting to each other that we managed to keep the boats together. There was no sleep for anybody owing to the severe cold, and we dare not pull fast enough to keep ourselves warm since we were unable to see more than a few yards ahead.

Occasionally the ghostly shadows of silver, snow, and fulmar petrels flashed close to us, and all around we could hear the killers blowing, their short, sharp hisses sounding like sudden escapes of steam. The killers were a source of anxiety, for a boat could easily have been capsized by one of them coming up to blow. They would throw aside in a nonchalant fashion pieces of ice much bigger than our boats when they rose to the surface, and we had an uneasy feeling that the white bottoms of the boats would look like ice from below. Shipwrecked mariners drifting in the Antarctic seas would be things not dreamed of in the killers' philosophy, and might appear on closer examination to be tasty substitutes for seal and penguin. We certainly regarded the killers with misgivings.

Early in the morning of 12 April the weather improved and the wind dropped. Dawn came with a clear sky, cold and fearless. I looked around at the faces of my companions in the *James Caird* and saw pinched and drawn features. The strain was beginning to tell. Wild sat at the rudder with the same calm, confident expression that he would have worn under happier conditions; his steel-blue eyes looked out to the day ahead. All the people, though evidently suffering, were doing their best to be cheerful, and the prospect of a hot breakfast was inspiriting. I told all the boats that immediately we could find a suitable floe the cooker would be started and hot milk and Bovril would soon fix everybody up. Away we rowed to the westward through open pack, floes of all shapes and sizes on every side of us, and every man not engaged in pulling looking eagerly for a suitable camping place. I could gauge the desire for food of the different members by the eagerness they displayed in pointing out to me the floes they considered exactly suited to our purpose. The temperature was about 10° Fahr., and the Burberry suits of the rowers crackled as the men bent to the oars. I noticed little fragments of ice and frost falling from arms and bodies. At eight o'clock a decent floe appeared ahead and we pulled up to it. The galley was landed, and soon the welcome steam rose from the cooking food as the blubber stove flared and smoked. Never did a cook work under more anxious scrutiny. Worsley, Crean, and I stayed in our respective boats to keep them steady and prevent collisions with the floe, since the swell was still running strong, but the

other men were able to stretch their cramped limbs and run to
and fro "in the kitchen", as somebody put it. The sun was now
rising gloriously. The Burberry suits were drying and the ice was
melting off our beards. The steaming food gave us new vigour,
and within three-quarters of an hour we were off again to the
west with all sails set. We had given an additional sail to the
Stancomb Wills and she was able to keep up pretty well. We could
see that we were on the true pack edge, with the blue, rolling sea
just outside the fringe of ice to the north. White-capped waves
vied with the glittering floes in the setting of blue water, and
countless seals basked and rolled on every piece of ice big enough
to form a raft.

We had been making westward with oars and sails since 9
April, and fair easterly winds had prevailed. Hopes were running
high as to the noon observation for position. The optimists
thought that we had done sixty miles towards our goal, and the
most cautious guess gave us at least thirty miles. The bright
sunshine and the brilliant scene around us may have influenced
our anticipations. As noon approached I saw Worsley, as navigating officer, balancing himself on the gunwale of the *Dudley Docker*
with his arm around the mast, ready to snap the sun. He got his
observation and we waited eagerly while he worked out the sight.
Then the *Dudley Docker* ranged up alongside the *James Caird* and
I jumped into Worsley's boat in order to see the result. It was a
grievous disappointment. Instead of making a good run to the
westward we had made a big drift to the south-east. We were
actually thirty miles to the east of the position we had occupied
when we left the floe on the 9th. It has been noted by sealers
operating in this area that there are often heavy sets to the east in
the Belgica Straits, and no doubt it was one of these sets that we
had experienced. The originating cause would be a north-
westerly gale off Cape Horn, producing the swell that had already
caused us so much trouble. After a whispered consultation with
Worsley and Wild I announced that we had not made as much
progress as we expected, but I did not inform the hands of our
retrograde movement.

The question of our course now demanded further consideration. Deception Island seemed to be beyond our reach. The
wind was foul for Elephant Island, and as the sea was clear to the

south-west, I discussed with Worsley and Wild the advisability of proceeding to Hope Bay on the mainland of the Antarctic Continent, now only eighty miles distant. Elephant Island was the nearest land, but it lay outside the main body of pack, and even if the wind had been fair we would have hesitated at that particular time to face the high sea that was running in the open. We laid a course roughly for Hope Bay, and the boats moved on again. I gave Worsley a line for a berg ahead and told him, if possible, to make fast before darkness set in. This was about three o'clock in the afternoon. We had set sail, and as the *Stancomb Wills* could not keep up with the other two boats I took her in tow, not being anxious to repeat the experience of the day we left the reeling berg. The *Dudley Docker* went ahead, but came beating down towards us at dusk. Worsley had been close to the berg, and he reported that it was unapproachable. It was rolling in the swell and displaying an ugly ice foot. The news was bad. In the failing light we turned towards a line of pack, and found it so tossed and churned by the sea that no fragment remained big enough to give us an anchorage and shelter. Two miles away we could see a larger piece of ice, and to it we managed, after some trouble, to secure the boats. I brought my boat bow on to the floe, whilst Howe, with the painter in his hand, stood ready to jump. Standing up to watch our chance, while the oars were held ready to back the moment Howe had made his leap, I could see that there would be no possibility of getting the galley ashore that night. Howe just managed to get a footing on the edge of the floe, and then made the painter fast to a hummock. The other two boats were fastened alongside the *James Caird*. They could not lie astern of us in a line, since cakes of ice came drifting round the floe and gathering under its lee. As it was we spent the next two hours poling off the drifting ice that surged towards us. The blubber stove could not be used, so we started the Primus lamps. There was a rough, choppy sea, and the *Dudley Docker* could not get her Primus under way, something being adrift. The men in that boat had to wait until the cook on the *James Caird* had boiled up the first pot of milk.

The boats were bumping so heavily that I had to slack away the painter of the *Stancomb Wills* and put her astern. Much ice was coming round the floe and had to be poled off. Then the

Dudley Docker, being the heavier boat, began to damage the *James Caird*, and I slacked the *Dudley Docker* away. The *James Caird* remained moored to the ice, with the *Dudley Docker* and the *Stancomb Wills* in line behind her. The darkness had become complete, and we strained our eyes to see the fragments of ice that threatened us. Presently we thought we saw a great berg bearing down upon us, its form outlined against the sky, but this startling spectacle resolved itself into a low-lying cloud in front of the rising moon. The moon appeared in a clear sky. The wind shifted to the south-east as the light improved and drove the boats broadside on towards the jagged edge of the floe. We had to cut the painter of the *James Caird* and pole her off, thus losing much valuable rope. There was no time to cast off. Then we pushed away from the floe, and all night long we lay in the open, freezing sea, the *Dudley Docker* now ahead, the *James Caird* astern of her, and the *Stancomb Wills* third in the line. The boats were attached to one another by their painters. Most of the time the *Dudley Docker* kept the *James Caird* and the *Stancomb Wills* up to the swell, and the men who were rowing were in better pass than those in the other boats, waiting inactive for the dawn. The temperature was down to 4° below zero, and a film of ice formed on the surface of the sea. When we were not on watch we lay in each other's arms for warmth. Our frozen suits thawed where our bodies met, and as the slightest movement exposed these comparatively warm spots to the biting air, we clung motionless, whispering each to his companion our hopes and thoughts. Occasionally from an almost clear sky came snow showers, falling silently on the sea and laying a thin shroud of white over our bodies and our boats.

The dawn of 13 April came clear and bright, with occasional passing clouds. Most of the men were now looking seriously worn and strained. Their lips were cracked and their eyes and eyelids showed red in their salt-encrusted faces. The beards even of the younger men might have been those of patriarchs, for the frost and the salt spray had made them white. I called the *Dudley Docker* alongside and found that the condition of the people there was no better than in the *James Caird*. Obviously we must make land quickly, and I decided to run for Elephant Island. The wind had shifted fair for that rocky isle, then about one hundred miles away, and the pack that separated us from Hope Bay had closed up during the night from the south. At 6 a.m. we made a distribution of stores among the three boats, in view of the possibility of their being separated. The preparation of a hot breakfast was out of the question. The breeze was strong and the sea was running high in the loose pack around us. We had a cold meal, and I gave orders that all hands might eat as much as they pleased, this concession being due partly to a realization that we would have to jettison some of our stores when we reached open sea in order to lighten the boats. I hoped, moreover, that a full meal of cold rations would compensate to some extent for the lack of warm food and shelter. Unfortunately, some of the men were unable to take advantage of the extra food owing to seasickness. Poor fellows, it was bad enough to be huddled in the deeply laden, spray-swept boats, frost-bitten and half frozen, without having the pangs of seasickness added to the list of their woes. But some smiles were caused even then by the plight of one man, who had a habit of accumulating bits of food against the day of starvation that he seemed always to think was at hand, and who was condemned now to watch impotently while hungry comrades with undisturbed stomachs made biscuits, rations, and sugar disappear with extraordinary rapidity.

We ran before the wind through the loose pack, a man in the bow of each boat trying to pole off with a broken oar the lumps of ice that could not be avoided. I regarded speed as essential. Sometimes collisions were not averted. The *James Caird* was in the lead, where she bore the brunt of the encounters with lurking fragments, and she was holed above the waterline by a sharp spur of ice, but this mishap did not stay us. Later the wind became stronger and we had to reef sails, so as not to strike the ice too heavily. The *Dudley Docker* came next to the *James Caird* and the *Stancomb Wills* followed. I had given orders that the boats should keep 30 or 40 yds. apart, so as to reduce the danger of a collision if one boat was checked by the ice. The pack was thinning, and we came to occasional open areas where thin ice had formed during the night. When we encountered this new ice we had to shake the reef out of the sails in order to force a way through. Outside of the pack the wind must have been of hurricane force.

Thousands of small dead fish were to be seen, killed probably by a cold current and the heavy weather. They floated in the water and lay on the ice, where they had been cast by the waves. The petrels and skua gulls were swooping down and picking them up like sardines off toast.

The Boat Journey

F. A. Worsley

On taking to their lifeboats (see pp285–97), Shackleton's men made their way to Elephant Island in the South Shetlands. This was not salvation, however, for Elephant Island was barren and uninhabited. Relief would have to be secured from further across the seas; it was determined that six men – Shackleton himself, Crean, McNeish, Vincent, McCarthy and the Endurance's *captain Worsley – would sail to South Georgia, 800 miles away, across the most savage waters in the world. Their transport was the 22-feet-long lifeboat, the* James Caird.

After noon the gale and sea increased, with intense cold. We rolled the sails up and stowed them below in the already confined space, to prevent them freezing, holding a mass of ice and capsizing the boat with top weight. The seas breaking on the boat froze and cased her heavily with ice, but we should have been worse off without the sea anchor.

To keep a boat afloat in very heavy weather, two things are almost necessities – oil to mollify the seas, and a sea anchor to ride to. Of oil we had ample for one day's gale – we had ten days' gales on this passage. A sea anchor consists of a canvas cone or bag, three to four feet long, the mouth nearly as wide and a small hole at the other end. Four small lines at the mouth are spliced into a "thimble", to which the rope is attached. When a gale is so heavy that a boat cannot run before it, she takes in sail and heaves to by throwing the sea-anchor over, with one end of the rope passed through the thimble, and the other end fast in the bows. Having no other rope, we used the painter. By dragging in the sea – the water escaping through the small hole – the sea anchor holds the boat head to wind and sea, the best position for riding out a gale.

We saw a few penguins in the afternoon, three hundred miles from any land. They were quite indifferent to the gale or the cold; we felt envious of them. By the bitter cold of the gale we reckoned it blew straight off pack ice not far away.

We drank our seal oil, black and odoriferous, as it was not worth keeping for one day of the gale and its calories were so valuable. A matter of latitude – what would have made us ill in the tropics was nectar here!

The ice increased on the boat till we had to excavate the four oars from a mound of it. They caught so much freezing water that we were forced to throw two overboard, and lash the others one on each side, for a railing from the mainshrouds to the mizzen-mast, eighteen inches above the "deck". They held very little ice then, and there was less danger of falling overboard. This was a serious sacrifice, but we could not get the other two oars below.

All night the breaking seas froze over her. This had one advantage; it stopped intermittent bucketsful pouring through the "deck" and down our necks, but pumping and bailing had still to be done at frequent intervals.

The eighth day the gale held steadily throughout from south-south-west, with a very heavy, lumpy sea. It was impossible to write – even a few remarks. These would have been illegible – but anyway unprintable – owing to the violent jerky contortions of the *Caird*. She was heavily iced all over outside, and a quantity of ice had formed inside her.

Sir Ernest had the Primus going day and night as long as we could stand the fumes, then it would be put out for an hour. This and a generous drink of life-giving hot milk every four hours, at the relief of the watches, kept all hands from any ill effects.

All gear was wet through. The sleeping-bags had a nasty sour-bread kind of smell, and were on the point of fermenting. I believe, in fact, that a certain amount of fermentation had started, and so prevented us feeling the cold quite so much in our sleep, as we called it.

We all smelt as well, or rather as ill, as our bags. We used to long for a hot bath or clean, dry clothes.

May Day. The ice on the boat got so thick and heavy that she was riding deep and had a tendency to capsize. Something had

to be done, and quickly, so we took it in turns to crawl out with
an axe and chop off the ice. What a job! The boat leaped and
kicked like a mad mule; she was covered fifteen inches deep in a
casing of ice like a turtleback, with slush all over where the last
sea was freezing. First you chopped a handhold, then a knee-
hold, and then chopped off ice hastily but carefully, with an
occasional sea washing over you. After four or five minutes –
"fed up" or frost-bitten – you slid back into shelter, and the
next man took up the work. It was a case of "one hand for yourself, and one for the King", for if a man had gone overboard
then, it would have been goodbye. Finally, we got the bulk of it
off, and were satisfied. All night the gale continued heavily from
south-south-west.

The ninth day. In the forenoon a heavy sea struck the *Caird*.
Almost immediately her bows fell off till the sea was abeam. The
great cake of ice that had formed on the painter at the bows, in
such a position that we could not smash it off, had swung to and
fro, round and round, till it had sawed and chafed through the
painter. So we lost both rope and sea anchor, which seemed a
double disaster to us.

We beat the ice off the jib, reefed and set it on the mainmast.

By 11 a.m. the gale had eased enough for us to set the reefed
lug and jib and run drunkenly before the wind and sea.

This fierce, cold gale had lasted at its height for forty-eight
hours. During that period we had, no fewer than three times –
once practically in the dark – to crawl out on top of the boat to
chop and scrape the ice off. We all agreed it was the worst job we
had ever taken on in our lives.

I estimated that day's drift at thirty-six miles – sixty-six miles
to north-east during the time we were hove to. The boat's antics
were almost as bad as before. The dead reckoning figures were
made one at a time by jabbing with the pencil as occasion offered.
By strict economy I confined their numbers to twenty-five. It was
impossible to write – perhaps I should say it was impossible to
force oneself to try.

The reindeer bags were now so miserable to get into that
when we had finished our watch and it was time to turn in, we
had serious doubts as to whether it was worthwhile. The smell
of cured skin constantly soaked and slept in was appalling. First

you undressed; that is, you took off your boots, and throwing back the flap of the bag thrust your legs in hurriedly. It felt like getting between frozen rawhide – which it was. You kicked your feet violently together for two minutes to warm them and the bag, then slid in to the waist. Again you kicked your feet and knocked your knees together and then like a little hero made a sudden brave plunge right inside. At first, while you knocked your feet together, it felt like an icehouse, and then it began to thaw out and you wished it hadn't – it smelt so, and the moulting hairs got into eyes, mouth, and nose. So, coughing, sneezing, and spluttering, you kicked your feet valiantly together till there was enough warmth in them to allow you to sleep for perhaps an hour. When you awoke you kicked again till you fell asleep, and so on.

After this gale the bags were in such a hopeless, sloppy, slimy mess, and weighed so heavily, that Sir Ernest had the worst two thrown overboard.

All that day and night we held on our erratic course before the gale.

In steering a small boat before a heavy gale don't look back – it may disconcert you. Fix your eye on a cloud or breaking sea right ahead and keep her straight – if you can. When you hear a roaring Bull of Bashan, with a wet nose, galloping up behind you, keep your shoulders hunched up to your ears – till you get it, then yell, "Pump and bailers." There's no need to, for they're hard at it already, but it shows you're alive, all right.

A great find – an inch of candle in the socket of the compass lamp. At night I lit it and, dropping a few spots of grease on the compass glass, stuck it three inches to the right of the centre. Then the procedure was to strike a flaming match once a watch at night for a smoke, and to light this piece of candle for a few minutes. Sheltered by our hands, its flickering light enabled the helmsman to correct the course and check it off by the sea, wind, and fluttering pennant. No need to blow it out, the wind did that, then all was darkness again, except for Tom Crean or Macarty's dully glowing pipe. About this time the compass glass got broken. We mended it with strips of sticking plaster from the medicine chest.

After my "trick" at the helm in the middle watch, when extra cold and wet, I got stiffened in the crouching position I had assumed to dodge the seas, and had to be hauled inside, massaged, and opened out like a jackknife before I could get into my sleeping-bag.

A few scribbled remarks in my navigating book ran: "Bags and finneskoe moulting at a great rate – 'feathers' everywhere – most objectionable in hoosh. My finneskoe are now quite bald. We are all suffering from superficially frost-bitten feet, Macarty is the most irrepressible optimist I've ever met. When I relieved him at the helm, boat iced over and seas pouring down our necks, one came right over us and I felt like swearing, but just kept it back, and he informed me with a cheerful grin 'It's a foine day, sorr.' I had been feeling a bit sour before, but this shamed me. His cheeriness does brighten things up."

As a rule, when a sea wets a sailor through, he swears at it, and comprehensively and impartially curses everything in sight, beginning with the ship and the "old man" – if he's not within hearing; but on this passage we said nothing when a sea hit us in the face. It was grin and bear it; for it was Sir Ernest's theory that by keeping our tempers and general cheeriness we each helped to keep one another up. We all lived up to this to the best of our ability, but Macarty was a marvel.

After the third day our feet and legs had swelled, and began to be superficially frost-bitten from the constant soaking in sea water, with the temperature at times nearly down to zero; and the lack of exercise. During the last gale they assumed a dead-white colour and lost surface feeling.

Our footgear consisted of two pairs of Jaeger wool socks, homemade felt shoes, ankle-high (mine were Greenstreet's handiwork), and, over all, finneskoe (reindeer-skin boots), hair out and skin in, when we started – now it was skin inside and out. When your feet got unbearably cold you took off your footgear and, rinsing your socks in the sea, wiped your feet, wrung out your socks, and again wiped your feet before replacing your footgear. This was the wag's opportunity. While busily engaged with your socks he would prick your toe with a Primus pricker. Getting no response he would prick higher and higher up foot and leg, till the victim suddenly jumped, yelled, or swore according to temperament. This was not merely horseplay or idle curiosity

– it was also an index as to how one's feet and legs were standing the rigours of the passage.

To prevent my feet getting worse, I adopted a system of wriggling them constantly, contracting and relaxing my toes until quite tired, waiting a minute, then wriggling them again, and so on. I think it saved my feet a good deal.

At midnight Shackleton relieved me. The south-west gale had been steadily increasing with snow squalls for eight hours and there was a heavy cross sea running which caused us to ship more seas over the boat even than usual. Just before he crawled out from under the canvas a sea struck me full in the face and the front as I stood aft steering with the lee yoke line to keep her out of the wind. The water was running out of me as he relieved me at the helm and then another sea dashed over the two of us. "Pretty juicy," he said, and we both forced a laugh. I crawled below and into my sodden sleeping-bag. In spite of wet and cold I fell asleep instantly, but soon after something awakened me. Then I heard Shackleton shout "It's clearing, boys!" and immediately after, "For God's sake, hold on! It's got us!" The line of white along the southern horizon that he had taken for the sky clearing was, in fact, the foaming crest of an enormous sea. I was crawling out of my bag as the sea struck us. There was a roaring of water around and above us – it was almost as though we had foundered. The boat seemed full of water. We other five men seized any receptacle we could find and pushed, scooped, and bailed the water out for dear life. While Shackleton held her up to the wind, we worked like madmen, but for five minutes it was uncertain whether we would succeed or not.

We could not keep that pace up – gradually we eased off as we realized that we had saved our lives. With the aid of the little homemade pump and two dippers it took us nearly an hour to get rid of the water and restore the boat to her normal state of having only a few gallons of water washing about the bilges through the stones and shingle. The wave that had struck us was so sudden and enormous that I have since come to the conclusion that it may have been caused by the capsizing of some great iceberg unseen and unheard by us in the darkness and the heavy gale.

The tenth day. In the morning the south-west gale moderated

and backed to west with great white cumulus clouds racing over-head, and clear weather. "Old Jamaica" showed his face through the clouds and I made the position 56° 13' S and 45°38' W. The run was N 55° E sixty-two miles, 444 since leaving Elephant Island. We had done more than half the distance, and had a happy feeling of certainty that we should succeed in our adventure.

Crossing South Georgia

Ernest Shackleton

After Shackleton's boat journey to South Georgia (see pp 298ff), his rescue mission was still faced with the challenge of traversing the island to reach the whaling station at Stromness.

A fresh west-south-westerly breeze was blowing on the following morning (Wednesday, 17 May), with misty squalls, sleet, and rain. I took Worsley with me on a pioneer journey to the west with the object of examining the country to be traversed at the beginning of the overland journey. We went round the seaward end of the snouted glacier, and after tramping about a mile over stony ground and snow-coated debris, we crossed some big ridges of scree and moraines. We found that there was good going for a sledge as far as the north-east corner of the bay, but did not get much information regarding the conditions farther on owing to the view becoming obscured by a snow squall. We waited a quarter of an hour for the weather to clear but were forced to turn back without having seen more of the country. I had satisfied myself, however, that we could reach a good snow slope leading apparently to the inland ice. Worsley reckoned from the chart that the distance from our camp to Husvik, on an east magnetic course, was seventeen geographical miles, but we could not expect to follow a direct line. The carpenter started making a sledge for use on the overland journey. The materials at his disposal were limited in quantity and scarcely suitable in quality.

We overhauled our gear on Thursday, 18 May and hauled our sledge to the lower edge of the snouted glacier. The vehicle proved heavy and cumbrous. We had to lift it empty over bare patches of rock along the shore, and I realized that it would be too heavy for three men to manage amid the snow plains, glaciers, and peaks of the interior. Worsley and Crean were coming with me, and after consultation we decided to leave the sleeping-bags behind us and make the journey in very light marching order. We would take three days' provisions for each man in the form of sledging ration and biscuit. The food was to be packed in three sacks, so that each member of the party could carry his own supply. Then we were to take the Primus lamp filled with oil, the small cooker, the carpenter's adze (for use as an ice-axe), and the alpine rope, which made a total length of fifty feet when knotted. We might have to lower ourselves down steep slopes or cross crevassed glaciers. The filled lamp would provide six hot meals, which would consist of sledging ration boiled up with biscuit. There were two boxes of matches left, one full and the other partially used. We left the full box with the men at the camp and took the second box, which contained forty-eight matches. I was unfortunate as regarded footgear, since I had given away my heavy Burberry boots on the floe, and had now a comparatively light pair in poor condition. The carpenter assisted me by putting several screws in the sole of each boot with the object of providing a grip on the ice. The screws came out of the *James Caird*.

We turned in early that night, but sleep did not come to me. My mind was busy with the task of the following day. The weather was clear and the outlook for an early start in the morning was good. We were going to leave a weak party behind us in the camp. Vincent was still in the same condition, and he could not march. McNeish was pretty well broken up. The two men were not capable of managing for themselves and McCarthy must stay to look after them. He might have a difficult task if we failed to reach the whaling station. The distance to Husvik, according to the chart, was no more than seventeen geographical miles in a direct line, but we had very scanty knowledge of the conditions of the interior. No man had ever penetrated a mile from the coast of South Georgia at any point, and the whalers I knew regarded the country as inaccessible. During that day, while we were walking to the snouted glacier, we had seen three wild duck flying towards the head of the bay from the eastward. I hoped that the presence of these birds indicated tussock land and not snow fields and glaciers in the interior, but the hope was not a very bright one.

We turned out at 2 a.m. on the Friday morning and had our
hoosh ready an hour later. The full moon was shining in a practically cloudless sky, its rays reflected gloriously from the pinnacles
and crevassed ice of the adjacent glaciers. The huge peaks of the
mountains stood in bold relief against the sky and threw dark
shadows on the waters of the sound. There was no need for
delay, and we made a start as soon as we had eaten our meal.
McNeish walked about 200 yds with us; he could do no more.
Then we said goodbye and he turned back to the camp. The first
task was to get round the edge of the snouted glacier, which had
points like fingers projecting towards the sea. The waves were
reaching the points of these fingers, and we had to rush from one
across to another when the waters receded. We soon reached the
east side of the glacier and noticed its great activity at this point.
Changes had occurred within the preceding twenty-four hours.
Some huge pieces had broken off, and the masses of mud and
stone that were being driven before the advancing ice showed
movement. The glacier was like a gigantic plough driving irresistibly towards the sea.

Lying on the beach beyond the glacier was wreckage that told
of many ill-fated ships. We noticed stanchions of teakwood,
liberally carved, that must have come from ships of the older
type; ironbound timbers with the iron almost rusted through;
battered barrels and all the usual debris of the ocean. We had
difficulties and anxieties of our own, but as we passed that grave-
yard of the sea we thought of the many tragedies written in the
wave-worn fragments of lost vessels. We did not pause, and soon
we were ascending a snow slope, heading due east on the last lap
of our long trail.

The snow surface was disappointing. Two days before we had
been able to move rapidly on hard, packed snow; now we sank
over our ankles at each step and progress was slow. After two
hours' steady climbing we were 2,500 ft above sea level. The
weather continued fine and calm, and as the ridges drew nearer
and the western coast of the island spread out below, the bright
moonlight showed us that the interior was broken tremendously.
High peaks, impassable cliffs, steep snow slopes, and sharply
descending glaciers were prominent features in all directions,
with stretches of snow plain overlaying the ice sheet of the

interior. The slope we were ascending mounted to a ridge and our course lay direct to the top. The moon, which proved a good friend during this journey, threw a long shadow at one point and told us that the surface was broken in our path. Warned in time, we avoided a huge hole capable of swallowing an army. The bay was now about three miles away, and the continued roaring of a big glacier at the head of the bay came to our ears. This glacier, which we had noticed during the stay at Peggotty Camp, seemed to be calving almost continuously.

I had hoped to get a view of the country ahead of us from the top of the slope, but as the surface became more level beneath our feet, a thick fog drifted down. The moon became obscured and produced a diffused light that was more trying than darkness, since it illuminated the fog without guiding our steps. We roped ourselves together as a precaution against holes, crevasses, and precipices, and I broke trail through the soft snow. With almost the full length of the rope between myself and the last man we were able to steer an approximately straight course, since, if I veered to the right or the left when marching into the blank wall of the fog, the last man on the rope could shout a direction. So, like a ship with its "port", "starboard", "steady", we tramped through the fog for the next two hours.

Then, as daylight came, the fog thinned and lifted, and from an elevation of about 3,000 ft we looked down on what seemed to be a huge frozen lake with its farther shores still obscured by the fog. We halted there to eat a bit of biscuit while we discussed whether we would go down and cross the flat surface of the lake, or keep on the ridge we had already reached. I decided to go down, since the lake lay on our course. After an hour of comparatively easy travel through the snow we noticed the thin beginnings of crevasses. Soon they were increasing in size and showing fractures, indicating that we were travelling on a glacier. As the daylight brightened the fog dissipated; the lake could be seen more clearly, but still we could not discover its east shore. A little later the fog lifted completely, and then we saw that our lake stretched to the horizon, and realized suddenly that we were looking down upon the open sea on the east coast of the island. The slight pulsation at the shore showed that the sea was not even frozen; it was the bad light that had deceived us. Evidently we were at the top of Possession Bay, and the island at that point could not be more than five miles across from the head of King Haakon Bay. Our rough chart was inaccurate. There was nothing for it but to start up the glacier again. That was about seven o'clock in the morning, and by nine o'clock we had more than recovered our lost ground. We regained the ridge and then struck south-east, for the chart showed that two more bays indented the coast before Stromness. It was comforting to realize that we would have the eastern water in sight during our journey, although we could see there was no way around the shoreline owing to steep cliffs and glaciers. Men lived in houses lit by electric light on the east coast. News of the outside world waited us there, and, above all, the east coast meant for us the means of rescuing the twenty-two men we had left on Elephant Island.

The sun rose in the sky with every appearance of a fine day, and we grew warmer as we toiled through the soft snow. Ahead of us lay the ridges and spurs of a range of mountains, the transverse range that we had noticed from the bay. We were travelling over a gently rising plateau, and at the end of an hour we found ourselves growing uncomfortably hot. Years before, on an earlier expedition, I had declared that I would never again growl at the heat of the sun, and my resolution had been strengthened during the boat journey. I called it to mind as the sun beat fiercely on the blinding white snow slope. After passing an area of crevasses we paused for our first meal. We dug a hole in the snow about three feet deep with the adze and put the Primus into it. There was no wind at the moment, but a gust might come suddenly. A hot hoosh was soon eaten and we plodded on towards a sharp ridge between two of the peaks already mentioned. By 11 a.m. we were almost at the crest. The slope had become precipitous and it was necessary to cut steps as we advanced. The adze proved an excellent instrument for this purpose, a blow sufficing to provide a foothold. Anxiously but hopefully I cut the last few steps and stood upon the razorback, while the other men held the rope and waited for my news. The outlook was disappointing. I looked down a sheer precipice to a chaos of crumpled ice 1,500 ft below. There was no way down for us. The country to the east was a great snow upland, sloping upwards for a distance of seven or eight miles to a height of over 4,000 ft. To the north it fell away steeply in glaciers into the bays, and to the south it was broken by huge outfalls from the inland ice sheet. Our path lay between the glaciers and the outfalls, but first we had to descend from the ridge on which we stood.

Cutting steps with the adze, we moved in a lateral direction round the base of a dolomite, which blocked our view to the north. The same precipice confronted us. Away to the north-east there appeared to be a snow slope that might give a path to the lower country, and so we retraced our steps down the long slope that had taken us three hours to climb. We were at the bottom in an hour. We were now feeling the strain of the unaccustomed marching. We had done little walking since January and our muscles were out of tune. Skirting the base of the mountain above us, we came to a gigantic bergschrund, a mile and a half long and 1,000 ft deep. This tremendous gully, cut in the snow and ice by the fierce winds blowing round the mountain, was semicircular in form, and it ended in a gentle incline. We passed through it, under the towering precipice of ice, and at the far end we had another meal and a short rest. This was at 12.30 p.m. Half a pot of steaming Bovril ration warmed us up, and when we marched again ice inclines at angles of 45 degrees did not look quite as formidable as before.

Once more we started for the crest. After another weary climb we reached the top. The snow lay thinly on blue ice at the ridge, and we had to cut steps over the last fifty yards. The same precipice lay below, and my eyes searched vainly for a way down. The hot sun had loosened the snow, which was now in a treacherous condition, and we had to pick our way carefully. Looking back, we could see that a fog was rolling up behind us and meeting in the valleys a fog that was coming up from the east. The creeping grey clouds were a plain warning that we must get down to lower levels before becoming enveloped.

The ridge was studded with peaks, which prevented us getting a clear view either to the right or to the left. The situation in this respect seemed no better at other points within our reach, and I had to decide that our course lay back the way we had come. The afternoon was wearing on and the fog was rolling up ominously from the west. It was of the utmost importance for us to get down into the next valley before dark. We were now up 4,500 ft and the night temperature at that elevation would be very low. We had no tent and no sleeping-bags, and our clothes had endured much rough usage and had weathered many storms during the last ten months. In the distance, down the valley below us, we could see tussock grass close to the shore, and if we could get down it might be possible to dig out a hole in one of the lower snowbanks, line it with dry grass, and make ourselves fairly comfortable for the night. Back we went, and after a detour we reached the top of another ridge in the fading light. After a glance over the top I turned to the anxious faces of the two men behind me and said, "Come on, boys." Within a minute they stood beside me on the ice ridge. The surface fell away at a sharp incline in front of us, but it merged into a snow slope. We could not see the bottom clearly owing to mist and bad light, and the possibility of the slope ending in a sheer fall occurred to us; but the fog that was creeping up behind allowed no time for hesitation. We descended slowly at first, cutting steps in the hard snow; then the surface became softer, indicating that the gradient was less severe. There could be no turning back now, so we unroped and slid in the fashion of youthful days. When we stopped on a snow bank at the foot of the slope we found that we had descended at least 900 ft in two or three minutes. We looked back and saw the grey fingers of the fog appearing on the ridge, as though reaching after the intruders into untrodden wilds. But we had escaped.

The country to the east was an ascending snow upland dividing the glaciers of the north coast from the outfalls of the south. We had seen from the top that our course lay between two huge masses of crevasses, and we thought that the road ahead lay clear. This belief and the increasing cold made us abandon the idea of camping. We had another meal at 6 p.m. A little breeze made cooking difficult in spite of the shelter provided for the cooker by a hole. Crean was the cook, and Worsley and I lay on the snow to windward of the lamp so as to break the wind with our bodies. The meal over, we started up the long, gentle ascent. Night was upon us, and for an hour we plodded along in almost complete darkness, watching warily for signs of crevasses. Then about 8 p.m. a glow which we had seen behind the jagged peaks resolved itself into the full moon, which rose ahead of us and made a silver pathway for our feet. Along that pathway in the wake of the moon we advanced in safety, with the shadows cast by the edges of crevasses showing black on either side of us. Onwards and upwards through soft snow we marched, resting now and then on hard patches which had revealed themselves by glittering ahead of us in the white light. By midnight we were again at an elevation of about 4,000 ft. Still we were following the light, for as the moon swung round towards the north-east our path curved in that direction. The friendly moon seemed to pilot our weary feet. We could have had no better guide. If in bright daylight we had made that march we would have followed the course that was traced for us that night.

Midnight found us approaching the edge of a great snow field, pierced by isolated nunataks which cast long shadows like black rivers across the white expanse. A gentle slope to the north-east lured our all-too-willing feet in that direction. We thought that at the base of the slope lay Stromness Bay. After we had descended about 300 ft a thin wind began to attack us. We had now been on the march for over twenty hours, only halting for our occasional meals. Wisps of cloud drove over the high peaks to the south-ward, warning us that wind and snow were likely to come. After 1 a.m. we cut a pit in the snow, piled up loose snow around it, and started the Primus again. The hot food gave us another renewal of energy. Worsley and Crean sang their old songs when the Primus was going merrily. Laughter was in our hearts, though not on our parched and cracked lips.

We were up and away again within half an hour, still down-ward to the coast. We felt almost sure now that we were above Stromness Bay. A dark object down at the foot of the slope looked like Mutton Island, which lies off Husvik. I suppose our desires were giving wings to our fancies, for we pointed out joyfully various landmarks revealed by the now vagrant light of the moon, whose friendly face was cloud-swept. Our high hopes were soon shattered. Crevasses warned us that we were on another glacier, and soon we looked down almost to the seaward edge of the great riven ice mass. I knew there was no glacier in Stromness and realized that this must be Fortuna Glacier. The disappointment was severe. Back we turned and tramped up the glacier again, not directly tracing our steps but working at a tangent to the south-east. We were very tired.

At 5 a.m. we were at the foot of the rocky spurs of the range. We were tired, and the wind that blew down from the heights was chilling us. We decided to get down under the lee of a rock for a rest. We put our sticks and the adze on the snow, sat down on them as close to one another as possible, and put our arms round each other. The wind was bringing a little drift with it and the white dust lay on our clothes. I thought that we might be able to keep warm and have half an hour's rest this way. Within a minute my two companions were fast asleep. I realized that it would be disastrous if we all slumbered together, for sleep under such conditions merges into death. After five minutes I shook them into consciousness again, told them that they had slept for half an hour, and gave the word for a fresh start. We were so stiff that for the first two or three hundred yards we marched with our knees bent. A jagged line of peaks with a gap like a broken tooth confronted us. This was the ridge that runs in a southerly direction from Fortuna Bay, and our course eastward to Stromness lay across it. A very steep slope led up to the ridge and an icy wind burst through the gap.

We went through the gap at 6 a.m. with anxious hearts as well as weary bodies. If the farther slope had proved impassable our situation would have been almost desperate; but the worst was turning to the best for us. The twisted, wave-like rock formations of Husvik Harbour appeared right ahead in the opening of dawn. Without a word we shook hands with one another. To our minds the journey was over, though as a matter of fact twelve miles of difficult country had still to be traversed. A gentle snow slope descended at our feet towards a valley that separated our ridge from the hills immediately behind Husvik, and as we stood gazing Worsley said solemnly, "Boss, it looks too good to be true!" Down we went, to be checked presently by the sight of water 2,500 ft below. We could see the little wave ripples on the black beach, penguins strutting to and fro, and dark objects that looked like seals lolling lazily on the sand. This was an eastern arm of Fortuna Bay, separated by the ridge from the arm we had seen below us during the night. The slope we were traversing appeared to end in a precipice above this beach. But our revived spirits were not to be damped by difficulties on the last stage of the journey, and we camped cheerfully for breakfast. While Worsley and Crean were digging a hole for the lamp and starting the cooker I climbed a ridge above us, cutting steps with the adze, in order to secure an extended view of the country below. At 6:30 a.m. I thought I heard the sound of a steam whistle. I dared not be certain, but I knew that the men at the whaling station would be called from their beds about that time. Descending to the camp I told the others, and in intense excitement we watched the chronometer for seven o'clock, when the whalers would be summoned to work. Right to the minute the steam whistle came to us, borne clearly on the wind across the intervening miles of rock and snow. Never had any one of us heard sweeter music. It was the first sound created by outside human agency that had come to our ears since we left Stromness Bay in December 1914. That whistle told us that men were living near, that ships were ready, and that within a few hours we should be on our way back to Elephant Island to the rescue of the men waiting there under the watch and ward of Wild. It was a moment hard to describe. Pain and ache, boat journeys, marches, hunger and fatigue seemed to belong to the limbo of forgotten things, and there remained only the perfect contentment that comes of work accomplished.

My examination of the country from a higher point had not provided definite information, and after descending I put the situation before Worsley and Crean. Our obvious course lay down a snow slope in the direction of Husvik. "Boys," I said, "this snow slope seems to end in a precipice, but perhaps there is no precipice. If we don't go down we shall have to make a detour of at least five miles before we reach level going. What shall it be?" They both replied at once. "Try the slope." So we started away again downwards. We abandoned the Primus lamp, now empty, at the breakfast camp and carried with us one ration and a biscuit each. The deepest snow we had yet encountered clogged our feet, but we plodded downward, and after descending about 500 ft, reducing our altitude to 2,000 ft above sea level, we thought we saw the way clear ahead. A steep gradient of blue ice was the next obstacle. Worsley and Crean got a firm footing in a hole excavated with the adze and then lowered me as I cut steps until the full 50 ft of our alpine rope was out. Then I made a hole big enough for the three of us, and the other two men came down the steps. My end of the rope was anchored to the adze and I had settled myself in the hole braced for a strain in case they slipped. When we all stood in the second hole I went down again to make more steps, and in this labourious fashion we spent two hours descending about 500 ft. Halfway down we had to strike away diagonally to the left, for we noticed that the fragments of ice loosened by the adze were taking a leap into space at the bottom of the slope. Eventually we got off the steep ice, very gratefully, at a point where some rocks protruded, and we could see then that there was a perilous precipice directly below the point where we had started to cut steps. A slide down a slippery slope, with the adze and our cooker going ahead, completed this descent, and incidentally did considerable damage to our much-tried trousers.

When we picked ourselves up at the bottom we were not more than 1,500 ft above the sea. The slope was comparatively easy. Water was running beneath the snow, making "pockets" between the rocks that protruded above the white surface. The shells of snow over these pockets were traps for our feet; but we scrambled down, and presently came to patches of tussock. A few minutes later we reached the sandy beach. The tracks of some animals were to be seen, and we were puzzled until I remembered that reindeer, brought from Norway, had been placed on the island and now ranged along the lower land of the eastern coast. We did not pause to investigate. Our minds were set upon reaching the haunts of man, and at our best speed we went along the beach to another rising ridge of tussock. Here we saw the first evidence of the proximity of man, whose work, as is so often the case, was one of destruction. A recently killed seal was lying there, and presently we saw several other bodies bearing the marks of bullet wounds. I learned that men from the whaling station at Stromness sometimes go round to Fortuna Bay by boat to shoot seals.

Noon found us well up the slope on the other side of the bay working east-south-east, and half an hour later we were on a flat plateau, with one more ridge to cross before we descended into Husvik. I was leading the way over this plateau when I suddenly found myself up to my knees in water and quickly sinking deeper through the snow crust. I flung myself down and called to the others to do the same, so as to distribute our weight on the treacherous surface. We were on top of a small lake, snow-covered. After lying still for a few moments, we got to our feet and walked delicately, like Agag, for 200 yds, until a rise in the surface showed us that we were clear of the lake.

At 1:30 p.m. we climbed round a final ridge and saw a little steamer, a whaling boat, entering the bay 2,500 ft below. A few moments later, as we hurried forward, the masts of a sailing ship lying at a wharf came in sight. Minute figures moving to and fro about the boats caught our gaze, and then we saw the sheds and factory of Stromness whaling station. We paused and shook hands, a form of mutual congratulation that had seemed necessary on four other occasions in the course of the expedition. The first time was when we landed on Elephant Island, the second when we reached South Georgia, and the third when we reached the ridge and saw the snow slope stretching below on the first day of the overland journey, then when we saw Husvik rocks.

Cautiously we started down the slope that led to warmth and comfort. The last lap of the journey proved extraordinarily difficult. Vainly we searched for a safe, or a reasonably safe, way down from the steep ice-clad mountainside. The sole possible pathway seemed to be a channel cut by water running from the upland. Down through icy water we followed the course of this stream. We were wet to the waist, shivering, cold, and tired. Presently our ears detected an unwelcome sound that might have been musical under other conditions. It was the splashing of a waterfall, and we were at the wrong end. When we reached the top of this fall we peered over cautiously and discovered that there was a drop of 25 or 30 ft, with impassable ice cliffs on both sides. To go up again was scarcely thinkable in our utterly wearied condition. The way down was through the waterfall itself. We made fast one end of our rope to a boulder with some difficulty, due to the fact that the rocks had been worn smooth by the running water. Then Worsley and I lowered Crean, who was the heaviest man. He disappeared altogether in the falling water and came out gasping at the bottom. I went next, sliding down the rope, and Worsley, who was the lightest and most nimble member of the party, came last. At the bottom of the fall we were able to stand again on dry land. The rope could not be recovered. We had flung down the adze from the top of the fall and also the logbook and the cooker wrapped in one of our blouses. That was all, except our wet clothes, that we brought out of the Antarctic, which we had entered a year and a half before with well-found ship, full equipment, and high hopes. That was all of tangible things; but in memories we were rich. We had pierced the veneer of outside things. We had "suffered, starved, and triumphed, grovelled down yet grasped at glory, grown bigger in the bigness of the whole." We had seen God in his splendours, heard the text that Nature renders. We had reached the naked soul of men.

Shivering with cold, yet with hearts light and happy, we set off towards the whaling station, now not more than a mile and a half distant. The difficulties of the journey lay behind us. We tried to straighten ourselves up a bit for the thought that there might be women at the station made us painfully conscious of our uncivilized appearance. Our beards were long and our hair was matted. We were unwashed and the garments that we had worn for nearly a year without a change were tattered and stained. Three more unpleasant-looking ruffians could hardly have been imagined. Worsley produced several safety pins from some corner of his garments and effected some temporary repairs that really emphasized his general disrepair. Down we hurried, and when quite close to the station we met two small boys ten or twelve years of age. I asked these lads where the manager's house was situated. They did not answer. They gave us one look – a comprehensive look that did not need to be repeated. Then they ran from us as fast as their legs would carry them. We reached the outskirts of the station and passed through the "digesting-house", which was dark inside. Emerging at the other end, we met an old man, who started as if he had seen the Devil himself and gave us no time to ask any question. He hurried away. This greeting was not friendly. Then we came to the wharf, where the man in charge stuck to his station. I asked him if Mr Sorlle (the manager) was in the house.

"Yes," he said as he stared at us.

"We would like to see him," said I.

"Who are you?" he asked.

"We have lost our ship and come over the island," I replied.

"You have come over the island?" he said in a tone of entire disbelief.

The man went towards the manager's house and we followed him. I learned afterwards that he said to Mr Sorlle: "There are three funny-looking men outside, who say they have come over the island and they know you. I have left them outside." A very necessary precaution from his point of view.

Mr Sorlle came out to the door and said, "Well?"

"Don't you know me?" I said.

"I know your voice," he replied doubtfully. "You're the mate of the *Daisy*."

"My name is Shackleton," I said.

Immediately, he put out his hand and said, "Come in. Come in."

"Tell me, when was the war over?" I asked.

"The war is not over," he answered. "Millions are being killed. Europe is mad. The world is mad."

The "Boss", as Shackleton was known, then went back and rescued every man of his party.

Waiting for Salvation

Thomas Orde-Lees

A captain in the Royal Marines, Orde-Lees was in charge of the
Endurance *expedition's motor-sledges. He was amongst the* Endurance
party who waited for rescue from Elephant Island.

June 15th: Mild but wet 31 degrees. Blackborrow has toes ampu-
tated. All hands except doctors, Wild and Hurley remain outside
for 3 hours taking shelter in cave. Bakewell cuts hair. Very dull
and monotonous in bags. Able to read for an hour or two at
noon. Very full [dull?] menu.

16th: Still mild and wet, rain in night thawing everywhere. In
bags all day. Very monotonous.

17th: Very mild 30 degrees some snow. SE wind much pack but
no swell. All rather weak through the lying in bags so much.
Daylight 9 a.m.–3 p.m. Open water visible from hill. Great craving for carbohydrates.

18th: Beautiful day. 2 hours sunshine. All exchanges stopped. I
am ordered to surrender all further claim on the sugar for which
I had paid NF. By this order I am a loser. There is a clique against
me to whom Wild gives too much heed. I am called a Jew.

June 29th: Cold calm both bays full of very loose pack. We kill a
young elephant [seal]. Much scarred blubber underneath. Meat
only enough for one day. 2 paddies. Another seal in water.

30th: SW blizzard. In bags all day. 16 penguins up. Not killed,
weather too severe.

July 1st: Beautiful sunny day but very cold. Both bays clear but much pack on E horizon drifting in. Penguins leave in morning by W bay, very unusual. 11 penguins come up in E bay in afternoon. 7 only killed. Skin, heart and liver only kept. Breast and legs thrown away with carcasses. Wild says we have fuel to mid August and too much meat. 13 degrees.

2nd: Wet and gloomy but able to read in hut until 3 p.m. by light reflected from fresh snow at door and through wet walls.

July 3rd: Terribly monotonous and weakening lying in bags so much. Get quite bed ridden. Vitiated air caused headache. Smoke from stove injures eyes. Food, rubbish etc. fall on me all day long. Piece of old tent affords me some protection. Anxiety re Sir E. We invent ideas to suit events and now expect *Aurora* to relieve us about 1st August. Blackborrow progressing well. Hudson rather ill with pain in his back. 25 penguins up but weather too bad to kill. W blizzard and all men cold and wet.

Blizzard of 7th July turned my lump sugar Venesta box upside down scattering contents and shaking strap off. I find the lid 100 yards away down by NW rocks.

On 8th about 150 shags on NW rocks. Wild says *Aurora* will have been very quick if she gets here before end of July and that he will not get uneasy until middle of Aug. I say I shall not be anxious until end of Sept. Wild also says that the spit will be free from snow by middle of August with subsequent cold snaps. I say middle of September. My berth in hut once considered the worst is now much envied owing to its proximity to stove and facilities for cooking, warming up hoosh and running down oil from penguin fat. I exchanged places with Kerr two months ago. Hither too have had no lamp now Wild has granted me the use of nightlight directly after supper.

July 9th: Strong SW wind in night. 31 degrees cold but fine. Light increasing noticeable. I am able today to write this by daylight reflected from snow through open door at 8.30 a.m. No ice in sight and few bergs. E bay quite clear. Some glacier brash in W Bay.

Men all out of tobacco makes them very irritable and impertinent. They sit about moping and cursing. Wild kindly gives them a small piece each which they immediately consume. Wild tells me that they have been very improvident but as they are always being told that "the ship" will be here tomorrow it is hardly to be wondered at that they have not put any tobacco by. My snoring is very bad, it quite exasperates Wild who pulls string attached to my arm unmercifully swears at me.

July 10th: 30 degrees but very wet snow all day. In bags all day. Yesterday the water in E bay was wonderfully clear and no ice in sight. Today both bays full of brash ice. No penguins up.

July 11th: Heavy surf during night. Many falls from glacier. Ice gradually goes out of bay during day. Beautiful weather. Bright sunshine. No wind 27 degrees. Much thaw in hut, very wet under my bed. 31 penguins killed (one an Adélie).

July 15th: Mild both bays full of loose pack some of it very heavy. A tremendous glacier fall creates 40 foot wave which would have overwhelmed us but for its being damped by the loose brash in bay. 1 penguin up and killed.

July 16th: Beautifully fine, quite warm in sun 28 degrees. 1 penguin up, not killed.

17th: I catch and eat snow petrel. Very tough. We cut legs off frozen carcasses of penguins throwing away the 46 carcasses with *breasts* on! = 4 days food. I work for an hour with pick axe and get quite hot and tired digging out the penguin carcasses which shows how comparatively weak one is. Hudson and Blackborrow having complained that my feet touch theirs at night. Wild orders me to reverse my bag. This enables me to disperse with my "halter" which has been a d—d nuisance for I think I was often awakened out of pique and not because my snoring was keeping either Wild or McIlroy awake, for both of them often sit up and read for an hour during the night and sleep in the afternoons. 24 degrees no penguins. Very fine. Much ice.

Unpublished diary.

The Death of Shackleton

Frank Wild

*In 1921 Sir Ernest Shackleton, known always to his men as "The
Boss" set sail in the* Quest *on his third Antarctic expedition, but died
on the way south of a heart attack.*

On Thursday, January 5th, I was awakened about 3 a.m. to find
both of the doctors in my cabin. Macklin was lighting my oil
lamp. McIlroy said:

"We want you to wake up thoroughly, for we have some bad
news to give you, the worst possible."

I sat up, saying:

"Go on with it, let me have it straight out!"

He replied: "The Boss is dead!"

It was a staggering blow.

Roused thus in the middle of the night to receive this news, it
was some minutes before I felt its full significance. I remember
saying mechanically:

"The Boss dead! Dead, do you mean? He can't be dead!"

On asking for particulars, I learned from Macklin that he
was taking the 2–4 a.m. anchor watch. He was patrolling the
ship, when he was attracted by a whistle from the Boss's
cabin, and on going in, found him sitting up in his bunk. His
own account, written almost immediately after, is as follows:

*Was called at 2 a.m. for my watch. A cold night but clear and
beautiful, with every star showing. I was slowly walking up and
down the deck, when I heard a whistle from the Boss's cabin. I
went in, and he said: "Hullo, Mack, boy, is that you? I thought
it was." He continued: "I can't sleep tonight, can you get me a
sleeping draught?" He explained that he was suffering from
severe facial neuralgia, and had taken fifteen grains of aspirin.*

"That stuff is no good; will you get me something which will act?"

I noticed that although it was a cold night he had only one blanket, and asked him if he had no others. He replied that they were in his bottom drawer and he could not be bothered getting them out. I started to do so, but he said, "Never mind tonight, I can stand the cold." However, I went back to my cabin and got a heavy Jaeger blanket from my bunk, which I tucked round him. He was unusually quiet in the way he let me do things for him . . . He talked of many things quite rationally, and finding him in such a complacent mood, I thought it a good opportunity to emphasize the necessity of his taking things very much more quietly than he had been doing . . . " You are always wanting me to give up something. What do you want me to give up now?" This was the last thing he said.

He died quite suddenly.

I remained with him during the worst of the attack, but as soon as I could leave him I ran to McIlroy and, shaking him very roughly I am afraid, said: "Wake up, Mick, come at once to the Boss. He is dying!" On my way back I woke Hussey, and told him to get me certain medicines. It must have been rather a shocking awakening for both of them, but they leapt up at once. Nothing could be done, however. I noted the time: it was about 2.50 a.m.

I had Worsley called and informed him of what had occurred. To the rest I said nothing till the morning.

At 8 a.m. I mustered all hands on the poop, and told them the bad news. Naturally it was a great shock to them all, especially to those who had served with him before and thus knew him more intimately. I added briefly that I now commanded the expedition, which would carry on.

On that day, and on the several that followed, rain fell heavily, fitting in with our low spirits.

I immediately set about making arrangements for sending home the sad news to Lady Shackleton, and for notifying Mr Rowett.

I sent for Watts, our wireless operator, and asked him if he could establish communication. He said he would try. From his log: "My ambition was to get the type 15 set working, so as to pass the news as quickly as possible. The whole set I stripped and tested thoroughly, and 'made good' minor defects, but luck was still against me. The dynamo was run at 5.45 p.m., and whilst testing the installation the machine suddenly raced, and fuses were blown out, so further working of the set had to be abandoned."

I went ashore to see Mr Jacobsen, who was deeply shocked at the news. I learned from him that there was no wireless apparatus on the island other than those carried by the oil transport steamers, none of which, however, had a sending range sufficient to get into touch with a receiving station from here. He told me that the *Albuera*, a steamer lying at Leith Harbour farther round the coast, was due to sail in about ten days. He said that if I cared to go to Leith and make arrangements with her captain for sending the news, he would put at my disposal the *Lille Karl*, a small steam whaler used by him for visiting different parts of the island.

I accepted his offer, and whilst the vessel was being got ready went with McIlroy and Macklin to notify the resident magistrate. He was away at another station, but I saw Mr Barlas, the assistant magistrate. It is curious how one notices small things at a time like this. One incident stands out vividly in my memory. At the moment of my telling him he was lighting a cigarette, which he dropped on the table-cloth, where it continued to burn. I remember picking it up for him and placing it where it could do no harm. This done I left for Leith with McIlroy, who during the whole of this time was of the greatest help and assistance. Everyone at Leith showed the greatest kindness and sympathy, and Captain Manson, of the *Albuera*, readily undertook to send off the message as soon as he got within range of any wireless station.

Arrangements for the disposal of the body I left to Macklin, and to Hussey I entrusted the care of papers and personal effects.

At first I decided to bury Sir Ernest in South Georgia. I had no idea, however, of what Lady Shackleton's wishes might be, and so ultimately decided to send him home to England. The doctors embalmed the body, which was placed in a lined coffin kindly made for us by Mr Hansen, of Leith. There was a steamer named *Professor Gruvel* lying in Grytviken Harbour, which was due to sail in about ten days, and her captain, Captain Jacobsen, offered to carry the body as far as Monte Video, from where it could be sent on by mail boat.

As soon as the necessary arrangements had been made we carried him ashore. All hands mustered quietly and stood bare-headed as we lifted the coffin, covered by our silk white ensign, to the side of the *Quest*, and passed it over into a motor launch. All the time the rain soaked heavily down. From the pier we carried him to the little hospital and placed him in the room in which we had lived together seven years before.

The next day we carried him to the little church, which is situated so romantically at the foot of towering snow-covered mountains, over ground which he had so often trod with firm, eager steps in making the final preparations for the start of the *Endurance* expedition.

Here I said goodbye to the Boss, a great explorer, a great leader and a good comrade.

I had served with him in all his expeditions, twice as his second-in-command. I accompanied him on his great journey which so nearly attained the Pole, shared with him every one of his trials and vicissitudes in the South, and rejoiced with him in his triumphs. No one knew the explorer side of his nature better than I, and many are the tales I could tell of his thoughtfulness and his sacrifices on behalf of others, of which he himself never spoke.

Of his hardihood and extraordinary powers of endurance, his buoyant optimism when things seemed hopeless and his unflinching courage in the face of danger I have no need to speak. He always did more than his share of work. Medical evidence shows that the condition which caused his death was an old standing one and was due to throwing too great a strain upon a system weakened by shortage of food. I have known personally and served with all the British leaders of exploration in the Antarctic since my first voyage in the *Discovery*. For qualities of leadership and ability to organize Shackleton stands foremost and must be ranked as the first explorer of his day.

I felt his loss, coming as it did, most keenly.

In order to ensure safe disposal of the body, and to arrange for its transference at Monte Video, I detailed Hussey to accompany it home. I could ill spare him, but I considered him the most suitable man I could select for the purpose. Naturally it was a disappointment to him to give up the expedition, but he accepted the responsibility without demur, and I am grateful to him for the spirit in which he complied with my arrangements.

As subsequent events turned out, Hussey received a message at Monte Video from Lady Shackleton expressing her wish that Sir Ernest should be buried in South Georgia, which was the scene of one of his greatest exploits, and which might well be described as the "Gateway of the Antarctic". The coffin was returned to Grytviken by the *Woodville*, through the courtesy of Captain Least, and Sir Ernest was ultimately buried in the little cemetery beside our old "dog-lines". Of his comrades, only Hussey was present at the funeral, for the rest of us had already sailed into the South, but there were many amongst the hardy whalers of South Georgia who attended, men who knew him and could, better than most people, appreciate his work. Nor was the sympathetic presence of a woman lacking, for at the funeral was Mrs Aarberg, wife of the Norwegian doctor at Leith, who with kindly thought had placed upon his grave a wreath made from the only flowers on the island, those which she had cultivated with much care and patience inside her own house. She was the only woman on South Georgia.

I have not the least doubt that had Sir Ernest been able to decide upon his last resting-place, it is just here that he would have chosen to lie, and would have preferred this simple funeral to any procedure carried out with greater pomp and ceremony.

> *Not here! the white South has thy bones; and thou,*
> *Heroic sailor-soul,*
> *Art passing on thine happier voyage now*
> *Toward no earthly Pole.**

* Adaptation from Tennyson's lines on Franklin.

Flying Over the Pole

Richard E. Byrd

The American adventurer Richard Byrd had a dubious claim to having been the first to fly over the North Pole; that he was the first to overfly the South Pole is definite.

[*28 November*]. It was an awesome thing, creeping (so it seemed) through the narrow pass, with the black walls of Nansen and Fisher on either side, higher than the level of the wings, and watching the nose of the ship [i.e. the aeroplane] bob up and down across the face of that chunk of rock. It would move up, then slide down. Then move up, and fall off again. For perhaps a minute or two we deferred the decision; but there was no escaping it. If we were to risk a passage through the pass, we needed greater manoeuvrability than we had at that moment. Once we entered the pass, there would be no retreat. It offered no room for turn. If power was lost momentarily or if the air became excessively rough, we could only go ahead, or down. We had to climb, and there was only one way in which we could climb.

June, anticipating the command, already had his hand on the dump valve of the main tank. A pressure of the fingers – that was all that was necessary – and in two minutes 600 gallons of gasoline would gush out. I signalled to wait. Balchen held to the climb almost to the edge of a stall. But it was clear to both of us that he could not hold it long enough. Balchen began to yell and gesticulate, and it was hard to catch the words in the roar of the engines echoing from the cliffs on either side. But the meaning was manifest. "Overboard – overboard – 200 pounds!"

Which would it be – gasoline or food? If gasoline, I thought, we might as well stop there and turn back. We could never get back to the base from the Pole. If food, the lives of all of us would be jeopardized in the event of a forced landing. Was that fair to McKinley, Balchen, and June? It really took only a moment to reach the decision. The Pole, after all, was our objective. I knew the character of the three men. McKinley, in fact, had already hauled one of the food bags to the trapdoor. It weighed 125 pounds. The brown bag was pushed out and fell, spinning, to the glacier. The improvement in the flying qualities of the plane was noticeable. It took another breath and resumed the climb.

Now the down-currents over Nansen became stronger. The plane trembled and rose and fell, as if struck bodily. We veered a trifle to the right, searching for helpful rising eddies. Balchen was flying shrewdly. He maintained flight at a sufficient distance below the absolute ceiling of the plane to retain at all times enough manœuvrability to make him master of the ship. But he was hard-pressed by circumstances; and I realized that, unless the plane was further lightened, the final thrust might bring us perilously close to the end of our reserve.

"More," Bernt shouted. "Another bag."

McKinley shoved a second bag through the trapdoor, and this time we saw it hit the glacier, and scatter in a soundless explosion. Two hundred and fifty pounds of food – enough to feed four men for a month – lay strewn on the barren ice. The sacrifice swung the scales. The plane literally rose with a jump; the engines dug in, and we soon showed a gain in altitude of from 300 to 400 ft. It was what we wanted. We should clear the pass with about 500 ft to spare. Balchen gave a shout of joy. It was just as well. We could dump no more food. There was nothing left to dump except McKinley's camera. I am sure that, had he been asked to put it overboard, he would have done so instantly; and I am equally sure he would have followed the precious instrument with his own body . . .

At six minutes after one o'clock, a sight of the sun put us a few miles ahead of our dead-reckoning position. We were quite close now. At 1.14 o'clock, Greenwich civil time, our calculations showed that we were at the Pole. I opened the trapdoor and dropped over the calculated position of the Pole the small flag which was weighted with the stone from Bennett's grave. Stone and flag plunged down together. The flag had been advanced 1,500 miles further south than it had ever been advanced by any American expedition.

For a few seconds we stood over the spot where Amundsen had stood, 14 December 1911; and where Scott had also stood, thirty-four days later, reading the note which Amundsen had left for him. In their honour, the flags of their countries were again carried over the Pole. There was nothing now to mark that scene: only a white desolation and solitude disturbed by the sound of our engines. The Pole lay in the centre of a limitless plain. To the right, which is to say to the eastward, the horizon was covered with clouds. If mountains lay there, as some geologists believe, they were concealed and we had no hint of them.

And that, in brief, is all there is to tell about the South Pole. One gets there, and that is about all there is for the telling. It is the effort to get there that counts.

We put the Pole behind us and raced for home.

Leviathan

F. D. Ommanney

F. D. Ommanney went south as a scientific officer on the "Discovery" Expedition organized by the Government of the Falkland Islands. His "business" was the study of whales and whaling.

The whale catcher *Narval* lay at the jetty, her mooring ropes creaking gently and the water from her condensers making a rushing sound that was unkind to the dark stillness of the night. Her pumps whined and her fore-truck moved very gently to and fro among the stars. From the adjacent whaling station a few lights winked and occasionally the clatter of iron rods came from the furnace room. When I went on board with my kit-bag and my camera, clumping over the steel decks in my sea-boots, the *Narval* was deserted. I clattered up a companion ladder into the small cabin under the bridge and, dumping my kit-bag on the deck, lay down on the narrow settee. The atmosphere was stifling and felt as though the little cabin had been lived in by dozens of people for weeks and none of them had ever washed. Against one bulkhead stood an enormous wireless transmitting and receiving set, a confusion of bulbs and switches which my mind made no attempt to encompass. Besides this, which seemed almost to fill the cabin, there was a table with some old magazines and a calendar advertising tooth paste from which a young woman smiled down dentally at me. Near the wireless apparatus a door led into another much smaller cabin on the starboard side where the gunner slept. I looked in and saw that it contained a bunk, with no bedclothes but several rugs on it, some heavy coats and an oilskin hanging on hooks, a basin and mirror and a photograph of the gunner's wife. It did not as yet contain the gunner himself, since he was "up at the villa" calling upon the manager.

The pumps whined, the condenser water rushed and presently I slept.

I was awakened by the gentle heaving of the settee beneath me and the dull throb of engines. The stars had paled and the mountains above Grytviken were receding against a pastel sky. They slid past and slowly fell away and soon we were bucking in the open sea. No motion is quite like the motion of a whale catcher. She does not roll, she bounces. She does not pitch, she bucks. She dances and kicks her heels. She wallows so that the open steel decks at her waist are always awash. Now in the lovely, cold, clear, blue morning she was dancing a jig. I went out on deck, feeling that the cabin with its unwashed smell might presently have an unpleasant effect on me. Also because it was no longer possible to lie on the settee. In the near distance stood the black and white mountains of South Georgia, their skirts painted with mid-summer greens and their tops white and flashing under the clear blue sky. All along the coast glaciers came down to the sea, presenting to it great jagged cliffs of ice and long, immobilized streams that poured down from the upper snows. Out to sea stood two tabular icebergs, looking infinitely forlorn and lonely as icebergs do. The foam leapt about their feet. A thousand sea birds crowded in our wake with a leisurely swooping, or a hurriedly fluttering, or insect-like skimming flight.

We danced on thus for three hours and the mountains grew less upon the horizon until they were a tooth-like row forty miles away. Then it was breakfast-time and I clattered down the steel companion ladder to the mess-room which, with the galley, was below the cabin where I had slept. The little table had room for six and one sat at it and ate at it with difficulty because space was so cramped and because of the bucketing motion of the ship. The gunner, the mate and the chief engineer were already there eating porridge and holding their plates up underneath their chins because, if the plate were placed on the table, the milk ran over the edge. They all said "*Morgen*" to me as I made my awkward entry and squeezed myself in among them. In the galley a young cook-steward ladled out porridge from a pot and bore the plate towards me with the poised swooping motion, bent at the knees, which becomes necessary and habitual in a heavily-rolling ship.

The gunner looked like a farmer. He had, it seemed, inserted his enormous bulk into the narrow space between the table and the bulkhead with a shoe horn. I looked at him as he balanced his plate of porridge and ate loudly therefrom, wondering how he would get out again. When he had finished he waved his plate in the air and called out "Steward!" and the steward came and took the plate from him, substituting another on which were four white fish-balls – *fiskeboller* – done in milk, a particularly Norwegian dish. When the gunner had finished he put both enormous hands on the fiddles and hunched his shoulders. He looked down at me and roared with laughter. Or he seemed to look down at me for actually I am as tall as he was, but his immense breadth and his way of hunching his shoulders with his arms straight and his hands upon the fiddles gave him the appearance of being above me.

"Ja, Ja!" said he. "So you wish to see a whale caught – eh?" He did not say "my little man", but it was there. "Well, we must see what we can do. You are not sea-sick? That is good. It is a bad sickness. Ja, Ja!" And he burst into laughter again. Then he forgot all about me and started to talk rapidly in Norwegian to his mate, who was quiet, dark and not at all Scandinavian in appearance. Indeed, he looked more like a Frenchman. The chief engineer was a horny old man who said very little but "Well, well. Ja, Ja. Well, well," and always had a piece of cotton waste with him, even at meals, on which he wiped his hands. When my fish-balls were put in front of me I said "Ah! *Fiskeboller!*" which seemed to put everybody at ease for they all laughed, including the steward, who leaned in the doorway of his galley and joined in the conversation, frequently interrupting the gunner. The gunner takes his own mate and steward with him whenever he takes command of a new catcher, so that these three in the *Narval* knew each other well. Restraint disappeared with the fish-balls and, when I had finished and extracted myself from the table, there was much laughter at my efforts to get my booted legs out from under it. And there was such mirth when I said "*Fand!*" that I returned to the outer air feeling that I had been a success. Which was vanity because a fortnight later, when I passed by the *Narval* as she lay at the jetty, the gunner and his mate gazed down at me from the bridge without recognition, having forgotten my existence.

On the bridge a young man stood at the wheel, bending his knees to the motion of the ship and gazing with keen eyes over the blue, white-flecked, limitless spaces from under a leather fur-lined cap. The ear-flaps of the cap hung down on each side of his face like the ears of a spaniel. He took no notice of me when I came on to the small space of the bridge, bending double under the canvas dodger in order to do so. I stood there for some time watching the men on the gun platform in the bows loading the harpoon gun. It was a deadly, vicious-looking instrument, a short cannon of three inches bore mounted on a swivel which turned easily. Two men rammed a harpoon down the muzzle. The harpoon was like a spear some six feet long with a swivelled head. Three barbs on the swivelled head were kept in place by lashings which, when the harpoon struck, would break so that the barbs would stick outwards and prevent the withdrawal of the harpoon. On the front of the head was a pointed conical bomb which would be exploded inside the whale by a time-fuse. A long line was attached to the harpoon. A length of this was coiled down on the platform on which the gun was mounted. The rest, of greater thickness, ran up the foremast over pulleys, over the drum of a winch on the foredeck and down into a hold. This was the harpoon line – the fishing line – and the mast was the rod. They rammed the harpoon down into the muzzle of the gun until only the swivel head showed. Then they turned the gun round, opened the breech and pushed in a cartridge. The gun was loaded, pointing menacingly at the dancing water, a thing of death. Silver spray flew over it.

"No good!" said the young man beside me, suddenly and surprisingly.

"What's no good?"

"That island! All of it." He made a movement with his head in the direction of South Georgia far away on the horizon. "Hell of a place that! Joost dam rock and snow. I have been there ten years. A long time, eh?"

"It's a long time to be at this game. But you get home in the winter?"

"Oh, ja. Oh, sure I get home. My wife – she live in Sandefjord. My kiddle – he go to school now. Sure I get home. You been to Norway?"

"Never."

"It is God's country. One day I leave this bloddy island and go home. Yessir, ten years. But soon I go home!"

Then suddenly there was a cry from the barrel at the mast-head.

"*Hvalblast!*"

I looked and saw nothing. Just dancing sunlight on wastes of water. But the young man at the wheel had seen it. Even while he was talking his keen eyes had been alert. "There, to port," he said. I strained my eyes to port and there, presently, far off there rose up three little plumes one after the other. They hung for a moment and disappeared. Hard a-port. The little ship turned, heeling over sharply, and was off on a new course, dancing gaily in the path of the sun, the smoke streaming from her funnel. Then again ahead the plumes rose up, nearer this time and larger. The ship danced on. The gunner came up on the bridge and the third time they blew he looked at them through glasses and said "*Blåhvaler* – Blue whales." You could see now, after the blows, the three dark backs, curving over slowly like three great submarine unhurrying wheels. They turned over one behind the other and immediately the sea-serpent legend became understandable to me, for they looked for all the world like three parts of a continuous whole. Then they disappeared and, for what seemed an eternity, my eyes wandered about the empty sunlit sea. Spray flew in showers across the gun platform. Foam leapt about the feet of an iceberg. The mountains of South Georgia gathered to themselves a mantle of cloud and drew it about their shoulders. "*Sagte!* – slow," said the gunner, and we waited, wallowing and uncertain.

"Yes," said the young man at the wheel. "Ten years. I have been in a *kokeri* (floating factory), too, in the South Shetlands. There it is light all the time so we work always. Always. But the weather is not so bad as here. You can sleep in your watch below. But often in the ice the lines and tackles they freezes up. Often you must cut the ice off the bow. Too much ice too heavy for the damn ship and she turn over. No good, eh? But here it is the worst. More weather. More sea. Longer to tow. Harder work. But soon perhaps I go home and live in Sandefjord and go fishing in the summer."

Suddenly there was a whistling rushing explosion which made

me jump. Not a hundred yards away a great burst of spray shot into the air. Then another and another. They went drifting away on the wind threaded by arching rainbows. After each a great flat grinning head with wide open blow-holes was for a moment visible, followed by a broad curving back, turning and turning. There was a whistling intake of breath and each vanished, leaving upon the water an oily smooth place to mark where it had been. This was the "slik". One of them had fouled the water with a yellowish-brown stain.

"*Fuld fart forover* – full speed ahead!" And away we danced again after them.

But now they were scared and vanished again for nearly ten minutes.

"They will come back," said the young man at the wheel, "they've sounded. They've gone two hundred fathoms, I bet."

"As much as that? I doubt it."

"Yes? I have been whaling ten years. I know how deep they go. I have seen whales take out two or three hundred fathoms of line straight down. I know."

He looked at me and laughed. "Discovery! What you discover?"

The gunner walked down the narrow gangway which led from the bridge to the gun platform, spanning the foredeck. He walked easily and lightly down it, and I followed clutching at the stanchions and wires all the time to steady myself. At the foot, near the gun platform, I braced myself with my camera ready, my body against one stanchion, my foot against the other. The gunner stood behind his gun, immense, impassive, calm, doing his daily job. As the whales came up ahead with their three whistling bursts of spray one after the other, he signalled calmly to the bridge, now a little to port, now a little to starboard. Once they came up close to the ship on the starboard side with a whistling explosion and I could see in that instant every detail, the vast grin, the grid-like plates in their mouths, the little knowing eye at the corner of the grin, the wide open blow-holes and then the great curving back. They were gone, leaving three oily patches, and the spray from their blow, which is sea-water from the back of the throat, mucus from the nasal passages and condensed vapour, drifted over me and over my camera. It stank, the stink

of whales' breath, hot and whaly. "*Fand!* No good," said the
gunner, "*Ganske sagte* – very slow!" and for a little we wallowed.
There were moments when I and my camera hung perilously
between the sky and sea like the thief whom Theseus threw over
the cliff, but who was rejected by both earth and sea as unworthy
of either.

Suddenly the three broad backs burst through the dancing
water immediately ahead. The gunner swung his gun. There
was a deafening crack and my ears sang. The black streak of the
harpoon flying out. The coiling whip outwards of the line. And
then a cataclysmic, hurtling, headlong rush down. Got him!
Down went the line, rattling out, and down, down, down. The
chief engineer was there on the foredeck, wiping his hands on a
piece of waste and saying "Well, well. Ja, Ja. Well, well." There
was the steward, a ladle in his hand. There was a fireman in a
peaked cap, singlet and sweat cloth. Though this killing was
their daily job, it never lost interest and all hands were always
on deck at the kill. It meant more money, anyway, in the pockets of every man. And Jonassen was the best gunner on the
station. There was a sudden strange silence, a suspension of
activity. The *Narval* wallowed, the waves flopping and flapping
against her sides, and the harpoon line no longer running out of
the hold but hanging taut from the bows, straight up and down.

Then began a thrashing disturbance in the water a mile away
to starboard. The terrible, lonely and titanic death struggle
began. Dark against the lashed smother of foam there wheeled
and thrashed now a forked tail, now a pointed head still grinning;
now a ribbed belly showed, now a pointed flipper, raised on high,
smacking down upon the water. Then a red fountain burst
upwards, and another. He was spouting blood. It meant the end.
"Ah!" they said on the foredeck. They were reloading the harpoon
gun. The smoking breech swung open and the empty cartridge
was removed. The gunner turned to me.

"You got a picture – ja?"

"No," I admitted. The loud crack of the gun had made me
pull the trigger too late. When you take photographs of a whale
hunt you need to be as calm and collected as the gunner himself.
"No matter," said Jonassen. "We will get some more, I think."

Still the Leviathan fought for his life, his harmless, free and joyful life that had suddenly been struck from him at one dreadful blow. His comrades had disappeared and he fought his battle out, deserted and alone. He whirled in a fury of crimson foam. The winch rattled and the slack harpoon line came in until it curved to him across the mile of water. Now it grew tight and pulled him. He drew towards us and suddenly he was still, his ribbed belly upwards, the crimson sea where he lay suddenly calm and a cloud of birds hovering above. In the distance a solitary iceberg, remote, forlorn and lonely, stood off and watched him die.

There was something strangely impersonal about him when they got him alongside. It was hard to believe that he really was once a huge and powerful animal, forging through the water with vertical sweeps of that great forked tail. He became just one of the shapes that waited for us every morning at the "plan" and which became several times daily before our eyes a scattered mass of meat.

With a long lance they punctured his ribbed under-surface and then pushed into the wound the nozzle of an air pump on the end of a pole. Thus they blew him up with air to prevent him from sinking and plugged up the hole where the nozzle had been with a piece of tow. Then they jabbed into him a flag on a long staff. On the flag were the letters C.A.P. (*Compania Argentina de Pesca*). So we left him wallowing, the flag pole wagging from side to side in the swell and, as we drew away, off on the chase again, the sea birds gathered in a cloud above him. Soon he was just a shape in the water and presently you could only mark the place where he lay by the cloud of birds.

Somewhere in that broad stretch of sea the companions of our victim must still be. Probably by now they had forgotten the sudden and inexplicable disaster which had overtaken their brother and were snorting and blowing through the waves as gaily as ever. We must find them. The mountains of South Georgia had shrouded themselves from view and, with that suddenness which is characteristic of the weather in those seas, the beauty of the day had disappeared. A grey mistiness overspread the sky and an icy, bitter wind had arisen. It whipped the sea into short, sharp waves which flew in bursts of spray over the bows of the *Narval*. I went into the cabin to get a leather waistcoat out of my kit-bag. The gunner was at the wireless set, calling the whaling station.

"Hallo, Grytvik. Hallo, Grytvik. Hallo, hallo, hallo. *Narval. Narval.*" And then a (to me) incomprehensible rush of Norwegian, spoken with great rapidity into the instrument. It was his noon report. He was telling them that he was forty-five miles east of Cape Vakop and had taken one large bull Blue whale, which he had flagged, and was now off after more; that the weather had worsened and was blowing sharply from the south-west. Then came a crackling and (again to me) incomprehensible reply from the metal throat of the loud-speaker.

"Hallo, hallo. Hallo, *Narval.* Hallo, *Don Miles.* Hallo, *Orca.* Hallo, *Morsa.* Grytvik. Grytvik. Grytvik." The brazen voice ran on. Then Jonassen rose from the instrument. "Ja!" he said. "*Orca* has one Fin. The others have nothing yet. So far we win. Ja."

In the afternoon we came upon the other whales. At least we came upon two other Blue whales and we chose to think they were the companions of our former victim, though there was nothing to indicate whether they were or not. The young man at the wheel had been relieved and his place had been taken by a giant with an immense red beard which spread all over his chest. He said never a word and took no notice of me at all. In the distance every now and again, ever nearer, the two whales shot up their plumes of spray against the grey sky. We gained upon them, but we were not alone. For on our port bow was another catcher, on which all our eyes were turned. She was far off and it was at first difficult to make her out. She was a coal-burner since, from her funnel, a long trail of black smoke streamed away, making a bar above the horizon. "A Leith boat," said the gunner. "Ja! A Leith boat. Only the Leith boats burn coal." And he looked at her through glasses. She was running down the same whales as we were following. It would be a race. As she drew nearer and converged upon us, she became more clearly visible so that we could, with glasses, make out her name, printed in large black letters on a white ground across her upper-works in the way that all Leith boats wore it. *Shouma.* She dipped and plunged. The foam rose in a splendid curve at her bows where, minute and venomous, we could now make out her harpoon gun pointing downwards at the water. The black smoke streamed away from her funnel. The whales were close ahead now, their broad backs visible as they rose. Go it, *Narval*! We sped dancing through the water and the spray slashed over our bows, icy cold. The gunner went down the gangplank again to his platform and I followed, bracing myself again against the stanchions. The wind was so cold that it seemed to burn my fingers as I held the camera. On the ever-nearing *Shouma* we could see the small dark figure of the gunner also walk down his gangplank to the platform. With a whistling explosion the two whales broke surface on our port bow not two hundred yards away. And from the starboard bow of the *Shouma* they were also not two hundred yards away. Their great backs wheeled over. "*Ganske sagte* – very slow!" Then there they were bursting up astern. They had doubled back. "*For Fand!*" said everybody. "Hard a-starboard!" and we spun round like a saucer, heeling over. I clung to the stanchions like grim death. The *Shouma* went hard a-port and swung round away from us, heeling over too, and the heavy trail of her smoke bent itself into a loop. The whales came up again farther ahead. "*Fuld fart forover!*" *Narval*! "*Fuld fart forover!*" *Shouma*! Full speed ahead. And the two whalers bore down upon each other. Then suddenly Jonassen swung his gun to starboard. The small crouching figure on the gun platform of the *Shouma* swung his gun to port. Where the two guns pointed, sure enough, the two whales burst up, tall columns of spray rushing up from their heads like steam from two locomotives. The guns cracked out together and the harpoons flew out and down to meet each other, whipping out their lines. The two catchers, shooting simultaneously, were within a hundred yards of each other. The *Narval* had hit and her harpoon line rattled out and down. Both ships paused wallowing. But the *Shouma* had missed. Jonassen straightened himself at his gun. "Again we win." And he waved across to the other gunner who waved back. The *Shouma* hauled in her spent harpoon. We could see the figures of her men reloading the gun. Then, with a shout and a farewell wave, she was off again. Her screw churned up the water at her stern and she made a lovely sweeping curve across our bows as we stood with our harpoon line still running out. She was off after the other whale. "*God fangst! Shouma.*"

This whale did not fight. He just went down and down. And

then as the *Shouma* crossed our bows, his bluntly-pointed nose pushed quietly up through the water ahead. He was dead. They hauled him close, and as the *Shouma*, triangular now in stern view, diminished to port, they pumped him up with air. Through hawse-holes they made him fast by the tail to the port bow and, with a flensing knife, cut off his great triangular tail fins. They flopped down into the water, a legacy for the birds. Then we were off again, listing to port a little, with the great, ribbed, shining, balloon-like carcass billowing through the water beside us. The daylight was fading. There would be no more whales today and we were on our way to pick up our earlier victim. Though the wind still blew icy and strong, the weather had cleared and the mountains of South Georgia were visible again to southward, darkling and sullen. At the western end of their long, toothed ridge the sun sank behind dark clouds, sending out bright rays, and in the east there shone a pale daylight moon. To the north the *Shouma* was only a pencil of smoke poised on the horizon.

Whale number one lay as we had left him. Far off you could just see the flag wagging and fluttering in the distance and the cloud of birds about him. As we approached they rose up screaming. We made him fast by the tail to the starboard bow and then, followed by our attendant throng of birds, we turned westwards towards the mountains.

At the wheel the man with the beard had been replaced by the young man who had been whaling ten years. The flaps of his fur cap hung down like the ears of a spaniel.

"You like this?" he said. "How you like to do it every day? Not so much damn fun, eh? How you like to do it every day for ten years? No good, eh? When I go home to Norway I say 'Olafsen! You are a bloddy fool. This is the last time you go south.' But here I am again. Ja! Every year."

He said more than that but I was not listening for, on our port quarter, there rose up two gigantic, black, triangular fins like knives. The water where they cut the surface flew outwards fanwise on each side of them. "Good God! What are those?" I said.

The young man turned his head for a moment and saw them. "Those? *Spekkhugger*. Killers."

They were making after us, making after the carcasses we towed. As they gained upon us with rushing, swooping dives through the water, we could see their black shapes beneath the surface. They made one or two swift sweeps towards the mouths of the dead whales from which the tongues lolled out. There was something terrible and sinister in the rush they made, the tigers of the sea. Then, as suddenly as they came, they vanished and we saw their knife-like fins no more.

"They go for the tongues," said the man at the wheel. "If you was in the water they would go for you. Sure they would!"

The dark mountains drew up to us and we crept home close in shore. The sky turned from pale blue to indigo and the clouds vanished from it, leaving it free for the stars, which came out one by one. Here one above the mountain-tops, there one out to sea, poised above an iceberg, until like dust they hung over us. The moonlight increased upon the water and upon the never-moving rivers of ice that wound from the peaks down to the sea.

Alone

Richard E. Byrd

For five months in 1934 Richard Byrd was alone at the Bolling Advance Weather Base, 125 miles south of the Ross Ice Shelf. Despite its grandiose name, the Base, sited at 80 degrees 08', was a rudimentary hut. Outside the temperature dropped to as low as -83 degrees below.

Out of the cold and out of the east came the wind. It came on gradually, as if the sheer weight of the cold were almost too much to be moved. On the night of the 21st the barometer started down. The night was black as a thunderhead when I made my first trip topside; and a tension in the wind, a bulking of shadows in the night indicated that a new storm centre was forming. Next morning, glad of an excuse to stay underground, I worked a long time on the Escape Tunnel by the light of a red candle standing in a snow recess. That day I pushed the emergency exit to a distance of twenty-two feet, the farthest it was ever to go. My stint done, I sat down on a box, thinking how beautiful was the red of the candle, how white the rough-hewn snow. Soon I became aware of an increasing clatter of the anemometer cups. Realizing that the wind was picking up, I went topside to make sure that everything was secured. It is a queer experience to watch a blizzard rise. First there is the wind, rising out of nowhere. Then the Barrier unwrenches itself from quietude; and the surface, which just before had seemed as hard and polished as metal, begins to run like a making sea. Sometimes, if the wind strikes hard, the drift comes across the Barrier like a hurrying white cloud, tossed hundreds of feet in the air. Other times the growth is gradual. You become conscious of a general slithering movement on all sides. The air fills with tiny scraping and sliding and rustling sounds as the first loose crystals stir. In a little while they are moving as solidly as an incoming tide, which creams over the ankles, then surges to the waist, and finally is at the throat. I have walked in drift so thick as not to be able to see a foot ahead of me; yet, when I glanced up, I could see the stars shining through the thin layer just overhead.

Smoking tendrils were creeping up the anemometer pole when I finished my inspection. I hurriedly made the trapdoor fast, as a sailor might batten down a hatch; and knowing that my ship was well secured, I retired to the cabin to ride out the storm. It could not reach me, hidden deep in the Barrier crust; nevertheless the sounds came down. The gale sobbed in the ventilators, shook the stovepipe until I thought it would be jerked out by the roots, pounded the roof with sledge-hammer blows. I could actually feel the suction effect through the pervious snow. A breeze flickered in the room and the tunnels. The candles wavered and went out. My only light was the feeble storm lantern.

Even so, I didn't have any idea how really bad it was until I went aloft for an observation. As I pushed back the trapdoor, the drift met me like a moving wall. It was only a few steps from the ladder to the instrument shelter, but it seemed more like a mile. The air came at me in snowy rushes; I breasted it as I might a heavy surf. No night had ever seemed so dark. The beam from the flashlight was choked in its throat; I could not see my hand before my face.

My windproofs were caked with drift by the time I got below. I had a vague feeling that something had changed while I was gone, but what, I couldn't tell. Presently I noticed that the shack was appreciably colder. Raising the stove lid, I was surprised to find that the fire was out, though the tank was half full. I decided that I must have turned off the valve unconsciously before going aloft; but, when I put a match to the burner, the draught down the pipe blew out the flame. The wind, then, must have killed the fire. I got it going again, and watched it carefully.

The blizzard vaulted to gale force. Above the roar the deep, taut thrumming note of the radio antenna and the anemometer guy wires reminded me of wind in a ship's rigging. The wind direction trace turned scratchy on the sheet; no doubt drift had short-circuited the electric contacts, I decided. Realizing that it was hopeless to attempt to try to keep them clear, I let the instrument be. There were other ways of getting the wind direction. I tied a handkerchief to a bamboo pole and ran it through the outlet ventilator; with a flashlight I could tell which way the cloth was whipped. I did this at hourly intervals, noting any change of direction on the sheet. But by 2 o'clock in the morning. I had had enough of this periscope sighting. If I expected to sleep and at the same time maintain the continuity of the records, I had no choice but to clean the contact points.

The wind was blowing hard then. The Barrier shook from the concussions overhead; and the noise was as if the entire physical world were tearing itself to pieces. I could scarcely heave the trapdoor open. The instant it came clear I was plunged into a blinding smother. I came out crawling, clinging to the handle of the door until I made sure of my bearings. Then I let the door fall shut, not wanting the tunnel filled with drift. To see was impossible. Millions of tiny pellets exploded in my eyes, stinging like BB shot. It was even hard to breathe, because snow instantly clogged the mouth and nostrils. I made my way towards the anemometer pole on hands and knees, scared that I might be bowled off my feet if I stood erect; one false step and I should be lost for ever.

I found the pole all right; but not until my head collided with a cleat. I managed to climb it, too, though ten million ghosts were tearing at me, ramming their thumbs into my eyes. But the errand was useless. Drift as thick as this would mess up the contact points as quickly as they were cleared; besides, the wind cups were spinning so fast that I stood a good chance of losing a couple of fingers in the process. Coming down the pole, I had a sense of being whirled violently through the air, with no control over my movements. The trapdoor was completely buried when I found it again, after scraping around for some time with my mittens. I pulled at the handle, first with one hand, then with both. It did not give. It's a tight fit, anyway, I mumbled to myself. The drift has probably wedged the corners. Standing astride the hatch, I braced myself and heaved with all my strength. I might just as well have tried hoisting the Barrier.

Panic took me then, I must confess. Reason fled. I clawed at the three-foot square of timber like a madman. I beat on it with my fists, trying to shake the snow loose; and, when that did no good, I lay flat on my belly and pulled until my hands went weak from cold and weariness. Then I crooked my elbow, put my face down, and said over and over again, You damn fool, you damn fool. Here for weeks I had been defending myself against the danger of being penned inside the shack; instead, I was now locked out; and nothing could be worse, especially since I had only a wool parka and pants under my windproofs. Just two feet below was sanctuary – warmth, food, tools, all the means of survival. All these things were an arm's length away, but I was powerless to reach them.

There is something extravagantly insensate about an Antarctic blizzard at night. Its vindictiveness cannot be measured on an anemometer sheet. It is more than just wind; it is a solid wall of snow moving at gale force, pounding like surf.* The whole malevolent rush is concentrated upon you as upon a personal enemy. In the senseless explosion of sound you are reduced to a crawling thing on the margin of a disintegrating world; you can't see, you can't hear, you can hardly move. The lungs gasp after the air sucked out of them, and the brain is shaken. Nothing in the world will so quickly isolate a man.

Half-frozen, I stabbed towards one of the ventilators, a few feet away. My mittens touched something round and cold. Cupping it in my hands, I pulled myself up. This was the outlet ventilator. Just why, I don't know – but instinct made me kneel and press my face against the opening. Nothing in the room was visible, but a dim patch of light illuminated the floor, and warmth rose up to my face. That steadied me.

Still kneeling, I turned my back to the blizzard and considered what might be done. I thought of breaking in the windows in the roof, but they lay two feet down in hard crust, and were reinforced with wire besides. If I only had something to dig with, I could break the crust and stamp the windows in with my feet. The pipe cupped between my hands supplied the first

---

* Because of this blinding, suffocating drift, in the Antarctic winds of only moderate velocity have the punishing force of full-fledged hurricanes elsewhere.

inspiration; maybe I could use that to dig with. It, too, was wedged tight; I pulled until my arms ached, without budging it; I had lost all track of time, and the despairing thought came to me that I was lost in a task without an end. Then I remembered the shovel. A week before, after levelling drift from the last light blow, I had stabbed a shovel handle up in the crust somewhere to leeward. That shovel would save me. But how to find it in the avalanche of the blizzard?

I lay down and stretched out full length. Still holding the pipe, I thrashed around with my feet, but pummelled only empty air. Then I worked back to the hatch. The hard edges at the opening provided another grip, and again I stretched out and kicked. Again no luck. I dared not let go until I had something else familiar to cling to. My foot came up against the other ventilator pipe. I edged back to that, and from the new anchorage repeated the manœuvre. This time my ankle struck something hard. When I felt it and recognized the handle, I wanted to caress it.

Embracing this thrice-blessed tool, I inched back to the trapdoor. The handle of the shovel was just small enough to pass under the little wooden bridge which served as a grip. I got both hands on the shovel and tried to wrench the door up; my strength was not enough, however. So I lay down flat on my belly and worked my shoulders under the shovel. Then I heaved, the door sprang open, and I rolled down the shaft. When I tumbled into the light and warmth of the room, I kept thinking, How wonderful, how perfectly wonderful.

My wrist watch had stopped; the chronometers showed that I had been gone just under an hour. The stove had blown out again, but I did not bother to light it. Enough warmth remained for me to undress. I was exhausted; it was all I could do to hoist myself into the bunk. But I did not sleep at first. The blizzard scuffled and pounded gigantically overhead; and my mind refused to drop the thought of what I might still be doing if the shovel hadn't been there. Still struggling, probably. Or maybe not. There are harder ways to die than freezing to death. The lush numbness and the peace that lulls the mind when the ears cease listening to the blizzard's ridiculous noise, could make death seem easy.

The hut, however, was not a complete sanctuary, for Byrd was frequently forced to inhale fumes, containing high levels of carbon monoxide, from his stove.

As I saw the situation, the necessities were these: to survive I must continue to husband my strength, doing whatever had to be done in the simplest manner possible and without strain. I must sleep and eat and build up strength. To avoid further poisoning from the fumes, I must use the stove sparingly and the gasoline pressure lantern not at all. Giving up the lantern meant surrendering its bright light, which was one of my few luxuries; but I could do without luxuries for a while. As to the stove, the choice there lay between freezing and inevitable poisoning. Cold I could feel, but carbon monoxide was invisible and tasteless. So I chose the cold, knowing that the sleeping-bag provided a retreat. From now on, I decided, I would make a strict rule of doing without the fire for two or three hours every afternoon.

So much for the practical procedure. If I depended on this alone. I should go mad from the hourly reminders of my own futility. Something more – the will and desire to endure these hardships – was necessary. They must come from deep inside me. But how? By taking control of my thought. By extirpating all lugubrious ideas the instant they appeared and dwelling only on those conceptions which would make for peace. A discordant mind, black with confusion and despair, would finish me off as thoroughly as the cold. Discipline of this sort is not easy. Even in April's and May's serenity I had failed to master it entirely.

That evening I made a desperate effort to make these conclusions work for me. Although my stomach was rebellious, I forced down a big bowl of thin soup, plus some vegetables and milk. Then I put the fire out; afterwards, propped up in the sleeping-bag, I tried to play Canfield. But the games, I remember, went against me; and this made me profoundly irritable. I tried to read Ben Ames Williams' *All the Brothers Were Valiant*; but, after a page or two, the letters became indistinct; and my eyes ached – in fact, they had never stopped aching. I cursed inwardly, telling myself that the way the cards fell and the state of my eyes were typical of my wretched luck. The truth is that the dim light from the lantern was beginning to get on my nerves. In spite of my earlier resolve to dispense with it, I would have lighted the pressure lantern, except that I wasn't able to pump up the pressure. Only when you've been through something like that do you begin to appreciate how utterly precious light is.

Something persuaded me to take down the shaving mirror from its nail near the shelf. The face that looked back at me was that of an old and feeble man. The cheeks were sunken and scabrous from frost-bite, and the bloodshot eyes were those of a man who has been on a prolonged debauch. Something broke inside me then. What was to be gained by struggling? No matter what happened, if I survived at all, I should always be a physical wreck, a burden upon my family. It was a dreadful business. All the fine conceptions of the afternoon dissolved in black despair.

The dark side of a man's mind seems to be a sort of antenna turned to catch gloomy thoughts from all directions. I found it so with mine. That was an evil night. It was as if all the world's vindictiveness were concentrated upon me as upon a personal enemy. I sank to depths of disillusionment which I had not believed possible. It would be tedious to discuss them. Misery, after all, is the tritest of emotions. All that need be said is that eventually my faith began to make itself felt; and by concentrating on it and reaffirming the truth about the universe as I saw it, I was able again to fill my mind with the fine and comforting things of the world that had seemed irretrievably lost. I surrounded myself with my family and my friends; I projected myself into the sunlight, into the midst of green, growing things. I thought of all the things I would do when I got home; and a thousand matters which had never been more than casual now became surpassingly attractive and important. But time after time I slipped back into despond. Concentration was difficult, and only by the utmost persistence could I bring myself out of it. But ultimately the disorder left my mind; and, when I blew out the candles and the lantern, I was living in the world of the imagination – a simple, uncomplicated world made up of people who wished each other well, who were peaceful and easy-going and kindly.

The aches and pains had not subsided; and it took me several hours to fall asleep; but that night I slept better than on any night since 31 May [several days earlier]; and in the morning was better in mind and body both.

The First Men in the White Eden

John Rymill

*Rymill was the leader of a 1934 British expedition to Graham Land,
a hitherto unexplored region of Western Antarctica.*

Coming from the dark, heaving ocean into the quiet channels of
north Graham Land was an amazing contrast, for one was
suddenly transported from the dull, dreary expanse of a leaden-
coloured sea into the full beauties of a polar land. The day we
passed through De Gerlache Strait and Neumayer Channel on
our way to Port Lockroy was clear and sunny with a cloudless sky,
giving us a good opportunity to appreciate the grandeur of the
scenery amongst which we should make our home for the next
two years. These channels, though deep, are in places less than a
mile wide, and are fringed with ice-cliffs some hundred feet high,
with serrated edges following the shore-line and forming little bays
and points. Behind the ice-cliffs the mountain ranges rise to snowy
peaks 4,000 or 5,000 feet above the water. There is dark rock
exposed on the mountain sides, but the most striking features are
the hanging glaciers and ice-falls, showing every shade of blue and
green as they are caught by the sun's rays, or else darkened by
shadows. The sea itself was oily calm with that strange misty glow
which seems peculiar to the cold water of the polar regions when
there is no wind. On the surface small icebergs and smaller growl-
ers, newly broken from the cliffs, lay sparkling in the sun like vast
jewels set in the long winding channel. The only sounds that could
be heard were the occasional roar of an avalanche, or a dull grum-
bling as an ice-cliff calved, and perhaps the cry of a Dominican
gull going to or from its breeding-ground near by.

 We had a wonderful view this afternoon. When the sky cleared,
the clouds over the Graham Land mountains to the east remained

dark, but took on lighter shades as they faded into long streamers towards the zenith, where their edges were touched with the reds and orange of the sunset light from the north. Down the western horizon the great mountain ranges of Alexander I Island stood out mysteriously, showing a pale copper colour against a dark grey haze into which they gradually disappeared further south, while the soft winter twilight made the whole scene look coldly beautiful, but rather awe-inspiring. As we sledged along I was impressed by the thought that here was all this strange grandeur round us, and we – people of the 20th century who had left an overcrowded land only a few months before – were the first to see it since the world began.

We were still 130 miles from home, but this first sight of well-known landmarks and the sea – always a thing of life even when frozen – gave us a pleasant sensation of familiarity which was a relief after the austere country through which we had been travelling for the last forty-five days: a country which had known eternal peace until we, two puny little black dots in its vastness, had the impudence to lift the curtain for a few brief days and look upon its beauty. Now that we were leaving it behind I had a feeling of intense pleasure in knowing that we had travelled its glaciers and scaled its mountains and come through safely. But this feeling was tinged with one of loss as though a friend had died, for the curtain had again dropped, and, in dropping, had hidden a scene difficult to put into words. Day after day we had travelled through silence which was absolute, not a depressing silence as of the dead, but a silence that had never known life. Even more impressive had been the sheer immensity of the country, and the atmosphere of mystery which seemed to dwarf us – the great mountains which have stood there untroubled for countless years, and the glaciers slowly forcing their way downwards, occasionally muttering in their depths to remind us that even here time goes on. And to think that when we return to England one of the first questions we shall be asked – probably by a well-fed businessman whose God is his bank-book – will be, "Why did you go there?" How can one reply other than flippantly to such a mentality? But the high plateau of Graham Land is no place to indulge in daydreams, and we hurried on.

Storms and Wonders

W. Ellery Anderson

A former regular Army officer, Ellery Anderson joined a 1954 Falklands Islands Dependencies expedition to Hope Bay, then one of the least known corners of Antarctica.

By the end of May we began preparations for the 250-mile depot-laying journey down the Crown Prince Gustav Channel to Cape Longing. It was part of my build-up for the main journey, with the added objective of surveying the north-west coast of James Ross Island. Those selected to undertake it, apart from myself, were Massey, Precious and Leppard, with the Players and the Gangsters as our dog-teams.

Preparations took a week. Route maps were drawn: sledges stripped and reassembled. Camp equipment, traces, met instruments, medicine bags and wireless sets were checked and new sets of harness were made for both teams. I can still see us grouped round the stove every evening like seamen of old mending sails on a windjammer, puffing at our pipes as we stitched away with our needles and thread and wearing sailmaker's palms.

We started out in fine weather on the morning of 7 June, Massey and Leppard leaving at eleven o'clock with the Gangsters pulling "Bloody Mary", and Precious and I an hour later with the Players and "Burlington Bertie". The surface was good, and with light sledges we made the seventeen miles to View Point by three that afternoon. We fed the dogs seal, camped on the sea ice near the tide crack and went to have supper with Lewis and Taylor, who were occupying the hut.

Early next morning we set out for Beak Island to pick up our rations, with Taylor and Lewis accompanying us. They were completing the store-hauling with an electrical strain-gauge attached to their sledge, which Taylor was using to test the work output of his team.

We reached the depot on Beak Island by twelve, loaded up with 1,050 pounds on each sledge and, after saying goodbye to Taylor and Lewis, we headed south-west down the Crown Prince Gustav Channel, which is like a glacial valley, roughly five miles wide, bounded on the west by the mainland and on the east by the cliffs of a chain of islands. The southern entrance to the channel is blocked permanently by the Larsen Ice-shelf, with the result that it has become a backwater crowded with a wide assortment of bergs and brash which never get swept out to sea.

This journey down the Crown Prince Gustav Channel represents the most back-breaking and soul-destroying work I have ever done in my life. There were days when our sledges overturned literally every few yards, and they would have to be unloaded before they could be lifted back on their runners. An advance of a quarter of a mile in any direction, other than the way we had come, was considered an achievement and, at first, our daily runs averaged a little under a mile and a half.

From a distance as we headed south-west from Beak, it looked a little rough, something like an area of concrete blocks put down as an anti-tank obstacle. But no sooner were we in it than both sledges started overturning, and "Burlington Bertie" broke its cow-catcher.

"Not a particularly good start," I observed gloomily to Precious, as we pitched our tent that evening.

"Don't worry, we'll soon be out of it," he said optimistically.

"I hope you're right, but somehow I doubt it."

As I was "inside" man, I wriggled through the entrance and on to an illuminated square of ice, like ground glass, admitting a bluish green luminosity from the sea beneath us. Our camping equipment and rations were handed in to me. I made the tent comfortable and began to prepare our evening meal.

Our basic diet was pemmican, a beef extract made by Bovril, which came in pound blocks, each packaged in an air-tight plastic bag. It was a hard, dark-brown stuff that had to be scraped off the block into the cooking pot. Boiling water was poured on top, dehydrated onions and potatoes added and it was allowed to simmer. We ate it with thickly buttered biscuits, washing it down with cocoa or tea.

Pemmican is satisfying; it has a high calorific content and contains all the vitamins necessary to keep the Antarctic traveller nourished and healthy. Theoretically it may have been the ideal sledging food, since it packed a large number of calories into a relatively light weight, but it was not particularly appetizing and, night after night on a long journey, it became very monotonous indeed. There was also a small tin of bacon which we had as a change once in ten days, but I do think some calories could very well have been sacrificed for the morale value of a more varied diet. The ration boxes contained 120 bars of chocolate, or six a day, and these were usually eaten during the midday halt or on the march.

The alarm clock roused us at eight next morning. Precious stopped it and lit the candle, and as the flame flickered and steadied I saw the interior of the tent, with our clothes hanging from the top, and our sleeping-bags all white with frost. He started the Primus, exposing as little of himself as possible in the act. He put on a pot of snow for an early morning mug of tea, and slid back under the hood of his sleeping-bag to wait until the pot boiled. As the heat rose from the Primus, our frozen garments began to steam and thaw out.

Breakfast that day and every succeeding morning of the journey consisted of Quaker Oats, with plenty of sugar. Sometimes we added a peppermint-tasting sweet called Kendal mint, which left a pleasant fresh taste in the mouth. We ate the porridge, with thickly buttered biscuits, and rounded off the meal with another mug of tea and a satisfying pipe of tobacco.

For our "handle-bar" lunch, Precious prepared a vacuum flask of coffee, taking care that the screw-top was thoroughly dry before putting it on, as any moisture freezing on the threads could make it impossible to remove. He buttered biscuits, smearing Marmite on them, and wrapped the snack in a piece of cloth to put in our sledging-bag on the handle-bars. Butter was a very necessary part of our diet. The ration was three pounds each for ten days, and still we craved for it, particularly towards the end of a journey.

The sun was rising over the islands as we emerged from our

tent at ten-thirty that morning. The cliffs of Graham Land were lighting up and the bluish haze and purple shadows were rapidly dissolving from the silent icescape around us. Five lonely shag flighted southwards over us as we climbed a small berg nearby to look at the way ahead. What we saw was the depressing vista of the brash extending on either side of the centre islands of the channel for practically twenty miles.

Now that we were in it, the brash was far worse than it had appeared from the outside. When we came down from the berg, it was difficult to pick a route for more than a few yards ahead. It was the sort of view a ploughed field must present to an ant.

We repaired the broken cow-catcher as best we could, by lashing the broken ends together, and we started out with Massey and Leppard going ahead. Half a mile out of camp we struck a small pool a hundred yards long by twenty-five yards wide with a colony of crabeaters lying on the ice round it and one lonely paddy. We detoured and continued southwards for about four miles, passing Tail and Egg Islands. Then, beside Red Island, "Burlington Bertie" suddenly overturned in a wind scoop, breaking her cow-catcher beyond repair. It was about three o'clock now and getting dark so I sent Massey and Leppard on to pick a camp site while Precious and I unloaded and righted our sledge. We caught them up after a while and the dogs were fed and the tents pitched.

I was "outside" man that night and almost asleep when I heard our dogs fighting. I cursed them as I climbed out of the tent in my long johns and belaboured them for being so damned inconsiderate. The moon was up, very bright and large in a clear sky, with the brash shapes all round me reflecting a weird supernatural luminosity. Wraiths of gossamer cloud clung to the islands, seeping down to the silver mist that lay like motionless ectoplasm over the strange world. The scene possessed a haunting dream-like quality, yet there was something about it that was uneasy and baffling, and I felt curious. The silence was so intense that my ears picked up a barely audible whisper. It was a faint movement of air through the labyrinth on that still night, and I realized that the strangeness was due to there being no wind. Then, as a puff of air touched me, the cold gripped me through my underwear, and I hurried back to the tent shivering.

The tent flapping angrily woke me next morning. The wind

was blowing about thirty knots and visibility was so bad that I decided we should lie up all day rather than tackle the brash in such conditions. The wind dropped the following day, and we continued; but the brash got steadily worse, with both sledges overturning every hundred yards or so. By the time we camped we had covered no more than one and a half miles. Next day, 12 June, we advanced a further three miles, but after yet another day's punishing travel we discovered to our great disappointment that "Bloody Mary" had damaged all her bridges.

There was no alternative but to patch up the sledge as best we could and send Massey and Leppard back to View Point to exchange it for "Ice Cold Katie" which Taylor was using for his tests. It would mean the loss of four or five valuable days to our expedition, but we could not possibly risk taking a load any farther on the damaged sledge. The arrangement would of course inconvenience Taylor, but he had better repair facilities at View Point; besides, he was only seventeen miles from base.

Massey and Leppard set out for View Point the following morning, carrying the barest essentials, while Precious and I settled down to pass the time as best we could. We tried reconnoitring a route, and walked through the brash, climbing a berg to get a better view down the channel.

The prospect was not encouraging. The brash seemed to stretch away south to where a chain of large tabular bergs were strung across our path from James Ross Island to the coast of Graham Land, and from where we stood there appeared to be no passage past them.

"Hell," I said, "will we ever get out of this bloody brash?"

"It looks pretty bad," Precious agreed.

"Why do we have to muck about in here when a helicopter could lay a string of depots right down the channel?" I demanded. "The *Biscoe* could bring a helicopter down on her first call, and take it away on her second call. In that time it could be used to lift all the stuff that's needed for the season's journeys, and we could get twice the amount of surveying done."

Precious eagerly responded to the idea. Between us we worked out the details of a supply operation, and cursed the FIDS administration for not having had the gumption to think of it before.

It was two o'clock when we returned from our recce. Within the last couple of hours the temperature had risen from about -10° F. to +38° F. so that the brash was now weeping and the snow was slush beneath our feet.

Presently the wind increased and was soon up to gale force. Then it was past it, and by the time darkness fell gusts of seventy and eighty knots were hitting us mercilessly. Our tent was flapping alarmingly, and although we had shovelled plenty of snow and piled blocks of ice round the skirt flaps, I was afraid the wet snow would not be able to hold it. I thought of Taylor and Willis when their tent blew away on Summit Pass, but at least they had another tent to shelter in a few yards away. We had no second line of defence.

We had supper and lay in our bags, unable to sleep for the flapping of the tent. The gale seemed to increase, and at 4.30, at the height of it, the dogs started fighting. I went outside, to find that they had pulled the forward picket out of the melting ice and had overturned the sledge in the mêlée that followed. In driving snow I had to disentangle them and when I crawled back into the tent half an hour later Precious had brewed a mug of tea. It was the only cheering moment of that long unhappy night.

I can think of only one less welcome obligation in a blizzard than breaking up a dog-fight – answering a call of nature. If you faced the wind the drift got in your eyes, and if you turned the other way it got in your trousers. You had your choice and nobody lingered over it, save the "inside" man in the morning when camp was struck. After everything had been passed to the "outside" man to load on the sledge, it was the "inside" chap's privilege to take advantage of the security of the tent.

When daylight came after the night of storm, the wind had died down and the temperature had dropped to 6° F., so that the tent was now pitched on what looked like the ice-rink at the Empress Hall, with the skirt flaps frozen deep in the ice.

We spent the morning drying out our sleeping-bags and sheepskin rugs over the Primus, and moved the dogs to a new and better site. Not satisfied with our recce the day before, we climbed a second berg and, from the top, 150 feet up, we chose what we hoped would be the best route out of the brash, which seemed to continue for at least another twenty miles.

We lay up, playing cards and sleeping most of the next day, save for another climb up the berg. We had tried each night to contact base and View Point by radio, without success. All we picked up on these occasions was Moscow putting out Communist propaganda in a marked American accent.

"For God's sake, turn it off," I would tell Precious. "I came down to the Antarctic to get away from all that."

Next day, 16 June, found us still waiting. We saw mother-of-pearl clouds high above the peninsula in the afternoon, and killed a crabeater one and a half miles due east. The dogs had part of it, and we fried the liver and onions for our supper that night.

Early the following morning we were setting out to put a red depot flag on a prominent bergy bit as a guide for the other two, when we spotted them a mile away to the north-west and walked out to meet them. It was lunchtime when we got back to our camp, and too late to think of continuing our journey, with only a couple of hours of daylight left, so we all climbed the berg again and after a lengthy discussion agreed that probably the best course would be to head for the coast of James Ross Island and hope for a better surface in the lee of its vertical red sandstone cliffs. As we were coming down from the berg a giant petrel flew past, stroking the air most gracefully with its wings. It seemed to prove my point about the helicopter.

On 18 June, after a hold-up of five days, we continued the journey southwards, but accomplished only one and a half miles in about five hours. We were now up to the first of the big tabular bergs, and before continuing next morning Leppard and I climbed it to make a recce. There appeared to be a possible route to the south-east in the direction of James Ross Island, and coming down we followed it for a short distance to see if it would be suitable for the sledges.

We found that the route improved the nearer we got to the island, so after a while we turned and retraced our steps. We must have got to within a mile and a half of camp, when I scrambled up on to a low ridge and suddenly saw an enormous leopard seal on a flat area of ice just below me.

It reared itself up, looking at us fiercely and expelled its breath in an open-mouthed snarling hiss. It was almost thirteen feet long, beautifully stream-lined, with a sleek pointed head and long terrifying teeth. Normally we would kill a leopard seal by shooting it from a very safe distance, but now our only weapons were ice-axes.

I jumped down and faced it as it hissed again and went down on its flippers. It bared its teeth and began swaying its head from side to side. Twice I went forward and struck at its head with my ice-axe, but missed each time. I could see that it was going to come at me.

Out of the water a leopard moves differently from other seals. While a crabeater or a Weddell pulls itself forward with both flippers together, bringing its tail up under it, in a series of flopping caterpillar-like movements, a leopard uses its flippers alternately to propel itself with a quick snake-like movement.

Now it rushed at me with a hiss, and I hit it as hard as I could, driving the pick end of the ice-axe into its skull. A moment later I felt the ice-axe wrenched out of my hand as the seal shook its head in a desperate attempt to get it out, and spouts of crimson blood began to stain the snow.

It was almost silent in its mortal agony. Its movements became weaker and weaker until Leppard ran up with a knife and cut the jugular vein in its throat. Its head sank down on the ice with the blood welling out, and it seemed to relax. It gave one last sigh, the back bent in a final spasm, and finally it lay dead.

When later we gutted it we found the stomach quite empty. Leopard seals are not gregarious animals, but what, we asked ourselves, was a lone leopard doing in the middle of the Crown Prince Gustav Channel? We had known them to inhabit small pools in the tide cracks in the winter, but there did not appear to be a pool anywhere for several miles. We could only guess at the answer; that the sea had frozen very quickly, leaving it high and dry.

Leppard and I returned to camp, and we set out together, making for the seal. That mile and a half took us up to nearly three o'clock, so we decided to camp near the seal and let the dogs have a good feed.

We started late next day as Leppard was surveying with the plane table, fixing the height and position of Lachman Crags. After climbing yet another berg, I decided that our best course lay due east from here, and we started out at 2.30 with Leppard and I leading the way. As he wanted to continue his survey, we camped an hour later, having made 2.3 miles, for which we congratulated ourselves.

However, we could now see the end of the brash, and our spirits were high. We were clear of it by two o'clock the following afternoon and, as it was 21 June, and Midwinter Day, we celebrated by opening our "perks" box, and the four of us feasted together on noodle soup, pemmican hash, Kendal mint, chocolate biscuits, coffee and a cigar each. We little realized, as we yarned and listened to news on the radio, that a short distance away was the spectacle of a strange and baffling mystery of the Antarctic.

There was something sinister about that morning. The sky was overcast, the channel gloomy. We were loading up our sledges, and I looked southward to see how far we could hope to get before dirty weather hit us and we had to go to ground. The ice stretched away flat to Carlson Island in the distance, with the promontory of Cape Lagrelius behind it on the left. About 500 yards away jets of steam appeared to be rising from the ice. Presently I saw a large blunt snout-like shape push up about seven feet above the surface, and then there was another jet.

Soon we were ready to move off. I pointed out what I had seen to the others, and we set out towards the spot. As we got near enough we saw that there was a hole in the ice. I stopped my sledge and walked to the edge of the pool. As I looked down into the dark water something seemed to be taking shape; I bent over further, there was a sudden roar and the huge head of a whale shot upwards through the hole, towering above me. I gazed at it too awestruck to do anything but stand and stare. Suddenly, I was drenched with spray as it exhaled with a deep sigh and slowly slid back into the water. It was like the last sad moments of a sinking ship, but in that brief second I had seen its eyes and they were the most intelligent I have ever seen in any animal.

Like the leopard seal, the whale posed a curious question. What was it doing in the Crown Prince Gustav Channel in midwinter? Whales need open water and have to come up at least every half-hour, and normally every few minutes in order to breathe. But it was all of seventy miles from here to the open sea.

We photographed the whale which we later identified as a Lesser Rorqual, and continued towards Carlson Island with Leppard carrying out a running survey. Soon we passed another whale blow-hole, then another; until presently we were in an area where there were about twenty blow-holes, from four to ten feet in diameter. Some were used by more than one whale – in one I counted four snouts squeezed up through an aperture about eight feet square. The thickness of the ice round the holes varied from about one and a half to two and a half feet, but so beautifully controlled were the movements of these huge but gentle creatures, that never once did I see them touch the edge.

At about 2.30 when we were approximately half a mile north of Carlson Island, I was driving the second sledge when I saw Leppard hold up his hand, I repeated the signal and we stopped. Then he pointed. Ahead of us I saw open water stretching across our route from Pitt Point on the mainland to Carlson, and then south-east to Cape Lagrelius.

As we went nearer we saw that there were three leads or pools, the largest of which was about six square miles in area, the smallest about 300 yards long by fifty yards wide. In these pools were a large number of whales – at a rough estimate, a couple of hundred. They were mainly Rorquals, but also quite a lot of Killers; and I noticed a few of the rarer bottle-nosed whales. Lying around on the ice were thousands of crabeaters.

The sight was awe-inspiring. We were a little apprehensive at first as we approached, and the breathing of the whales became louder and louder. Each blow was like the sigh of escaping steam from a railway engine, so that when we got close enough the place sounded like a crowded marshalling-yard. Some of the whales were cruising about on the surface of the leaden black water, others would come up to blow and dive again, but they were all so unhurried and natural in their movements that presently we felt reassured. It was as if we had come to an oasis full of life and sound in the silent, sterile Antarctic desert.

The explanation, we concluded, was that the animals had come into the Crown Prince Gustav Channel to feed and had been trapped by the sudden forming of the sea ice. They had been coralled into these pools, and as far as we could make out their survival depended on their keeping them open, but at the time we were not struck by anything unusual about their behaviour.

As we would have to change course and possibly skirt the edge of James Ross Island to get past these leads, we decided to camp. It was not a good spot because our sleep was disturbed by the bubbling and snorting of seals through a small blow-hole a few feet away from our tent. Then at 4.30 in the morning a wind sprang up without warning, and we were subjected to spasmodic gusts of gale force striking at two- or three-minute intervals, with a calm between each gust, as though the wind was pausing to get its breath back. As I lay half asleep, I felt uneasy; the brash, the broken sledge, the open water, the whales, and now the blizzard, all seemed to serve as a warning.

Bad weather kept us confined to our tents for the next two days. Sunday, 26 June, dawned fine and clear with exquisite mother-of-pearl cloud high over Lachman Crags to our north. The snow on the ice was soft and sticky with salt which had seeped through from the sea, making it heavy going for the dogs; however, by one-thirty we were under the majestic shape of Cape Lagrelius, like the bow of a massive ship breaking through the ice.

A little to the west was yet another area of open water, two miles long and half a mile wide, and this was also teeming with whales. On the ice we could see fat black Weddell seals lying alongside silver-grey shapes of crabeaters.

Suddenly I saw a whale jump clean out of the water like a gigantic salmon. A moment later another, a little nearer to us, did the same. Then a third went up. We immediately got out our cameras hoping to photograph a jumping whale, but none obliged.

We were getting used to the sight of whales, but were certainly not prepared for what we encountered in the next pool, a short distance away. It was a small pool, perhaps a hundred yards long by fifty yards wide, and in it were about twelve Adélie penguins, four crabeaters, one leopard seal, and occasionally two Killer whales, all swimming about together in perfect harmony. Such a scene in Hope Bay would have been unbelievable.

Then, as we watched, a pack of five Killers appeared from under the ice less than six feet from where we stood. There was no mistaking them. They were certainly Killers, yet they went porpoising through the group of seals and penguins, without harming them, and we saw a swirl of glistening backs and the flash of dorsal fins as they dived under the ice on the other side.

We looked at each other in amazement. Had we seen aright? Up to that moment we had believed that Killers attacked whatever creature they saw in the water with terrifying ferocity. We had been warned that if Killers appeared when we were out in a boat, we should make for the land or climb on to the nearest iceberg. But here they were acting quite contrary to their sinister reputation. What was the explanation? We did not know, but it did not stop us guessing. As Massey pointed out, this discovery of ours was going to upset the marine biologists.

"We'll need to take a lot of photographs to substantiate our story or nobody will believe us," he said.

We camped under the lee of the cliffs as the sun was setting over the peninsula, turning the mist that lay across the channel into beautiful pastel pink. It rolled and billowed southward before the gentle wind like an incandescent smoke-screen.

This was indeed an enchanted place. The air was full of echoes, our voices being thrown back at us from the ice-cliffs. The dogs were fascinated. They began growling, listening to the echo and growling again. Pluto, my biggest dog, became particularly belligerent and excited.

From that point the snow surface was perfect and by three o'clock next day we made Cape Obelisk, on the south-west corner of James Ross, where the crevassed pressure ridges of the Larsen Ice-shelf rose seventy feet before us, barring our route due south towards Cape Longing, which was now a blue outline in the distance.

After camping for the night we turned east, skirting the ice-shelf for three miles, to a point where it sloped gently down to the sea ice and the sledges could be taken up.

As we climbed on to the glacial ice of the shelf, we encountered another Antarctic riddle. This was the presence of a number of black boulders lying about in the snow, varying in size from a brick to a car but without a vestige of snow covering them. Obviously the snow that had fallen on them had melted, possibly because they retained some heat from the sun during the day.

Yet, on the other hand, they had not caused any melting in the ice below them. We had at first mistaken them for seals, since they lay completely exposed on the surface. They looked as though they had just been put there, but they must have lain on the shelf-ice for hundreds of years. They could not have been blown into that spot, as some were too big, and the nearest land was over three miles away. One possible explanation is that they had been brought down from a glacier and carried to their present position by the barely perceptible movement of the ice-shelf. But why were they still exposed? The secret remains locked in the heart of the Crown Prince Gustav Channel.

We camped for the night, and continued towards our objective twenty-five miles away, making fifteen miles in the best day's sledging so far, though the temperature dropped to the minus thirties and we all suffered from frost-bitten noses, cheeks and ears.

By two o'clock next day we could see Longing Col ahead of us in a wide saddle running out from the mainland to the tip of the cape. Soon we began the gradual climb to the summit of the col. We reached the top, and there, less than a mile away, was a tattered red pennant and a small pile of boxes. We had reached our objective, the Longing Col Depot. Ahead of us lay the desolate vista of the cliffs of Graham Land and the ice-shelf stretching for miles and miles into the grey south. This was the sort of country we had to explore on the main journey. The prospect was not encouraging.

We spent the next day catching up with minor repairs, and checking the depot. It consisted of three boxes of man-rations, fifteen boxes of dog pemmican and eight gallons of paraffin – enough for four men and two dog teams for fifteen days. We added our contribution which, after all our efforts, merely increased the depot by another twenty days' supply. It looked a pathetic little mound in such a vast wilderness. A helicopter could have delivered that and returned to base in three hours.

Going All the Way

Vivian Fuchs

The sometime director of the Falkland Islands Dependencies Survey, Fuchs was both the mover and leader of the 1955–8 Commonwealth Trans-Antarctic Expedition, the belated British bid to fulfil Shackleton's dream of an overland crossing of the entire southern continent.

Camp Life

Below Fuchs recounts the expedition's second winter holed up doing preparations for the crossing.

We were concerned for our dogs. At Scott Base, where there were sixty, they were able to live outside all through the winter and, again when the moon came up each month, they were harnessed to their sledges and given a run. Racing over the rough sea ice was an exhilarating experience for both dogs and men as it was impossible to pick out obstacles in the moonlight – for the driver the only thing to do was to cling to the sledge and hope for the best.

At Shackleton, as the winds rose and the temperatures fell, they lay curled up on the snow above our buried hut, with only their fur and blubber to protect them. As the wind continually swept the snow from the hard compacted surface, they were even denied the usual protection of accumulating drift to keep them warm. Sometimes when we went to visit them they would rise to greet us, but often their warmth had melted the snow, which had then frozen again and tore the hair from their bodies as they struggled to their feet.

We decided to dig new tunnels for their protection and

determined that there must be plenty of headroom as well as space to saw up the seal-meat under shelter. Making a tunnel 140 feet long by 8 feet deep and 4 feet wide, we cut alcoves in the walls on alternate sides to prevent the dogs reaching each other at the ends of their chains. Later on, the main power system provided the tunnel with electricity for twelve hours each day, and the dogs lived in considerable comfort and relative warmth – for even with an outdoor temperature of -60°F, the heat from their bodies kept the tunnel just above zero.

One of the least popular chores was cutting up the seal-meat. The carcass had first to be dug out from the snow and then cut into pieces by two men using a great cross-cut saw. These were then split up with an axe or sawn into "logs" weighing four to six pounds. One such "log" was fed to each dog every other day . . .

All the bases were carrying out scientific work. At South Ice a Dexion lattice mast was erected which soon became festooned with recording instruments, including anemometers and thermometers every few feet right down to the surface. These provided Hal Lister with wind and temperature records for his glaciological work. At the top of the mast was a small red light which could be switched on from inside the hut to call an absorbed scientist in when lunch was ready.

Jon Stephenson was studying ice crystals, and to obtain the specimens he dug a pit 50 feet deep from inside one of the snow tunnels. From this depth he bored a hole for another 100 feet down, bringing up a core of ice in sections 18 inches long. By studying the snow strata both in the walls of the pit and in the cores, much was learnt about the annual snow fall for centuries past. In fact, the snow recovered from the deepest point fell at the time of the Battle of Agincourt!

At Shackleton Allan Rogers had some complicated instruments called Integrating Motor Pneumotachographs (known as "IMPS" for short), with which he could measure and study the energy expended by a man both at work and at rest – provided, of course, that he could persuade any of us to put up with the discomfort of wearing a mask over his face and a pack on his back while going about his normal work. Soon, members of the party could be seen cooking or sweeping, hauling sledges or building, while wearing IMPS.

Geoffrey Pratt very helpfully undertook to wear the instrument day and night (except at meals) for a whole week. He found it an irksome and uncomfortable experience and even suffered from frost-bite on his face through wearing the mask long hours out of doors, in temperatures below -50°F. However, in the end it was poor Allan who had the worst of it, because he had to follow Geoffrey about all day to see that the IMP was working, and so had to help his energetic subject with all kinds of tasks which were certainly nothing to do with a doctor. Then at mealtimes Allan had to weigh all the food that Geoffrey ate besides questioning the cook to find out what had gone into making the various dishes. This was necessary so that the energy consumed by Geoffrey in the form of food could be compared with energy he expended. So it was that mealtimes passed with Geoffrey eating heartily and poor Allan still hard at work in the kitchen, with often the prospect of little left for him to eat!

After one sleepless night due to the gurgling noises made by Geoffrey and the IMP while he slept, we banished him from the bunk-room to the attic. Still there was no rest for Allan, for he had to follow him and even remain awake to see that the mask was not displaced by his "guinea-pig" while he slept. At the end of the week it was the doctor who was exhausted!

An outdoor task undertaken by David Pratt was the measurement of friction between different types of sledge-runner materials in varying temperatures and on different types of snow surfaces. He used small manhauled sledges carrying a known load, the amount of effort required to keep the sledge in movement being measured electrically by strain gauges. He was constantly looking for unsuspecting people to act as hauliers. I was lucky to do my stint of forty hauls in good conditions, with the temperature at only -19°F, but a few days later Allan Rogers found himself doing the same thing in -60°F. Suddenly he realized that he could make use of the same activity for his IMP work and, in no time at all, the unfortunate Taffy Williams found himself torn from his nice warm radio-room, wearing an IMP and manhauling a sledge in the outer darkness. As he stumbled from one invisible snowdrift to another, Allan and David each cried his own directions, until the protesting Taffy was at last discharged from duty (exhausted), and another victim found . . .

The sun left us on 23 April, but inside our huts we were always busy. At Shackleton each man was duty cook for four days at a time, helped by two "gashmen" who were responsible for bringing in the snow to be melted for our water supply, keeping the stoves supplied with fuel, washing up, keeping the hut tidy, and – perhaps the worst chore of all – disposing of the rubbish. This entailed carrying a twelve-gallon bucket of kitchen waste up a flight of snow steps to the surface where, more often than not, the wind would whip the contents over the gashmen as they staggered away into the drift.

After a time we could bear this no longer, so we dug out an extension tunnel from the bottom of the snow steps, and made a deep waste-pit in an unusual manner. First we made a small hole about 18 inches deep in the snow. Into this we poured a pint of petrol which soaked in immediately. Taking care that there were no small pools of petrol on the surface, a match was applied, and the petrol burnt slowly, gradually melting a cavity. Each time the flames went out more petrol was poured into the deepening hole and set alight, and in two hours, with the use of four gallons of petrol, we had a pit 24 feet deep. This served us excellently as a waste-pit until the base was abandoned in November.

After a few weeks we noticed that when a bucket of water had been tipped into this waste-pit, there was a pause followed by a distant rumbling gurgle. Then we found that cold air was rising from the pit, and we realized that the bottom of the pit had broken through into a crevasse which ran almost under the base hut.

At Scott Base they had a full-time cook, helped by two duty "gashmen" who were on for a week at a time. On Sundays the cook was given a complete rest and the gashmen prepared the meals, which led to keen competition for original menus.

Many firms had given us labour-saving equipment which greatly added to our comfort at base. Both at Scott and at Shackleton the Singer sewing machines were never idle as we made hundreds of trail flags and mended or modified clothing and tents. During the winter, sledges were stripped down and repaired, dog traces spliced and new dog harnesses made. As there were thirteen of us sharing the hut at Shackleton, each man had the bathroom in turn for a day at a time. At the same time he did his personal laundry with the Hoover washing machine which we had been given.

Installing our bathroom had presented us with some unexpected problems. When an Antarctic hut is built on rock, as at Scott Base, it is very unwise to allow the bathwater to run away through the normal waste-plug as it will freeze on the rock below, gradually building up ice beneath the floor and very soon preventing any further escape. We had therefore expected to bail out our bathwater and empty it outside, but finding our hut at Shackleton built on a great depth of snow, we now thought that it would accept the bath waste – as indeed it did. Unfortunately the bath supplied to us had no waste-plug!

David Stratton told us he had discovered that this type of bath was made specially for sale in Aden, as Arabs apparently did not require waste-pipes. But why not? We spent a great deal of time inventing stories of a long camel caravan winding over the hot sands of Arabia, each camel bearing two white enamelled cast-iron baths like panniers on either side of its swaying humps. But what on earth did the Arabs do with the waste water when the baths were finally in use?

We never did find out, but our engineers decided to try to make a hole in the normal place in the bath and to drain the waste water away beneath the hut. This was not an easy task without chipping the enamel or cracking the iron, and during their initial experiments in devising a suitable plug for the hole, the bather was frequently left sitting in the empty bath, high, dry, soapy, and unamused . . .

One of the busiest places at each base was the garage workshop. Here the engineers worked long hours preparing and modifying the vehicles for the testing time ahead of them. At Scott Base the original plan was for the depots towards the Pole to be established by dog teams and for the supplies to be flown in by air. But Ed Hillary had been very impressed with the performance of his small Ferguson tractors and finally decided to use these also for the southern journey. It was a large-scale operation preparing them. Over the driver's seat was welded a powerful crash bar to give some protection should the vehicle go down a crevasse or roll over. Around this a cab, or rather a windbreak, was constructed from canvas to keep out a little of the

Antarctic wind. The track system was strengthened and an enormous amount of work was done on the tracks themselves to try and improve their grip in soft snow. The motors were overhauled, the electrical wiring system simplified, and any unnecessary parts of the body were cut away to save weight. A light, portable garage was constructed out of canvas, with a collapsible framework of three-quarter-inch piping, in case of a major breakdown; a strong towbar was welded to the front of each vehicle, and sixty-foot lengths of Terylene towrope, with an eight-ton breaking strain, were cut and spliced.

At Shackleton David and Roy worked on the vehicles one after the other, stripping down tracks, welding on recovery equipment for use should they fall into crevasses, and overhauling all the engines. The days were not long enough for everything that had to be done.

As a relaxation our engineers had made a large fish trap out of wire netting which they had lowered through a hole cut in the sea ice, although as the water was three thousand feet deep, there was no hope of bottom fishing. One evening George Lowe and I went down with them to visit this trap. Leaving Shackleton in a brisk wind and heavy snow, we found it difficult to find our way along the two-mile route in the dark, but, helped by the marker stakes and stretches of the old track which had not been drifted over, we reached the edge of the sea ice. The hole through which the trap had been let down was frozen over and when we broke through, countless clusters of ice crystals an inch or more in diameter floated to the surface. When at last we obtained a patch of clear water, we could see hundreds of pink, shrimp-like creatures in the light of our torches. These were *euphausea*, or krill, the main food of many species of whale, and this was all that the trap contained. Not intending to return empty-handed, we collected as many of them as we could, thinking they would make a surprise dish for David Stratton's birthday the next day.

Suddenly there was a swirl of water and a seal surfaced to breathe, but he was as startled as we were and disappeared in an instant. As we turned back towards the Shackleton beacon light shining through the driving snow, it occurred to me that people at home might think us slightly mad to go shrimping in a snowstorm at dead of night in the Antarctic winter – but to us it was a relaxation to leave base and do something different from the daily routine.

Our special dish of sea-food was duly prepared in honour of David's birthday and looked most attractive. We all gathered round as manfully he tackled the delicate pink pile, only to find that each multi-legged corpse contained no more than a few drops of pink oil! . . .

On 21 June – Midwinter Day – we rose late for breakfast, and then everybody helped with the normal chores of sweeping, cleaning and bringing in ice and coal, before dressing to go to the Pratt-Homard cocktail party – although it was darkly rumoured by the non-engineers that the "cocktails" would consist mainly of petrol, flavoured with grease and oil! We set out for the workshop fully clothed in windproofs and gloves, expecting to stumble over the intervening snowdrifts, but to our surprise the snow reflected the flickering light of dozens of paraffin flares marking the 200-yard route.

Inside the workshop it was beautifully warm, for the small coal fire in the annexe was roaring and the temperature of the whole building had been raised to + 35°F. We were able to strip off our outdoor clothing and stand about in comfort admiring the new photographs and coloured posters which decorated the walls. The shouts of welcome which greeted each new arrival and the general air of gaiety was enhanced by a background of Irish jigs from the record-player, and soon someone thought of fixing a large meteorological balloon to the exhaust of a Weasel and starting the engine. Slowly at first, but with increasing speed, it grew to gigantic proportions before exploding with a satisfying bang!

This entertainment was followed by the explanation of Gordon Haslop's strange behaviour during the previous few days. The "Haslop Firework Display" began with a series of detonations spelling "TAE" in morse and continued with flares and rockets, while the flitting figure of Gordon could be seen silhouetted against the lights, clearly clutching a beer mug in one hand while setting off fireworks with the other. It was a fine show.

South Ice came through on the radio to exchange greetings and tell us about the roast beef lunch they had just finished and how they were already looking forward to chicken for dinner. At

3.30 p.m. we sat down to a splendid meal which included green turtle soup, roast turkey, plum pudding and ice-cream. The table was decorated with crackers and presents and in due course most of us were wearing paper hats and playing musical instruments.

Later that evening, after a suitable pause for digestion and recovery, we enjoyed a buffet supper, which included even mustard and cress sandwiches (grown in boxes in the loft of the hut), the first fresh vegetable we had tasted since the *Magga Dan* left us. Ralph Lenton felt inspired to entertain us with a wonderful version of the Dance of the Seven Veils, while an improvised band – I imagine the first Antarctic Skiffle Group – played vigourously on any available article.

Such was our Midwinter, and after it we settled down to the second half of the long dark night, always looking forward to the return of the sun in August. We went back to our regular routine of tending our instruments, looking after the dogs, working on the vehicles, digging out buried sledges and the thousand other things which made the time of preparation for spring all too short. We worked hard on the camping equipment, mending tents, binding tent poles with tape or balloon cord to strengthen them, checking and repacking ration boxes, overhauling field radio equipment – all labourious jobs which took many hours.

By the end of July the temperature at Shackleton dropped to -64°F with a 25 knot wind. At South Ice it was -71°F. But by the beginning of August both bases enjoyed the faint glow of the returning sun reflected from below the horizon. Day by day the light on the clouds became more colourful and steadily increased until it was possible for us to move about outside without the aid of lanterns to light our way.

Sno-Cats and Crevasses

With a party of ten Fuchs set out by snow tractor from Shackleton Base, Weddell Sea, on 24 November 1957.

In spite of our late start we made 15 miles before pitching camp for the night, and after 14 miles next day we thought that we were well set for a long run. Then, as if to laugh at such optimism, a snow bridge fell away beneath Rock 'n' Roll, leaving

David Stratton and myself suspended in mid-air over an enormous hole – it was about 15 feet wide and 60 feet deep to the first step in the walls of the crevasse below. Peering out of the driving seat was distinctly alarming, for I did not know how firmly the vehicle was wedged against the sides, and in any case there was nothing on to which I could step out – even the pontoons were inaccessible. However, David found that on his side he could just about reach the rear pontoon and we were able to crawl to firm snow across the ladder-like track as it hung in space over the abyss.

At first sight it looked as if we would have to abandon the vehicle – a real catastrophe at this early stage of our journey – and we began to remove everything from inside the cab. Then we determined to "have a go" and thought out a plan to recover it. David Pratt and Roy moved the two other Sno-Cats side by side behind Rock 'n' Roll and attached them by steel cables to the rear towing hook. Next, after careful prospecting along the length of the crevasse, we found a point where George and Allan could take their Weasels over and bring them round in front of Rock 'n' Roll. There they were joined in tandem and attached by another cable to the Sno-Cat's front axle. In this way they formed an anchor, preventing the front of the vehicle from falling vertically into the crevasse when an attempt was made to pull it out backwards.

On a Sno-Cat each track runs round a pontoon. These pontoons are themselves free to swivel about the axles in a vertical plane, which made it very difficult for us to move the front ones into the correct position to rise over the edge of the crevasse. The Muskeg was hitched to one of the front pontoons so that it could swing it as the two Sno-Cats hauled slowly backwards. The other was helped into position by David Stratton, whom we lowered into the crevasse on a rope so that he could cut out a ledge to receive it. When everything was ready we had five vehicles to control simultaneously.

On a given signal the two Sno-Cats brought their total of 400 horse-power to bear, using the emergency low gear known to us as "Grandma", while the Weasels kept their lines taut to hold up the front of Rock 'n' Roll as she gradually moved backwards, and the Muskeg (driven in yet a third direction) brought the free pontoon safely over the edge and into position. It seemed to require a gargantuan effort and we held our breath as the vehicles strained to perform their tasks. When the recovery was at last safely accomplished, it was discovered that we had left Rock 'n' Roll in forward gear all the time! The whole incident had delayed us five hours.

Next day we pressed on over many more crevasses. From our previous experience over the route we believed them to be quite small, but then we received another warning when a crevasse lid 15 feet wide collapsed only a few feet in front of Roy's County of Kent, after all the other five vehicles had passed safely over it. When Roy stopped, his tracks were only three feet from the brink. He now had to reverse away from the hole and find another place where the crevasse could be crossed safely – a very difficult and tedious operation as the two sledges behind him could not be pushed backwards and he could therefore only reverse a few feet at a time. After that we went ahead on skis over the route, probing for crevasses every few yards, and finding a great many which had not been there on our first journey to South Ice. Undoubtedly, during the intervening weeks, the sun had weakened the snow bridges, and now, with more vehicles to worry about, we had to be doubly careful, for we began to find monstrous black caverns beneath the seemingly smooth surface.

By the evening of the 29th we had reached the old 50-Mile Depot, but a number of minor mechanical troubles had arisen; David Pratt and Roy were constantly changing radiators, hunting for coolant leaks in the very complicated engine systems, or trying to cure obstinate ingnition troubles. We were particularly worried by the appearance of considerable wear on the rollers of Rock 'n' Roll's front left track which had not been seen before she fell into the first crevasse. We were unable to find the cause (later it proved to be nothing to do with the crevasse accident), but I decided we must have a new pontoon and rollers sent out by air from Shackleton.

After leaving the depot we cleared the remaining four miles of crevasses in that particular belt and covered 27 miles in the day. On 1 December we moved 41 miles, but that night County of Kent drove into camp misfiring badly, and needing attention; we also began to dismantle the damaged pontoon on Rock 'n' Roll to inspect the bearings. Maintenance work held us up until the 3rd when we travelled for thirteen hours and covered sixty-five miles over the broad undulations of the ice shelf; at the time it seemed only a fair distance, but it proved to be the best mileage we were to make until long after we had passed the South Pole.

We were now only seven miles from the eleven-mile wide crevasse belt lying in front of the ice wall, and with confidence we set out to find the chequered flag which we had planted in October to mark the first of the crevasses. As we saw it and just as I was about to say to David Stratton, "I should stop a little way before you get there", we felt again that horrible, prolonged sinking sensation. The bonnet rose up and up in front of us, then there was a jolt and a pause, long enough to make us think we had settled, followed by a further sickening lurch as the back sank still further. Once more we were down a hole. Carefully we crept out and scrambled to the firm snow surface, where we found the front pontoons holding grimly to the other edge of the chasm while the back of the "cat" was nearly level with the surface. When the others came up they reported that we had been breaking a number of small holes through the surface, and that they had been trying unsuccessfully to attract our attention. Here again was an area where the later season was revealing dangers we had not seen on our reconnaissance run.

As we worked to recover the vehicle it was discovered that the cause of our second lurch was the breaking of four bolts holding the towing hook, for this had torn away from the Sno-Cat and allowed the back to drop deeper. When we had Rock 'n' Roll on the surface again we found that the large cast aluminium steering platform for the rear pontoons had been snapped on both sides. Fortunately David Pratt had brought a spare and repair work began at once. This went on late into the night and during the next day, while the rest of us began the endless business of probing our way through the eleven miles of crevasses – it was clear that in spite of our knowledge of the route, it was still going to be slow work.

Owing to lack of time the engineers had been unable to make three more of the complicated forward towing attachments which had been devised for Haywire on the reconnaissance journey. Therefore our three Sno-Cats could not be roped together and were in greater danger of falling into crevasses than the other vehicles. For this reason, and because the loss of a Weasel was less important than the loss of a "cat", we now sent the two Weasels and the Muskeg ahead, roped together. In this way the leading Weasel acted as a crevasse detector.

On the 9th, we were moving forward in this new order over a section of the probed route, when David Stratton, who was skiing ahead to guide my leading Weasel over the prepared track, suddenly pointed back. There behind us we could see two loaded sledges but no third Sno-Cat. At first I feared that David Pratt had dropped right down a crevasse, but then I could just make out a part of the vehicle standing up in front of the sledges. Clearly he was in a bad position and figures could be seen moving about and waving, presumably to call us back.

As we returned on skis, Hal Lister met us to say that all the vehicles would be needed for the recovery, so we unhitched from our various sledges, prodded a turning space for each vehicle, and started back over a course like a switch-back, where the numerous smaller crevasse bridges had sunk or broken through. Arriving at the scene we found Able resting in the crevasse with only the very tips of the front pontoons on the surface, the main weight of the vehicle being supported by the back of the body, and the rear pontoons hanging free.

Here was a very different recovery problem. It would be necessary to support the rear pontoons from below when the vehicle was drawn forwards, for there was certainly no possibility of hauling her out backwards. Luckily, directly beneath Able and about 25 feet down, the walls of the crevasse came very close together, so we all set to with shovels to fill in the hole below, until it was possible for men to stand on the snow filling we had made, and to set lengths of aluminium crevasse bridging in place beneath the pontoons. To secure them, ledges were cut into the walls of the crevasse upon which the aluminium spans could rest at a sloping angle beneath the tracks. The spans had been specially constructed in 14-foot lengths, each weighing 125 lbs and strong enough to carry four tons.

It was impossible to put the bridging into position on both sides at exactly the same angle so the whole structure looked even more precarious than it really was. To be on the safe side steel rope slings were placed round the ends of the bridging pieces and fastened to "dead-men", stout timbers buried several feet below the surface to act as anchors. When all was ready, Rock 'n' Roll and County of Kent began to pull ahead, while two Weasels, acting as a drag anchor behind Able, gradually gave way at the back. As Able started slowly to move, the cables taut, there was suddenly a loud crunch as the ledges under the bridging gave way and the vehicle lurched sideways to sink deeper – but, to our great relief, the dead-men held. Then, like some monster rising from the deep, she seemed to heave and wallow her way to the surface, and finally came clear.

When reloading was complete, and all the tools, steel cable, shackles, boards, bridging, ropes and other equipment had been returned to the various vehicles, we set off for the third time over the broken and sagging crevasse bridges along the trail we had already made. With a few diversions, and great care in driving, everyone reached the sledges, hooked up and continued safely to the end of the probed route.

Travelling via the Pole and Depot 700, and with the aid of Sir Edmund Hillary, Fuchs reached the far side of Antarctica on 2 March 1958. He had travelled 2,158 miles across the white desert.

Ghosts

Noel Barber

The journalist Noel Barber became the first Briton to reach the South Pole since Scott's party of 1912, when he was flown into witness the arrivals of the Commonwealth Trans-Antarctic Expedition. During his sojourn in Antarctica, he also visited Scott's old hut at Cape Evans.

The weather was beautiful, the temperature plus five, no wind, a vivid, aching sun. A helicopter was making a trip to Cape Evans, twenty-five miles or so along the Ross Sea, facing the open sea from the other side of Ross Island. Would I care to go along? I most certainly would. We spun out in the chopper, always so much more exciting than flying in an ordinary aircraft, and half an hour later landed on a patch of black earth, sending up swirls of dust, within ten yards of the black water of the Ross Sea. Near by were three small nylon bivouac tents, each big enough for one man. Fifty yards away was an old wooden shack.

This was the base established by Scott in 1910, and living there temporarily was one of the grand old men of Antarctica, Sir Hubert Wilkins, now sixty-nine, but as tough as leather, and who probably knew more about the Antarctic than any man alive. He had flown out to Cape Evans to spend some time there with two companions living in tents and eating nothing but dehydrated survival rations to test their effects on men. I looked forward to an incredibly bad meal, but I could not have been more mistaken.

The helicopter whirred into action, blanketing us in black dust – dust in the Antarctica, it really was too ridiculous – with the promise of returning to pick me up later that day.

Wilkins, sporting a trim goatee beard and with a nose which the cold had turned as red and shiny as a small apple, was a most engaging character. His tests with dehydrated food, he explained, were over. He was now camping at Cape Evans for a few days longer while his companions collected geological specimens and he took a holiday. Next to his small camp stood the solid wooden shack that Scott had planted there forty-seven years ago, still in excellent condition, though filled with packed snow so that one could not enter. The bones of some of his Manchurian ponies lay around.

"But I'll give you a meal you'll never forget," said Wilkins, and he most certainly did, for I ate the strangest meal of my life, a meal cooked and tinned at least fifty years ago, but which, due to the natural refrigeration of the Antarctic, was just as good as new. When Wilkins arrived at Cape Evans he found an enormous cache of food in tins left by Scott in case of emergencies. How little the Antarctic really changes, for at this very time the descendant of Scott and Shackleton, Sir Edmund Hillary was doing just the same thing, laying in food stocks at depots along the trail.

At Cape Evans, there seemed to be everything. We opened a tin of cooked mutton, heating it on a modern cooking tablet from the American survival ration bag, and followed this with some excellent Stilton and biscuits. Then some more biscuits and marmalade – the very same brand of Oxford marmalade I eat at home each morning, and in just as good condition.

The meal was excellent and there were hundreds of tins of it. The cheese was rather high, and tended to crumble when we opened the tin, but it was quite edible. The biscuits still retained much of their original crispness. There were scores of tins of English vegetables, some wonderful greengage jam (I tested that too), boxes of Quaker Oats, Cerebos salt and Colman's mustard in huge tins and all in well-nigh perfect condition. The only thing that had gone off was some corned beef.

The store of food was not buried. Scott had left it in a small hollow halfway up the hillside and surrounded by snow. This had kept it in almost perfect condition, and the natural dehydration of the Antarctic air had stopped it from going bad. We found bars of chocolate, even some old showcards for Fry's, and when I was rummaging around, I opened a carton of ordinary boxes of matches which I struck into a flame without any trouble. I would have sorely liked to take back a selection of souvenirs – there were so many, nobody would have missed any – but the thought of overweight from New Zealand to London prevented me. I did take some boxes of matches though, remembering how short of matches I had been at the Pole when my lighter refused to work. They would be very useful if I returned. (They were also very useful on my return to England when I lost my lighter.)

It was a wonderful, happy afternoon, hand in hand with the past. I would have dearly liked to remain at Cape Evans ("Stay by all means," offered Wilkins, "I'm sure we have a spare tent!"), but one of the chores of being a reporter is that you can't always do what you want. You can be the best newspaperman in the world and it will avail you nothing if you do not keep open your lines of communication and make your daily checks on news that might develop at any moment. So the helicopter flew me back into the present and more hamburgers for supper at McMurdo, and to pass the evening I went, as usual, to the camp cinema for my nightly hour or so of stale romance (each film being up to ten years old).

Cape Adare

David Lewis

A New Zealander, Lewis became, in 1973–4, the first person to sail single-handedly to Antarctica. Three years later he returned to the Antarctic in the yacht Solo *with an eight-person expedition funded by the Oceanic Research Foundation. Among the landfalls of the* Solo *expedition was Cape Adare, where Carsten Borchgrevink had made the first over wintering on the continent (in 1899) and where Scott's Northern Party had made their base (1911).*

Midnight had passed. It was now 23 January. A flutter of excitement was caused when Pieter Arriens spotted an Emperor penguin, the only one seen on the entire voyage. Emperors share with Adélies the distinction of being truly Antarctic but, unlike the latter, they breed on the fast ice itself, not on the land at all. The eggs are laid and the chicks reared on the Emperors' enormous vascular feet, where they are enfolded by a protective layer of skin. The little creatures need all the protection they can get for the eggs are laid in the fearful cold of the Antarctic mid-winter blizzards.

Beyond Cape Adare was a snow saddle, behind which the land rose gradually to a gentle rounded summit. The slopes were obviously easy going.

"How about that for a good afternoon's stroll?" I suggested to Fritz, "if you and I can get away."

"Glad to, skipper. Only too pleased to get my feet on something solid after this rocking stuff."

My chagrin was complete when I looked more closely at the map. Me, who really should have known the scale of this Antarctic land! The "hill" I had proposed to stroll up in an afternoon was twenty miles from the landing place. It was as high above sea level as Mount Kosciuszko, the summit of Australia!

A more serious cause for concern as we closed in was the inshore pack ice that could now be seen to form a possibly impenetrable barrier between us and the land. Some enormous icebergs came into view, several of which were clearly grounded on the "shoals reported to extend from three to four miles westward of Cape Adare". The prospects of a landing which, hours before, had looked so bright, were now doubtful in the extreme. It was with a heavy heart that I came off watch at 2 a.m. and handed over to Lars.

I was all the more delighted, when awakened at 5 a.m., to find that Lars and Pieter between them had managed to weave their way back and forth across the mouth of Robertson Bay, sometimes down the narrowest of leads, and had now brought *Solo* inside the shoals whereon the bergs were grounded and into a polynia five cables off a rock spire in the shelter of the beetling promontory.

Ridley Beach, a triangular spit of gravel cemented by millennia-old deposits of penguin guano, and a dozen hectares in extent, could be made out from the rigging. It was the site of the old huts. But between us and the beach lay seemingly impenetrable pack, which extended as far as the eye could see. Moreover the pack was moving out towards us at around two knots. Since no open water was visible in the depths of Robertson Bay, it was clear that a current must be sweeping the ice into the bay along the southern shore, which seemed a stone's throw away in that clear atmosphere but was actually eighteen miles off. After their long circuit the floes were emerging past the northern cape where *Solo* lay so uneasily.

Looking to seaward, I saw with some misgiving how the line of grounded bergs revealed more graphically than any chart the presence of the shoals the *Pilot Book* had warned against. The risk of being trapped between the drifting pack and immovable bergs was obvious. Nevertheless, our polynia seemed more or less stationary. Although no open passage to the beach was apparent, I resolved to try for a landing in the Beaufort inflatable.

Pieter, Peter, Ted and I pushed off without any very sanguine hopes. When in doubt try for the shore lead, I thought. And sure enough, right in under the beetling cliff, where the swell boomed hollowly and the backwash sucked noisily away from the ledges, there was a meandering broken passage between the close pack and the land. Time and again brash ice rafted underneath the inflatable until she was brought to a standstill, lifted almost out of the water. We blessed the propellor guard on the Evinrude, for all that was necessary was to go into reverse and pole with the paddles to win free – until the next time. I was more than grateful too for the Beaufort's stout fabric, since a bad puncture that would set us floundering in the icy water and scrambling for the dubious refuge of the nearest floe was no cheerful prospect.

Before long the cliffs receded, to be replaced by steep snow slopes and a shoreline fronted by an impenetrable jumble of massive floes grounded on the shelving bottom. Judging by the height – a metre or more – of their flotation lines above the water, the tide was low. Further out the drifting mass of floes went spinning by. In and out along the leads we weaved and, before we knew it, we were off Ridley Beach itself, searching for an opening between the close-set grounded floes.

"There's a gap!" called Ted, who was in the bow with his movie camera. He pointed and I swung the tiller and turned down the lane he had indicated between the undercut green walls of ice. As the Beaufort surged up to the shingle we tumbled out dry shod and ran it up out of reach of the waves. To make doubly sure the painter was looped round a block of ice. A group of Adélie penguins emerging from the water (this was clearly their access road too) made grudging way for us. For Peter Donaldson and Ted this was their first landing on the Antarctic mainland.

Peter wrote:

I was elated as I jumped from the inflatable on to an icy beach. Antarctica has fascinated me ever since reading about Scott and Amundsen as a boy and now I thought "Bloody hell, I've finally got here". Ted seemed quite surprised when I solemnly shook his hand. On topping a small rise, we saw an almost surrealistic sight: an enormous penguin rookery of perhaps a million Adélies and, right in the middle of this teeming life, sat our goal – three old wooden huts. Walking across the rookery towards them, most penguins ignored us. Many adults were away fishing whilst the chicks sheltered in nurseries from marauding skuas. However, to our great amusement, one adult took an instant dislike to David: perhaps it was his bright red insulated suit, but everywhere he went, it followed – snapping at a most uncomfortable height. David maintained some semblance of dignity for a while but this dissolved when the penguin's chick joined the fray for a few snaps.

This last was delightful. After intently watching its elder, the chick waddled up to me with a comical air of bravado. Having delivered its token peck against my heavily quilted thigh, it swaggered back to its parent, so obviously preening itself at its daring as to leave us helpless with laughter.

Before setting out for the huts we called up *Solo* on the walkie-talkie: "*Solo, Solo*, this is Rubber Duck calling *Solo*. Come in please, Over." No reply. "*Solo*, this is Rubber Duck. We have landed on Ridley Beach. Are you all right? Come in please. Over."

But there was still no answer. The transmitter, tested only half an hour before, was no longer working. (This was the only radio failure on the entire trip.) There was no way of knowing whether Lars was receiving us (he was, it turned out) but, in any case, I was anxious for the safety of the ship.

"Let us get over to the huts as fast as we can and do some double-quick time filming. Then we must be on our way back. There isn't even time to climb Cape Adare to look for Hansen's grave," I decided.

The enormous Adélie rookery was far more crowded than the one at Sabrina Islet. Overcrowded, judging by the aggressive behaviour of some of the "nursemaids" and parents, to say nothing of the obviously undesirable sites of nests on the edges of melt pools, and the legions more that stretched as far as one could see up the steep 300-metre slopes of the cape itself. Priestley in 1911 had also noted this overcrowding. Dead chicks lay everywhere, though there was no way of telling in that below-zero climate how many years or even centuries some of them had been there. Certain it was that the ever-attendant skuas were well fed, because they showed little interest in potential strays on the fringes of the crèches.

As we neared the huts and observed that the westernmost had but two walls standing, we naturally assumed it to be the oldest.

"No, that must be Scott's," insisted Pieter. "Look at the construction of this intact hut – tongued and grooved at the corners like a log cabin, heavy half-rounded timbers. It is typical Norwegian." He was obviously right. The thinner boarding and more prodigal use of nails in the tumble-down hut was confirmation if any had been needed. It was with considerable respect that we looked at Borchgrevink's 79 year-old hut and store room (the latter unroofed, as it had been in Priestley's day, but otherwise unchanged) and noted the intact shutters and door, the sand and snow-blasted woodwork and the rusted supporting cables. As we fossicked around it became clear that, while iron and steel rusted in the salt sea air – nails and barrel hoops, for instance – woodwork and even the unidentifiable contents of varnished food cans were preserved intact from decay.

Peter Donaldson conjures up the scene:

As we examined the amazing row of old barrels, bottles, cases of briquettes and food tins buried in the penguin guano, the old faded photographs and verbose descriptions of the inhabitants sprang to life. Perhaps the most interesting relic was half of the boat that had been wrecked and dragged across sea ice in a desperate struggle in 1899. Everywhere penguins sheltered, in boxes and even in the toilet pit. What a place to be when the ship and the penguins have departed, when the wind starts blowing pebbles amongst the desiccated carcasses of long-dead birds. Perhaps venturing here in a small boat made us feel akin to those pioneers but the sight of the small wind-buffeted huts in that desolate place with its pervading aura of death, was startling and extremely moving.

One of the most disturbing sights for me was the extraordinary 15-metre-high ridge of pressure ice, floes distorted and packed one on top of the other, that reared up high above the *inner* margin of Ridley Beach. Suppose we *had* succeeded in bringing *Solo* into Robertson Bay and she had been caught in *that* – to become a compressed filling in a deadly sandwich! Suppose we had lingered too long in the Sturge Island anchorage. The same unimaginable forces that had piled up those five-metre-thick floes would have crushed *Solo* as flat as a tin can under a steam roller!

"Sorry, Ted. We must finish the filming now and get back to *Solo*." The unfortunate cameraman wrote later: "I was perspiring profusely as I literally ran around trying to cram into one hour's shooting what I had hoped to have several days to do."

We hastened to the Beaufort and pushed off. Back in the narrow leads I was not at all cheered to see that fresh pancake ice, like one-metre-wide waterlily leaves with upturned edges, was forming between the old floes. Despite its being high summer, the sea was beginning to freeze. A cold snap here could trap us.

I was not too anxious to fail to be amused at the clumsy attempts to take-off of the giant petrels that wandered about the floes. These huge birds, larger even than the smaller albatross species, were known to the old sailors as stinking nellies. All birds of the petrel family will regurgitate their stomach contents, with considerable force and accuracy, at intruders who disturb them. Considering the size of the nelly and presumably of its stomach, and the fact that it is a scavenger, the reason for its nickname is not far to seek.

Being so heavy, the nelly needs a long take-off run. We watched them careering over the irregular surfaces of the floes, wings waving wildly, slipping and stumbling and scattering the indignant Adélies in their path and, as often as not, ending ignominiously in the sea in a cloud of spray.

It was no small relief to find *Solo* in much the same place as we had left her, though in a much shrunken polynia. There was time for the rest of the crew to go ashore, but they would have to hurry. As Dot put it in her diary: "Pack seemed to be closing in again but on seeing Jack's face, David decided it should be our turn to go ashore. Fritz, Jack, Lars and me." It was true, as Dot recognized, that I was very conscious of the "rewards" (in terms of time ashore in the Antarctic) that everyone had more than earned during the weary, uncomfortable months at sea, but safety was the primary consideration. A spare walkie-talkie accompanied Rubber Duck so that the party could be recalled at will.

Just as we had, the second shore party found the impact of the enormous penguin rookery overwhelming. "We counted forty or fifty chicks with four or five adults on guard at each nursery, of which there were hundreds, going nearly to the top of Cape Adare," Dot wrote. She noted that drifted snow, seeping in around the doors and shutters, had filled Borchgrevink's hut. She was impressed too with the splayed-out staves of the barrels, whose hoops had rusted away, and with the penguins nesting within them. Indeed, there was never a box nor a cranny innocent of its round-eyed little denizen to greet the towering intruder with a belligerent "Ark, Ark".

Dot found the huge ridge of pressure ice that towered over the inner side of Ridley Beach as ominous as I had and was not too surprised when I radioed that the pack was moving in rapidly. The returning party found a lot more ice on the way back to *Solo*, but on the way they made one observation which was particularly interesting. In Dot's words: "If we followed the Adélies going to sea via the leads, the way was clear all through the bigger pieces."

In the interim we had not been idle aboard *Solo*. As mentioned earlier, when sea water freezes to form pack ice the salt takes no part in the process and subsequently leaches out, leaving fresh "drinkable" ice, usually by the end of the first season. This ice can be "quarried" for drinking water but the snag is that, if left to itself in the Antarctic, it will not melt but remain on deck as useful as so many blocks of granite. Pieter Arriens had designed a most ingenious but simple device to melt the ice without using extra fuel. A copper coil had been constructed that just fitted inside a large plastic container about twice the size of a bucket. The waste engine cooling water was led into one end of the coil. After circulating through the spirals, a rubber tube carried the waste water to a cockpit drain, where it ran away into the sea. Blocks of ice were packed round the coil. If Pieter was right, the warmth of the engine-cooling water would melt the ice. Now was a good time to put the apparatus to test.

Solo's bow was nosed hard into a large floe, upon which the two Peters, armed with ice saws, axes and crowbars, landed. Soon they were cutting out great snow and ice blocks, with which they staggered back to the yacht. Before long the foredeck was piled so high that it looked like a tumble-down igloo and the melting process was commenced. It worked like a charm. The ice chunks melted with unbelievable rapidity and the melted water was poured into plastic containers. Peter's salinometer came into play.

"Almost pure," he announced, and read off the figures.

"Why, that is a good deal purer than the Adelaide water supply!" exclaimed the delighted Pieter.

But by now the pack was closing in with a vengeance and it was time to recall the second shore party if we were not to be beset. Being beset – held immovably in the pack – is one thing in clear water; I had had four peaceful days of it in *Ice Bird*. It is quite another when the pack is likely to come up against an obstruction and become compressed into the terrifying pressure ridges that can destroy the strongest ship. The grounded bergs and shoals off Cape Adare afforded an excellent setting for such a drama.

As soon as the rest of the crew were aboard, and while the Beaufort was still being manhandled onto the coach roof and the Evinrude lashed in place by the rails, *Solo* was got under way. It was 11.30 a.m., just under six hours since the first party had set out for the shore. The next two and a half hours were anxious ones while the yacht was manoeuvred from lead to lead, always at the direction of someone aloft. As Dot says: "It was a long slow trip out to clear water. Ted did a great job with Lars and Pieter Arriens up the ratlines. Intense concentration all the time. Of course I was, as usual when the men were worried, in the way, so I stayed silently in the stern. Made a cuppa and lay down for a while."

Now was the time for decision. Once *Solo* was in open water outside the pack, the dredge was lowered in an effort to obtain a bottom sample, while I retired below to mull over the charts, sailing directions and ice reports and to decide on our future plan of action. I was amused to note that the compass variation, which is 12° E in Sydney, was 100° E here off Cape Adare, which was beyond – to the south of – the South Magnetic Pole. Thus if the compass had been more sensitive and still working, its north-seeking needle would have pointed a little south of east. That would be a sight not many sailors had seen!

This Awful Place

Michael Parfitt

*The American writer Michael Parfitt spent a full season in Antarctica,
journeying to places unknown and known. Amongst the latter was the
Pole itself.*

(1)

I staggered coming up out of the tunnel into the light. It was less
than twenty-four hours after the Dry Valleys, but Antarctica had
changed again. We were at the Pole.

Equilibrium was gone. Something odd was happening to my
breath. It collected in my face. Though I could see it, every crystal, there was not enough substance there for my lungs. I gulped
at it. *Mawsoni.* Crabeater. I'd lost my way on the ice. In all the
blue-and-white world there was no water sky. A hand touched
my arm. Whose was it? My white wool mask was like blinders. I
could not see for the cloud I made and the sun in it. A woman's
voice: "You okay?" Yes, yes.

"A white desolation and solitude," Richard Byrd said of this
place. He flew over the South Pole in 1929, and when he came
back that's what he said to Paul Siple, the Boy Scout. In January
1956 a Marine Corps pilot flew across the Pole as an advance
scout for United States Task Force 43, which was planning to
build a base there. The marine dropped smoke flares, a balloon
full of ink, and cutout cardboard models of penguins into the
white desolation. He circled. They had disappeared. It was the
snow, he thought. Up in this stunning cold the snow must be
powder. He could imagine the aircraft sweeping closer and closer
to this deceiving brilliant surface, touching down with exquisite
gentleness, and being enveloped in frozen fluff. A large white

flower would bloom on the high plateau and would slowly drift away, and the pilot's soul would join those of Titus Oates, Edgar Evans, Henry Bowers, Edward Wilson, and Robert F. Scott, enshrined in legend and eternal cold.

The marine pilot returned to the fledgling US base on McMurdo Sound carrying the bad news. For a short time it added to the fears that some raised against the occupation of the Pole: It was very cold; people could not live there. The sun would set in March and rise in September; people could not remain sane there. And now the surface was untrustworthy; people could not land there.

Soft snow and strange sunshine. The sun sets once, rises once. It goes down slowly into a sea of snow, sidling around the horizon and taking the late red sky of west to all points of the compass, every one of which is north. It leaves twilight hanging in the sky for a month and a half. It rises fierce, flinging arms of light around the cold world. "It rolled, heaved and surged like a distant forest fire or like a restless, flaming tidal wave . . . And we saw strange flashes of light," Paul Siple wrote of the five days before sunrise. The sun sets once, and the temperature goes to a hundred below, but the snow is hard as iron. When the planes touched down there was no catastrophic cloud. Men walked unimpeded on the hard surface, pounded on stakes to get them to stick, made foundations for buildings so big you could get lost in them, took possession of a place that seemed solid as land. They laughed at the rumours. The men were sane; they kept warm.

But the snow moved. It gathered. It felt hard and reliable; it was hard and shifty. Everything the planes brought and everything built was slowly consumed, grain by windblown grain.

The South Pole was a dream, a nightmare. "The Pole . . . Great God! this is an awful place and terrible enough . . ." Scott cried out to his diary while he was camped at the Pole in defeat, words to be read only months after his death. Scott walked up the Beardmore Glacier, pulling a sledge. He walked back down the Beardmore Glacier, pulling a sledge that bore the tent that would be his tomb and the pages of the diary that would sweep away his foolishness with glory. The Pole was a nightmare, a dream. Comfortable, confident, our group of journalists had flown south in an LC-130. The Beardmore was a staircase no longer, just a checkpoint passing under the wing.

"What else do you have up here as a landmark?"

"The Prudential Rock."

The pilot was quizzing the copilot.

"How much fuel at Pole?"

"They got a 10K bladder that's full and a 24K one pretty near full."

"How much time do you have to report?"

"You have thirty minutes to get hold of them. After an hour You're said to be overdue."

The Transantarctic Range approached and passed under the plane. Glaciers poured down between mountains like water over a five-hundred-mile-long dam of loose rocks. The plane crossed the range at an angle. The glaciers looked smooth, seamed with lines of stress and blue icefalls, pouring water stilled and softened by a time exposure of centuries. The range rolled away close to the course, like a freight train on another track slowly drawing away to a siding a thousand miles away on the Weddell Sea. Behind it the surface was flat and high. The ice was dammed, and behind the range it grew and grew and grew, expanding under our gaze until the mountains were gone and from twenty-four thousand feet the horizon in all directions was an unbroken curve of snow. It was six, eight, nine, eleven thousand feet deep, two miles of snow packed to ice, the storehouse of the world's fresh water; the cap of reflection that tossed the sun's light back in its face, fed winter winds across the globe, and sent its creeping fingers of cold into the depths of all the world's seas; the face of the earth that shone.

Get out of the plane. Walk slowly. Put on your fur-backed bear-paw mittens. Put on your balaclava mask. Pull up your hood. In your enthusiasm do not walk into the propellers. Your enthusiasm may be hypoxia, the drunkenness of too little air. You may be sick with joy. Walk slowly. The air is very thin. Amundsen–Scott South Pole Station is at 9,300 feet above sea level. It has an effective altitude of 10,600. Walk slowly. Do not run up the stairs. Do not run. "You will have strange feelings here. You may have a headache, nausea, shortness of breath. Anything beyond that, see me," Dr Michael Beller, station physician. All arrivals are the same: the doors open, the warmth of the cabin makes a fog at the doors. You feel the sting of the cold. You stagger out with your survival bag. You are high, you are heavy. Your space suit is ungainly; your arms stick out from your sides. You look around. Flags; a tiny barber pole with a silver ball on it in the middle of the flags. A huge silver dome; steam rising from vents. A ramp of snow down into a big square door in the dome. A sign above the door: United States Welcomes You to the South Pole.

(2)

"It was 47 degrees below zero Fahrenheit when you landed. It was minus 67 when the first flight came in this year. The highest temperature ever recorded at the South Pole was minus 7.5 degrees. The lowest was minus 117." The standard briefing was given in the South Pole library. Shell within shell, the people at the South Pole lived warm. The dome was shelter. It was calm in there, but the frost remained. You could drive a front-end loader through the door, and people did. The cold came in, too, stronger than a D-9 Cat. The light within was dim, shaded from the glare by the overhead expanse of aluminium. This metal sky coloured day and night inside; within the dome the light was a cool metallic blue, like twilight on a quicksilver sea. The lights of the interior buildings shone warmly out onto the snow floor. The air looked as if it should taste like water stored in a can.

The sun came harshly into the dome through a cluster of openings at the peak. A shaft of light blazed in at a shallow angle at this time of the spring, and moved slowly around the huge room, making a spot of light on the upper reaches of the dome. The light swung like a planet around the central fire. At the edges of the holes in the roof was a growth of bright white rime ice, as if the light drove in so hard it scraped on the metal. Through the dazzling holes could be seen, if the angle was right, the American flag that flew at the dome's peak. From the twilight inside the dome the flag looked bleached; all those stalwart colours blown pale and inconsequential by the raging antarctic light.

Long orange buildings were stacked up like cargo containers

on the snow, one and two stories high. Their precious cargo was warmth. Their doors were like air locks. The warmth was like oxygen. Without it we would all soon die. We would go spinning away into the whiteness, pale and stiff in our red jackets.

Within the containers were people. The population of the South Pole today was sixty-nine souls, including the visitors: Malcolm, Bob, Ellen, Guy Guthridge, and me. Outside the containers was the food – boxes of frozen beans and frozen bread; cans of frozen sauerkraut. It was dinnertime in the mess hall: Chinese chicken and egg rolls. The cooks were the antarctic CIA contacts – they were graduates of the Culinary Institute of America. After the bland Navy food at McMurdo, the South Pole cuisine was magnificent.

There were stairs outside the buildings. Up the stairs, down the stairs. Our footsteps rang, bunny boots on metal. Through the fuel arch, where great black bladders lay on the snow like huge hot-water bottles, blanketed with insulation. Dick Cameron was here too, bearded and happy. We followed Guy Guthridge around. We never took off our coats; we sweated in the warm rooms, grew chilly in the dome. The grand accumulation of South Pole science piled up against us, drifts of golden leaves. We were like children, stuffing pockets that were too small: Give us time to understand. There is no time. Listen, take notes. You reach the South Pole once in your life.

Elmer Robinson, University of Washington, studied the way the ice surface reacted with trace gases in the atmosphere: "Like most antarctic research I'm familiar with, an investigator begins looking at some general aspects of the field, then finds there is little known at all about conditions in Antarctica." The public address system interrupted: "Mike Beller, please call 006. Mike Beller, please call 006."

Eric Siefka, communications chief, was twenty-two. He had been coming here since he was nineteen. He would winter here next year. "We do most of the flight following for the continent," he said. "We talk to helicopters around McMurdo." A large wooden mallet hung above an array of radios, labelled Acme Noise Suppressor. Siefka: "We talk to everybody. We're going to have a sign made: Antarctica Control."

Gary Foltz, US Geological Survey, monitored seismographs.

"This machine can pick up earthquakes from all over the world. We also pick up a tractor in the dome, or a Here arriving."

Malcolm: "Can you detect an underground nuclear explosion?"

Foltz: "Yes."

"What do you do?"

"Just pick it and send it to Colourado."

Foltz was solid and unemotional. This year would be his second winter. The first time he spent a year here he and a colleague, figuring their display of modest humming machines bored Distinguished Visitors, made up a control panel with flashing lights and switches that said things like Engage Satellite. The panel was still there. It had no real function at all.

The South Pole was stairs and shortness of breath; glimpses outside of the dazzling permanent day; glimpses inside of the work that progressed here, day to day.

F. Tom Berkey, of Utah State University, looked up into the cusp of the ionosphere, where the earth's magnetic fields, curving to the Pole, made a window in which he could stare into the eye of the solar wind. Ensign Frank Migaiolo, with the National Oceanic and Atmospheric Administration, tested this remote air for any trace of changes in the quality of air on the globe. Migaiolo, also the fire officer of the South Pole Station, watched for the most frightening enemy of explorers of the cold land.

Francis Navarro, a Spaniard and a graduate student from the University of California at Los Angeles, listened to the reverberations of the earth's mantle in response to earthquakes on the surface. When we came to see him he stood in a cluttered room with a globe in one hand and a spool of solder in the other, demonstrating the creation of twenty-seven-day tides in rock and ice and deep, hot liquid: "For our studies we need an earthquake of more than 7.9 on the Richter scale." Navarro would spend the winter. He had recently started a beard. He was waiting for the beard to grow thick. He was waiting, with equal certainty, for the crash of devastation and tragedy that must happen somewhere on the globe, waiting to catch the echoes but not the tears.

The public address system interrupted again: "XD 03 has departed McMurdo Station. Estimated arrival, 10.55 local. Zero mail, zero pax." It was the second half of the double shuttle, coming to take us away. There was a saying in MacTown: "Never wait for the second shuttle." It might not come. But this one would not fail.

Malcolm had carried his Christmas cards in his survival bag; he took them to the post office. The postmaster was Mike Beller, the doctor. Doctors in the Antarctic had to find something else to do or go crazy bored. Beller had a box of cachets, verification of our presence here. We sat at a table in the library, putting "South Pole" all over postcards.

And then nothing was left on the schedule. In the library were shelf after shelf of books, and a television set hooked to a video cassette recorder. Some of the residents were watching a movie. Slowly our eyes were drawn to the screen, to the little blue window on our distant world. The movie was *The Godfather, Part II*. Malcolm, Bob, and Ellen slid into chairs. On the little screen a man was shot in the forehead. He died. On the screen another man got into a car. Poison took effect. He went into convulsions. His heel kicked out the window of the car. He died. Someone was shouting. Someone was screaming, crying. Someone was being buried.

Whose dream was this? Not mine. I dreamed about Antarctica. I left the library. I walked alone through the cold air of the dome. I put on my bear-paw mittens, my balaclava mask, my hood. My eyes flinched from the brightness of the big door. I walked out into the sunshine. It was so strong I felt washed by it, cleansed by the solar wind. Looking in the direction of the sun I could see a very faint glitter in the air. Fine ice crystals, light as molecules, drifted down from the clear sky. The glitter fell all around, almost invisible, dusting the surface of the immense whiteness with a dew of light.

(3)

The barber pole with the mirrored globe that represented the South Pole was surrounded by the sixteen flags of the Antarctic Treaty nations – the original twelve plus four new members. Near it was the stand of arrows, common to all antarctic stations, that bore signs pointing in assorted directions, each sign to the home of someone who had been here. Memphis, London,

Lisbon, Los Angeles, Miami, Tehachapi, Billings, Eugene. The flags were official. The arrows represented longing. Here home mattered more than country. The taller of two stands was topped with a wooden fish and pointed to Salmon, Idaho.

This was not the real South Pole. Where was it? In the neighbourhood of the barber pole was a one-acre grove of bamboo stakes. Within these transplanted tropical woods was hidden the South Pole, the real pole, the true axle of the earth. I wandered around. I found it. The real Pole was modest. It turned out to be a little imitation of the big barber pole stuck into the snow. It reached my waist. On top of it was a small knob. That was it, the heart of the whirl.

The real Pole was not celebrated with international flags. Next to it on a bamboo stake flew a single drab, dark blue flag bearing the insignia of the US Geological Survey: crossed hammer and pick.

I stood out on the hard snow, looking around. My head hurt, softly, dully. My eyes ached. I wrote notes on my notebook. The pen froze and faded away. I got out a pencil and wrote with it clamped in my mitten. In the distance was the faint mutter of generators. A plume of steam rose from the vents and drew together in a long, low cloud that drifted – north. The paper of the notebook crackled as I turned a page. It was brittle. It tore; it broke. Nearby noises seemed very loud, loud as all others were distant. The flapping of the USGS flag. The sound of the paper. The scratch of the pencil. The harsh sound of breathing, like the puffing of a lung made of tin cans and parchment.

The South Pole was advancing across the ice. Its position from year to year was marked by metal posts. Each stood about ten metres in front of the previous one and was labelled with copper: "Jan 1, 1983," "Jan 1, 1982. Set by T. Henderson, K. Covert. USGS." The posts cast long shadows in the low sunlight, the golden morning sun of spring. The earth's core remained in one place. The ice moved, thirty feet a year. Nine thousand vertical feet of ice, a thousand miles wide, moving ten metres a year, moving towards South America, moving towards the distant sea, cold, hard and alive.

As I stood at the Pole, it seemed that someone was walking in the distance. The single figure was alone. It strode across the ice three hundred yards away. It did not pause or wave, although I was the only other figure on the white expanse. It appeared to be coming out of the featureless distance and walking with simple resolve back into the featureless distance. It was up-light, a silhouette made thin by the glare of the sun. It was Shackleton, finally making the last ninety-seven miles to the south. It was Amundsen, looking for the glow of light on the snow. It was Scott, free of the sledge at last. It was Titus Oates. "I am just going outside. I may be some time." I will be forever. I will walk through the meaningless years in the light of the Pole and cast a long shadow.

The figure was a South Pole scientist. He passed, following a distant line of flags, and went into an outlying building where machines monitored the cleanliness of the air. I knew where he had been, and perhaps that is why the silhouette had made no sign to me. He had been down an illicit hole.

The place he had come from was called Old Pole. It was the labyrinth of structures that Paul Siple and his men had built and lived in during the winter of 1957 and others had occupied until 1974. Old Pole was now a hatch over a well in the snow fifty feet deep. Old Pole was finished. Old Pole was drawing away from the Pole itself with the ice, being inexorably removed from its setting of glory.

Old Pole was out of bounds. It was invisible from the surface, buried and nearly crushed. It was buckling and collapsing under the smothering of that snow that had seemed so solid a foundation. At another base that was dying under the snow, people had reported rivets popping out of bent steel like bullets, firing down the frosty halls. Shot by the wall, crushed by the ice: somebody could be killed. You are a USARP; you are forbidden to go down Old Pole. Do not go down Old Pole. Do not go.

(4)

You were not permitted to go down Old Pole. But people went down anyway. The life everyone led in Antarctica was so strange that even the most recent past was legendary. People went down through the hatch to glean valuable hardware from the debris, or to bring up food that had been frozen there since 1974; but mainly they climbed down the blue ice tunnel to wander through the cold hallways of the ghost town that was the first city at the bottom of the world; to be a part of Antarctica's history.

An arrangement was made. In the interests of history I was escorted to Old Pole. It was possible that someone wanted me to expose government waste; Old Pole was littered with thousands of dollars of equipment that might have been salvaged. But I was already bewitched by the continent, too enthralled to worry about money. Antarctica was hope and hardship and beauty; it was worth the price. So in the collapsing clutter of Old Pole there was nothing more important than the glimpse of lives that had once also been captured by this terrible, enchanting landscape.

There were four of us. We had bunny boots and wool masks and coats and double layers of underwear and headlamps lit by batteries warmed by our bodies. We carried hissing gasoline lamps that steamed and cast a cloudy light. The faces of the other three were hidden by the masks, where the frost grew at their mouths like stone crystals. They were, for the sake of protecting the guilty, Robert F. and Ernest and Roald, and I was Titus. We were ghosts, floating among the ruins.

We moved rapidly through the buried halls. We walked so fast it seemed we were pursued. We were. We were chased by the cold. We moved urgently, like criminals. The cold was the officer of the law.

It was sixty below zero. When Paul Siple arrived at the South Pole he dug a hole to measure the temperature within the ice. That would be roughly the annual mean temperature at the Pole. He dug for four days and excavated a pit eighteen feet deep. The thermometer registered sixty-two below zero. Now that had become the temperature in his old home, where he and seventeen other men had spent the first winter, 1957. It was winter there forever, down the blue walls of the hole by ladder and rope to the snow-dusted plywood at the bottom and the shadowed memories of ghost towns and ice.

"The roof had sagged under the crushing weight of ice," Richard Byrd wrote of January 1934, when he returned to Little America on the Ross Ice Shelf, which had been abandoned for four years. "Several of the main beams had cracked. They lay splintered across the top bunks. A film of ice lay over the walls, and from the ceiling hung thick clusters of ice crystals, which were brighter than jewels when the light caught them." In Byrd's old station the telephone rang when cranked, and the lights glowed faintly, and there was a frozen piece of roast beef with a fork stuck in it resting on a table. Men left in haste and the things that seemed part of life stood and cooled. In Old Pole the plywood floors were strewn with T-bone steaks, white beans, and a fine gravel of frozen broken eggs. The place was strewn with artefacts of the twentieth century:

Bean with bacon soup. Plastic bags of hot dogs. A sign on a door: "Check electrolyte level at least once/week." A room entirely lined with copper mesh. An exercise bicycle. "All aboard!" shouted Roald. "Hell with that," said Ernest. "Look at this fan," said Robert F. "Is that ancient or what?"

A table was strewn with playing cards. "Operation Deep Freeze," it said on the back of each card. "Task Force 43." There was a Christmas card: "Love, Mother and Dad." In his old camp Byrd noticed an accordion, boxing gloves, and a phonograph that played "The Bells of St Mary's." In Old Pole the debris was the same. We rushed from room to room. The cold pressed closer behind.

Walls of white leaned in upon us. Leaves of frost grew from the walls. We brushed against them and flakes glittered in the lamp, falling in the fog we made with our breath. Wires hung across us, brushed against us like webs, glistening with frost. Doors had the names of offices painted on them. We walked on tilted wooden catwalks. We hastened, hastened, the cold marching at our heels. The steel arches were crumpled like tinfoil under the weight of the snow. Ice crystals grew on the roof and formed on the electrical wiring. Ice crystals grew in blooms. The head-lamp caught a little fake garden behind a picket fence, a garden made of plastic flowers. Next to it was someone's vegetable garden, growing big green plastic peppers. Everywhere were photographs of women. Most wore nothing in the cold. Their skin colours tended to blues; their smiles were antique.

A bowl of cereal stood on a table in the galley, flakes in a puddle of ice. The town was a labyrinth; here and there, rarely, a shaft reached up to the outside world, and a little spot of blue light filtered through the snow. Floors humped up into the rooms. Ceilings were crooked, bending to meet the floor. How deep would this little city go before it was crushed to a flat layer of wood and meat and photographs of women, a smudge of the twentieth century moving slowly north towards South America? Some of the support beams were split, showing fresh jagged wood. Wires festooned the place, caught us around the throat, brushed against our heads and dropped ice down our necks. Robert F., Ernest, Roald, and I rushed in the white halls. I tripped on steaks and frozen instruction manuals. The library was almost empty. There was one remaining rack of Ellery Queen. Roald followed the shelves around, speculating about what literature the departing Americans thought important: "The religious stuff is still all here." Ernest was the boss; he swept up a handful of hard candies, two cans of Pream, and a box of beef jerky. "What a score!" he said. The words were muffled in his mask.

My head hurt. I got out of breath easily. A thermometer reading down to 30 was just a little glob of red nestled in its bulb. It was here to record warmth, to record the pressure of that life that had gone. We moved in a fog of our own making; the lanterns smoked and steamed and our breath made huge clouds. The headlamps cut through it in beams. Everywhere small electric motors were stored in closets, waiting to whir. Stuff was scattered right and left. Someone had ransacked it, but there was a sense of wild abandonment, as if suddenly it was too much – the dark, the loneliness, the weight, the slide of the brute ice – they all threw up their hands and chucked the books and the meat out in the halls and fled, mouths open to the killer wind, out into the snow to run north in all directions and disappear.

There was a smell down here, a bad smell, like something rotting, but without ferment. It was a hard flaking away of odour. It was the smell of dried fear and frozen excrement. At one place where steaks were splayed out of a box, someone long ago crapped a hard mound.

In the bar a can of Piels Real Draft Premium Beer had exploded and made a permanent head of frozen foam on the side of the can. It looked like insulating foam but smelled of beer. My feet were starting to get cold; I must keep moving, pacing around. Keep moving, keep moving. The flexible cable from my headlamp to the batteries at my chest was hard as copper from cold. It whacked me in the nose. It knocked frost from the mask onto my cheeks behind the stiff wool. Frost grew all over my face. My eyelashes tried to freeze together. I took my hands out of the big mittens to take a photograph and they got covered with frost too. Surely the wood was splitting around us and the steel buckled just from the cold.

In some of the rooms there was snow on the floor. In some places it was as fine as talcum powder, in some places it was like beach sand – but everywhere it was dry, dry as dust. Then we opened a door into a room where the ceiling had broken and there it was: snow cascading down and forming a little glacier, dense and deadly. It filled the room. It was as if I had opened a door on a live malevolence, the awful thing hidden behind all these doors decorated with humorous remarks and naked women: the antarctic nightmare. Scott had stood here and felt it pressing down on the arch of his courage, distorting it, crippling it, breaking it in: this terrible place.

A chill that was not just the raw cold ran through me. There was no mercy in this moving ice. I looked at the ice-filled room. I could not pull away. I saw an ending:

The snow is pressure. The nightmare grows. Roald and Ernest and Robert F. are ghosts. I am Titus Oates, inside Old Pole. I may be some time. I am running through snow. The snow is light as powder, deep as the sea; I sink. At the bottom of this sea will be white living trilobites, huge, armoured seals. I am running, running, running through these halls, accompanied by cardboard penguins and balloons full of ink, and I open the last door at the end and call out to see it there – the bland, hard face of death.

No, it cannot be. Roald! Ernest! Does it look this way? Did it come upon you this way? They are gone. They were never here at all. I have been stumbling in the wind. I open door after door and there it is: cold, white, implacable, heaping down from above. The shaft up has clamped shut. The ceiling has fallen in. I have waited too long. Old Pole is going down in the sea of ice.

The hissing dies. The lanterns go out. The headlamp goes dim. The batteries at my heart go quiet. Still I open doors to stare at rooms filled with snow. The structure cracks as the ice moves. Rivets fire down the halls, ping and whine. I am flowing towards South America. I have time now, time to get there. I find matches and cook steaks over heaps of smouldering instruction books, filling the air with the smell of meat and killing gas. Byrd sat in his hut alone at Advance Base on the great Barrier in 1934, breathing carbon monoxide from his stove; they came and found him in August when he was almost dead. No one will find me. I am a thousand feet down. The ice creaks in its journey. I can hear the groan of the earth below. I slice green peppers. I sit on the bar and eat the steak and gnaw on the frozen beer, and it gets completely dark, until at last my eyes, wide open, see dimly by the soft, deep, permanent blue.

(5)

The man I called Ernest came to get me. My feet were cold. We climbed back up out of Old Pole and hoisted a big hunk of copper – some kind of valve – out with us. On the way back to the dome our Spryte broke down, but Ernest opened it up, played with the engine, and got it going again. Inside the dome the light was metal blue, and the lights of the little buildings were warm. Outside, snow drifted gently against the walls.

The Killer Under the Water

Gareth Wood

Accompanied by Robert Swan and Roger Mear, Wood undertook the "In the Footsteps of Scott" expedition in 1984–5. The expedition was a signal success; it was the aftermath that was a disaster. Wood's support ship was crushed by ice, leaving him stranded for a second winter in Antarctica. Then, hiking over frozen Backdoor Bay with companions Tim Lovejoy and Steve Broni, Wood was attacked from under the ice.

The going was easy and as I moved over the ice I had no idea that I was being stalked from beneath its surface.

Ahead was a working crack which was slightly more than one stride in width – too far to comfortably cross without jumping. It was covered with a very thin layer of unblemished ice. Innocently, I stepped closer. Would it hold my weight, I wondered, or would I have to jump? Stretching one foot down, I probed it with the tip of my crampon, much as I'd done with dozens of other working cracks in similar circumstances. Suddenly, the surface erupted as the massive head and shoulders of a mature leopard seal, mouth gaping in expectation, crashed through the eggshell covering. It closed its powerful jaws about my right leg, and I fell backward, shocked and helpless in its vice-like grip. Feeling myself being dragged towards a watery grave, I locked my left crampon onto the opposing edge. I knew that once I was in the water, it would be all over.

"Help, help, Steve, Tim, help," I screamed repeatedly. It seemed an age before I finally caught sight of their running figures.

"Kick it, kick it, kick it, get the bloody thing off me, hurry, hurry for Christ's sake, you bastard, you bastard," I yelled hysterically, my gloved hands scrabbling fruitlessly for purchase on the smooth ice behind me as I strained against the seal's prodigious weight.

For one tiny fraction of a second our eyes met. These were not the pleading eyes of a Weddell seal nor the shy glance of a crabeater seal – they were cold and evil with intent. What fear the seal must have recognized in my own during this brief moment of communication, I can only imagine.

"Bloody hell, it's a leopard seal," Steve shouted breathlessly as he leapt across the crack to attack the brute from the opposite side.

"Get the bloody thing off me, kick it, for Christ's sake," I screamed again.

"Aim for its eye, its eye," Tim shouted, his voice verging on panic.

"Bastard! Bastard! Bastard!" Steve chanted in rhythm to his swinging boot.

"Get its eye, blind it," Tim shouted again.

I watched, dazed, as the front tines of Steve's cramponed boot made small, fleshy wounds in the side of the beast's head near its eye. Fifteen or 20 times his foot swung with crushing impact. Blood streamed from the wounds and spattered to the ice with each sickening smack of the boot. The impact of the violent attack vibrated through my body. Stubbornly, the beast continued to grip my leg, which appeared tiny in its jaw. I felt as powerless as a mouse caught by a cat.

"It's backing off," Tim shouted triumphantly as the seal suddenly released its hold and slipped slowly back beneath the surface.

Numbed, confused, and mesmerized by the concentric ripples slapping the edge of the bloodstained hole, I stared entranced at the spot where the frightening beast had disappeared.

"Quick, get him back from the edge," Tim gasped.

Arms had just grabbed me when the seal's monstrous form leapt once more from its watery lair. Lunging at me, it crossed the ice with an awkward gait, streams of bloody water cascading to the ice around it. Its large, interlocking teeth crushed down on my plastic boot.

"My God, we've blown it," I gasped. "Kick it, kick it, for Christ's sake, kick it," I shouted, the fear in my throat threatening to choke me.

"Its eye, get its eye," Steve shouted as he and Tim again booted its head with the lance-like front tines of their crampons.

Irrational thoughts careered madly about my brain. What would the ice look like from beneath the surface? What would death be like? As if divorced from life already, I pictured the seal swimming down with my limp, red-coated body in its jaws. I could see pale, green sunlight filtering down through the ice as I descended into the gloom of certain oblivion. It all seemed so real, so peaceful – a silent movie with myself as the reluctant hero.

Tim's tugging at my shoulders pulled me swiftly back to reality – finally vanquished, the animal had retreated to its nether world. They skidded me quickly over the ice a safe distance from the crack. I stood up shakily.

"Lie down, let's have a look," Steve implored, motioning me down.

"No, I'm all right. Thank God it's not broken," I gasped, as I tested my wounded leg by stumbling backward, away from the terror I had just experienced. Glancing down at my torn clothing I saw blood on my leg – whether it was mine or the seal's I was not sure. I unzipped my outer Gore-Tex and fibre-pile pant.

"Oh, my God," I trembled, horrified at the blood and puncture wounds on the front and back of my leg just below my knee.

Abyss

Mike Stroud

A British adventurer and doctor, Mike Stroud teamed up with Ranulph Fiennes in 1992 for the first unsupported crossing of Antarctica from coast to coast. To aid their crossing, Stroud and Fiennes determined to harness the power of the wind with "up-ski sails".

To inflate the sail, I had to pull on a control cord which closed the centre hole while the canopy was still on the ground. Then, a flick at one of the risers allowed the edge to catch the wind and, almost immediately, the thing rose up like a huge coloured beast and I was off, racing across the ice, and desperately opening the centre hole to try and slow down. It had no apparent effect. Full speed was maintained right up to the stage when the hole was so big that the sail wouldn't fly at all, at which point it would collapse and promptly tangle itself up. This necessitated a period of frustrating and intensely cold macramé, inevitably with bare fingers. Furthermore, while I was hurtling forwards, the sail flew very close to the ground, almost completely obscuring the view ahead and catching on small surface features to tangle itself up anyway. Although they were clearly of great potential benefit, the sails were going to need considerable skill in their use, and they would be limited by strong winds or difficult terrain.

All the same, they were compulsive. Compared with the toil of manhauling, to be pulled forward at high speed was a delight so intense that to ignore it, merely because it was difficult and dangerous, was near impossible. Instead of stopping once we had learned of the difficulties, we went on, in strong winds and poor visibility, regardless of being in a crevassed zone. It was a stupid thing to do, but we were desperate to take advantage of a ride that we knew might not occur again for a couple of months. The light was poor and it was impossible to discern the tell-tale dips in the snowfields that marked hidden crevasses. It was also difficult to be sure that rising ground wasn't obscuring the view. It was the latter that almost spelt disaster.

Ran was just ahead of me when I saw him fall just to the left of a long open crack – a blue slash in the white that joined ground to sky. Ahead of him, it looked firm and so, steering left, I carried on, aiming to pass close by. I didn't realize that he had not fallen by chance. He had thrown himself over when he had seen that the crack extended in front of him and his chute had collapsed, a coloured flag, draped over the entrance to an icy coffin. I was going much faster when I saw it, and the gaping chasm filled my vision with its darkness and my mind with horror. I tore at the control cord release, but it was far too late, and as my gloved hands fumbled fruitlessly at the toggle, I heard Ran shout, "No-o-o . . . !" – the short word extending into a long wail that followed me over the edge as my mind echoed the same pointless denial and I rushed towards black depths that lay to either side.

I didn't fall freely. Instead I hung beneath the partially inflated chute and swung forward to smash into the wall on the far side of the cleft. It was rough blue-ice and my forehead struck hard, dazing me slightly. I scrabbled at the wall, trying to grasp at something to hold, anything rather than be pulled down. It was useless. Although I did get my hand around a protrusion, it was smooth as glass, and the weight of the sledge came on to me, ripped me off and I fell backwards. At that moment, I was sure I was going to meet my death. I knew that behind there was nothing; I had seen the bottomless pit.

I was wrong. Instead of plummeting into the darkness, I dropped another ten feet or so before I landed hard on a surface, my back crashing painfully into the front of my sledge. For a moment I lay still, winded, confused, scarcely able to believe my luck. Then I looked around, not daring to move, trying to assess my situation. I was perched on a narrow snow platform, where the crevasse had been choked by drift. It was about twenty feet down, and the walls of shimmering blue rose almost vertically above me. To either side, just a few feet away, the crevasse was open and the same walls went on down, darker and darker until they passed out of sight. The blackness beckoned. In front of me, just beyond my feet, the snow surface was punctured by a yard-wide hole, another entrance to the void. I could see from its edges that my platform was horribly thin. It was a precarious position and I gazed up at the band of sky, wondering how to get out.

"Mike!" The shout came from above. "Are you okay?"

I had forgotten about Ran. He had seen me disappear, and perhaps half a minute had passed. Later he told me that he was sure I was dead.

"I'm fine," I shouted back in reassurance. "Fine, but it's not too clever and I need some help."

Although I was virtually unhurt, the alloy traces of my sledge, rigid tubes that made the sledge turn and follow me closely, were crumpled and smashed beyond repair. The sledge itself was also damaged, the carbon-fibre/kevlar shell cracked at the front and creased across the middle. Still, the hull was essentially in one piece and we could go on if only I could get it and myself out safely. I tried to move, but my skis were wedged beneath me, dug awkwardly into the fragile snow, and when I struggled I heard pieces of my bridge falling away beneath. I broke into a sweat that instantly turned to frost on my forehead. If I tried too hard I would destroy this thin meringue that supported me. I didn't know what to do. I couldn't move with the skis on, but in boots alone it would be very easy to fall through. It seemed hopeless but I had no choice – I had to take them off, keep close to the wall and hope for the best.

I unstrapped one of the skis and pulled the foot free. I was half-kneeling, with the knee of the ski-shod foot on the snow and the ski tip stuck in behind me. I tentatively put some weight on the booted foot. The surface was quite soft and it sunk in, but then held. Slowly I pressed more heavily, intending to stand up and then pull the ski out from behind me. Without warning, the foot suddenly went through and I pitched forwards. My mind made another silent cry of denial – no, not *now*! It was heard. My face hit the snow and a hole appeared, my outstretched arm went through it, but the bridge still held as dislodged pieces of ice fell away and disappeared under my gaze. I felt sick with fear, trans-fixed, and had to quash the panic that flooded up within me.

"You've got the rope, Mike. Tie yourself on and get it up to me."

Of course . . . I had to get the rope. I eased back into a kneeling position and released the other binding while staying with my weight on the ski. Then I turned round and slowly bent over towards the sledge. I couldn't reach the sledge zip without moving and had to lean quite hard on the hull as I did so. As my weight came on to it, the sledge lurched downwards, and life stopped. Underneath me I heard the sound of more ice falling.

"Christ! This is no place to stick around . . ." I muttered, and then I almost laughed at the inadequacy of my verbal assessment.

I undid the sledge cover and the rope was right in front of me. I had put it there in case I needed to get Ran out. He had been ahead, and we followed a policy of the rear man always carrying the rope.

"Ran, I'll try to throw it up," I shouted, my voice sounding alien with tension. "Can you get over the crack to the other side."

"Yes, I won't be a minute," the answer came from an invisible source. "I reckon I can cross about fifty yards away."

I kept quite still as I heard footsteps receding. Looking along the length of the crevasse, I could see that thirty or forty yards away the blue ravine became a black tunnel, roofed over by another snow bridge on the surface. That was where Ran was going to cross. Underneath, there was an immense emptiness. My God! Was that really what we'd been crossing?

Ran reappeared at the other lip. "Okay," he said. "Chuck it up here."

I took the rope and tied one end to one of the carrying loops of the sledge cover, and I also tied myself on about halfway along. Then I checked that the other coils were free and threw it with all my strength. It snaked up and over the top and I saw Ran catch it. As the rope brushed the lip some pieces fell and went straight through my support. It really was very thin in places, and another sickening wave of panic gripped my stomach. I had to force it down, and then shouted far too loudly.

"Anchor it off on your sledge or something and I'll throw up some of the food and stuff. We'll never get it out of here without reducing the weight."

I heard Ran's muffled acknowledgement. He was already doing it and didn't need to be told. When he was ready, I began to unload, trying not to move my feet, or to press too heavily on the sledge. I threw up one ration, one fuel bottle, one piece of equipment at a time. Each one disappeared as Ran caught them at the edge twenty feet above and piled them safely to one side. As I worked, concentrating on the activity, the inner churning subsided, but all the time I was conscious of just how little lay between me and the gulf.

It took about twenty minutes to empty the load and then Ran called down. "Just hang on a moment and I'll get in a position to pull." He tied himself up close to his sledge anchor and then braced his feet against the snow while taking up the slack to give me a tight rope. Then, with him pulling, and me climbing as best I could, I slowly scaled the wall of the crevasse at a point where it wasn't quite so steep. Finally, grunting with the effort, I emerged from the gateway to death and lay panting on the surface, my cheek on the cool snow. I felt a strange combination of elation and joy mixed with a crushing sense of vulnerability. My life had been so close to an end and I thought of my children, fatherless into the future.

Neither of us spoke for a moment. There was nothing to say. We pulled up the empty sledge in silence, watching as the snow bridge on which I had lain collapsed, rumbling into eternity. I turned and looked ahead. The sun was shining now and the wind had dropped. The scene was remarkably peaceful. Then Ran looked at me and saw that I was shocked by what had happened. Just for a moment he put his arm around my shoulders in the briefest of reassuring gestures. It was the most that our upbringing and a stiff upper lip would allow. He smiled.

"I don't know what I'd have told Thea," he said. "Shall we go?"

There was no wind for further sailing and so we resumed manhauling. I was now pulling on rope instead of the rigid traces which had been buckled and consigned to the black depths of the crevasse from which I'd escaped. When we started to go down-hill after the Pole in two months' time, ropes would allow the sledge to catch up with me and knock me off my feet. Still, that was a long way ahead and we might never get as far. For the moment we had more acute worries. Looking back at the sledge, I noticed that it flexed as I moved and realized that we would be lucky if it held together. If it fell apart now, or even soon, there was no way in which we would be able to carry its load. One or even one and a half sledges wouldn't have the capacity to sustain us both all the way. I could only hope that it would last. In any case, it was a gorgeous evening in the sunshine and if a break did precipitate a premature end to the expedition, I didn't mind. I was just happy to be alive.

In 2003 Stroud and Fiennes both completed seven marathons on seven continents in seven days in the Land Rover 7×7×7 Challenge for the British Heart Foundation.

Toughing it Out

David Hempleman-Adams

Over the course of 1995–6 Hempleman-Adams became the first Briton to walk unsupported and solo to the South Pole. One of the world's greatest explorers, Hempleman-Adams has also climbed the highest mountain on each continent, and reached the North Pole, as well as the South and North magnetic poles.

When I woke up on day six it was clear that the blizzard was still with me but, on further inspection, I decided that the winds had died down to a still dangerous but manageable level. The weather meant another slow day's trek, not helped by constant sastrugi formed by the whipping winds. After six hours the sledge suddenly hit the lip of a sastrugi. For nearly six days I had been dragging the sledge smoothly over them, but this time it stuck and stopped dead in its tracks. For a split second I kept going before suddenly being jerked backwards, almost off my feet, straight on to my arse. I lay there, with my skis in the air, crying out in agony. The whole of the area around my coccyx had been jarred. I felt a piercing pain and immediately knew I was in trouble.

The day's walk ended abruptly at this moment. Having slowly erected my tent, and discovered through my GPS that I had covered yet another six miles, I started to take painkillers. The tablets seemed to make no initial impact. The pain was excruciating, which only served to worsen my morale and make me wonder how badly I had damaged my back. My attempt at the North Pole back in 1983 failed partly due to a fall on the ice which resulted in two cracked ribs. Was history about to repeat itself in the Antarctic? Ignoring the advice on the bottle, I chucked a load of extra painkillers down my throat. This may not have been the cleverest action to take, but these were desperate moments on the expedition, and they required desperate actions. Then, leaning back and trying to find the least uncomfortable position, I began to take stock of my worsening situation.

The facts were not encouraging. I was well behind schedule, and it was clear that I was never going to be able to catch up on lost ground in such pain. I was feeling extremely sorry for myself and, after virtually a year without seeing my family due to horrendous business commitments abroad, very homesick. It would make complete sense to pull out right there. I was close to Patriot Hills and it would have been a cheaper exercise to quit there because Adventure Network would not charge to pick me up. Few would ever get to hear of the failure, because I had made a point of keeping the publicity down until I had succeeded, and I would simply return the following year, re-evaluate and, no doubt, have another crack at the South Pole.

All it would have taken was one push of the "emergency evacuation" button on my Argos position transmitter and a plane would have flown me out within hours. My God, it was an incredible temptation. It could all be over with just a simple prod of my finger. I called up Geoff Somers at base back at Patriot, and discovered that despite my slow going I was faring better than both Roger Mear and Feodore. Both had covered less mileage than me, and were suffering in the uncompromising conditions the Antarctic had decided to throw at us all. I had become so caught up in my personal obsession to reach the Pole, and my resultant hardship, that I had forgotten I was involved in a race with Roger Mear to become the first Briton ever to reach the South Pole solo and unsupported. Despite everything that had happened to me, I was clearly winning the race.

Geoff proved once again to be priceless. If I had ever been a heavyweight boxer, I would have had him in my corner for every fight. He told me he respected me, and that I was doing all right. He went on to refer to the others out there on the ice as "poor bastards", whereas he referred to me as "wonderful". He probably meant none of it, but it was so good to hear. Even so, my gut feeling was to hell with it all. So what if I was winning the race? The fact remained that I was in terrible pain, and I could not see how I could even get close to the Pole in my condition, and at the pace I had been plodding at. I could not see Mear succeeding either, so there did not seem an awful lot of point in walking a little further than my rival to record an ultimate failure. My old reasoning – better to be a living failure than a dead hero – seemed once again to be making sense.

I experienced quite a few moments during the trip when I felt like packing it all in, but the night of day six undoubtedly proved to be the major turning point. It was a complete accident that I had brought Mrs Thatcher's autobiography along in the first place. It was the thickest and best value-for-money book on sale at Heathrow airport, and as I admired the woman enormously and required a large book to provide reading material for as long as possible during my trip, I bought it. Idly flicking through the pages that night, prolonging the moment when I was going to push the button on the Argos, I came to a phrase her father often said to her, something which stuck in Mrs Thatcher's mind ever since: "It is easy to be a starter," she wrote, "but are you a finisher?" I looked at this sentence, and then read it over and over again, before putting the book down beside me.

My thoughts then turned to my eldest daughter, Alicia, and all her friends at school. They were plotting my course on a map in the classroom, and I thought of that map and how pathetic it would look if the little girls' line was to come to an abrupt end after just six days. Then I remembered Jock's pleas not to come on this trip. He could be guaranteed to turn round later and say, "I told you so." Then I thought of all the others, the friends and the doubters, all of whom were expecting the moment when I pushed the emergency button. I would be following in a long line of failed British expeditions. While explorers and adventurers from countries like Norway and Russia continued to break down barriers, the British seemed to have this knack of cocking up.

I picked up the book again, found my place and ripped out the page with the quotation on it. Instead of burying it in the snow together with the rest of the pages I had read, I placed it in my top pocket. From then on, I would look at those words each day to remind myself that I had started, so I was bloody well going to finish. I accepted that I was well behind schedule, and that I was making a total pig's ear of the attempt to reach the Pole, but I had made the decision right then that I was not going to give up until my food had run out.

I am not sure whether it was the huge dose of painkillers or the distraction of this new-found motivation derived from Mrs Thatcher but, whatever the case, the pain seemed to ease and I started to plan ahead. Let's just get over that first degree, I told myself. I had another nine to cross, of course, but suddenly that moment when eighty degrees south turned to eight-one degrees south became a vital goal for me to attain. After that, I worked out, I would walk an extra half hour, whatever the hardship, until eighty-two degrees. Once past that mark, I would add a further thirty minutes to the day and so on until, by the time I reached the Pole, I would be walking an extra four hours each day. How I envisaged I could do this given the facts of the trip up to that point I will never know, but it is surprising what a mixture of cold, pain and motivation can do for you. If it could be bottled, it would gain incredible results in the sporting arena. I went to sleep safe in the knowledge that the trip was still on.

It was just as well I was in such a positive frame of mind, because I woke up on the morning of day seven to discover my first true white-out in the Antarctic. Surrounding my tent was a very thick, totally white fog, walking through which messes up your balance so much that you experience a sensation of being upside down.

I had taken my three painkillers and was beginning to notice some weight loss. I knew there would be more crevasses out there, somewhere in the swirling cotton wool that lay ahead of me, but my mind had been made up the night before, and a furtive glance at the ripped-out page in my top pocket only served to confirm my conviction. It was desperately frustrating that on a day when I hoped to walk twelve miles I was stuck again, this time in a white-out, but I started walking nonetheless, confused in the fog and a little scared.

As I trudged through the thick soup, I even convinced myself that I deserved everything that was happening to me. I looked back on my other adventures and came to the conclusion that on trips such as Everest I had been incredibly lucky. I had reached the summit when many far more accomplished climbers had perished. I had come through everything in my life with nothing more than a few cracked ribs. This, I reasoned, was pay-back time.

I was therefore upbeat when I pitched my tent that night and discovered that, despite the pain and the white-out, I had managed to cover another seven miles. By now I think I had released the pressure placed upon myself by the desire to reach the Pole. That goal had been changed to just lasting out the sixty days before my food supplies ran out. Looking back, this clearly helped my mental state. Each day I was falling further and further behind schedule, but it somehow stopped bothering me. The point was I was still there, alive and hanging in.

On any trip I believe what really makes you able to survive is the ability to address any problem that suddenly confronts you. After all, you are there on your own, and nobody else can help you. I realized that simply chucking painkillers down my throat would not be enough to enable me to speed up my pace. I therefore made a corset for my back, which I wrapped around my body, by ripping up a sleeping mattress and tying it together using sticky tape. This kept my back straight in one position for the rest of the time, even if it meant that I waddled across the continent like one of the hundreds of thousands of penguins who live on its shores.

For day nine, read day five. Another blizzard made it impossible to trek anywhere, and although I was obviously concerned about how long the severe weather conditions would last, I was also thankful that it would give my back, and the rest of my body, a day of much-needed rest. It also gave me time to think. Although my sights had been reset, I found myself up to my old trick of working out how I could still make it to the Pole. If the load of the sledge was reduced to half its original weight by, say, 85lb, I should in theory be able to pull it twice the distance. I had achieved this on my Magnetic North Pole trip and, at a push, past experience had taught me that I might be able to cover as much as eighteen miles in a day.

Every hour my thoughts would be broken and I would stick my head out of the tent to see if the blizzard was calming down. Then I would return to my nest, either to read more of Mrs Thatcher or to make further plans. The reduction of the sledge's weight was never far from my mind. During the day I decided to get rid of my Sony Walkman and all my tapes. Then I decided to sling out my crampons which, for a climber, was a big move to make. I was now stripping down to the most trivial possessions. Out went a spare pair of shoelaces, the ties on the sleeping-bags, and so on until I was convinced I was not carrying a single ounce of excess weight.

Midway through the day the winds eased sufficiently for me to get going. Under normal circumstances I might have remained in the tent, but I wanted to record some distance by the end of the day, and was therefore amazed when, a few hours later, I discovered that I had covered six and a half miles.

That night I made what turned out to be one of my longest radio calls to Patriot. It was incredible how I was stuck in the middle of the loneliest place on Earth, and yet the most mundane messages were being sent or received. Claire, apart from sending her love, wanted to know whether she should pay for three cases of Rothschild wine which had not yet been delivered. Jock was saying that some of the sponsors had not paid up yet for the trip, and asked what he should do about it. And I was developing a raunchy rapport with a girl called Sue, who was a cook back at Patriot Hills.

It began with me asking her to make me an apple and blackberry pie for when I finally returned. Food, understandably, became an obsession as the trek towards the Pole went on. She agreed, but wanted to know what I was going to give her in exchange. And so the theme of the conversation, relayed backwards and forwards by Geoff, went on, with the whole of British Antarctica listening in, ready for the next instalment as if it was the Gold Blend advert. It was all innocent fun, of course, but even little details like these help to keep up your morale.

The wind blew from the west on day ten, and with the altitude dropping from 2,700 feet to 2,600 feet, the walking was relatively easy, at least compared to my previous excursions. The back was holding up thanks to the painkillers and the corset, and my mood was amazingly good. By that evening I calculated that I had only nine and a half miles to go until I crossed over from eighty to eighty-one degrees, and that would signal my first celebration on the trip, and a good excuse for a brandy which, conveniently, I had refused to discard while lessening the sledge's load. Another seven miles the following day meant that I was just two and a half miles away from a point which was fast becoming as significant as reaching the South Pole itself.

I had no difficulty starting out bang on eight o'clock on the morning of the twelfth day. This time I needed no radio calls from Geoff Somers, or any motivation from Mrs Thatcher. This was the day when I knew I was going to pass through one vital degree. This was going to be the equivalent of my birthday. The weather conditions were kind to me, and the day and the miles seemed to fly past. By six o'clock it was time to stop and face the moment of truth.

By that time I had settled nicely into a routine. I would get the cooker going, and then start taking my clothes off. This would take up to half an hour, by which time the pot would be boiling. I would place my gloves on top of the cooking pan in order to melt off the snow, and then the flask of piping hot soup would be made up. It all boiled down to time management, but on this night it went out the proverbial window. As soon as I had erected the tent I took the GPS out of my pocket and, still fully clothed, peered excitedly at the reading. Not only had I crossed over into eighty-one degrees, but by recording eight miles for the day I had produced my best walk of the trip.

It was time to celebrate. I found the bottle of brandy, packed purposefully at the very bottom of the sledge, and took a swig. The bottle had lines drawn on it, denoting each degree point I would pass on my way to the Pole. It was tempting to down the lot, but I drank the amount up to the next line, and returned the bottle to the depths of the sledge. Then I opened my "special treat" bag, which consisted of a packet of pork scratchings and an Earl Grey tea bag, and sucked on each scratching as if it were nectar. Boy, did I know how to throw a party!

Looking at the situation in a logical light, I had no cause to celebrate. For a start, eighty-one degrees was merely an imaginary line, but I was treating it as if it were a glass entrance through which I had just come. It was just one degree, and I had another nine to go. I should have been there within five days, not twelve, so in theory I had three emergency days left of supplies, assuming I could maintain a pace of twelve miles a day from that point on, right the way up to the Pole. When one considered that I had just recorded my best mileage, and this was four miles down on what I would now have to produce, it was a tall order. Yet logic, thankfully, did not come into my thinking that night. I had this funny feeling that someone, maybe my late grandfather or late father, was watching over me. It almost became a spiritual moment for me.

There were hundreds of dangers ahead of me: more fields of crevasses, a higher altitude to reach, and plummeting temperatures. I could easily get frost-bite and, of course, there was the big question mark over my back.

But this was the moment, huddled up alone in my tent with my brandy and pork scratchings, that I knew, deep down inside, that I would make it to the South Pole.

Melting Point

David Helvarg

Helvarg, an American environmental activist and journalist, visited Antarctica on behalf of the Sierra Club to witness the effects of global warming at first hand.

Clouds, snow, rock, and water hard as black marble are all we can see as we approach Antarctica at the end of our four-day, 900-mile voyage from Punta Arenas, Chile. Up on the bridge the first mate, Robert, is playing Led Zeppelin and talking on the radio with Palmer Station. "Never been this far south without seeing ice," he says.

"That's 'cause we cleared it for you," the base's radioman teases. "Went out in our Zodiacs with blowtorches." We round Bonaparte Point and there it is – Palmer Station, one of three US Antarctic bases administered by the National Science Foundation, prefab blue and white metal buildings with fuel tanks and heavy equipment scattered about, and a boathouse flanked by black rubber Zodiac boats. Behind the station's rocky outcropping looms a calving blue and white glacier; on the surrounding boulder field by Hero Inlet on Anvers Island, we find a greeting committee of Adélie penguins, brown skuas, and elephant seals.

Anvers is 38 miles of granite covered by ice up to 2,000 feet thick. It is part of the Antarctic Peninsula, a 700-mile-long tail to the coldest, driest, highest continent on Earth, a landmass bigger than the United States and Mexico combined, containing more than 70 per cent of the world's freshwater and 90 per cent of its ice. Marine and polar climates converge on the peninsula, making it Antarctica's richest wildlife habitat. Researchers jokingly refer to it as "the banana belt".

And that was before global warming.

Bill Fraser, a rangy, weathered, 48-year-old ice veteran from Montana State University, is chief scientist at Palmer, one of 35 researchers and support personnel working there during my visit in the austral summer of 1999. "When I was a graduate student, we were told that climate change was occurring, but we'd never see the effects in our lifetime," Fraser says. "But in the last twenty years I've seen tremendous changes. I've seen islands pop out from under glaciers, species changing places, and landscape ecology altered."

He points upslope. "The Marr glacier used to come within a hundred yards of the station. Its meltwater was the source of our freshwater." Today the glacier is a 400-yard hike across granite rocks and boulders; gull-like skuas splash in the old melt pond while the station is forced to desalinate saltwater. Periodically the artillery rumble of moving ice signals continued glacial retreat, as irregular ice faces collapse into Arthur Harbour amid a blue pall of ice crystals and rolling turquoise waves.

Globally, 1998 was the warmest year on record, breaking previous records set in 1997 and 1995; eight of the ten hottest years in history have occurred in the 1990s. The clue that this warming is related to human activity is that there's more carbon dioxide (from burning fossil fuels) in our atmosphere today than at any time in the past 400,000 years. One of the ways we know this is through ice cores taken from Siple Dome, Vostok, and other sites in the Antarctic interior, which contain trapped bubbles of ancient air. We also know that climate is far less stable than we've imagined, and that the past 10,000 years – the period that's seen the rise of civilization – has been a period of atypical climate stability.

For the past 30 years, climatologists have predicted that planetary warming, when it began, would be most prominent in the polar regions. While the world's average temperature has risen by about one degree Fahrenheit in the past century, the Antarctic Peninsula has warmed by more than 5 degrees in only 50 years – including an incredible 10-degree warming during the winter months. In recent years, pieces of the Larsen B Ice Shelf the size of Rhode Island have calved off the peninsula's eastern shore. That's a sideshow if some predictions are borne out:

global-warming scenarios positing a 5-degree temperature rise in the next century project a rise in world sea levels of one to three feet from melting ice. Should the great Western Antarctic Ice Sheet melt – as it apparently has in the past – sea levels could rise by up to 20 feet. Most of the experts who believe the ice will melt don't expect it to do so until sometime after the 21st century. By the time they know for sure, it will be too late to do anything about it.

I may be learning a survival skill for the next millennium, then, when the first thing I do upon arrival is learn how to drive a Zodiac, the fast inflatable boat that, along with thick boots and crampons, provides the main means of transport at Palmer. Soon I'm steering a 15-foot Zodiac through the floating fragments known as brash ice. Spotting a leopard seal on an ice floe, I manoeuvre to photograph the snaky, blunt-headed predator. A moment later a panicked penguin jumps into my boat, tripping over the gas can. We exchange looks of mutual bewilderment before it leaps onto a pontoon and dives back into the icy blue water.

A few days later I'm out with Bill Fraser and his "Schnappers" (the boat-radio moniker for his seabird researchers, named after a Wisconsin polka band). We tie off on the rocky edge of Humble Island, remove our orange "float coats", and walk to a wide pebbly flat past a dozen burbling 800-pound elephant seals. One rises up just enough to show us a broad pink mouth and issue a belching warning to stay back lest it rouse itself from complete stupor. The elephant seal population, once restricted to more northerly climes, is booming along the now-warming peninsula.

The seals' belches and grunts are soon complemented by the hectic squawking and flipper flapping of thousands of Adélie penguins and their downy chicks, who occupy a series of rocky benches stained clay-red by their droppings. Skuas, looking for a weak chick to feed on, glide overhead.

"These penguins are extremely sensitive indicators of climate change," Fraser says. The pebbled area we're standing on, he explains, is an abandoned Adélie colony. He's been studying the colonies over the past 25 years, and has watched at least one go extinct in the Palmer area every year since 1988. In that time, 15,200 breeding pairs of Adélies declined to 9,200, while the population of chinstrap penguins, who share Adélies' taste for tiny shrimp-like krill, has increased from 6 pairs to 360 pairs. "Here you have two krill predators," says Fraser. "The question we asked ourselves was, why the different trends?"

A clue came in 1988 when the National Science Foundation authorized the first winter cruise in the frozen Weddell Sea on the far side of the peninsula. "We saw trails made by thousands of passing penguins," Fraser recalls. "After about a day and a half, we caught up to this huge line of penguins walking single file toward the edge of the sea ice. They were all Adélies, not a chinstrap among them. We got to the edge and there were about 10,000 birds per square mile."

The population shifts, they concluded, might be a result of abruptly altered habitats. The Adélie feed along the sea ice, the chinstraps in open water. Four out of five Antarctic winters are marked by heavy sea ice, according to Robin Ross, a biological oceanographer from the University of California at Santa Barbara, but in the early 1990s "the cycles of high and low ice began to fall apart. This year's winter sea ice was the lowest on record."

Like the Adélie penguins, plankton-eating krill are dependent on sea ice. The most abundant animal on Earth in terms of total biomass and the base of Antarctica's food web, these crustaceans are consumed by penguins, seals, and whales alike. (A blue whale can consume four tons of krill a day.) "The ice is like an upside-down coral reef," says Ross. "There are lots of bumps and crevasses and caves for krill to hide in. The bottom of the ice is where 70 per cent of their larvae are found. Without access to the ice, krill shrink, lose weight, and become more vulnerable."

Ross works off the 240-foot research boat *Laurence M. Gould*, which brought us to Palmer. Her recent trawls along the peninsula have brought up more salps than krill. Salps are open-water jelly creatures that look a bit like floating condoms. Unlike krill, salps reproduce in open water – and may soon fill krill's ecological niche if sea ice continues to decline. Since relatively few creatures feed on salps, a long-term decline in krill could be disastrous for the Antarctic ecosystem.

Back on Humble, I'm waving off a dive-bombing skua while

Fraser confers with Rick Sanchez of the US Geological Survey, who clutches a global positioning system unit. Sanchez also has a satellite antenna sticking out of his backpack and a magnesium-shelled laptop computer strapped to an elabourate folding-table rig hanging from his waist and shoulders. He's trying to pace the perimeter (he calls it "the polygon") of an extinct colony of Adélies, but a pile of elephant seals is blocking his way. If he tries to move them they might stampede and crush penguin chicks. Such are the quandaries of high-tech research in Antarctica.

Using 3-D aerial and satellite computer mapping, Fraser and Sanchez are trying to document how global warming is changing the ecology of Antarctica. "We see winter sea ice declining, but we also see warming creating more precipitation in the form of snow," Fraser says. "This snow accumulates on the southern, leeward side of islands, which is where the Adélie colonies are all going extinct, and which is what we're now trying to map. These birds need dry ground to lay and hatch their eggs, but the increased snow is altering the available nesting and chick-rearing habitat. Chinstraps breed later in the season after the snow melts, and so they do better. They're a weedy species. They adapt well to disturbed habitat and can also take fish and squid when krill aren't available because they can dive deeper and feed at night. They're the dandelions of the penguin world."

A similar dynamic is at work among other species. Fur and elephant seals coming in from the north threaten to displace more specialized, ice-dependent seals like Weddells, crabeaters (actually krill eaters), and leopard seals (which eat krill, penguins, crabeaters, and the occasional Zodiac bumper). Worldwide, rapid warming could exacerbate the spread of highly adaptable species like pigeons, rats, deer, and elephant seals and hasten the loss of more specialized endemic creatures like tigers, monarch butterflies, river dolphins, and Adélie penguins.

Climate change is not the first warning issued from the icy continent. In 1981, scientists with the British Antarctic Survey sent up research balloons that detected lower-than-expected levels of protective ozone in the stratosphere. After checking their equipment (they assumed at first their readings were in error) the researchers asked NASA to look at its satellite data, which confirmed a springtime thinning of ozone over Antarctica. Most of the depletion was tracked to chlorofluorocarbons (CFCs), synthetic chemicals widely used in air-conditioning and industrial processes. Without stratospheric ozone, more ultraviolet radiation penetrates the atmosphere, causing genetic damage to plants and animals, including eye damage and higher rates of skin cancer among humans. In response, most of the world's nations signed a treaty banning CFCs and other ozone-depleting chemicals in 1987.

Tad Day, a sandy-haired, thirty-nine-year-old professor of plant biology at Arizona State University, drives his Zodiac, *Lucille*, like a race car. For the past five years, Day has been studying how hairgrass and pearlwort, Antarctica's only two native flowering plants, react to increased ultraviolet radiation and a warmer atmosphere. The main study site he and his researchers (radio handle: "Sundevils") use is Stepping Stone Island, a surprisingly green and rocky isle several miles south of Palmer, surrounded by pale blue icebergs and rumbling glacier, and blessed by a lack of the barnyard odour of penguin colonies.

Amid nesting giant petrels the size of eagles and a friendly skua that he calls Yogi, Day maintains two gardens – fenced to keep fur seals out – with over 90 wire plant frames containing banks of hairgrass and mosslike pearlwort. Each frame has various Aclar, Mylar, and press-polish vinyl filters to control the amount of ultraviolet light and warmth it receives.

Day says he has found that ultraviolet B radiation causes genetic damage and reduces growth somewhat in pearlwort and substantially in hairgrass, while warming improves growth in pearlwort but appears to stunt the grass. "Still, both plants are expanding their range, colonizing new areas where the glaciers are retreating. Both are flowering earlier and producing more seeds, but the relationship is changing. Hairgrass, which was the dominant species, is being displaced by pearlwort."

I ask him what this phenomenon might mean in terms of the rest of the world. "Global warming," he says, "has the capacity to shift the competitive balance of species in ways that we don't understand yet, and that could have important consequences on our ability to produce food and fibre."

"So basically with these greenhouse gases we're doing a kind of giant experiment on the planet?" I suggest.

"Hey," he says, grinning. "You want me to start getting calls from Rush Limbaugh's listeners?"

Day is well aware of the political ramifications of his work. Limbaugh's Dittoheads are just some of the more boisterous targets of a $45 million campaign waged over the last decade by the fossil-fuel industry to promote the idea that there is still no conclusive proof of human impact on climate change. This has included personal attacks on leading scientists, which has made other researchers gun-shy about speaking out in nonprofessional forums. "Scientific uncertainty doesn't play well in politics," explains Robin Ross. "Someone with a strong position has more credibility, even if they're wrong."

Bill Fraser has chosen to speak out about what's happening to Antarctica at climate-change conferences and congressional hearings. His testimony, like that of other mainstream scientists, was challenged by Patrick Michaels, one of a handful of climate "skeptics" regularly paraded through Washington hearings and the media by the fossil-fuel industry. Michaels edits World Climate Report for the Western Fuels Association, an organization of coal producers, and is a senior fellow at the conservative Cato Institute.

"He used data pooling on the whole Antarctic to say there was no warming, but that's not how ecosystems work," complains Fraser. "You can't use those techniques the way he did. These lobbyists are really out to discredit science."

Despite the increasingly grim implications of climate research in Antarctica, it's hard to maintain a sense of gloom and doom on the last wild continent for more than a few hours at a time. At Palmer you need at least two people with radios if you want to take out one of the Zodiacs, so on days when I wasn't working with the Schnappers or Sundevils I'd spend my time looking for a boating partner. Doc Labarre, the station physician who used to work in the emergency room in Kodiak, Alaska, was among those always up for an adventure. One day I headed us towards Loudwater Cove on the far side of Norsel Point. The following seas allowed us to surf the 15-foot craft past the rocky spires of Litchfield Island and around the big breaking waves at Norsel. We then motored around a few apartment-size icebergs, crossing over to a landing opposite the glacier wall. We tied off our bowline, watching a leopard seal sleeping on an adjacent ice floe. We dumped our "float coats" and climbed several hundred feet up and over rocky scree and down a snowfield splotched with red algae to reach the opening of an ice cave. Inside, the cave was like a dripping blue tunnel, with a clear ice floor showing down to the rocky piedmont. Hard blue glacier ice formed the bumpy roof with its stalactite-like icicles and delicate ice rills forming pressure joints along its edges. Outside we hiked the loose granite, feldspar, and glacial sand until we encountered a fur seal hauled up on shore, several hundred yards from the water on the sharp broken rocks. He barked and whined a warning at us. Nearby ponds and 100-year-old moss beds had attracted brown skuas, who were nesting and soon began dive-bombing us. I got whacked from behind by one of the five-pound scavengers; it felt like a hard slap on the back of the head. We quickly moved away from their nests, climbing back over the exposed glacier rock, past middens of limpet shells and down a rock chimney to where our boat was tied up. The leopard seal was awake now, scrutinizing us as we took off.

We next dropped by Christine, a bouldery island where we walked past a large congregation of elephant seals lounging opposite a colony of Adélies. Crossing the heights we found mossy green swales with ponds full of brine shrimp, then lay out on a rocky beach at the end of a narrow blue channel, sharing the space with two elephant seals that looked to weigh about 500 and 900 pounds. The southern ocean was crystal clear; the sun emerged and turned the sky cobalt blue. Our perch felt almost tropical, the sound of the waves rolling and retreating across smooth, fist-size stones. The elephant seals were blowing, and blinking their huge red eyes, their pupils the size of teaspoons for gathering light in deep diving forays after squid. A fur seal came corkscrewing through the channel's water before paddle-walking ashore and scratching itself with a hind flipper, a blissful expression on its wolfy face. There we were, just five lazy mammals enjoying a bit of sun.

Driving the Zodiac back to Palmer Station we were accompanied by a flight of blue-eyed shags and squads of dolphin-diving penguins in the water. Doc steered while I kept an eye out for whales. The sky clouded over again, turning the water the colour of hammered tin. Each buck of the boat sent a slap of icy saltwater spray in our faces. But instead of repelling us, the untempered contact with Antarctic reality invigourated us. We felt right with the wild.

Antarctica is vast and awesome in its indifference to the human condition. At the same time it's become a world centre for scientific research and provided us warning of two of our greatest follies: destruction of the ozone layer and the human impact on climate. Through international action we're well on the way to solving the first problem but remain in denial about the second. But the message from the ice is as plain as the penguin bones I found scattered around a dying Adélie colony. Our world, and theirs, are more intertwined than we imagine.

Mind Over Matter

Catharine Hartley

A thirty-something TV stage-manager with no previous polar experience, Hartley joined an extreme tourism expedition to the South Pole, led by the explorer Geoff Somers.

Over the next three days the pattern became painfully apparent. Eight fit and strong members of the expedition skied at a reasonable rate for eight hours a day, covering a distance of around eleven miles, battling against blasting, icy winds and temperatures of down to -48°C, taking account of wind-chill. We pulled everything behind us in sleds weighing around eleven stone. Imagine that you spend your entire day dragging a full-grown man behind you as you walk about. There were no injuries yet, and although tired at the end of the day, the team was comfortable, and made camp quite happily. The next morning, we would pack everything up into the sleds and set off for another eight hours. Surprisingly, Justin, who had known nothing about Antarctica, was completely comfortable. He was exceptionally strong and his cavalier attitude of "training as you go" seemed to be working. I sensed he found my pace irritating. I was especially conscious I was an obstacle to his obsession with reaching the Pole for the Millennium.

The ninth member – that was me – was in quite a different position. I continued to find the conditions absolutely awful. I developed a chest infection and was coughing up a sinister fluid. No doubt this was because I only gave up smoking after Punta. I was completely unable to keep up with the apparently gentle pace, and this meant the team had to wait on average three times an hour for me to catch up. I had pain in every muscle and was completely annihilated by the end of each day. I knew the team was getting cold waiting for me. In addition, we only had limited food, so we had target mileages, and I could not ask for longer breaks, let alone days off. Least of all could I "finish early" if I was too tired. I felt doomed. I also noticed that the tip of each finger had turned white and felt strangely wooden, a middle finger in particular. I decided to ignore the fact that I was probably getting frost-bite.

Four days from Patriot Hills we came across a crevasse field. Geoff was aware this existed from a Japanese adventurer's hand-drawn map. He did not, however, know the exact locality. That day was a whiteout, I was miserable, and my mind felt unconnected to my body. In the afternoon, the wind started to pick up and the terrain became very icy. It became impossible to ski without sliding over so we took our skis off and walked. At this point Geoff was leading, and seeing a change in the surface twenty feet in front, he went ahead. With a ski pole, he probed a line of softer snow. The pole went straight through, opening up a small crevasse of about two feet wide. Below there was a yawning hole at least fifty feet deep. Geoff collected us together and told us to step over the crevasse and not be fooled by the soft snow bridge on top.

We found and crossed a number of such crevasses until we came across one almost four feet across, again, thinly covered with snow. This time Geoff spanned the crevasse with his sled to act as a handrail and had each of us make the step. I was utterly oblivious to my surroundings, locked in my own mind, concentrating on putting one foot in front of the other and keeping up with the sled in front of me. I was coughing continually now and my lungs and chest felt as if they would explode.

In this state of mind and because of the loud wind, I did not register what Geoff had said. Instead of stepping right across the crevasse I put one foot right on the snow bridge at the weakest point. As my foot plunged through I felt Geoff's hands just yank me into the air and on to the safe ice the other side. Crevasses narrow into a V shape as they deepen. Once jammed inside, rescue is extremely difficult. But for us to rope together in the way glaciers are normally crossed could have been as dangerous. Standing around and sorting out equipment could have very quickly brought on frost-bite and hypothermia in such cold conditions. On the crevasse field, the line between control and disaster was a very fine one.

The next day, Fiona took one of my food boxes. It was an extremely kind gesture even though she was one of the strongest. Now I comprehended the enormous swallowing of pride attached to giving up a part of my load. First, it acknowledged that I was actually as slow as I thought I was. The others must have been discussing how to speed me up. Second, it was hard to accept help. Most of us want to be strong and capable, few enjoy being needy and vulnerable. I was used to helping and supporting others in everyday life. Finding myself helpless was a torment. But I gratefully accepted Fiona's offer.

We were now travelling eight hours every day, with four breaks. The breaks themselves proved to be stressful for me. In ten minutes I might have to go to the loo in front of seven men. Invariably, my hands were so cold I would fumble helplessly with the zips of my four layers of trousers. With my huge mittens I would often fail to tuck in the four layers of thermal underwear properly, so for the next session would have a bitter wind grinding into my skin.

I would have little time left to stuff as much food and drink into my mouth as I could with increasingly frozen hands. It took all my effort to undo the zip of my bum bag, pull out a frozen Nutrigrain, Pepperami or chocolate bar and put it into my mouth. The temptation was to pull off my gloves to make the whole procedure quick and simple, but to expose my hands at this point would have meant possible frost-bite. They were already in agony simply because I had stopped moving for a few minutes. The breaks were strictly timed by one of the team members and at ten minutes there would be a shout of "Time!" We would have to put our skis on, and then haul ourselves up for the next two-hour march. My breaks were often shorter – I had used, perhaps, four minutes catching up with everyone while they were eating. At this point I was generally on the verge of tears, because I was so tired. But there was a real disadvantage if I actually cried. I found tears would freeze round my eyes and make it difficult for me to see properly.

I would spend the first ten minutes after each break moving my hands wildly to get the blood back in them and warm them up. I remember my friend Liza, whom I had met on Pen's selection course, and who had already had polar experience, advising me to "play the piano with my fingers" to keep them from freezing. Because I was exerting myself so much, my goggles would fill up with condensation. The condensation would then quickly freeze and ten minutes into the march I would be almost blind, unable to distinguish much through the thick film of ice.

That evening I set up the tent with Steve. I got out my pee bottle and discovered I stupidly had not emptied it from the morning. It was frozen solid. I put it by the stove to thaw; Steve did not bat an eyelid. A little later, we were having our first warm drink of the evening when Geoff poked his head through the tent door. He looked very serious. "Go for a walk for five minutes," he told Steve. "I need to talk to Catharine."

Quite where Steve was going to walk I don't know, but I knew immediately I was in trouble. It was that tap on the shoulder I had been waiting for. Hurriedly and awkwardly Geoff expressed grave concerns about my ability to continue. It was clear he felt I was quite incapable of making the trip and wanted me off the expedition. He left my tent with the words, "The plane is only sixty miles and a radio call away, I suggest you think about taking it." Steve came nervously back in. "Are you all right, Cath?" he asked. No, I was absolutely shattered. As ever, Steve was kind. I should not go, he argued, things would get better. Not wanting to impose myself on him at that moment, when he was so constantly supportive, I reapplied my five layers of clothing, three pairs of gloves, face mask and goggles and finally reached for a Nicorette chewing gum. Then I visited Mike and Fiona for counselling.

Mike and Fiona could have been sympathetic, but in agreement with Geoff. Then I would be off their backs and the team could continue without my holding them up. Instead, they were extremely supportive. Mike said: "Change your mindset, Catharine. You must have determination just to have come this far, so rather than feeling sorry for yourself, wake up tomorrow with a positive attitude. Geoff hasn't chucked you off; he's simply suggested you go. Show him that you won't, show him that what you lack in physical ability you have tenfold in mental determination. Fight him!"

Their encouragement was enough to strengthen my resolve to continue. I was overwhelmed by their support, especially by Fiona's. Their sponsorship relied on her breaking that record of being the first British woman to the Pole and she had been the only woman on the trip until just a fortnight before we left. Suddenly to have to share the possibility must have been galling and I had always been uncertain how she must feel about me. A lesser person would have wanted me off at the earliest moment. How selfless she must be.

I could hear the entire "zoo" of Zoë Ball's breakfast show. Knowing I was a fan of it, Steve was recreating it for me in the confines of a tent in the middle of the Antarctic wastelands to give me the best possible start to my day. It worked. I got up terrified but with a fighting attitude. I knew it was very likely my last chance. So my plan was to keep up with the sled in front of me, come what might. I would show Geoff.

I lined up between Steve and Fiona. Steve whispered, "Good luck." Fiona told me to stick to the back of her sled like glue and not let it get more than three feet away from me. Mike gave me a squeeze on the arm and reminded me, "Just fight him." It felt like a self-assertiveness class I had attended some years before. I did as they instructed and out of nowhere I found physical strength. I thought about nothing except not allowing Fiona's sled to get away from my skis. My legs were burning and I was absolutely exhausted but I kept up. At the end of the day, Geoff gave me an approving nod before going into his tent. I went to bed so much happier.

Hartley and companion Fiona Thornewill became the first British women to walk to the South Pole. The following year they walked to the North Pole.

Swimming to Antarctica

Lynne Cox

Holder of the record for swimming the English Channel, the first person to swim the Bering Strait from Alaska to Siberia, Lynne Cox also became, in 2002 the first person to swim a mile off the coast of Antarctica. The water temperature was 32 degrees.

When I hit the water, I went all the way under. I hadn't intended to do that; I hadn't wanted to immerse my head, which could over-stimulate my vagus nerve and cause my heart to stop beating. Dog-paddling as quickly as I could, I popped up in the water, gasping for air. I couldn't catch my breath. I was swimming with my head up, hyperventilating. I kept spinning my arms, trying to get warm, but I couldn't get enough air. I felt like I had a corset tightening around my chest. I told myself to relax, take a deep breath, but I couldn't slow my breath. And I couldn't get enough air in. I tried again. My body wanted air, and it wanted it now. I had to override that reaction of hyperventilating. I had to concentrate on my breath, to press my chest out against the cold water and draw the icy air into my lungs.

My body resisted it. The air was too cold. My body didn't want to draw the cold air deep into my lungs and cool myself from the inside. It wanted to take short breaths so the cold air would be warmed in my mouth before it reached my lungs. I was fighting against myself.

I noticed my arms. They were bright red, and I felt like I was swimming through slush. My arms were thirty-two degrees, as cold as the sea. They were going numb, and so were my legs. I pulled my hands right under my chest so that I was swimming on the upper inches of the sea, trying to minimize my contact with the water. I was swimming fast and it was hard to get enough air.

I began to notice that the cold was pressurizing my body like a giant tourniquet. It was squeezing the blood from the exterior part of my body and pushing it into the core. Everything felt tight. *Focus on your breath,* I told myself. *Slow it down. Let it fill your lungs. You're not going to be able to make it if you keep going at this rate.*

It wasn't working. I was labouring for breath harder than on the test swim. I was in oxygen debt, panting, gasping. My breath was inefficient, and the oxygen debt was compounding. In an attempt to create heat, I was spinning my arms wildly, faster than I'd ever turned them over before. Laura later told me that I was swimming at a rate of ninety strokes per minute, thirty strokes per minute quicker than my normal rate. My body was demanding more oxygen, but I couldn't slow down. Not for a nanosecond. Or I would freeze up and the swim would be over.

An icy wave slapped my face: I choked and felt a wave of panic rise within me. My throat tightened. I tried to clear my throat and breathe. My breath didn't come out. I couldn't get enough air in to clear my throat. I glanced at the crew. They couldn't tell I was in trouble. If I stopped, Dan would jump in and pull me out. I still couldn't get a good breath. I thought of rolling on my back to give myself time to breathe, but I couldn't. It was too cold. I closed my mouth, overrode everything my body was telling me to do, held my breath, and gasped, coughed, cleared my windpipe, and relaxed just a little, just enough to let my guard down and catch another wave in the face. I choked again. I put my face down into the water, hoping this time I could slow my heart rate down. I held my face in the water for two strokes and told myself, *Relax, just turn your head and breathe.*

It was easier to breathe in a more horizontal position. I thought it might be helping. I drew in a deep breath and put my face down again. I knew I couldn't do this for long. I was losing too much heat through my face. The intensity of the cold was as sharp as broken glass. I'd thought that swimming across the Bering Strait in 38-degree water had been tough, but there was a world of difference between 38 degrees and 32. In a few seconds, the cold pierced my skin and penetrated into my muscles. It felt like freezer burn, like touching wet fingers to frozen metal.

Finally I was able to gain control of my breath. I was inhaling and exhaling so deeply I could hear the breath moving in and out of my mouth even though I was wearing earplugs. I kept thinking about breathing, working on keeping it deep and even; that way I didn't have time to think about the cold.

My brain wasn't working as it normally did. It wasn't flowing freely from one idea to another – it was moving mechanically, as if my awareness came from somewhere deep inside my brain. Maybe it was because my body was being assaulted with so many sensations, too different and too complex to recognize. Or maybe it was because my blood and oxygen were going out to the working muscles. I didn't know.

For the next five or six minutes, I continued swimming, telling myself that I was doing well, telling myself that this was what I had trained for. Then something clicked, as if my body had gained equilibrium. It had fully closed down the blood flow in my skin and fingers and toes. My arms and legs were as cold as the water, but I could feel the heat radiating deep within my torso and head, and this gave me confidence. I knew that my body was protecting my brain and vital organs. Staring through the clear, silver-blue water, I examined my fingers; they were red and swollen. They were different than when I'd been swimming in the Bering Strait, when they'd looked like the fingers of a dead person. They looked healthy, and I thought their swollenness would give me more surface area, more to pull with.

I smiled and looked up at the crew, who were in the Zodiacs on either side of me. Each of them was leaning forward, willing me ahead. Their faces were filled with tension. Gabriella, Barry, Dan, and Scott were leaning so far over the Zodiac's pontoon I felt as if they were swimming right beside me. I was sprinting faster than I ever had before, moving faster than the Zodiac, and I was getting fatigued quickly. The water was thicker than on the test swim, and it took more force to pull through on each stroke. My arms ached. I didn't feel right; I couldn't seem to get into any kind of a rhythm. Then I sensed that something was wrong.

We were heading to the left, towards some glaciers. This didn't make sense; we couldn't land there. It was too dangerous. The glaciers could calve and kill us.

"Barry, where are we going?" I shouted, using air I needed for breathing.

He pointed out our direction – right towards the glaciers. I didn't understand. I didn't want to go that way. I wanted to aim for the beach. I was confused. I was moving my arms as fast as they would go, and it was taking all I had. From each moment to the next, I had to tell myself to keep going. The water felt so much colder than on the test swim. It had already worked its way deep into my muscles. My arms and legs were stiff. My strokes were short and choppy. But I kept going, telling myself to trust the crew and focus on the glaciers to watch the outcropping of rocks that was growing larger. I couldn't get into any kind of pace.

Abruptly the Zodiacs zagged to the right. I looked up and thought, *Wow, okay; we're heading for the beach now.* For a moment, I started to feel better. I was able to extend my reach farther, and I could see passengers from the *Orlova* walking along the snowbanks. In the distance, their clothes lost their colour and they looked black, like giant penguins. I saw smaller black figures, too – real penguins nesting near the edge of the shore. For a few moments, I felt like I was going to be okay, like I was going to make it in to shore, but then the Zodiacs abruptly turned farther to the right, and we were headed past the beach for another range of glaciers.

Finally, it occurred to me that the *Orlova* had anchored too close to shore for me to swim a mile, so Barry was adding distance by altering the course. And the ship's captain was on the bridge monitoring our course on his GPS and radioing our Zodiacs, updating them on the distance we had travelled. One of the passengers, Mrs Stokie, who was on the bridge with him, told me later, "The captain was watching you and he was shaking his head. He was an older man, and he had experienced everything. And now he was seeing something new. It was good for him. Still, I think he couldn't believe it."

We continued on right past the beach, towards more glaciers.

"How long have I been swimming?" I asked.

"Fifteen minutes," Barry said.

I had swum a little more than half a mile. I looked up at the shore. If I turned left, I could make it in. I could reach the shore. This struggle could be over. But I wouldn't complete the mile. I had swum farther two days before. But I was tired now, and this was so much harder. I just didn't feel right. I couldn't figure out what the problem was. I kept talking to myself, coaching myself to keep going. Then I felt it; it was the water pressure, and it was increasing on my back. It meant there was a strong current behind me. I looked at the glaciers onshore, using the fixed points to gauge how fast the current was flowing. It was flowing at over a knot. I wondered if I would have enough strength to fight it when we turned around and headed back for the beach. It would cut my speed by half and could cause me to lose heat more rapidly.

Barry and the crew in the Zodiacs couldn't feel what was happening. They had no idea we were moving into a risky area. If the current grew any stronger, it could cost us the swim. Barry motioned for me to swim past a peninsula and across a narrow channel. I lifted my head and pulled my hands directly under my chest, to gain more lift, so I could look across the bay and see if we had any other options for landing. There were no alternatives. This made me very uncomfortable. Chances were good that there would be a strong current flowing into or out of the narrow bay. And if we got caught in that current, all would be lost.

We started across the inlet, and within a moment I could feel that second current, slamming into our right side at two knots, pushing us into the inlet. Without any explanation, I spun around, put my head down, dug my arms into the water, and crabbed into the current. I focused on repositioning myself so I could parallel shore again and head towards Neko Harbour. Barry knew I knew what I was doing. But the abrupt course change caught the Zodiac drivers by surprise. They scattered in different directions, trying to avoid ramming into each other and trying to catch up with me. The motor on the lead Zodiac on my left sputtered and stopped. The second Zodiac immediately pulled up beside me. I sprinted against the current.

"How long have I been swimming?"

"Twenty-one minutes," Barry said. He and all the crew were watching me intently, their faces filled with tension and concern.

I put my head down, and something suddenly clicked. Maybe it was because I knew shore was within reach, or maybe because I got a second wind; I don't know. But I was finally swimming strongly, stretching out and moving fluidly. My arms and legs were as cold as the sea, but I felt the heat within my head and contained in my torso and I thrilled to it, knowing my body had carried me to places no one else had been in only a bathing suit. I looked down into the water; it was a bright blue-grey and so clear that it appeared as if I were swimming through air. The viscosity of the water was different, too; it was thicker than any I had ever swum in. It felt like I was swimming through gelato. And I got more push out of each arm stroke than I ever had before. I looked at the crew. They were leaning so far over the pontoons, as if they were right there with me. I needed to let them know I was okay.

I lifted my head, took a big breath, and shouted, "Barry, I'm swimming to Antarctica!"

I saw the smiles, heard the cheers and laughs, and I felt their energy lift me. They were as thrilled as I was. I swam faster, extending my arms, pulling more strongly, reaching for the shores of Antarctica.

Appendix I

The Last Letters of Robert Falcon Scott RN

In addition to his famous journal of the doomed South Pole expedition, discovered in the tent alongside Scott's corpse were a handful of last letters.

To Kathleen Scott [his wife]

The Great God has called me and I feel it will add a fearful blow to the heavy ones that have fallen on you in life. But take comfort in that I die at peace with the world and myself – not afraid.

Indeed it has been most singularly unfortunate, for the risks I have taken never seemed excessive.

. . . I want to tell you that we have missed getting through by a narrow margin which was justifiably within the risk of such a journey . . . After all, we have given our lives for our country – we have actually made the longest journey on record, and we have been the first Englishmen at the South Pole.

You must understand that it is too cold to write much.

. . . It's a pity the luck doesn't come our way, because every detail of equipment is right.

I shall not have suffered any pain, but leave the world fresh from harness and full of good health and vigour.

Since writing the above we got to within 11 miles of our depot, with one hot meal and two days' cold food. We should have got through but have been held for *four* days by a frightful storm. I think the best chance has gone. We have decided not to kill ourselves, but to fight to the last for that depot, but in the fighting there is a painless end.

Make the boy interested in natural history* if you can; it is better than games; they encourage it at some schools. I know you will keep him in the open air.

Above all, he must guard and you must guard him against indolence. Make him a strenuous man. I had to force myself into being strenuous, as you know – had always an inclination to be idle.

There is a piece of the Union Jack I put up at the South Pole in my private kit-bag, together with Amundsen's black flag and other trifles. Send a small piece of the Union Jack to the King and a small piece to Queen Alexandra.

What lots and lots I could tell you of this journey! How much better has it been than lounging in too great comfort at home! What tales you would have for the boy! But what a price to pay!

Tell Sir Clements I thought much of him and never regretted his putting me in command of the *Discovery*.

To Sir James Barrie

We are showing that Englishmen can still die with a bold spirit, fighting it out to the end. It will be known that we have accomplished our object in reaching the Pole, and that we have done everything possible, even to sacrificing ourselves in order to save sick companions. I think this makes an example for Englishmen of the future, and that the country ought to help those who are left behind to mourn us. I leave my poor girl and your godson, Wilson leaves a widow, and Edgar Evans also a widow in humble circumstances. Do what you can to get their claims recognized. Goodbye. I am not at all afraid of the end, but sad to miss many a humble pleasure which I had planned for the future on our long marches. I may not have proved a great explorer, but we have done the greatest march ever made and come very near to great success . . . We are in a desperate state, feet frozen, etc. No fuel and a long way from food, but it would do your heart good to be in our tent, to

---

* Kathleen Scott succeeded admirably in the request; their son, Peter, grew up to be a world-famous ornithologist.

hear our songs and the cheery conversation as to what we will do when we get to Hut Point.

Later. – We are very near the end, but have not and will not lose our good cheer. We have had four days of storm in our tent and nowhere's food or fuel. We did intend to finish ourselves when things proved like this, but we have decided to die naturally in the track.

As a dying man, my dear friend, be good to my wife and child. Give the boy a chance in life if the State won't do it. He ought to have good stuff in him . . . I never met a man in my life whom I admired and loved more than you, but I could never show you how much your friendship meant to me, for you had much to give and I nothing.

To Mrs E. A. Wilson [wife of Dr Wilson]

If this letter reaches you, Bill and I will have gone out together. We are very near it now and I should like you to know how splendid he was at the end – everlastingly cheerful and ready to sacrifice himself for others, never a word of blame to me for leading him into this mess. He is not suffering, luckily, at least only minor discomforts.

His eyes have a comfortable blue look of hope and his mind is peaceful with the satisfaction of his faith in regarding himself as part of the great scheme of the Almighty. I can do no more to comfort you than to tell you that he died as he lived, a brave, true man – the best of comrades and staunchest of friends.

My whole heart goes out to you in pity . . .

To Mrs Bowers [mother of Lieutenant Henry Bowers]

I am afraid this will reach you after one of the heaviest blows of your life.

I write when we are very near the end of our journey, and I am finishing it in company with two gallant, noble gentlemen. One of these is your son. He had come to be one of my closest and soundest friends, and I appreciate his wonderful upright nature, his ability and energy. As the troubles have thickened his

dauntless spirit ever shone brighter and he has remained cheerful, hopeful, and indomitable to the end.

The ways of Providence are inscrutable, but there must be some
reason why such a young, vigourous, and promising life is taken.

To the end he has talked of you and his sisters. One sees what
a happy home he must have had, and perhaps it is well to look
back on nothing but happiness.

He remains unselfish, self-reliant and splendidly hopeful to
the end, believing in God's mercy to you . . .

To Vice-Admiral Sir George le Clerc Egerton [Scott's commanding officer]

I fear we have shot our bolt – but we have been to the Pole and
done the longest journey on record.

I hope these letters may find their destination some day.

Subsidiary reasons of our failure to return are due to the sickness of different members of the party, but the real thing that has
stopped us is the awful weather and unexpected cold towards the
end of the journey.

This traverse of the Barrier has been quite three times as
severe as any experience we had on the summit.

There is no accounting for it, but the result has thrown out my
calculations, and here we are little more than 100 miles from the
base and petering out.

To Vice-Admiral Sir Francis Charles Bridgeman, KCVO KCB

My Dear Sir Francis,

I fear we have shipped up; a close shave; I am writing a few
letters which I hope will be delivered some day. I want to thank
you for the friendship you gave me of late years, and to tell you
how extraordinarily pleasant I found it to serve under you. I want
to tell you that I was not too old for this job. It was the younger
men that went under first . . . After all we are setting a good
example to our countrymen, if not by getting into a tight place,
by facing it like men when we were there. We could have come
through had we neglected the sick.

Goodbye, and goodbye to dear Lady Bridgeman.
Yours ever,
   R. Scott.

Excuse writing – it is -40 deg., and has been for nigh a month.

To Right Honourable Sir Edgar Speyer, Bart.

Dated 16 March, 1912. Lat. 79.5 deg.
   My Dear Sir Edgar,
   I hope this may reach you. I fear we must go and that it leaves
the Expedition in a bad muddle. But we have been to the Pole
and we shall die like gentlemen. I regret only for the women we
leave behind.
   I thank you a thousand times for your help and support and
your generous kindness. If this diary is found it will show how we
stuck by dying companions and fought the thing out well to the
end. I think this will show that the Spirit of pluck and power to
endure has not passed out of our race . . .
   Wilson, the best fellow that ever stepped, has sacrificed himself
again and again to the sick men of the party . . .
   I write to many friends hoping the letters will reach them
some time after we are found next year.
   We very nearly came through, and it's a pity to have missed it,
but lately I have felt that we have overshot our mark. No one is
to blame and I hope no attempt will be made to suggest that we
have lacked support.
   Goodbye to you and your dear kind wife.
   Yours ever sincerely,
   R. SCOTT.

To J. J. Kinsey, Christchurch

24 March 1912.
   My Dear Kinsey,
   I'm afraid we are pretty well done – four days of blizzard just
as we were getting to the last depot. My thoughts have been with
you often. You have been a brick. You will pull the expedition
through, I'm sure.

My thoughts are for my wife and boy. Will you do what you can for them if the country won't.

I want the boy to have a good chance in the world, but you know the circumstances well enough.

If I knew the wife and boy were in safe keeping I should have little regret in leaving the world, for I feel that the country need not be ashamed of us – our journey has been the biggest on record, and nothing but the most exceptional hard luck at the end would have caused us to fail to return. We have been to the S. Pole as we set out. God bless you and dear Mrs Kinsey. It is good to remember you and your kindness.

Your friend,

R. SCOTT.

Message to the Public

The causes of the disaster are not due to faulty organization but to misfortune in all risks which had to be undertaken.

1. The loss of pony transport in March 1911 obliged me to start later than I had intended, and obliged the limits of stuff transported to be narrowed.

2. The weather throughout the outward journey, and especially the long gale in 83° S., stopped us.

3. The soft snow in lower reaches of glacier again reduced pace.

We fought these untoward events with a will and conquered, but it cut into our provision reserve.

Every detail of our food supplies, clothing and depots made on the interior ice-sheet and over that long stretch of 700 miles to the Pole and back, worked out to perfection. The advance party would have returned to the glacier in fine form and with surplus of food, but for the astonishing failure of the man whom we had least expected to fail. Edgar Evans was thought the strongest man of the party.

The Beardmore Glacier is not difficult in fine weather, but on our return we did not get a single completely fine day; this with a sick companion enormously increased our anxieties.

As I have said elsewhere, we got into frightfully rough ice and Edgar Evans received a concussion of the brain – he died a natural death, but left us a shaken party with the season unduly advanced.

But all the facts above enumerated were as nothing to the surprise which awaited us on the Barrier. I maintain that our arrangements for returning were quite adequate, and that no one in the world would have expected the temperatures and surfaces which we encountered at this time of the year. On the summit in lat. 85°, 86° we had -20°, -30°. On the Barrier in lat. 82°, 10,000 feet lower, we had -30° in the day, -47° at night pretty regularly, with continuous head wind during our day marches. It is clear that these circumstances came on very suddenly, and our wreck is certainly due to this sudden advent of severe weather, which does not seem to have any satisfactory cause. I do not think human beings ever came through such a month as we have come through, and we should have got through in spite of the weather but for the sickening of a second companion, Captain Oates, and a shortage of fuel in our depots for which I cannot account, and finally, but for the storm which has fallen on us within 11 miles of the depot at which we hoped to secure our final supplies. Surely misfortune could scarcely have exceeded this last blow. We arrived within 11 miles of our old One Ton Camp with fuel for one last meal and food for two days. For four days we have been unable to leave the tent – the gale howling about us. We are weak, writing is difficult, but for my own sake I do not regret this journey, which has shown that Englishmen can endure hardships, help one another, and meet death with as great a fortitude as ever in the past. We took risks, we knew we took them; things have come out against us, and therefore we have no cause for complaint, but bow to the will of Providence, determined still to do our best to the last. But if we have been willing to give our lives to this enterprise, which is for the honour of our country, I appeal to our countrymen to see that those who depend on us are properly cared for.

Had we lived, I should have had a tale to tell of the hardihood, endurance, and courage of my companions which would have stirred the heart of every Englishman. These rough notes and our dead bodies must tell the tale, but surely, a great rich country like ours will see that those who are dependent on us are properly provided for.

Appendix II

The Early Life of Robert Falcon Scott

James M. Barrie

Barrie – the author of Peter Pan *– was a friend of Scott's, and wrote the biographical essay below for the abridgement of Scott's journals edited by Charles Turley and published by Smith, Elder in 1914.*

On the night of my original meeting with Scott he was but lately home from his first adventure into the Antarctic, and my chief recollection of the occasion is that having found the entrancing man I was unable to leave him. In vain he escorted me through the streets of London to my home, for when he had said good-night I then escorted him to his, and so it went on I know not for how long through the small hours. Our talk was largely a comparison of the life of action (which he pooh-poohed) with the loathly life of those who sit at home (which I scorned); but I also remember that he assured me he was of Scots extraction. As the subject never seems to have been resumed between us, I afterwards wondered whether I had drawn this from him with a promise that, if his reply was satisfactory, I would let him go to bed. However, the family traditions (they are nothing more) do bring him from across the border. According to them his great-great-grandfather was the Scott of Brownhead whose estates were sequestered after the '45. His dwelling was razed to the ground and he fled with his wife, to whom after some grim privations a son was born in a fisherman's hut on 14 September 1745. This son eventually settled in Devon, where he prospered, for it was in the beautiful house of Outlands that he died. He had four sons, all in the Royal Navy, of whom the eldest had as youngest child John Edward Scott, father of the Captain Scott who was born at Outlands on 6 June 1868. About the same date, or perhaps a little earlier, it was decided that the boy should go into the Navy like so many of his forebears.

I have been asked to write a few pages about those early days of Scott at Outlands, so that the boys who read this book may have some slight acquaintance with the boy who became Captain Scott; and they may be relieved to learn (as it holds out some chance for themselves) that the man who did so many heroic things does not make his first appearance as a hero. He enters history aged six, blue-eyed, long-haired, inexpressibly slight and in velveteen, being held out at arm's length by a servant and painted plank, still rode the waters. With many boys this would be the end of the story, but not with Con. He again retired to the making of gunpowder, and did not desist from his endeavours until he had blown that plank sky-high.

His first knife is a great event in the life of a boy: it is probably the first memory of many of them, and they are nearly always given it on condition that they keep it shut. So it was with Con, and a few minutes after he had sworn that he would not open it he was begging for permission to use it on a tempting sapling. "Very well," his father said grimly, "but remember, if you hurt yourself, don't expect any sympathy from me." The knife was opened, and to cut himself rather badly proved as easy as falling into the leat. The father, however, had not noticed, and the boy put his bleeding hand into his pocket and walked on unconcernedly. He was really considerably damaged; and this is a good story of a child of seven who all his life suffered extreme nausea from the sight of blood; even in the *Discovery* days, to get accustomed to "seeing red", he had to force himself to watch Dr Wilson skinning his specimens.

When he was about eight Con passed out of the hands of a governess, and became a schoolboy, first at a day school in Stoke Damerel and later at Stubbington House, Fareham. He rode grandly between Outlands and Stoke Damerel on his pony, Beppo, which bucked in vain when he was on it, but had an ingratiating way of depositing other riders on the road. From what one knows of him later this is a characteristic story. One day he dismounted to look over a gate at a view which impressed him (not very boyish this), and when he recovered from a brown study there was no Beppo to be seen. He walked the seven miles home, but what was characteristic was that he called at police-stations on the way to give practical details of his loss and a description of the pony. Few children would have thought of this, but Scott was naturally a strange mixture of the dreamy and the practical, and never more practical than immediately after he had been dreamy. He forgot place and time altogether when thus abstracted. I remember the first time he dined with me, when a number of well-known men had come to meet him, he arrived some two hours late. He had dressed to come out, then fallen into one of his reveries, forgotten all about the engagement, dined by himself and gone early to bed. Just as he was falling asleep he remembered where he should be, arose hastily and joined us as speedily as possible. It was equally characteristic of him to say of the other guests that it was pleasant to a sailor to meet so many interesting people. When I said that to them the sailor was by far the most interesting person in the room he shouted with mirth. It always amused Scott to find that anyone thought him a person of importance.

I suppose everyone takes for granted that in his childhood, as later when he made his great marches, Scott was muscular and strongly built. This was so far from being the case that there were many anxious consultations over him, and the local doctor said he could not become a sailor as he could never hope to obtain the necessary number of inches round the chest. He was delicate and inclined to be pigeon-breasted. Judging from the portrait of him here printed, in his first uniform as a naval cadet, all this had gone by the time he was thirteen, but unfortunately there are no letters of this period extant; and thus little can be said of his years on the *Britannia* where "you never felt hot in your bunk because you could always twist, and sleep with your feet out at a porthole." He became a cadet captain, a post none can reach who is not thought well of by the other boys as well as by their instructors, but none of them foresaw that he was likely to become anybody in particular. He was still "Old Mooney", as his father had dubbed him, owing to his dreamy mind; it was an effort to him to work hard, he cast a wistful eye on "slackers", he was not a good loser, he was untidy to the point of slovenliness, and he had a fierce temper. All this I think has been proved to me up to the hilt, and as I am very sure that the boy of fifteen or so cannot be very different from the man he grows into, it leaves me puzzled. The Scott I knew, or thought I knew, was physically as hard as nails and flung himself into work or play with a vehemence I cannot remember ever to have seen equalled. I have fished with him, played cricket and football with him and other games, those of his own invention being of a particularly arduous kind, for they always had a moment when the other players were privileged to fling a hard ball at your undefended head. "Slackness" was the last quality you would think of when you saw him bearing down on you with that ball, and it was the last he asked of you if you were bearing down on him. He was equally strenuous of work; indeed I have no clearer recollection of him than his way of running from play to work or work to play, so that there should be the least possible time between. It is the "time between" that is the "slacker's" kingdom, and Scott lived less in it than anyone I can recall. Again, I found him the best of losers, with a shout of delight for every good stroke by an opponent: what is called an ideal sportsman. He was very neat and correct in his dress, quite a model for the youth who come after him, but that we take as a matter of course; it is "good form" in the Navy. His temper I should have said was bullet-proof. I have never seen him begin to lose it for a second of time, and I have seen him in circumstances where the loss of it would have been excusable.

However, "the boy makes the man", and Scott was none of those things I saw in him but something better. The faults of his youth must have lived on in him as in all of us, but he got to know they were there and he took an iron grip of them and never let go his hold. It was this self-control more than anything else that made the man of him of whom we have all become so proud. I get many proofs of this in correspondence dealing with his manhood days which are not strictly within the sphere of this introductory note. The horror of slackness was turned into a very passion for keeping himself "fit". Thus we find him at one time taking charge of a dog, a "Big Dane", so that he could race it all the way between work and home, a distance of three miles. Even when he was getting the *Discovery* ready and doing daily the work of several men, he might have been seen running through the streets of London from Savile Row or the Admiralty to his home, not because there was no time for other methods of progression, but because he must be fit, fit, fit. No more "Old Mooney" for him; he kept an eye for ever on that gentleman, and became doggedly the most practical of men. And practical in the cheeriest of ways. In 1894 a disastrous change came over the fortunes of the family, the father's money being lost, and then Scott was practical indeed. A letter he wrote at this time to his mother, tenderly taking everything and everybody on his shoulders, must be one of the best letters ever written by a son, and I hope it may be some day published. His mother was the great person of his early life, more to him even than his brother or his father, whom circumstances had deprived of the glory of following the sailor's profession and whose ambitions were all bound up in this son, determined that Con should do the big things he had not done himself. For the rest of his life Con became the head of the family, devoting his time and his means to them, not in an it-must-be-done manner, but with joy and even gaiety. He never seems to have shown a gayer front than when the troubles fell, and at a farm to which they retired for a time he became famous as a provider of concerts. Not only must there be no "Old Mooney" in him, but it must be driven out of everyone. His concerts, in which he took a leading part, became celebrated in the district, deputations called to beg for another, and once in these words, "Wull 'ee gie we a concert over our way when the comic young gentleman be here along?"

Some servants having had to go at this period, Scott conceived the idea that he must even help domestically in the house, and took his own bedroom under his charge with results that were satisfactory to the casual eye, though not to the eyes of his sisters. It was about this time that he slew the demon of untidiness so far as his own dress was concerned and doggedly became a model for still younger officers. Not that his dress was fine. While there were others to help he would not spend his small means on himself, and he would arrive home in frayed garments that he had grown out of and in very tarnished lace. But neat as a pin. In the days when he returned from his first voyage in the Antarctic and all England was talking of him, one of his most novel adventures was at last to go to a first-class tailor and be provided with a first-class suit. He was as elated by the possession of this as a child. When going about the country lecturing in those days he travelled third class, though he was sometimes met at the station by mayors and corporations and red carpets.

The hot tempers of his youth must still have lain hidden, but by now the control was complete. Even in the naval cadet days of which unfortunately there is so little to tell, his old friends who remember the tempers remember also the sunny smile that dissipated them. When I knew him the sunny smile was there frequently, and was indeed his greatest personal adornment, but the tempers never reached the surface. He had become master of his fate and captain of his soul.

In 1886 Scott became a middy on the *Boadicea*, and later on various ships, one of them the *Rover*, of which Admiral Fisher was at that time commander. The Admiral has a recollection of a little black pig having been found under his bunk one night. He cannot swear that Scott was the leading culprit, but Scott was certainly one of several who had to finish the night on deck as a punishment. In 1888 Scott passed his examinations for sub-lieutenant, with four first-class honours and one second, and so left his boyhood behind. I cannot refrain, however, from adding as a conclusion to these notes a letter from Sir Courtauld Thomson that gives a very attractive glimpse of him in this same year:

> In the late winter a quarter of a century ago I had to find my way from San Francisco to Alaska. The railway was snowed up and the only transport available at the moment was an ill-found tramp steamer. My fellow passengers were mostly Californians hurrying off to a new mining camp and, with the crew, looked a very unpleasant lot of ruffians. Three singularly unprepossessing Frisco toughs joined me in my cabin, which was none too large for a single person. I was then told that yet another had somehow to be wedged in. While I was wondering if he could be a more ill-favoured or dirtier specimen of humanity than the others the last comer suddenly appeared – the jolliest and breeziest English naval Second Lieutenant. It was Con Scott. I had never seen him before, but we at once became friends and remained so till the end. He was going up to join his ship which, I think, was the *Amphion*, at Esquimault, B.C.

As soon as we got outside the Golden Gates we ran into a full gale which lasted all the way to Victoria, B.C. The ship was so overcrowded that a large number of women and children were allowed to sleep on the floor of the only saloon there was on condition that they got up early, so that the rest of the passengers could come in for breakfast and the other meals.

I need scarcely say that owing to the heavy weather hardly a woman was able to get up, and the saloon was soon in an indescribable condition. Practically no attempt was made to serve meals, and the few so-called stewards were themselves mostly out of action from drink or sea-sickness.

Nearly all the male passengers who were able to be about spent their time drinking and quarrelling. The deck cargo and some of our top hamper were washed away and the cabins got their share of the waves that were washing the deck.

Then it was I first knew that Con Scott was no ordinary human being. Though at that time still only a boy he practically took command of the passengers and was at once accepted by them as their Boss during the rest of the trip. With a small body of volunteers he led an attack on the saloon – dressed the mothers, washed the children, fed the babies, swabbed down the floors and nursed the sick, and performed every imaginable service for all hands. On deck he settled the quarrels and established order either by his personality, or, if necessary, by his fists. Practically by day and night he worked for the common good, never sparing himself, and with his infectious smile gradually made us all feel the whole thing was jolly good fun.

I daresay there are still some of the passengers like myself who, after a quarter of a century, have imprinted on their minds the vision of this fair-haired English sailor boy with the laughing blue eyes, who at that early age knew how to sacrifice himself for the welfare and happiness of others.

Appendix III

The Antarctic Treaty

The Antarctic Treaty was made on 1 December 1959.

Text of the Antarctic Treaty

The Governments of Argentina, Australia, Belgium, Chile, the French Republic, Japan, New Zealand, Norway, the Union of South Africa, the Union of Soviet Socialist Republics, the United Kingdom of Great Britain and Northern Ireland, and the United States of America,

Recognizing that it is in the interest of all mankind that Antarctica shall continue for ever to be used exclusively for peaceful purposes and shall not become the scene or object of international discord;

Acknowledging the substantial contributions to scientific knowledge resulting from international cooperation in scientific investigation in Antarctica;

Convinced that the establishment of a firm foundation for the continuation and development of such cooperation on the basis of freedom of scientific investigation in Antarctica as applied during the International Geophysical Year accords with the interests of science and the progress of all mankind;

Convinced also that a treaty ensuring the use of Antarctica for peaceful purposes only and the continuance of international harmony in Antarctica will further the purposes and principles embodied in the Charter of the United Nations;

Have agreed as follows:

Article I

1. Antarctica shall be used for peaceful purposes only. There shall be prohibited, inter alia, any measure of a military nature, such as the establishment of military bases and fortifications, the carrying out of military manoeuvres, as well as the testing of any type of weapon.

2. The present Treaty shall not prevent the use of military personnel or equipment for scientific research or for any other peaceful purpose.

Article II

Freedom of scientific investigation in Antarctica and cooperation toward that end, as applied during the International Geophysical Year, shall continue, subject to the provisions of the present Treaty.

Article III

1. In order to promote international cooperation in scientific investigation in Antarctica, as provided for in Article II of the present Treaty, the Contracting Parties agree that, to the greatest extent feasible and practicable:

   (a) information regarding plans for scientific programs in Antarctica shall be exchanged to permit maximum economy of and efficiency of operations;
   (b) scientific personnel shall be exchanged in Antarctica between expeditions and stations;
   (c) scientific observations and results from Antarctica shall be exchanged and made freely available.

Article IV

1. Nothing contained in the present Treaty shall be interpreted as:

- (a) a renunciation by any Contracting Party of previously asserted rights of or claims to territorial sovereignty in Antarctica;
- (b) a renunciation or diminution by any Contracting Party of any basis of claim to territorial sovereignty in Antarctica which it may have whether as a result of its activities or those of its nationals in Antarctica, or otherwise;
- (c) prejudicing the position of any Contracting Party as regards its recognition or non-recognition of any other State's rights of or claim or basis of claim to territorial sovereignty in Antarctica.

2. No acts or activities taking place while the present Treaty is in force shall constitute a basis for asserting, supporting or denying a claim to territorial sovereignty in Antarctica or create any rights of sovereignty in Antarctica. No new claim, or enlargement of an existing claim, to territorial sovereignty in Antarctica shall be asserted while the present Treaty is in force.

Article V

1. Any nuclear explosions in Antarctica and the disposal there of radioactive waste material shall be prohibited.

2. In the event of the conclusion of international agreements concerning the use of nuclear energy, including nuclear explosions and the disposal of radioactive waste material, to which all of the Contracting Parties whose representatives are entitled to participate in the meetings provided for under Article IX are parties, the rules established under such agreements shall apply in Antarctica.

Article VI

The provisions of the present Treaty shall apply to the area south of 60 deg. South Latitude, including all ice shelves, but nothing in the present Treaty shall prejudice or in any way affect the rights, or the exercise of the rights, of any State under international law with regard to the high seas within that area.

Article VII

1. In order to promote the objectives and ensure the observance of the provisions of the present Treaty, each Contracting Party whose representatives are entitled to participate in the meetings referred to in Article IX of the Treaty shall have the right to designate observers to carry out any inspection provided for by the present Article. Observers shall be nationals of the Contracting Parties which designate them. The names of observers shall be communicated to every other Contracting Party having the right to designate observers, and like notice shall be given of the termination of their appointment.

2. Each observer designated in accordance with the provisions of paragraph 1 of this Article shall have complete freedom of access at any time to any or all areas of Antarctica.

3. All areas of Antarctica, including all stations, installations and equipment within those areas, and all ships and aircraft at points of discharging or embarking cargoes or personnel in Antarctica, shall be open at all times to inspection by any observers designated in accordance with paragraph I of this Article.

4. Aerial observation may be carried out at any time over any or all areas of Antarctica by any of the Contracting Parties having the right to designate observers.

5. Each Contracting Party shall, at the time when the present Treaty enters into force for it, inform the other Contracting Parties, and thereafter shall give them notice in advance, of

(a) all expeditions to and within Antarctica, on the part of its ships or nationals, and all expeditions to Antarctica organized in or proceeding from its territory;

(b) all stations in Antarctica occupied by its nationals; and

(c) any military personnel or equipment intended to be introduced by it into Antarctica subject to the conditions prescribed in paragraph 2 of Article I of the present Treaty.

Article VIII

1. In order to facilitate the exercise of their functions under the present Treaty, and without prejudice to the respective positions of the Contracting Parties relating to jurisdiction over all other persons in Antarctica, observers designated under paragraph 1 of Article VII and scientific personnel exchanged under sub-paragraph 1(b) of Article III of the Treaty, and members of the staffs accompanying any such persons, shall be subject only to the jurisdiction of the Contracting Party of which they are nationals in respect of all acts or omissions occurring while they are in Antarctica for the purpose of exercising their functions.

2. Without prejudice to the provisions of paragraph 1 of this Article, and pending the adoption of measures in pursuance of sub-paragraph 1(e) of Article IX, the Contracting Parties concerned in any case of dispute with regard to the exercise of jurisdiction in Antarctica shall immediately consult together with a view to reaching a mutually acceptable solution.

Article IX

1. Representatives of the Contracting Parties named in the preamble to the present Treaty shall meet at the City of Canberra within two months after the date of entry into force of the Treaty, and thereafter at suitable intervals and places, for the purpose of exchanging information, consulting together on matters of common interest pertaining to Antarctica, and formulating and considering, and recommending to their Governments, measures

in furtherance of the principles and objectives of the Treaty, including measures regarding:

(a) use of Antarctica for peaceful purposes only;
(b) facilitation of scientific research in Antarctica;
(c) facilitation of international scientific cooperation in Antarctica;
(d) facilitation of the exercise of the rights of inspection provided for in Article VII of the Treaty;
(e) questions relating to the exercise of jurisdiction in Antarctica;
(f) preservation and conservation of living resources in Antarctica.

2. Each Contracting Party which has become a party to the present Treaty by accession under Article XIII shall be entitled to appoint representatives to participate in the meetings referred to in paragraph 1 of the present Article, during such times as that Contracting Party demonstrates its interest in Antarctica by conducting substantial research activity there, such as the establishment of a scientific station or the despatch of a scientific expedition.

3. Reports from the observers referred to in Article VII of the present Treaty shall be transmitted to the representatives of the Contracting Parties participating in the meetings referred to in paragraph 1 of the present Article.

4. The measures referred to in paragraph 1 of this Article shall become effective when approved by all the Contracting Parties whose representatives were entitled to participate in the meetings held to consider those measures.

5. Any or all of the rights established in the present Treaty may be exercised as from the date of entry into force of the Treaty whether or not any measures facilitating the exercise of such rights have been proposed, considered or approved as provided in this Article.

Article X

Each of the Contracting Parties undertakes to exert appropriate efforts, consistent with the Charter of the United Nations, to the end that no one engages in any activity in Antarctica contrary to the principles or purposes of the present Treaty.

Article XI

1. If any dispute arises between two or more of the Contracting Parties concerning the interpretation or application of the present Treaty, those Contracting Parties shall consult among themselves with a view to having the dispute resolved by negotiation, inquiry, mediation, conciliation, arbitration, judicial settlement or other peaceful means of their own choice.

2. Any dispute of this character not so resolved shall, with the consent, in each case, of all parties to the dispute, be referred to the International Court of Justice for settlement; but failure to reach agreement on reference to the International Court shall not absolve parties to the dispute from the responsibility of continuing to seek to resolve it by any of the various peaceful means referred to in paragraph 1 of this Article.

Article XII

1.–(a) The present Treaty may be modified or amended at any time by unanimous agreement of the Contracting Parties whose representatives are entitled to participate in the meetings provided for under Article IX. Any such modification or amendment shall enter into force when the depositary Government has received notice from all such Contracting Parties that they have ratified it.

(b) Such modification or amendment shall thereafter enter into force as to any other Contracting Party when notice of ratification by it has been received by the depositary Government. Any such Contracting Party from which no notice of ratification is received within a period of two years from the date of entry into force of the modification or amendment in accordance with the provision of sub-paragraph 1(a) of this Article shall be deemed to have withdrawn from the present Treaty on the date of the expiration of such period.

2.–(a) If after the expiration of thirty years from the date of entry into force of the present Treaty, any of the Contracting Parties whose representatives are entitled to participate in the meetings provided for under Article IX so requests by a communication addressed to the depositary Government, a Conference of all the Contracting Parties shall be held as soon as practicable to review the operation of the Treaty.

(b) Any modification or amendment to the present Treaty which is approved at such a Conference by a majority of the Contracting Parties there represented, including a majority of those whose representatives are entitled to participate in the meetings provided for under Article IX, shall be communicated by the depositary Government to all Contracting Parties immediately after the termination of the Conference and shall enter into force in accordance with the provisions of paragraph 1 of the present Article.

(c) If any such modification or amendment has not entered into force in accordance with the provisions of sub-paragraph 1(a) of this Article within a period of two years after the date of its communication to all the Contracting Parties, any Contracting Party may at any time after the expiration of that period give notice to the depositary Government of its withdrawal from the present Treaty; and such withdrawal shall take effect two years after the receipt of the notice by the depositary Government.

Article XIII

1. The present Treaty shall be subject to ratification by the signatory States. It shall be open for accession by any State which is a Member of the United Nations, or by any other State which may be invited to accede to the Treaty with the consent of all the

Contracting Parties whose representatives are entitled to participate in the meetings provided for under Article IX of the Treaty.

2. Ratification of or accession to the present Treaty shall be effected by each State in accordance with its constitutional processes.

3. Instruments of ratification and instruments of accession shall be deposited with the Government of the United States of America, hereby designated as the depositary Government.

4. The depositary Government shall inform all signatory and acceding States of the date of each deposit of an instrument of ratification or accession, and the date of entry into force of the Treaty and of any modification or amendment thereto.

5. Upon the deposit of instruments of ratification by all the signatory States, the present Treaty shall enter into force for those States and for States which have deposited instruments of accession. Thereafter the Treaty shall enter into force for any acceding State upon the deposit of its instruments of accession.

6. The present Treaty shall be registered by the depositary Government pursuant to Article 102 of the Charter of the United Nations.

Article XIV

The present Treaty, done in the English, French, Russian and Spanish languages, each version being equally authentic, shall be deposited in the archives of the Government of the United States of America, which shall transmit duly certified copies thereof to the Governments of the signatory and acceding States.

In witness thereof, the undersigned Plenipotentiaries, duly authorized, have signed the present Treaty.

Done at Washington this first day of December, one thousand nine hundred and fifty-nine.

Antarctic Treaty Parties

Country, Date Ratified or Acceded to Treaty
Argentina, June 23, 1961
Australia, June 23, 1961
Austria, August 25, 1987
Belgium, July 26, 1960
Brazil, May 16, 1975
Bulgaria, September 11, 1978
Canada, May 4, 1988
Chile, June 23, 1961
China, June 8, 1983
Colombia, January 31, 1989
Cuba, August 16, 1984
Czech Republic, June 14, 1962
Dem People's Rep of Korea, January 21, 1987
Denmark, May 20, 1965
Ecuador, September 15, 1987
Finland, May 15, 1984
France, September 16, 1960
Germany, February 5, 1979
Greece, January 8, 1987
Guatemala, July 31, 1991
Hungary, January 27, 1984
India, August 19, 1983
Italy, March 18, 1981
Japan, August 4, 1960
Netherlands, March 30, 1967
New Zealand, November 1, 1960
Norway, August 24, 1960
Papua New Guinea, March 16, 1981
Peru, April 10, 1981
Poland, June 8, 1961
Rep of Korea, November 28, 1986
Romania, September 15, 1971
Russian Federation, November 2, 1960
Slovak Republic, June 14, 1962
South Africa, June 21, 1960
Spain, March 31, 1982

Sweden, April 24, 1984
Switzerland, November 15, 1990
Turkey, January 24, 1995
Ukraine, October 28, 1992
United Kingdom, May 31, 1960
United States, August 18, 1960
Uruguay, January 11, 1980

Glossary

Ablation The loss of snow or ice by melting or evaporation

Anchor ice Submerged ice attached to the sea bed

Brash Wrecked ice from a larger formation

Cairn Marker made from ice, snow or stones

Calve The breaking off of an iceberg from a glacier or ice sheet

Crevasse Crack or gap

Fast ice Sea ice attached to the shore

FID British Antarctic worker (named from the Falkland Islands Dependency Survey)

Finnesko Boots made entirely of fur; worn by early explorers

Frazil ice Slush of pointed ice crystals in the water

Frost smoke Condensed water vapour which forms mist over open sea in cold weather

Hoosh Stew eaten on expedition; usually made from pemmican (q.v.), dry sledging biscuits and water

Ice blink Reflection of light off the ice and onto the underside of clouds

Ice window The breaking up of fast ice in the summer, which allows shipping to reach the Antarctic coast

Lead Open water in pack ice

Moraine Loose rock moved and deposited by a glacier

Mukluks Boots made of sealskin or moose hide (North America)

Névé Bed of frozen snow that has not turned to ice; literally "last year's snow"

Nunatak Rock or mountain standing up through an ice-field

Old ice Ice more than ten years old

Pancake ice Disks of young ice, formed by wave action

Pemmican Ground dried meat mixed with lard

Sastrugi Furrows or irregularities formed on the ice or snow by the wind

Snow blindness Temporary (usually) loss of sight caused by glare of sunlight off snow or ice

Snow bridge Windblown crust of snow over a crevasse

Tabular berg Recently calved iceberg with straight sides and flat top

Tide crack A crack separating land ice and sea ice

Whiteout The blurring between ground and sky, in which perspective becomes lost, caused by overcast sky descending to the horizon

Sources & Acknowledgements

The editor has made every effort to secure the requisite permission to reprint copyrighted material in this volume. In the case of any omissions or errors, please contact the editor c/o the publishers.

Roald Amundsen, *The South Pole: An Account of the Norwegian Antarctic Expedition in the* Fram, *1910–12*. Trans. A. G. Chater, London, John Murray, 1912.

W. Ellery Anderson, *Expedition South*. London, The Travel Book Club, n.d.

Noel Barber, *The White Desert*. London, Hodder and Stoughton, 1958. Copyright © Noel Barber 1958.

Edward Bransfield, reprinted from *The Oxford Book of Exploration*, ed. Robin Hanbury-Tenison. Oxford, Oxford University Press, 1994.

Richard E. Byrd, *Alone*. London, Macdonald & Co., 1987.

Skyward. New York, GP Putnam's Sons, 1928. Copyright © 1928 The Estate of Richard E. Byrd.

Apsley Cherry-Garrard, *The Worst Journey in the World*. London, Picador, 1994. Copyright © Angela Mathias 1922, 1965.

James Cook, *A Voyage Towards the South Pole*. London, 1777.

Lynne Cox, *Swimming to Antarctica*. London, Weidenfeld and Nicolson, 2005. Copyright © Lynne Cox 2005.

T. W. Edgeworth David, *Aurora Australis*. SeTo Publishing 1988. Copyright © SeTo Publishing 1988.

E. R. G. R. Evans, *South With Scott*. London, Collins, 1921.

Vivian Fuchs, *Antarctic Adventure*. London, Cassell, 1959. Copyright © The Trans-Antarctic Expedition 1959.

Catharine Hartley, *To the Poles (Without a Beard)*. London, Simon & Schuster, 2002. Copyright © Catharine Hartley 2002.

David Helvarg, "On Thin Ice", *Sierra*, November 1999. Copyright © Sierra Magazine 1999.

David Hempleman-Adams, *Toughing It Out*. London, Orion, 1997. Copyright © 1997 David Hempleman-Adams.

David Lewis, *Voyage to the Ice: The Antarctic Expedition of* Solo. Sydney, Australian Broadcasting Commission & William Collins Sons & Co., Lyd, 1979. Copyright © Australian Broadcasting Commission.

Douglas Mawson, *The Home of the Blizzard*. London, Hodder & Stoughton, 1930.

F. D. Ommanney, *South Latitude*. London, Longmans, 1938.

Thomas Orde-Lees, reprinted from *The Faber Book of Exploration*, ed. Benedict Allen. London, Faber and Faber, 2002.

Michael Parfitt, *South Light*. London, Bloomsbury, 1988. Copyright © Michael Parfit 1985.

John Rymill, *Southern Lights*. London, Chatto & Windus, 1938. (This selection of extracts originally aapeared in *From the Ends of the Earth*, ed. Augustine Coutauld, Oxford University Press, 1958).

Robert F. Scott, *The Voyage of the Discovery*. London, John Murray, 1929.

Scott's Last Expedition. London, The Folio Society, 1964.

Ernest Shackleton, *The Heart of the Antarctic*. London, Heinemann, 1911.

Mike Stroud, *Shadows on the Wasteland*. London, Jonathan Cape, 1993. Copyright © Mike Stroud 1993.

Gareth Wood & Eric Jamieson, *South Pole: 900 Miles on Foot*. Victoria, BC Horsdal & Schubert, 1996.

F. A. Worsley, *Shackleton's Boat Journey*. London, Pimlico, 1999. Copyright © The Estate of F. A. Worsley.